THE MAKING OF A DETECTIVE

THE MAKING OF A DETECTIVE

by
HARVEY RACHLIN

W. W. NORTON & COMPANY
NEW YORK   LONDON

The text of this book is composed in Baskerville
with the display set in Bisteck Bold and Serifa Bold
Composition and manufacturing by the Haddon Craftsmen, Inc.
Book design by Michael Chesworth

Library of Congress Cataloging-in-Publication Data
Rachlin, Harvey.
The making of a detective / by Harvey Rachlin.
p.   cm.
1. Detectives—New York (N.Y.) 2. Police—New York (N.Y.)
3. Homicide investigation—New York (N.Y.) I. Title.
HV8021.R33 1995
363.2′3′092—dc20
[B]   95-6148

ISBN 0-393-03797-5

W. W. Norton & Company, Inc., 500 Fifth Avenue, New York, N.Y. 10110
W. W. Norton & Company Ltd., 10 Coptic Street, London WC1A 1PU

1 2 3 4 5 6 7 8 9 0

For Marla, Elyssa, Lauren, and Glenn

—Harvey Rachlin

To Luciann and loving daughter Danielle

—David Carbone

INTRODUCTION

Having long been fascinated by the uniformed police officer on the street, six years ago I undertook a study at the New York City Police Academy in which I followed four recruits through training. The result was *The Making of a Cop,* a book that chronicled the remarkable process that transforms a civilian into a police officer.

Street cops are sometimes referred to as the "backbone" of a police department because they are the officers out there on the front lines, patrolling the streets, maintaining law and order, guarding the city from anarchy. As I followed my four recruits through their six months of training at the academy, I witnessed the emotional and psychological changes, as well as the growth of technical know-how, that prepared them for the job they would soon be doing—handling calls for crimes in progress, issuing summonses, rushing to emergencies, handling family disputes, arresting people, quelling riots, executing rescues, and so much more—and doing it all with the confidence, aplomb, and courage expected of police officers. The experience opened my eyes to the difficulty of the job the men and women in blue have and showed me how they grow into it, developing the required mental instincts, temperament, and skills. It whetted my appetite to learn about further steps in this extended metamorphosis, and I decided to take the next step and see what makes detectives tick.

Detectives had always intrigued me. They seemed able to work magic in identifying and bringing to justice the perpetrators of crime.

No crime seemed too difficult for them to solve. My notions, admittedly, bordered on the romantic, fueled by the folklore that had grown over the past century or two about the seemingly supernormal capabilities of sleuths, but today's detective had to be something special, given the increased sophistication and ruthlessness of society's criminals. Conducting a case study of one person's transmutation from cop to neophyte detective to seasoned criminal investigator promised to be a fascinating endeavor. As with my earlier study, the best place to do this seemed to be New York City, which is host to more murders—almost one-tenth of all the murders committed in this country—and other categories of crime than any other city in America.

After receiving permission from the New York City Police Department to conduct the study, I contacted the president of the Detectives' Endowment Association, Thomas Scotto, for his help in selecting an up-and-coming young detective who would be the focus of this book. He or she would have to be a very special detective, I stressed, one who had demonstrated early on a real talent for detective work and who would continue on that path successfully. The next day, Scotto called me back and said he had for me "one of the hottest young detectives in the Bureau." His name was David Carbone, and he worked out of the 75th Precinct in East New York, Brooklyn. "A rising star" was how the DEA president described this rookie detective.

Scotto's recommendation was better than I could have dreamed. I soon found that aside from being a terrific detective, David Carbone had another invaluable asset—the perfect personality to be the subject of this kind of book. Quick-witted, salty, energetic, garrulous, humorous, kindhearted, considerate, opinionated, compassionate, open-minded—he could be all these things, yet his detective smarts were always apparent. Carbone is a no-holds-barred person, and even a bit of a renegade in his own way. When it came to talking about any facet of his work with me, there was certainly no "blue wall" of secrecy about him. When asked to explain something, he would, brimming with enthusiasm, deliver an encyclopedic lecture on the subject.

Many of the other detectives in the Seven-Five squad were equally helpful. Both veterans and rookies were eager to see that I learned comprehensively and at first hand about the job of detective; they went out of their way to assist me in any way they could. On my very first day, in fact, after I had been warmly welcomed by several bosses and detectives, a supervisor told me to put a vest on. "What for?" I inquired, knowing he was of course referring to a bulletproof vest.

"Are you here to learn or not?" he demanded. "We're going on a stakeout to pick up a murderer, and it would be very embarrassing to us if you got killed.'' An adrenaline rush flowed through me, and I suited up.

The killer was not to be found that day, but the stakeout—I rode in an unmarked car with three detectives within radio distance of a beat-up old surveillance van carrying Carbone, another detective, and a confidential informant who was going to point out the killer—presaged an unusually adventurous course of study. It marked the beginning of a long and close working relationship with the 75th Precinct Detective Unit. For a year and a half I followed Carbone and other members of his team on their investigations, which turned out to be primarily for murders.

I preferred the late tours, because there was more action then, and some nights it was nonstop. On more than one evening there were three murders in the precinct, not to mention numerous other individuals shot, stabbed, beaten, torched, robbed, raped, run over, menaced, harassed, kidnapped, or conned.

When I saw my first shooting victim, I was horrified by the holes in the young man's body, the blood oozing out, his contorted face, writhing limbs, gasps for breath, and agonized groans. While we waited in the street for an ambulance, I kept my distance. But the detectives nudged me to move in and look close up. Reluctantly I agreed, trying to control my queasiness and thinking this was something I could never get used to. However, with such an extremely high rate of homicide in the precinct, it was only a matter of months before I'd walk into crime scenes and step over bodies indifferently, even crack a joke or two about the DOA. As I became inured to murder, I felt as if I were losing a bit of my humanity—although I could never quite bring myself to stick my face right up to a stab wound or peer into a head half blown off, like some of the other detectives.

The worst thing I saw haunts me to this day; I don't think it will ever leave me. A call came in late one afternoon about a baby found in a bag along the side of a road. We drove to the scene. I prayed it was a mistaken call, but sure enough, at the side of the dirt road was a black nylon gym bag. Inside, wrapped in clear plastic, was an infant, only hours old. He had an adorable, beatific smile. Fresh out of the womb, instead of being cradled in soft, motherly warmth, he had been greeted by a pair of cold human hands bent on choking the life out of him. A deep, dark depression set in, and my faith in human beings seemed irrevocably shaken. The next day I went to the morgue where the baby was to be autopsied. It was almost unbearable to watch. In the middle of a room of tables on which rested the bodies of deceased adults was the tiny infant. Then the pathologist opened him up.

The smell of the morgue lingered on my clothes. I went home and was tempted to burn them.

So busy were the detectives that many times they'd work all night, and, if a day tour followed, straight into the next day (that's seven additional hours in between). I must confess that about seven or eight in the morning I took off, in dire need of sleep, while the detectives were just beginning their next eight-hour tour, and perhaps overtime after that if they were still working an important case or another murder came in. I don't know how they did it.

My interaction with the squad was as close as any outsider could possibly hope to enjoy, clearly a once-in-a-lifetime opportunity. I had free rein at crime scenes behind the yellow tape; I accompanied the detectives on their investigations, stood by their side on canvasses, sat next to them during interviews of witnesses, observed interrogations, went out for meals with them, sat with them on breaks in the lounge, discussed cases and shot the breeze with them in the office. When out in the field, I always kept my mouth shut and never tried to pass myself off as a detective. When the big brass were around, I usually tried to make myself scarce. My goal at all times was to soak up the job and understand as much about it as possible.

I felt myself undergo changes. Having been to numerous homicide scenes and observed numerous emergency-room procedures, having seen carnage close-up and wholesale, I was no longer reticent about talking to a grieving family about the loved one who had been brutally murdered. I no longer cringed when walking into a bloody death scene. I no longer was afraid to confront death, although I would never get used to autopsies and the unforgettable smell of corpses.

Seeing East New York from a police perspective was a real eye-opener. Anyone not familiar with the conditions in the ghetto is in for a rude awakening. It's not just the poverty that is pervasive. Drugs are omnipresent, and gangs are an ever-threatening presence. I empathized with the people's terror of going outside, where at any moment one might be robbed, shot, even killed. There are many good people in East New York; indeed, most of the people there I believe are decent, hardworking citizens. I was, and still am, amazed at how they survive there, carrying on their lives with enthusiasm and optimism.

Seeing and talking to the "bad guys" (as the detectives call them) was also eye-opening. One drug dealer I spoke to in the squad room told me he wasn't afraid of the cops at all. Within twenty-four hours, he told me confidently, he could gather all the people and weapons necessary to blow up the station house or take over the precinct. True or not, he believed it and would have been willing to stake his life on it. This same drug dealer boasted that his people didn't like to use 9mm semiautomatic pistols because the bullets went right through the victim's body. Certain bullets break apart when penetrating bodies, he told me with zest, so if you shot somebody in the head, it would crack open and the brains would spill out. He and his associates liked that sort of thing. He was also thrilled to be interviewed for this book, but he'll never get to read it. He's doing time six feet under.

Then there was the time we arrived at a homicide scene and found that an Emergency Medical Service crew had preceded us. Said one tech, shaking his head over the brazenness of the local bad guys, "Ten minutes ago we were at a light when a group of drug dealers pulled up. Somebody rolled down the window and leaned his head out. He was grinning. He said, 'Stick around, you'll be needed.' "

At that same crime scene, Joe Vigiano, a robbery detective in the precinct, told me that just a few nights before he had been driving home when a car full of gang members had opened fire on him. He was alone and off duty and had only his five-chamber off-duty revolver on him. He floored the accelerator, and a high-speed chase ensued, bullets spewing from inside the pursuing car. Both vehicles reached speeds of a hundred miles per hour on the Southern State Parkway, the pursuing vehicle weaving in and out of traffic behind Vigiano or bouncing after him on the grassy shoulders of the highway. Finally, the car sped off. Throughout the ordeal, Vigiano claimed, he had never been terribly worried. He had known it was just a warning. (In August 1994, however, Vigiano was shot in the arm and chest in a housing project by a member of the same gang, which was based in the project and pulled robberies throughout East New York. A bulletproof vest saved his life.)

I'll never forget the phone call Detective Al Nesbot took from the sergeant at the 104th Precinct in Queens. A family had had dinner at a local restaurant the previous evening, the sergeant told him, and the owner of the restaurant had watched as the parents and their three kids traipsed through the parking lot to their car. The mother threw her infant and two-year-old into the trunk, and everybody else piled into the seats. As the car sped off, the restaurant owner took down the license plate number. Then he called the police, who ran the plate number and found that it came back to an address in East New York. The sergeant thought the people should be checked out. Since his team was occupied with a fresh murder, Nesbot requested patrol to respond to the address. After a canvass for the car and an interview with the mother, the officers took the children away and placed them with the Bureau of Child Welfare.

One of my last crime scenes was a dump job murder—an old man who had been killed elsewhere and was found wrapped in a blanket in an abandoned lot. That night we had already been to a firebombing and another murder. The detectives were talking to a freelance news crew waiting on the opposite side of the yellow tape for the Crime Scene Unit to arrive.

One of the cameramen observed, "You know, it's not just East New York that's being hit these days. In quiet sections of Queens and other boroughs, nice people are getting whacked for no reason, but these murders rarely make the news because there's nothing lurid or sensational about them or the victims." It was a freezing night with the wind howling and trains roaring high overhead on elevated tracks. Virtually the only illumination was provided by the moon. "If people really knew how bad it was here," he said resignedly, "there'd be a mass exodus out of New York."

Just then, a radio operator at Central called to tell the detectives patrol had just picked up another murder.

And so Carbone and the other detectives were soon off to another crime scene, where they'd collect details on the victim and what had happened to him, launching their hunt for the killer or killers. Undaunted by having to juggle three murders in one night, they set themselves on their new investigative journey, a little weary and stoically resigned to the incessant violence around them. Once again they were appointed to speak for the dead, and for the people of the city, to solve and avenge yet another misdeed in the metropolis's seemingly unending procession of wrongdoing.

AUTHOR'S NOTE

This is a book about real people and real events. Because of the violent nature of the areas where many of the scenes take place, some names of witnesses and victims have been changed.

David Carbone joined the 75th Precinct Detective Unit in 1989, and I met him and began following him around the squad three years later, in 1992. The events and dialogue portrayed in this book through 1992 are based on the recollections of Carbone and some of the other players, as well as police reports and other materials; after this time, I was present to observe and record what was happening firsthand. Some scenes have been dramatically re-created, and in a few instances a sequence of events has been compressed or slightly rearranged to expedite action or enhance clarity.

PROLOGUE

It's been said that of all the jobs in law enforcement in the world, there is one that has more mystique and prestige than any other. There's an aura about it, it's looked upon with a bit of awe, and it's even been the subject of countless Hollywood movies and television shows. It's not working as an FBI agent, nor as a CIA agent, nor as an undercover operative in a foreign country. The honor is owned outright by the New York City detective.

It's the mega-metropolis which is New York City that gives its detectives that distinction, of course. At once electrifying and threatening, glamorous and sinister, the city is one of the largest and—in some of its areas—most dangerous in the world. It has everything, and can be one's best dream or worst nightmare, but it is all too real. Indeed, there's no place on earth quite like it.

Corridors of skyscrapers rise from the asphalt trenches of Manhattan like giant cubes reaching to the heavens. It is the epicenter of finance, theater, fashion, advertising, publishing, jewelry, and many other industries. A vast network of tunnels carved underneath the city provides swift train passage to virtually any point inside its borders. Brackish, polluted rivers surround the island of Manhattan, and grimy gridiron bridges and long tunnels connect it to the other boroughs.

Radiating from midtown Manhattan outward 301 square miles are neighborhoods of every size, appearance, and economic condition, ranging from abject poverty to immense wealth. Ethnic communities abound, and people of every race, color, religion, ethnicity, nationality, sexual orientation, and political persuasion go about their daily lives on the bustling streets. There's tension and anger, controversy and unrest. There is drama everywhere.

With its great expanse and its millions of people, the city is host to virtually every kind of crime imaginable. And crime occurs with prodigious frequency. Each year, about 2,000 people are reported murdered in the five boroughs of New York City—approximately one of every ten murders committed in the United States. There are around 95,000 reported robberies (forceful taking of property), about 3,000 reported rapes, over 40,000 reported assaults (shootings, stabbings, and other attacks), more than 110,000 reported burglaries (unlawful entry of a building to commit crime), nearly 100,000 reported grand larcenies (felonious property thefts), and 130,000 or so cars reported stolen. Crime is rampant, crime is violent, and it is the detectives who are charged with solving it.

To become a New York City detective, a rookie cop must follow a career path. Various units exist for the officer to go into, each of which can plunge the budding cop deeper into the netherworld of crime in the city, each one a stepping stone to the "Bureau"—the revered, exalted Detective Bureau.

But advancement is a grueling and rigorous process. All the way along, evaluations, recommendations, and interviews determine whether the officer remains at a particular level, is demoted, or advances. Everyone from frontline supervisors to commanding officers appraises the cop's skills, professionalism, arrests, summons activity, demeanor, appearance, commendations, complaints, sick record. They want to see how the cop behaves in dubious circumstances, in stressful circumstances, in deadly situations. They want to see if the cop has what it takes to move up, to become that hunter of human beings known as a detective.

The detective's shield, the coveted gold shield, is a badge of distinction. For with it the bearer carries not just a symbol, but honor, a detective's honor, and that is extraordinarily special in the NYPD. They say cops would kill to get into the Bureau, a bit of hyperbole that illuminates the difficulty of doing so. Indeed, many try to join the city's elite corps of sleuths, but only a small portion ever make it.

PART ONE

There is no hunting like the hunting of man. And those who have hunted armed men long enough and liked it never care for anything else thereafter.

—quote attributed to Ernest Hemingway mounted in the 75th Precinct detective squad room, East New York, Brooklyn

1

A throng of dark suits milled nervously before a closed door on the thirteenth floor of One Police Plaza, down the hall from the office of the New York Police Department's chief of detectives. Most of the twenty or so young men clustered in small groups of three or four, while a few stayed seated or standing by themselves, tense but quiet, and seemingly lost in thought.

The men in the clusters tried to shunt off their disquiet by making idle chatter that occasionally erupted into boisterous laughter. One of the garrulous ones—crusty and tough, New York to the core—was regaling the others in his circle with a continuous supply of wisecracks. It was in the nature of this man, twenty-eight, earring implanted in his left lobe, legs entrenched in knee-deep black lizard cowboy boots, to weather even the most stressful situations with levity. But today, despite his machine-gun procession of jests, he was feeling a tugging sense of anxiety.

Fresh from the Anticrime unit, where he worked the streets as a plainclothes cop, usually in tattered jeans and a ripped sweatshirt, a three-day stubble gracing his cheeks, the young man on this occasion presented a much different appearance. His face was closely shaved, and he was dressed in a double-breasted navy-blue pinstripe suit with a decorously folded fluffy white handkerchief sprouting from the breast pocket. This businesslike attire was what he hoped would be his uniform of the future: a coat of arms of the job, an emblem of his prestige, an indication that he was a special cop. And of course it was appropriate that he was dressed today in these clothes, for the interview he was about to have was a necessary step on the path to becoming a New York City detective. Homicide.

David Carbone—thick brown hair brushed straight back and sprayed to Sassoonian perfection, square Italian jaw, compact nose and sparkling blue eyes, clear, fair skin—examined the others vying for promotion into the NYPD's Detective Bureau. Some looked sharp, some didn't. Not that he searched for faults in others; he just took measure of things around him. It was his habit.

For some brief moments, as his acquaintances made small talk in a conscientious pretense of forgetting why they were there, Carbone scanned the group. Unkempt hair, he observed. What'd he just wake up? Mismatched suit. Probably a horny bastard without any woman to dress him. Or maybe he's got one and she's a slob. Tassel shoes. Man, that's *guindaloony* stuff. Penny loafers. Hey, that shit went out in the ninth grade. Waist-length suit jacket. Okay, dude, maybe you should be tending bar at the corner catering hall.

It would not have occurred to Carbone to wonder what some of the guys checking *him* out might be thinking: macho, swaggering stud; preening peacock; Italian stallion.

The corridor resonated with soft idle babble and the sound of hard, rapid gum chewing; it was a scene of contained pacing and uninterrupted smoking. Yeah, we're all nervous, Dave thought, but smoking? C'mon! If you're here to make an impression, why gross out the interviewers with tobacco breath?

The din came abruptly to a halt when the door opened and a voice summoned an officer whose surname began with A. Suddenly, Dave shot his hand to his left ear and snatched off the diamond earring with the dangling gold cross. His trademark accouterment of the street, a small piece of paraphernalia that went a long way in helping him blend in with the area he patrolled as an Anticrime officer, it had no place here. Surely it would be over before he started if he went in for his detective interview with his earlobe sporting a glittering symbol of the Passion.

The nervous talk and the pacing resumed at a slightly more urgent level and continued until the first candidate emerged and dispatched the second into the interview room. The young man, previously unknown to Dave, was immediately surrounded and barraged with anxious queries. What did they ask? Who was doing the questioning? What kind of personal inquiries did they make? The interview had taken longer than anyone expected. If things had gone smoothly, the guy should have been in and out relatively quickly.

Dave timed the next candidate. His inexpensive watch was manifestly mismatched with his custom-made navy-blue silk suit, but ever since he had cracked the face of his best jewel-studded timepiece in the course of wrestling to concrete a burglar trying to escape from a building, he had always worn a cheap Timex.

Number two emerged from the room after only twelve minutes. Ah, thought Dave, now, there's a cop with no problems. But an active cop? Probably not. Active cops, those making lots of collars, those who really did the job as far as Dave was concerned, got rips: civilian complaints, department investigations, that sort of thing. He momentarily reflected on his own career. He could be in for some trouble. David Carbone, no regrets, was an active cop.

When the third candidate came through the door he announced, "Carbone, you're next." Dave withdrew from his group, his husky five-foot-eleven-inch frame cutting through the thick cloud of smoke now hovering in the hallway. He tried not to think about the interview—about what it would mean for him if it didn't go well. About wearing a uniform and pounding a beat for the rest of his career.

That would be a nightmare.

Moving quickly along the NYPD career path, Dave had spent only a year and a half on patrol. As a uniformed police officer in the 73rd Precinct in Brownsville and the 94th Precinct in Greenpoint, both in Brooklyn, he had performed regular police duties while walking a foot post and riding in a sector car. Patrol was the backbone of police work, but it hadn't been stimulating enough. He had needed more challenge.

Promoted to Anticrime, a plainclothes unit of the Patrol Services Bureau that targets street crimes and works out of precincts, he shed his uniform and donned raggedy clothing to blend in with the skels in the streets. A uniformed police presence acted as a deterrent to crime; plainclothes cops could catch the bad guys in action. Anticrime cops were the same rank as police officers, wearing (concealed beneath their street costume) the same silver shield, but the Anticrime assignment was usually a springboard to a specialized unit or detail. Dave's goal, crystallized in his mind after two years in Anticrime, was the Detective Bureau. If he didn't move on, it would still be another two years before he would be bounced back to patrol, but Dave saw no point in allowing such an unappealing possibility to remain open any longer than was absolutely necessary. It was time to exorcise that specter, time to settle his future.

He opened the door.

The first thing he saw in the room was a large beige Formica conference table. The seating arrangement intensified the coldness of the naked room. Across the width of the table, one empty chair faced three high-ranking officers—bosses, as the cops called them. Someday he himself might be conducting intimidating interrogations just like this, Dave thought, but not of other cops. Of perps.

Three men, all white, all in dapper business attire, faces impassive, stood up and extended their arms to introduce themselves. Leaning over the table, Dave shook each hand in procession and then sat down. Open files sat before each man, and at each end of the long table was a big stack of manila folders.

There was a brief pause before the questioning began, each interviewer's head fixed on the papers in front of him. Across the table to Dave's left was a captain with silver hair, prominent connecting eyebrows, and a dour look. Trouble, Dave thought. The archetypal ballbuster, he probably got off on exhuming skeletons. Directly across from Dave was another captain. His face was Irish plain, no distinguishing features, but stern and morose nevertheless under his half-glasses. He seemed to be in his early fifties, a few years younger than the other captain. This one could be trouble too. The older bosses went strictly by the rules and tended to forget what the street cop has to deal with. The one friendly-looking boss was to the right. A lieutenant wearing wire-rimmed aviation glasses, with wavy black hair parted on the left and a kinder, more expressive face, he was the youngest, about forty-five.

Dave sat at the edge of his chair, not because he was nervous, which he was, but because with his head forward he would be most alert. Reclining tends to make one drowsy.

Only one thought was in Dave's mind: Be succinct. Say what you have to, then shut up. Rambling shows indecisiveness, weakness, shows that you're not really sure how you should answer. Rambling gets you into trouble. Detectives, he knew, try to make perps ramble during interrogations.

The lieutenant began the questioning. He looked up from the folder and took off his glasses. "Tell us about your personal life," he said pleasantly. "You know, your family and friends."

"I'm married. I have a little girl, three years old," Dave began. "Danielle."

He thought for a second. He didn't know what was in his file, but a friend had told him they'd have a readout on his entire life. Not that he had anything to hide, but certain things might raise flags, however small. On the other hand, not being totally forthcoming might indicate a propensity toward dishonesty.

"I'm divorced from my first wife," he added.

"What was the problem?" asked the lieutenant, not unkindly.

"We just grew apart, so we decided to go our separate ways."

Before Dave had come on the job, background investigators had interviewed his ex-wife. He wasn't happy about it—they hadn't parted on the best of terms—but he figured the investigators wanted to see if he was a wife-beater or something. Not that her word would be gospel even if she made such an accusation, but the department always made thorough investigations and checked out any allegations.

"I kept the house," Dave continued, "because I grew up in the community. I wanted to stay in Merrick. My family's from there. I have four brothers and three sisters. My father works for Grumman. My mom—she's dead."

The lieutenant looked down at his file, and the captain with the connecting eyebrows slowly raised his head, shifted his eyes, and focused on Dave. The three bosses were spread far apart across from Dave, so he'd have to turn his head sharply to address each one.

"Officer Carbone," said the captain matter-of-factly, "why should we pick *you*? What makes you think you're better than the people outside?"

Dave smiled faintly and sighed, a delicate show of modesty that also bought him a second or two to figure out how the hell to answer the question. Shit, Dave thought as he cleared his throat, am I supposed to toot my own horn here or what?

"I think my record speaks for itself," Dave replied, thinking of the more than a hundred collars he had made during his three and a half years on the force. He had always prided himself on being a good, honest, hardworking cop, and his record reflected this self-perception. What else could he tell them that they didn't already know? "Above and beyond that," he ventured, "I think I have the kind of analytical mind needed to successfully work cases."

Dave thought momentarily and with satisfaction of the work he'd done on his home; it was an indication of the meticulous, careful type of person he was. He had built one of the bathrooms himself, complete with a Jacuzzi. He had tiled the kitchen, installed cabinets, gutted and rebuilt the living room with skylights, refinished the basement, and built a cedar deck. With no training whatsoever in household construction, he had been able to work his way through and analyze what he'd be doing several steps ahead. He knew he could channel this aptitude to detective work, shape his cop skills into the methodical precision a detective brings to solving cases.

"In doing police work, I've been able to think beforehand about what could develop down the line," Dave continued. "I keep an open mind. I don't get tunnel vision, thinking something can only be one way. And I believe I've developed the requisite street smarts. I've made so many arrests because I know how the mutts out there think."

Dave considered his medals. He could have had more, but he had hardly ever bothered writing himself up as the *Patrol Guide* required, the first step in being considered for a commendation. Some cops spent a lot of time singing their own praises, but Dave eschewed these self-congratulatory exercises, thinking them a waste of time. He hoped that wouldn't now prove a drawback.

"I'm meticulous, I'm zealous, and I'm dedicated," he said. "And I don't give a hundred percent. I give a hundred and ten percent."

Shit, I'm starting to ramble, he realized.

"I don't know if I'm better than the people in the hallway," he wound up, "but I think I'd make a damn good detective."

The three men looked down at their folders, and Dave wondered how they had taken what he said. Had he sounded too pompous?

The first captain, still gazing at the papers in front of him, remarked casually, "Police officers have many opportunities to take money." Then he looked up at Dave. "Why is taking money not right?"

Dave was not surprised by this straightforward inquiry about ethics. "First, it's dishonest," he said emphatically. "Second, I'm a cop, and cops have higher standards to live up to than anybody else. I'd never do something that would disgrace the department and my family."

The captain considered this for a moment, holding Dave's eyes. Then he said, "And how would you feel if you were offered a bribe?"

"Insulted," Dave shot back. "I can't be bought."

The captain returned to his folder for a second, then raised his eyes to Dave's again. "Do you own anything?"

Dave's lips tightened at the corners. "Yes. I own a home, two cars, a motorcycle. I think that's it."

What I own has nothing to do with the job, he thought, nothing to do with how I'd be as a detective. It's personal and I shouldn't have to justify it. But they had the authority to ask such questions, and he had to answer them. If they didn't like his answers, were they going to check out what he owned? Look into his finances? He knew they'd be comparing what he owned to what he earned. Background investigators had interviewed his neighbors when he applied to join the police department.

For a split second he contemplated saying, "What difference does it make?" He cleared his throat instead.

The captain was staring at him, his connecting eyebrows furrowed. "How are your bills?"

"Well, you struggle, but I make them every month. Overtime helps, and Luciann—my wife—works." Dave knew exactly what the captain was looking for. Was he or had he ever been on the take? If you had nice things, it looked as though you had stolen to get them. After all, you couldn't afford them on a cop's salary.

"What did you pay for your house?"

"Fifty-two thousand." The house was now worth at least $100,000, Dave thought. Would it be a problem that he owned a house at a relatively young age? He had worked damn hard all his life, sometimes two jobs, and he had earned everything he owned. He could feel his stomach tightening.

"What do you have outstanding?"

"Just the usual stuff. Mortgage, Visa, MasterCard, Sears. I have a home improvement loan." Dave told himself to relax, but the captain was relentless.

"How much savings do you have?"

"Three, four thousand dollars."

"You don't know exactly?" The eyebrows rose delicately.

"My wife handles the money. I just give her my checks." Dave looked directly into the captain's eyes and held his gaze steady.

"Okay. Now, let's say somebody actually offered you that bribe," said the captain. "What if somebody you locked up offered you fifteen hundred dollars? You'd be insulted. But what would you do?"

Dave knew they would be listening not only to what he had to say—there were proper procedures to follow in bribery cases—but how he said it. Of course, he had nothing to hide, but the job itself made for paranoia.

"I'd tell him I'd take the fifteen hundred to let him go," he responded. He fidgeted a bit in his seat, then straightened up. "Then I'd notify the duty captain and wait for IAD to come wire me."

The captain nodded at his reference to the Internal Affairs Division. Then the bosses flung at Dave one scenario after another in which a cop might find himself tempted to supplement his salary. It was all too easy. He might have to sit alone with a corpse for six hours waiting for the meat wagon to arrive, while cash, jewelry, and other valuables were staring him in the face. He might catch somebody selling drugs and be offered a few thousand cash to walk away. He might even pull over a motorist while off duty and suggest a payoff to walk away from a summons or an arrest.

"You have to be able to shave in the morning," Dave said. "I could never steal or take a bribe." He hated these questions; they made him feel demeaned.

Now the lieutenant started in, moving to other technical scenarios.

"It's three o'clock in the morning," he said, "and you just locked up a red-haired Spanish guy for rape. Where are you going to get your fillers?"

"Shelters, bodegas, pool halls, the street, cops in the precinct," Dave shot back instantly, relieved to be off the bribery and theft questions. He described police procedures in conducting lineups. He mentioned the six bodies, noted that the five fillers—people who appear in the lineup with the suspect—should look somewhat like the alleged perp, spoke of the one-way mirror. The lawyer got to view the lineup with the complainant or witness if he wanted, he added.

"Some cops use the squad to run their lineups," he continued, "but I run my own. I take the initiative. I don't like taking the backseat and letting other people do my work."

"If a detective called you in the middle of the night looking for information on a cop shooter, would you say you had to go to your office to get the information, or do you keep a diary in your house?"

"I write down information on a steno pad and keep that handy," Dave responded. "I might be able to say, "Yeah, I locked up Johnny Smith, whose street name is Scorpio. He carries a 9mm in his back pocket. We chased him, and he ran into a crack den. He's a fast runner, he puts up a big fight.' "

"You were never out sick, but you had a couple line-of-duty injuries," said the first captain.

"Yes," Dave said, recalling a sprained hand he had sustained in Anticrime while struggling with a robber. "But I was out only a short while. I had to be back for my team."

The bosses, Dave knew, were asking the kinds of questions that would help them decide whether he was a good team player, whether he had a knack for detective work, and how he had prepared himself for that work in his current detail.

"Tell us about the quality of your arrests."

"My arrests stick, and they're not bullshit arrests." Dave knew they weren't concerned here about quantity but quality. Some cops think that because they make tons of arrests, they should be in line for a detective detail. But locking up three-card monte guys doesn't make you a good investigator. "I've made good observation arrests for burglaries and robberies, and the perps generally plead guilty before going to trial."

Abruptly the captain leaned back, and the Irish captain smoothly took up the questioning, as if rehearsed. "Tell us about the most satisfying arrest you've made."

Dave thought for a moment. Of all the collars he had made, a few stood out in his mind: the machete-wielding drunk, the guy who had thrown a refrigerator down at him from a rooftop, the men who ran a stolen car ring. But there was one that always gave him tremendous satisfaction. It was as clear in his mind as the day it happened.

Bayard Street, in the heart of Greenpoint, Brooklyn, was a quiet Italian area with wide white asphalt sidewalks and thin lampposts painted red, white, and green. Three-story connecting apartment houses with cement front patios enclosed by steel fences and white gates lined the block, and at dinnertime the fragrance of Italian cooking invitingly filled the air. At one end of the block was an immaculate house with pristine brown aluminum siding and an American flag mounted on a long pole. Inside lived Carmine and Rose Babino. In this home Carmine had been born many years ago.

It was overcast that April morning, gray clouds hanging low, a light drizzle trickling down. A balmy breeze seemed to signal the beginning of spring. Carmine Babino, sixty-eight, had just awakened and was standing in boxer shorts in front of his bathroom mirror, his face fully lathered. He pressed the razor to his face and carefully drew off thick white cream.

Suddenly he heard a loud crash. What was it? Carmine thought he'd better take a look. He put down his razor and opened the bathroom door.

In the hall was a stranger, a stocky, unshaven man, crude-looking, strung-out, definitely strung-out, glaring at him. Before Carmine's anger could explode, the man yelled, "Where's my daughter? Where's my daughter?"

"What? Get out of here!" Carmine shouted.

He grabbed the intruder's arm to lead him out. The stranger in turn locked with Carmine, and the two wrestled to the ground. Rolling around the kitchen and corridor, they knocked over tables and objects.

The clamor woke Rose, who put on her bathrobe to see what the commotion was.

In the kitchen, Rose found a man on top of her husband, pummeling him. He was driving his fists hard into the elderly man.

Rose screamed and rushed to the struggling pair. She tried to push off the attacker, but he threw her across the room. Stumbling and off balance, she barely managed to avoid falling and striking her head on the porcelain sink.

Holding on to the sink for support, she stood there a second, frantic. Then, collecting herself, she ran to the phone in the hall and dialed 911.

"Help!" she cried when the emergency operator answered. She had difficulty talking; she couldn't catch her breath. She followed her husband and the intruder with her eyes as they rolled out of sight. She cried to the operator, "Help us, please help us!" and managed to blurt out her address.

Rose dropped the phone and ran down the long, narrow corridor to where the two men were still fighting. Carmine was pinned to the floor now, and the man was furiously pounding his head into the bottom steps of the stairway. Blood was starting to gush out of her husband's head. Rose, frail and petite, was hysterical, not knowing what to do. A crack addict was in her home killing her husband.

"Oh, God," she screamed. "Oh, my God!"

A patrol car sat at a light at the corner of Graham and Metropolitan avenues. It was a busy commercial area with a subway station, and inside the car two young uniformed cops were watching the people stroll by. There had been many robberies there recently, especially chain and pocketbook snatchings, and they were planning to catch anyone in the act of committing a crime.

Suddenly a beeping tone crackled over the radio. The partners exchanged wary looks. That tone indicated an important job like a 10-30 (robbery in progress), a 10-34 (assault in progress), or a 10-13 (police officer needs assistance). The man in the passenger's seat reached for the radio as Central's voice cut in.

"Nine-Four Adam, K."

"Four Adam, K," he barked in response.

"In David sector you got a ten thirty-one at 170 Bayard Street. Be advised that the caller states her husband is fighting with the perpetrator at this time. Adam read?"

A 10-31 meant a burglary in progress. Before the vehicle's recorder, Bill Carlson, could respond to Central, the NYPD's radio communications unit at One Police Plaza, the car was already in motion. The driver, David Carbone, had instinctively activated the siren switch and turned on the red-and-white turret lights.

"Adam read, K."

"Okay, Adam. If a bus [ambulance] is needed, notify us when you're eighty-four [on the scene]."

The static crackled, and Billy Carlson put the radio down. He checked his seat belt. Cars in the intersection came to a sudden halt as the radio car plowed through.

North on Graham Avenue, a right on Meeker under the Brooklyn-Queens Expressway, where the hollow sound of the siren reverberated like a passing train whistle. Just as the car made a left onto McGuinness Boulevard, David Carbone turned off the siren and lights. A crime was in progress, and he wanted to surprise the perp. One block up, he made a left onto Bayard.

The car pulled up to number 170, and the two officers jumped out. The front door was open; they ran up the pathway and swept right in. A few feet ahead, in the entranceway, was a middle-aged woman standing over a man, her hands pressed against her face, crying.

Dave winced when he saw the elderly man sprawled out on the floor and the bottom steps of the staircase, his face and neck covered in blood and gobs of shaving cream.

Rose Babino, sobbing, told the officers what had happened. There was no sign of the intruder; he had run out of the house before the police arrived.

Carmine could still talk. In fact, although his head was bleeding and his whole body was bruised, he was so angry that he insisted the cops put him in their car to look for the intruder.

"Slow down there, old-timer," Dave said. "Don't you think you'd better go to the hospital, get yourself checked out?"

"No. I want to look for him," Carmine growled hoarsely. He struggled to his feet, grabbed a towel from a basket of clean laundry sitting in the entranceway, and pressed it to his head. Then, ignoring Rose's protests, he turned and marched unsteadily out the door.

Dave and Bill exchanged glances. "Feisty old geezer," Bill remarked under his breath to Dave. Then he said to Rose, "Don't worry, we'll take care of him. You go back in the house, make yourself a cup of tea, try to relax, okay?"

Rose looked up at him, her face a mixture of pain and gratitude. Dave gave her arm a light squeeze. "I'm sorry this happened," he said, and he meant it.

The two cops put their wounded assault victim in the back of the patrol car and scoured the neighborhood. They didn't find the intruder, but Carmine gave a good description of him.

"Sounds like Mike Harrison," said Dave to his partner. The cops knew most of the neighborhood mutts.

Carlson nodded.

Dave turned the car around and headed for the suspect's home.

The two officers, one on either side of the still-unsteady Carmine, their hands on his elbows, made their way up the walk. A woman answered the doorbell, not all that surprised to see the cops. She eyed the disheveled Carmine with alarm.

"Good morning, ma'am. Where's Michael?" Carlson asked pleasantly.

"He was just here to get his raincoat," his mother answered warily. "He rushed out, and I may not see him for a couple days."

The three men looked at each other. Harrison had done the assault.

Driving Mr. Babino home, Dave thought the situation through. As old man Babino and Officer Carlson commiserated about a city in which drug-crazed punks beat up old men, he reviewed the precinct mentally: its geography, where the crackheads and skels hung out, which locations were populated by which different sorts. Finally, they pulled up to the Babino home. Still feeling sore, Mr. Babino held his hand to his head as he alighted stiffly from the car. "We'll find him soon," Dave promised, as his partner shot him an uneasy look. "Maybe even tomorrow."

Now a past assault, the Babino case would be handed over to the precinct detective unit. Detectives would interview the complainant and handle any investigation that followed. Patrol officers sometimes became attached to a particular case or victim, but once a job was over with, it was on to the next.

The next morning, Dave greeted his partner with an amazing coincidence. By a stroke of luck, Dave told Billy, a job away from their sector had just happened to come in for them. It was in sector George at the India Street piers, a popular hangout for dopeheads.

"What'd you say that job was?" Carlson asked, scratching his head.

"A ten-ten, suspicious person," Dave replied, eying his partner.

Carlson thought a moment and broke into a grin. "Yeah, a ten-ten. Let's go get him!"

The two officers headed out of Adam-David sector at nine-thirty. Fifteen minutes later, they entered sector Frank at the other end of the precinct. They cruised by the waterfront in Greenpoint, surveying the area from the car. It was a bright, clear day, and the tall buildings of Manhattan loomed majestically across the river.

Parking their RMP—radio motor patrol car—across the street from the waterfront, the two patrol officers strolled circumspectly toward the India Street piers. As they approached, they melted into the background as best they could. The cops appraised the scene, focusing on the denizens as their eyes swept slowly back and forth. A gaggle of people were spread out ahead, standing, sitting, leaning on fences, lying stretched out on the pier.

Several minutes passed, then Dave said quietly, "That's him."

As the two cops made their way out onto the pier, the folks loitering on it muttered insults and glowered at them. Cops weren't their favorite people.

The cops' prey was huddled in a corner, sniffing glue from a paper bag. He wasn't aware he was even being monitored until the officers were about to descend upon him.

"Mr. Babino," Dave said on the phone a short while later, "we just picked up somebody. We'd like you to come down to the station house, see if you can pick him out of a lineup."

An hour later, Carmine stood behind a one-way mirror and gazed at the six men who stood several feet away. He immediately recognized his assailant, selecting the man Dave and his partner had grabbed at the pier. Dave spent the rest of the day shepherding his prisoner through Central Booking. The man had been high from sniffing glue when he broke into the Babino home, apparently to boost his courage to commit burglary. He had no daughter; that was the first thing to pop into his muddled mind when Babino unexpectedly confronted him.

Because criminals often plead out at arraignments or hearings and their cases don't go to trial, cops often never find out the disposition of the collars. But because Dave took this case almost personally—old and young crime victims struck at the very core of his heart—he was determined to follow this one through. His collar was charged with burglary and assault, and he hoped the district attorney wouldn't reduce the charges just to get a conviction, as often happens, or drop them altogether.

It was with immeasurable satisfaction that Dave learned seven months later that his collar had been sentenced to three to five years in jail. When he dropped by the Babinos' house to congratulate them, they invited him for Thanksgiving dinner the following week—and they renewed the invitation every year thereafter.

There was also an equal, if not a greater, sense of personal satisfaction. This had been Dave's first real taste of detective work, and it had confirmed to him that being an investigator was the area of law enforcement he most wanted to pursue.

As he finished up an abbreviated version of this tale for his examiners, who gave almost imperceptible nods of approval, Dave noticed a peculiar look had come over the face of the Irish captain, emphasized by his half-glasses. Dave could feel it coming. This pleasant interlude was over, and the bombs—the questions about his disciplinary record—were about to be dropped. Two cases were pending against him and the city in the area of $50 million each.

The captain peered at Dave over his glasses. "You were charged with an assault," he stated flatly.

"Yes. But I was exonerated."

Dave's hands clenched and his jaw locked, not out of nervousness but in exasperation at the bullshit that came with the job. He tried hard not to display any signs of discomfiture.

"What happened?"

"I was in a patrol car with my partner and we got a call of a man with a gun. As we were on our way to the scene, Central told us the man had fled in a car, and a couple minutes later we saw a car that fit Central's description. The guy wouldn't pull over, and we had a high-speed chase. After a few miles the guy crashed his car and bailed out, and we chased him on foot. When we caught him he resisted arrest, but we subdued him. And then he tried to turn the tables and claimed we assaulted him."

There was silence. The captain wrote something in Dave's folder, and the other two began writing as well. What the hell could be wrong? Dave wondered. Not only had he done the right thing, he and his partner had acted heroically and should have written themselves up for a medal. But instead this mutt had turned the story around and sued the city. Dave searched for any warmth in his questioners' faces, but they were completely devoid of expression. His belly churned acid, which seemed intent on boring a hole through his stomach lining.

It wasn't for another minute that anyone spoke. Dave's hands were clammy. That also pissed him off, because he'd never reacted this way before. The importance of the interview was getting to him.

"You were also charged with a burglary, stealing ten thousand dollars," the other captain announced.

"Yes, but I didn't do it." Maybe it was futile, Dave thought. These guys were probably too far removed from reality to appreciate the rigors a cop goes through.

"What happened?"

The fingernails of Dave's hands dug into his palms, and his stomach tied itself in a knot. Against his will, he felt his temper rising. Some cops lost a lot of sleep over allegations like this, which could take years to investigate. Dave hadn't lost his cool, but the investigation that followed, like the assault charge, had really tried his patience. Each had

taken eight months, a long, painful eight months. Internal Affairs studied all the records associated with the cases—Dave's memo book, transcripts of the day, the arrest folders, the desk officer's blotter. IAD officers interviewed the complainants. With a tape recorder running, they interviewed Dave, with a PBA attorney present. Some jerk's work of fiction, and he went from doing his job to being put on trial.

Dave explained that he and his partner had received a call of a burglary in progress. When they arrived at the scene, they saw a man who fit Central's description come out of the building. He ran, and they chased him into another building, where he kicked down a door and entered an apartment. Dave had tackled him just as he was about to slip out a window and down the fire escape. When the occupant of the apartment later returned, the neighbors filled him in on what had happened. Later, the occupant charged the officers with taking $10,-000 from his apartment.

Although the charge was obviously a crock—what better way to extort money from the city than by claiming cops who entered the apartment when the resident wasn't home had absconded with a horde of cash?—Dave thought it was sickening that the department would spend so much time and money investigating it. Every creep who gets collared or summoned knew he could make a complaint about a cop just to bust his chops, and the department would take it seriously. It was a good arrest, and Dave was exonerated of this charge too.

"How do you feel about the charge?" the lieutenant asked when Dave had finished describing the incident.

With an effort, Dave kept himself from voicing his thoughts. "It comes with the job. People get mad when you lock them up, and they make complaints or fabricate stories. If I feel I'm right making the arrest, I don't worry about what they'll do."

"Do you worry about your complaints?"

"No," Dave said emphatically. All three bosses stared at him. "Because I've never done anything wrong where I've had to worry," he added. Three heads returned to their file folders.

The very last question was not unexpected, and it was the easiest. Dave could answer from the heart.

"Why do you want to be a detective?"

"I love being a cop," he said. "But I'm looking to better myself, challenge myself more, find out what I'm made of, what I could accomplish if I had the chance. And no disrespect," he added, "but I don't want to be a boss in this job. I want to be an investigator. That's what I've wanted from the start, and that's what I'd like to be when I retire."

There were no more questions. The three interviewers spent the next few minutes writing and conferring in low voices.

Dave sat there feeling helpless as they decided his fate. Acid flooded his stomach again. I've tried my best, he told himself. If they reject me, I can still hold my head up to my family.

The alternation of silence and hushed conversation was disconcerting. Dave kept his head mostly lowered, not even trying to read their faces. Not much ran through his mind. He was trying to settle his nerves.

Finally, the three men rose from their seats. Here it comes, Dave thought as he stood to face them, the moment of reckoning. So what will it be? PO or DT? He watched their lips curve upward, sudden smiles blooming on their faces. The men offered their hands as the dour captain intoned, "Welcome aboard, Carbone."

Dave returned their smiles and handshakes, trying to contain his exultation. His long-held aspiration had been granted. But he knew he had to temper his dream with patience. He'd passed the first hurdle, but the psychological interview loomed. And there was still the protracted stepping-stone of the Robbery Investigation Program.

David Carbone strode out of the room and told the next officer it was his turn up.

Moving his sleeve away from his wrist, he observed that precisely twenty-eight minutes had elapsed since he had entered the room—twenty-eight minutes that had opened one of the most significant doors of his life.

2

Three weeks later, in mid-July 1986, David Carbone cruised on his Honda Magna Special Edition from his home in Nassau County, Long Island, into the 90th Precinct in Brooklyn, a dense patchwork of tough black, Italian, Hispanic, and Hasidic neighborhoods in the Bushwick and Williamsburg sections. He was dressed nattily in designer jeans, a blue pullover shirt, and bullhide cowboy boots. It wasn't yet the detective's suit he coveted, but it was a step up from Anticrime.

This was only supposed to be a pit stop on the way to Homicide, Dave reminded himself for the umpteenth time as he parked his bike in back of the station house and removed his helmet. Looking in the bike's rearview mirror, he ran a comb through his hair. Then he walked around to the front and entered the station house, a modern two-story brick building attached to a firehouse at the intersection of Union Avenue and Broadway in Williamsburg. Gazing through a square window in the vestibule, he saw the desk officer and a few uniformed officers huddled in conversation.

Directly facing the officers, out of Dave's view, would be the muster area, where cops line up for formal inspection before each tour. Dave wondered if his new colleagues released their frustrations and anxieties by pulling pranks as those in other precincts occasionally did, such as assembling before the platoon sergeant in their raincoats while lumbering underneath in the buff.

Clutching his shield in his hand, Dave stepped inside and paused for a moment, looking around the vestibule. Occupying most of the chairs and benches was a selection of civilians in varying stages of dishevelment and apparent distress. The guy with the head wound was probably waiting to file an assault charge. The other people could be there for any number of reasons: to have an order of protection served, file a stolen car or vehicle accident report or a complaint against a landlord or neighbor, report a burglary or a missing spouse or a lost child or pet—anything for which police assistance was needed, either in reality or merely in perception. Dave remembered how during his patrol and Anticrime career people on the street would call him and his fellow officers names and generally behave rudely, only to turn up weeks, maybe months, later at the precincts entreating the aid of those same cops.

This tour might be just a pit stop, Dave reflected as he crossed the vestibule, but an assignment of over two years is more than a minor jaunt. This was the system, the career path the NYPD laid out for its detectives. To enter the NYPD's Detective Bureau, a cop had to serve a minimum period in an investigative unit: the Organized Crime Control Bureau, which was essentially narcotics investigation; the Robbery Identification Program, in which robbers were hunted down; the Internal Affairs Division or any of the Field Internal Affairs Units, in which corrupt cops were ferreted out; the Warrant Division, which tracked down people who skipped out after judges had issued bench warrants for their arrest; or the Applicant Background Investigation Unit, which checked on the backgrounds of prospective police academy recruits.

It was a bit like traveling from New York to Europe by way of Asia, but it was, Dave had to admit, the most judicious course; you have to learn to crawl before you can walk. In any case, there was no choice but to accept it. Inwardly brimming with impatience, Dave tried to look cheerful, hoping what he would gain in knowledge would more than make up for what he lost in time.

Having previously brought robbery collars to the Nine-Oh, Dave knew the layout of the place. As he moved out of the vestibule, Dave flashed his shield to a police aide, who was listening to a young woman make some kind of tearful plea. He made a quick left turn to a stairwell and, two steps at a time, climbed to the second-floor office of the Robbery Identification Program.

It was a few minutes before eight o'clock in the morning, and the other members of Dave's RIP team—one of four in the unit—were already assembled, drinking coffee and talking shop through mouthfuls of doughnuts.

As Dave entered the room, one of the older detectives spotted him and stepped away from the group. "You must be Carbone," he said, extending a welcoming hand as the others turned toward Dave, eying him with a mixture of curiosity and wariness. "I'm Joe Torres. This here is Billy Ciorciari, and this is Larry Shannon. Glad to have you aboard—we can use another body around here."

As Dave shook the detectives' hands and exchanged cordial pleasantries, he could sense their uneasiness. He understood. New guys always have to prove they can be trusted before they're accepted.

Dave was immediately drawn to the welcoming detective, José Ramón Torres, a veteran who looked more Italian or Arabic than Hispanic with his olive complexion, straight black hair, and prominent arcing mustache. His compelling eyes, large and black and sad, were crowned with surging eyebrows that conveyed profound sincerity. Everyone looked up to Joe Torres, as Dave was to discover, and it was immediately apparent to him that Torres was a shrewd and able detective.

Shannon handed Dave a paper cup of steaming strong coffee and passed him a box of doughnuts. After a little small talk, Torres drew him aside as the other two detectives went back to working on their cases.

Torres led Dave to a desk in the corner of the room, and they sat. "As you know, we investigate robberies in RIP," said Dave's new mentor. Born in Puerto Rico, and a resident there until he was nine, Torres nonetheless had no perceptible accent. Though bilingual, he was an acclimated New Yorker, and his patois was authentic Brooklynese. "A victim reports that he or she was robbed, and we go after the perp."

Dave raised his left hand and rested his chin between his thumb and first finger, a posture that from childhood he had used to signal his brain to prepare to absorb new material. As Torres went into more detail, Dave found himself relaxing. RIP would be a good place to become proficient in investigation, to learn to identify and search for criminals. Although looking for a murderer was more intense, a hunt was a hunt. The basic concepts of an investigation applied to any crime, whether a robbery, a burglary, or a murder.

"It's not like being a cop," Torres continued, "getting jobs, maybe chasing robbers, but then going on to other jobs. We get robberies after they happen—a few minutes, an hour, a day, maybe even a week later. They're committed, then we got out and try to find the perp and make an arrest. If it's a robbery, we got it.

"Most of the time there's a pattern, if you can find it. A robber doesn't just rob once. They rob numerous times until they get caught. They're creatures of habit. They strike the same way, they wear the same jacket, the same cap, the same footwear."

Dave smiled inwardly. It was a good thing most criminals weren't very smart—otherwise the cops would never catch them. He'd heard stories like the one about a motorist being pulled over for running a red light, then being identified as a killer when a routine run of his name through the computer turned up the arrest warrant. You'd think murderers would be model citizens on the road, but they were stupid enough to get caught on a lousy traffic violation.

"There's a lot of paperwork to learn now that you'll be investigating robberies," Torres told his young apprentice, riffling through the pile of forms on his desk. They included Detective Division (DD) Fives, On-Line Booking System arrest worksheets, complaint reports, Detective Bureau Unusual Occurrence Reports, and robbery worksheets, some of which Dave had never had to deal with before. "We'll spend the next few days going over the paperwork and how to conduct an investigation as the cases come in."

As a result of a successful pilot project in 1979 to identify robbery recidivists, or repeat robbers, in the 90th Precinct, the NYPD's Robbery Identification Program had been formally set up in 1981. Investigators had found that robbery suspects were territorial—they tended to operate in the same areas over and over again. Robberies had previously been handled by the precinct detective squads, which investigated all types of crime, but the RIP pilot program revealed that it would be more efficient to have separate units that concentrated exclusively on robberies and only in particular areas. After robbery recidivists had been identified, their photos went in a file of repeat offenders for a specific area. When a robbery—the use or threatened use of force to take property away from a victim—occurred in that area, the victim would be able to look through its file. Many identifications had resulted from this program.

There was never any shortage of cases for apprentice detectives in the Nine-Oh RIP unit to cut their teeth on. Robberies poured in daily, and the newcomers were immediately placed on the team rotation order to "catch" cases. The catching detective—the person the case was assigned to—went out to investigate the crime with whoever was available on the team to assist him. Sometimes it was just one other detective, sometimes the whole team. Following a robbery, either RIP investigators went to the crime scene, or patrol brought the victim to the station house.

Several hours after Dave arrived, a call came in about a man who had been approached by two thugs on a subway platform. The strangers had dragged the man down a staircase to the lower level of the station, where a third accomplice was waiting with a gun. The armed man had knocked the victim to the ground with the butt of his gun; as he lay helpless, all three perpetrators had kicked him, then they had removed his wallet and jewelry and fled on foot.

Patrol was waiting at the scene with the victim, and the case was Dave's—the other members of his team having just caught their own cases, he was already up on the rotation order.

"First you'll interview the victim," said Torres to Dave, beginning an explanation of the procedures for starting an investigation as the two drove in an unmarked car to the crime scene. As Dave listened intently, Torres offered tips on how to relax victims, build their confidence, gain their trust, use psychology to prod them to identify a perp. He explained what the interview should yield: a detailed explanation of what happened and what weapon was used, and a physical description of the perp, including gender, race, height, weight, clothing, and distinguishing characteristics. "Did the perp have a scar?" Torres asked. "Facial hair? A tattoo? Acne? Missing teeth?" He unrolled a laundry list of different peculiarities. "You'd be surprised how important these are to getting the perp."

With Torres coaching him discreetly, Dave carried out the initial interview. The victim refused medical attention, and Dave asked him to come back to the station house to sift through photographs in the RIP office.

The office was crammed with photograph books of perps—books categorized as male white, female white, male black, female black, male Hispanic, female Hispanic, guns, push-in robberies, mixed males with eyeglasses, common thieves, pimps, numbers, chop shops, smoke shops, shelters, nicknames. If someone was arrested for robbing a bodega, his mug was filed in the commercial robbery book. If a person had been collared for a street robbery and lived in a project, he went in one of the project books. There were books for just about every category of robbery, and if none of them quite fit, the perp would go into one of the 90th Precinct's eighteen zone books.

The main tool in RIP was photographs, Torres had explained to his protégé. Various techniques and psychology could be used when showing complainants the photos. Placing a piece of paper with a hole cut in it over a photo so just the face was visible kept hair and clothing from interfering with the victim's concentration on the mug's features. Having the victim describe in detail exactly what he or she had been doing immediately prior to the crime sometimes helped sharpen the victim's memory of the perp's appearance.

The complainant in the office combed the books in vain for photos of the guys who had robbed him. As he left, Torres leaned back in his chair and rubbed his eyes. "We have so many shots, you'd think every perp in the city would be in those books somewhere. But there are a

few who haven't had the courtesy to drop by for a photo session yet.''
He grimaced wearily at Dave and shook his head.

The two victims of the next robbery Dave caught had been working
in a gas station. Three gunmen had slipped into the premises after
dark and shot the guard dog when it had begun to bark. In the station
office, they had announced a stickup. Relieving the employees of their
personal cash, the gunmen had tied them up in a back room, then
emptied the cash register and fled. The victims couldn't identify their
assailants in the photo books either. There was nowhere else to go with
the case for the time being, and Dave began to feel a bit down.

Dave conducted his next interview in a hospital room. The victim
had been getting out of his late-model four-door sedan when two men
grabbed him and forced him into the car's backseat, removing all his
jewelry and his wallet. When the driver tried to struggle with his assailants, one of them pulled out a gun and shot him in the stomach. The
perpetrators then had tossed him onto the street and driven away in
the car.

From his bed, the complainant pointed to a photo in one of the
books the detectives had lugged to the hospital. "That's one of them,"
he said, his voice tense.

Back at the station house, Dave grabbed from a shelf a thick ring
binder—the master photo log, or the "bible," as Torres had called
it—to research his photo hit. The book contained sheets of information on the perps in the photo books: names, dates of previous arrests,
addresses, dates of birth, heights, accomplices, locations where they
operated, and their MO, or modus operandi—such as "Does hallway
robberies aided by an accomplice with a knife."

A canvass of the area of the crime had failed to turn up a suspect,
but now with the photo hit the RIP investigators had the perp's picture
and an address. The next day, Dave and Torres checked out the address, but the occupant said he had never heard the name they gave
him, and he didn't recognize the person in the photo. His neighbors
didn't either. Dave distributed copies of the perp's photo to patrol and
Anticrime officers in case they happened to spot him during their
tours.

"What happens now?" Dave inquired of Torres.

"We close out the case with a Wanted Card," answered Torres.
"Maybe six months from now, patrol—somewhere in the city—will arrest someone who fits the description of the perp, the Wanted Card
will pop, and we'll be notified. Then we'll call the victim to come in

and ID the suspect. But for now, the case is closed."

Closed, Dave thought, with a vicious pair of gunmen still at large. The next time one of their victims rashly decided to fight back, he might not be lucky enough to escape with merely a hole in his belly.

In these first weeks, while Dave was learning the ropes of RIP, there were shootings, stabbings, and beatings, most quite brutal, all assigned to RIP because the victims—ranging from young children to octogenarians, from the healthy to the enfeebled—had been robbed.

These bastards have no conscience whatsoever, Dave told himself. He interviewed robbery victims in hospitals, in the office, at crime scenes. He took them on canvasses, showed them the photo books. He tried to work as fast as he could while the crimes were still fresh in the victims' minds. As they left the office, he told them that if he found something, he would call.

But he never had anything to call about.

Dave couldn't find the perps. He made no arrests. He admitted to himself that the work was tougher than he had imagined. Some guy commits a robbery, and Dave was supposed to find him, when all he had to go on was a physical description from a terrorized victim? Torres was right; conducting investigations wasn't like being a cop. It wasn't like getting a job and taking a report, and going on to the next. You got the case after the crime happened, did investigative work, and built up the case. While street smarts were important in both lines of work, being a detective was quite different from being a patrol cop.

Now he began asking himself, if he couldn't handle robberies, how was he ever going to be able to handle murders? Captain Woods, the commanding officer in the Nine-Four, where Dave had been in Anticrime, had recommended the young officer highly to Sergeant Heffernan, the Nine-Oh RIP CO. Dave had been an active cop, had made plenty of collars. Now he was trying to live up to that recommendation, to build an impressive record toward his eventual promotion to Homicide—and he was coming up dry.

"Maybe I should go back to being a cop," he mused aloud to Torres.

"Don't worry," said Torres, resting a hand briefly on the young man's shoulder. "You'll get the hang of it. It just takes time."

Dave grinned wanly at the older man. He was having his doubts.

It was on Kent Avenue under the Williamsburg Bridge that the Nine-Oh cops found their release after work, trading tales of lust and war stories and swigging away their frustrations under clouds of smoke and stale air. The Water Front Bar was a dark and cozy haunt located in an industrial area along the East River, far enough off the crime-beaten path to permit the cops to drink in peace and seclusion.

For Dave, it was about trying to fit in, to be one of the guys. It was usually midnight or later when the tour ended, and he wanted nothing more than to crawl into bed next to his wife and lose consciousness. But his buddies would insist he join them at the Water Front. If Dave demurred, they'd implore him in tones impassioned enough to make him feel like a killjoy: "Come on, come on, we'll just go for one or two. What can it hurt? We all need to unwind." Of course, "one or two" meant all he could quaff and hours of nonstop gab.

Dave's after-tour beverage was draft beer. He could down six or so without any unsteadying effect, and he might go as high as two six-packs. Hard liquor, though, he avoided.

And so after too many tours, particularly the four-to-twelves, the soldiers descended on the precinct watering hole. There were twenty-year-olds just out of the academy and burned-out fifty-year-olds with mean scowls etched on hardened faces who hated the world and everything in it that moved. Their shirts hung loosely over their trousers, and their off-duty revolvers were tucked discreetly into waistbands and ankle holsters.

As the hours passed and the air grew heavier and mustier, the soldiers would loosen up. As a general rule, there were only two topics of conversation at the saloon: pussy and the job. Bragging competitions regularly erupted in which the combatants argued about who was nailing more pieces of ass during their tours. Occasionally conversation would drift to other topics such as the wife and kids, but it soon returned to rollicking bragfests about porking, muff-diving, BJs, and the job. Always the job. It was the J-O-B that owned them, mind and soul.

On any given night, one might hear a wide variety of stories.

"This lady called nine-one-one. Said her home had been burglarized. We were on another job and couldn't get there right away, so she calls back hysterical and says we had *better* get there immediately, because the burglar was there and he had a gun. So of course we drop everything and charge like the army on D-Day to get to her apartment. Our guns are drawn, the adrenaline's pumping a mile a minute—you know, the whole nine yards. When we get there she rushes us in and says, oh, she's really, really sorry, she was mistaken about the man with a gun, but now that we were there, her dishwasher was broken and could we fix it?"

"Before I rolled over into the city police, I was in Transit. A woman came up to me one day on a train and reported a man in the next car for smoking. She didn't like it that he was breaking the law, but more than that, she was allergic to smoke, and it was really bothering her. So I went into the car and told the guy to put the cigarette out. He knocked my memo book out of my hand and started slugging me. I wrestled him to the floor, and we rolled around until we got to the next stop and some station backups arrived and took the guy in.

"The next day, I discovered the woman who'd told me about the guy had reported me to the Civilian Complaint Review Board for using unnecessary force in getting him to stop smoking.

"Can you believe it? What a royal fuckover!"

"It was a really hot day out, and my partner and I got a call for a past burglary. We went to this beautiful apartment, a nice young couple, very affluent. My partner, Fred said, 'Excuse me, ma'am, do you mind if I use your bathroom?' She smiled, real gracious. 'No, not at all, officer,' she said. 'Right over there.'

"A minute later, we heard the shower running, and Fred was singing at the top of his lungs. The couple was looking at me, and I was looking at them. I tried to distract them by asking questions for the complaint report, and they were staring at each other. 'Is something wrong?' I kept asking, and they shook their heads and said, 'No, no, no.'

"Every time I looked up from what I'm writing, they were mouthing to each other, 'Is he really taking a shower?' and when they saw me looking, they froze. Finally, the husband got his nerve up. 'Officer,' he said, 'do you mind if I ask you something? Is your partner, uh, taking a shower?'

"I said I didn't know, but it sounded like it. 'Yo, Fred,' I yelled, 'you taking a shower?'

" 'Yeah,' he shouted. 'I'll be right out.'

"The husband was really disturbed by this, and he asked me if this sort of thing was routine. And I was, like, 'Well, he did ask if he could use your bathroom, and you said yes. If he wanted to use your toilet, he'd have specified 'toilet.' But he said 'bathroom,' which could have meant a bath. But we don't have time to lounge around, so, heck, he's just taking a fast shower. No big deal.'

"Finally, Fred came out in his pants and T-shirt, with a towel draped around his shoulders, and he was combing his hair. He said we'd better get a move on, because we had a lot to do. And I told him, 'You were the one taking the shower, and I was waiting for you!'

" 'Okay, so let's get going,' he said. Then he turned to the husband. 'Oh, by the way,' he asked, 'you got any cologne?' ' '

"This car crashed something bad, and the steering wheel went right through the driver's body. The woman on the passenger side went through the windshield and was lying on the hood. The glass had ripped her face off, but she was still alive. The guy's gurgling blood, and he asks if he's going to die. 'Yeah, you'll make it,' I said. 'You'll make it.' I never prayed so hard for anyone to die."

"We got a call once that there was a dispute going on at this apartment. When we got there, we saw these four girls, and when one of them saw me she started giggling and said, 'Oh, shit, it's Bill!' She knew my wife. So we asked them what was going on. 'Nothing,' one of them said. 'We just wanted to do some cops.' ' '

"This guy was run over by a train, and we were there collecting his parts. Me and my partner, we found a leg here, a couple of fingers there. We rounded up everything but the guy's head. We couldn't find the head. They turned the power off, but when you walked along the tracks or crawled underneath the train you could hear electricity sizzling. Real spooky, you know? So we were looking for the head, and there's a crowd of about three hundred people standing around now, waiting, growing real anxious. They must've thought this was some kind of party, like the Mardi Gras. Finally my partner picks something off the ground, and this kid yells out, 'He found the head, the cop found the fucking head!' You wouldn't believe the fucking reaction. Those folks clapped and cheered and whistled and hooted like it was the greatest entertainment they ever had."

The patrol cops busted Dave's chops sitting in the bar, smoking, drinking, unwinding, releasing frustrations. "So, how many runs did you do today?" one asked, as the rest snickered.

"I don't do runs anymore," he said, smiling. "I'm upstairs."

"Well, you must think you're pretty hot, now that you're in RIP."

"Yeah, I must be pretty hot now that I don't have to stuff my gut in a patrol car anymore. I dine in restaurants. And I don't make street-jump collars anymore either. I make cases." The patrol officers rolled their eyes and pretended to be unimpressed.

The place was always packed, people sitting at the long wooden bar and the small tables across from it, or just standing around, holding a drink, waiting for nothing more than for the time to pass, for an hour when it felt reasonable that guardians of the big city should slip out of the night and its loneliness. The smoke would cling to their clothing long after they left, a stale, musty odor that was a reminder of late-hour fraternizing in the private world of cops, a reminder that cop life didn't end after a day's shift. Luciann Carbone patiently endured her husband's late-night relaxing. As a cop's wife, she understood.

Dave's first arrest came in the fourth week. His team was in the RIP office when Central broadcast a 10-30, robbery in progress. The first sector car to arrive at the scene transmitted back to Central: "Confirmed robbery of a variety store. Have units slow down, it's in the past. Perps fled west on Grand Street in a blue auto."

With patrol giving back to Central a confirmation of the robbery, the RIP Team One was out the door. Dave was up on the rotation order to be assigned the next case. Over his portable radio, he informed Central, "Be advised the RIP unit is responding to the location. Have the patrol unit stand by with the complainant."

Joe Torres stayed behind to man the fort should anything else come in, and Dave, Ciorciari, and Shannon drove to the scene, making it there in five minutes. It was on Grand Street near Lorimer Street, and the store owner was waiting with two patrol officers.

The owner said he had been robbed by two Spanish men. One came in first and browsed, then the other entered and announced a holdup, brandishing a large black gun. The gunman demanded money, and the owner turned over the $400 in his cash register. The two stickup men then ran out of the store and fled in a car parked across the street.

"Can you describe the robbers?" Dave asked, flipping open his notebook.

After delivering vague descriptions of both men—"they had mustaches and one wore a cap"—the owner suddenly exclaimed, "Wait a minute, I can do better than that." He pointed to a videocamera mounted on a far wall and aimed at the cash register. He turned the videotape over to the detectives and promised to come to the station house to review the RIP photos.

Out on the street, the detectives decided to canvass the area. A few people said they had seen two suspicious men speed away in a blue Maxima, and one had taken down the license plate number. He turned it over to the officers, pleading that he wanted no further involvement with the crime.

Dave ran the plates at the station house. The car had been stolen from Queens. When he informed Torres, the detective took the slip with the number and went back to the computer.

"What are you doing?" Dave queried, insulted. "You don't think I know how to run plates?"

Torres grinned. "Relax, Carbone. I'm going to run it for summonses."

"How would that help?"

"A stolen car often gets summonses. Thieves don't bother moving it for things like alternate side of the street parking or expired meters. So maybe we'll get some locations where the car's been parked. Meanwhile, why don't you go to One PP"—One Police Plaza—"and start working what you've got?"

An hour later, Dave and Ciorciari were in the Technical Assistance Response Unit (TARU) office at NYPD headquarters in Manhattan. They played the videotape from the store's camera and made stills of the perps, but there was a problem. The tape was of poor quality, so the stills were not very clear either. But distinct facial features were visible when the camera caught the men's profiles.

The two young detectives returned to the RIP office to find the variety store owner perusing the photo books. He couldn't make a hit, but perhaps it didn't matter. Torres had some interesting news. The stolen vehicle used in the robbery getaway had received two summonses. Both locations were in the vicinity of Bedford Avenue. Dave gave a description of the car with its license number to a patrol sergeant to read at roll call for the three tours—the eight-to-four, four-to-twelve, and midnight-to-eight—and then with his team began canvasses of the cars at those locations, which they continued to pursue in between handling other cases that came in. On the third day, Dave and Ciorciari, riding in an unmarked vehicle, spotted the stolen car parked on Bedford at South Second Street.

"I'll call the precinct," Dave informed his partner, "on a public telephone." He was close to making his first robbery collar now and didn't want to see it blown. "If I use the radio, nosy fucking cops'll flood the area and scare the guy away." From a pay phone Dave told the commanding officer, Sergeant Joseph Heffernan, that he and Ciorciari would sit on the car. "Fine," answered Heffernan, "but I'll send Joe and Larry to back you guys up."

For two and a half hours, the detectives waited. Finally their quarry showed up. A man fitting the description of one of the variety store robbery perps waddled down the street and got into the car. Two unmarked police cars immediately screeched up next to it, and the man's jaw dropped. Dave took him out at gunpoint and frisked and cuffed him. After a half hour in the interrogation room back at the Nine-Oh, the suspect confessed to the variety store robbery and gave up his accomplice. And Dave had his first robbery collar.

A one-week hiatus from the rigors of RIP came shortly after when Dave was dispatched to his first detective training session, the "mini-CIC"—the miniature Criminal Investigation Course, an abridged version of the three-week CIC given later in a detective's career. The white shields—police officers in a detective detail awaiting their detective gold shields—learned how to track phone records, execute wiretaps, run checks on people and locations using the sundry units of the NYPD, employ resources out of the department, and work with other governmental agencies in conducting an investigation. While Dave found the subject material fascinating, by the week's end he was restless and anxious to get out of the classroom and back onto the street.

Dave was back in action starting with his next RIP tour. Covering the Nine-Oh and Nine-Four precincts, his RIP team was barraged with cases: carjackings, street robberies, store robberies, push-in robberies, taxicab robberies, chain snatchings, pocketbook snatchings—virtually every conceivable type of robbery. And the detectives were constantly astonished by the different means employed to execute robberies. Knives, guns, fists, chains, bats, sticks, fake guns, tire irons, rocks— these were all conventional weapons. The detectives had cases where the victims were injured or threatened with dogs, snakes, and hypodermic needles. In a tactic that was becoming more common, self-proclaimed AIDS carriers threatened to slash people and spill their own tainted blood into their victims' wounds if they didn't fork over their money.

After a while, Dave was able to tell virtually from the get-go whether a case would be solved immediately or put on the back burner until a lead developed. Several factors made a case readily solvable. Perhaps the victim or a witness could identify the perp or knew the person by name or nickname or knew somebody who knew the person; or evidence was recovered; or the license plate number or partial number of a vehicle used by the perp was observed. The easiest cases to solve, the ground balls, were those in which the victims knew their assailant or could identify him or her. But even these weren't necessarily easy, because a detective had to *prove* the person was guilty. A victim or witness might pick out a photo of someone who looked like the perp but hadn't actually done the robbery. At the time of the crime, the alleged perp might actually have been in jail or far away or at work, with witnesses to vouch for him. Often, robbery victims didn't get a good look at their assailants and couldn't identify them; if there were no witnesses or other evidence, the detective had very little or nothing to go on. These cases were extremely difficult to solve. The best that could be hoped for was to catch the guy doing another robbery using the same MO, with a complainant who could identify him.

The old man limped into the room, braced at the elbow by a sturdy young patrol officer. Deep creases lined his face, like the rings of a seasoned tree. The back of his pants was slit, leaving a pocket dangling that once had obviously cupped a wallet, and his hand pressed together the torn fabric, trying to prevent his right leg and buttock from being exposed.

"Please have a seat," said Dave, pointing to a chair next to his desk. He had heard the radio communication and was expecting the man.

The old man was sniveling. Dave asked him if he could get him a glass of water, and the man muttered something in Spanish. Dave looked over at Joe Torres, who stood up and swung his chair over next to the old man.

For the next ten minutes, Torres spoke to the man, the victim of a hallway robbery in one of the projects. He had been visiting a friend on his way home from work when a Hispanic man with a cane came up behind him and threw him to the ground, ripped his back pocket open, and snatched his wallet.

Torres got up and went across the room, returning with a small pile of photograph books, which he deposited on the table. "Look through these and see if you can find the man who robbed you," said Torres to the man in Spanish.

The old man combed the books, repeatedly shaking his head no.

"If we find anything, we'll call you," said Dave, without a glimmer of hope, as they escorted the old man down to patrol, which would drive him home. Another garden-variety mugging. Dave and Torres shrugged to each other after bidding the tired victim goodbye; these kinds of robberies came in all the time. Without the name of the perp or a photo hit, nothing more could be done. When the detectives got back to their office, they closed out the case.

The days passed, and an endless stream of cases poured into the Nine-Oh RIP unit. Robberies, Dave found, were often crimes of opportunity. Somebody decided on the spur of the moment he wanted to rip somebody else off. And as Papi—as his squad affectionately called Joe

Torres—had told Dave the first day, robbers were creatures of habit. They'd work the same area, prey on the same kind of victims, do their crimes the same way. So now Dave knew that if there was a broadcast of a robbery in progress near the Greenpoint Men's Shelter, instead of going to the scene he'd rush straight to the shelter. A minute or two later, he'd see the perp come huffing and puffing down the block, and he would be there to welcome him with open arms and handcuffs.

A lot of jobs came in as robberies but were actually either larcenies or grand larcenies. If force wasn't used or threatened—the provisos for robbery—it could be either larceny or grand larceny, depending on the amount stolen. Women came in complaining, for instance, that a man had run by and grabbed their pocketbook. If they weren't punched, knocked to the ground, or dragged—if they didn't resist—it was larceny or grand larceny.

Others fell victim to con artists who used various scams to separate people from their money. A con artist might, for example, produce a "winning" lottery ticket she said she couldn't cash because she had no green card, or a bag she'd "found" that was stuffed with bills. In each case, the marks or victims were prevailed on to put up money for a share—money they'd often have to go to their bank for because they didn't carry that much on them—and somewhere along the line, while the victim was in the lottery office trying to cash the spurious ticket, or in an alleyway where the alleged cache was to be divided up, the swindlers would do a disappearing act. The victims would come into the RIP office crying that they'd been robbed, but the crimes committed were only larcenies and were referred to a specialized unit.

Other people would claim they had been robbed while going to make a deposit. They were on welfare, and they were usually gaunt and hollow-eyed. They weren't so much interested in seeing justice served as in getting the Sixty-one (complaint report) number, which they needed to include in their claims to Welfare and Victim Services to recover their "stolen" money.

"Nine times out of ten, these people haven't been robbed," Torres told his young disciple. "They're junkies looking to hustle some money for drugs."

Their stories were always elaborate, and there were never any witnesses, of course.

"Can they get away with that?" Dave wondered

"Sure, as long as they don't do it too much. What can we do? Call them liars?"

Some time later, Dave noticed something unusual.

Each of the RIP teams had a pin guy, usually the youngest member of the team—Dave was Team One's pin guy—whose job it was to work the pin map, a detailed map of the precinct that hung on a wall. The pin guy would stick colored pins into the map to represent locations of different types of robbery. A red pin was for street robberies, blue for transit, yellow for commercial or stores, green for housing, white for gypsy or medallion cabs, and black for inside jobs such as push-ins or hallways, where people get pushed into their residence or a building.

"I think we've got ourselves a pattern," Dave announced to his co-workers and Sergeant Heffernan.

The men came to look at the map. There was a cluster of black pins around a project at the intersection of Moore Street and Bushwick Avenue. A cluster of same-colored pins might designate a pattern, but then again it wouldn't be unusual to have four or five same-colored pins in or around a particular location and not have a pattern. Furthermore, even if there was a pattern, not all the pins in a cluster might belong to that same pattern.

"Looks promising. See if you can come up with something," said Heffernan.

In Heffernan's office, next to the pin maps, was a clipboard with all the Sixty-ones—the complaint reports, filled out by patrol—for the year. Dave took them and pulled every robbery from around the cluster area.

"This is what I've got," he said, handing the papers over to Joe Torres.

On a large sheet of paper, Torres broke down every single robbery around Bushwick and Moore by day, time, location, victims, perps, weapons, and MO.

"Tuesday, 1645 hours, male Hispanic, five-six, put hypodermic needle to complainant's throat and demanded money, perp fled on foot into subway," went one entry. Torres listed all the robberies from the area. He called Dave, Billy, and Larry.

"Look at this," he said, pointing to the sheet. Placing his index finger on the perp column at the top of the page, he moved it slowly down.

"Male white, female Hispanic and male black, two male whites, male white and female white, male Hispanic and female black, female Hispanic and male black, two male Hispanics, male Hispanic and female black. . . . Now, under weapon—cane, knife, gun, cane, cane, bat, gun, cane."

"Shit," Dave said. "It's a pattern!"

"Yeah," said Torres, who had thrown out all the robberies that had nothing to do with the pattern—chain snatch with a male Hispanic on a bicycle, corner stickup by a male white, and so on. "I think we've got two teams, a female Hispanic and a male black, and a male Hispanic and a female black. On one of these teams is a guy with a cane."

A week later Dave was at Woodhull Hospital interviewing an elderly man who had been robbed and stabbed in the projects.

"What were you doing in the building?" Dave asked.

The man didn't want to talk. He just lay there, eyes half closed, lips clenched together. Finally he spoke.

"I was getting a blow job."

The man told Dave about a woman who had befriended him. She had used her hand to pet him awhile, then said she'd use her mouth for $20. They went to the fifth floor stairwell of a nearby building. While his pants were down, the woman about to perform fellatio, a man came by. The woman, whom he had paid up front, fled, and the man cut him up and took the rest of his money.

What a nice, easy rip-off, Dave thought, with the victim not likely even to report the crime. He'd be either too embarrassed or afraid his wife would find out.

The stabbing bothered Torres, and he issued a warning. "It looks like these crack addicts are getting really desperate now. We'd better get them before they kill somebody."

The latest victim said the woman was a dark-skinned Hispanic and the man a light-skinned black.

Something occurred to Dave. "You know, we might have only one team here," he told his coworkers. Reflecting on the Sixty-ones, he speculated that the Hispanic woman could have been mistaken for black, the black man for Hispanic. The others concurred. Most of the crimes located on the pin map could have been committed by one team of a male and female. It was just people's idea of what their race was.

Because the RIP teams worked only two tours—eight to four and four to twelve—robberies that occurred after midnight were written up by patrol or by police aides. When they interviewed victims, Torres now suggested, they might have misinterpreted the complainant's descriptions. After all, ghetto Spanish has its own vernacular, and precise meanings get lost in translation. The people who took the complaint reports might not have bothered to pin down victims or witnesses as to exactly who they had observed.

If a Hispanic perp was light-skinned, for example, his victim might say he was a white man; if he was dark-skinned, the victim might say the man was black. The victims were interviewed in the heat of emotion and might not have been pressed for clarification. Detailed interviews by RIP investigators would be necessary.

"We're gonna have to bring all the victims back," announced Torres, "and reinterview them closely. Find out what really happened and who robbed them."

With dozens of complainants, it was a slow and tedious process, but the people were sought out.

"Listen up," said Dave as they filed in. "We don't care if you were getting sucked off or having a conversation about the weather. It doesn't mean you have to get robbed. Tell us what happened, what really happened, and please don't take us for fools."

This worked with many, who admitted they had paid for sex and were mugged in the act. Some, though obviously lying, stuck to their original stories, afraid, perhaps, of family repercussions.

"You said black," Torres asked one victim. "Do you mean American black? Jamaican? Hispanic? What kind of black are we talking about?"

Team One needed a name, but no one in the projects would talk. Torres remembered a woman who had been robbed in a stairwell of the same building; he called her and told her about his team's investigation. She said she had heard about a woman in the building who was doing robberies. She knew who it was, everybody in the building knew. She just didn't want to say who.

"I helped you," said Torres, who had collared the perp who had robbed her. "Now I need your help."

After much hemming and hawing, the woman finally gave in. "They're called Sandra and Glenn. She's Hispanic," she said. "He's black, but he could pass for Dominican or Hispanic."

It was confirmed now: There was just one team. The RIP investigators bandied the case about in their office.

"Hey, a long time ago I locked up a girl in that building named Sandra Rivera for a larceny," said Larry Shannon. "Maybe it's the same one."

Shannon dug up a photo, and the reluctant informant said it was the same girl who was doing the robberies. Sandra, she said, lived on the fifth floor.

Dave checked the records of the apartment building. "No one named Sandra is recorded as living there," he announced.

"The tenants never give Housing a complete list," Torres responded. "They'd get kicked out and would have to move to a bigger place and pay more rent."

The RIP men went to the fifth-floor apartment and interviewed Sandra's stepfather. He hadn't seen Sandra in a while, he told them, but he thought she was staying somewhere in the Bronx.

"He's full of shit," said Torres.

A few days later the woman from the building called the RIP office. "She's out there now," she said, and gave a description of Sandra.

Dave and Torres jumped into an unmarked car. Pulling up in front of the building, they spotted a dark Hispanic woman. She could pass as black. Dirty and scrawny, she was obviously an addict. They got out and grabbed her.

Dave noticed her breath stank of semen.

At the precinct, Sandra said she and her boyfriend were strung out. He made her participate in the robberies to support his crack habit. She gave his name and made a full confession on most of the cases. She looked sick and starved, and Dave gave her a candy bar and cigarettes.

Dave called the NYPD's Identification Section (better known by its previous name, the Bureau of Criminal Investigation or BCI) and asked for a group search on the name Glenn Jimerson, a male black, DOB 1963. If Jimerson had been arrested before, BCI would have his New York State Inquiry Identification System (NYSIIS) number. This was a seven-digit number ending with a letter that was assigned to a person the first time he or she was arrested in the state and that stayed with the person until death. With Jimerson's number, Dave could order a picture of him from the Photo Unit at headquarters.

A tech input Jimerson's name into a computer and came back with six names. Of those, three were from Brooklyn. Dave requested photos of these men and showed them to Sandra, who identified one as her boyfriend. Now all he needed to do was to obtain a photo hit by a complainant. Dave called in one of the victims, did a photo array, and got a hit. Now it was only a matter of picking up the suspect.

Torres reminded everybody of his robbers-as-creatures-of-habit edict. "Just like they commit their robberies the same basic way," he said, "they frequent the same places."

Team One arranged to stake out the area where Jimerson hung out. On one corner, Dave and Torres idled by a bodega. Down the block, Billy Ciorciari and Larry Shannon sat on a bench or pretended to be talking on the telephone. All the team members tried not to call attention to themselves, but most people knew who they were. For three days the team members lurked, but to no avail. Glenn Jimerson never came by.

They had given up and resumed work as usual when the woman who had identified Sandra called.

"I just saw him walking toward the drug spot at Bushwick and Flatbush. I ran upstairs to call you."

The RIP team raced to the area. Sure enough, they saw a man with a cane who looked liked Glenn Jimerson on the east side of Bushwick Avenue walking toward the projects. He started to run when he saw the officers, but his bad leg kept him from getting very far.

Jimerson started whining almost the instant the cuffs closed around his wrists, blaming Sandra for the robberies. He had only done it to support *her* habit.

Jimerson was ID'd in person by a number of the complainants and put into the system. After that, all robberies fitting the MO stopped. Dave was elated.

As time passed, Dave gradually assimilated the detective's mind-set. He learned how to handle robbery victims adeptly, making them effective witnesses. Investigating the robberies became second nature—interviewing the victims, canvassing, showing photos, reading past arrest sheets for information, finding patterns, conducting stakeouts, grabbing the perps. Eventually it all began to click for him. But it wasn't by any means a perfunctory routine.

Getting to know the street is vital to solving crimes. It became a regular ritual for Dave and Billy Ciorciari, a loquacious detective with dirty-blond hair, to hang with the mutts, not that the mutts liked it. When robberies were occurring frequently in a certain location, the two would hop in a car, park near the location, get out, walk around, stand with the mutts, circle around them, and talk to them, over the course of several hours. They bothered the hell out of these people and for their efforts earned the nicknames Starsky and Hutch, but it paid off. They learned names and faces and even developed informants on the street. Although their activities were essentially peaceable, they dubbed these ventures "kicking ass and taking names." So when a robbery went down and a witness said, "Yo, Chino did it," they knew just who Chino was and where to pick him up.

More and more, Dave found himself thinking like a detective. When street cops arrest somebody, they have to fill out an On-Line Booking System arrest worksheet and list a plethora of information about their collar. In patrol, Dave would hear cops say, "So the guy has a scar on his left forearm. Why the fuck do I have to write that down?"

All the details, all the paperwork—Dave himself hadn't appreciated what a wealth of information the OLBS could be for investigators until he was in RIP. The scar listed on the OLBS arrest sheet could come in very handy when he was pulling reports and looking for a perp with a scar on his left forearm. Dave started paying close attention to details such as height, weight, complexions, nicknames, habits, associates—all of which, he found, made him a better investigator.

Now, after patrol locked people up, he would talk to them. The cops would say, "What are you talking to that piece of shit for?" But he found he could learn a lot from them, that these "pieces of shit" could teach him things he could never pick up unless he were a mutt himself hanging on the street all day long.

At the end of his first two years in RIP, Dave had made over 150 arrests. He had had his share of failures, but he usually averaged one or two collars a week, exceeding the unofficial quota of two a month, and he never had the slightest worry about being transferred out of the unit for lack of activity.

But by that time he was growing bored with doing robberies. Although there were always difficult cases, he had stopped finding them challenging and was frustrated by the limitations of his unit. When a robbery victim was critically injured, the case was investigated by RIP. But if the victim died, the case would immediately be assigned to the precinct detective squad, which worked the case with the Brooklyn North Homicide Task Force. When that happened, Dave felt like a second-class cop.

And so when Sergeant Heffernan announced that he had received word from the Detective Bureau that transfers were coming down and that he was to submit the names of officers he deemed qualified for transfer, Dave was exuberant. He was one of the selected officers, and Heffernan asked him to name three choices of precincts he'd like to work in.

At the start of a late-September day tour, Dave walked into Heffernan's office holding a piece of paper. He handed the paper over to the sergeant, who was seated at his desk. Heffernan was a large, stocky man in his early forties with a thick mane of sandy brown hair. Dave studied his reaction and watched his lips press together.

On the sheet of paper were the three precincts where Dave wanted to go—75th, 90th, and 83rd, in that order. These were in East New York, Williamsburg, and Bushwick, all in Brooklyn.

Heffernan stared at the paper for about half a minute. Then he looked up, registering an expression Dave had hoped he wouldn't see.

"Forget the Seven-Five, kid," he said, chuckling. "The place is a madhouse, one of the busiest houses in the city."

Dave knew that. Many young detectives wanted to go there for the work and experience and the opportunity to learn from the old-timers there, who had a reputation of being among the best detectives in the NYPD. He knew you could go to some precincts and collect twenty years' worth of paychecks without creasing your suit. That was not what he wanted to do. He wanted to learn. And to learn, he needed to work. Detectives who wanted to work went to the Seven-Five, where they could work more murders in a single year than entire squads do in other precincts.

"You have to have a lot of experience to get in there," Heffernan continued. "Most of the guys in the squad, they've been there for a while."

The sergeant paused to let his information sink in.

"You have to be real good to go there," he repeated when Dave didn't seem fazed. "You have to know someone to get in. Why don't you put another choice down?"

Dave knew he was good; after all, he led the Nine-Oh RIP unit in arrests. His mind was made up. He wanted to be in the best place in the city to learn to be a homicide detective. He knew there was no better place than the Seven-Five. He shook his head.

"Are you sure you want to go there?"

"Yes."

"It's a real shithole, you know."

"I know," Dave said, nodding.

Heffernan lowered his head, but Dave caught the slight lift at the corners of his mouth. "All right. I'll see what I can do," said Heffernan equably. The sergeant sat silently for a minute, as if mapping a campaign in his mind. He knew it might take some appealing to higher-ups. The Seven-Five didn't accept phone calls on such matters.

Dave was grateful but worried. Sergeant Heffernan was well liked by all the higher bosses, but a sergeant was not the greatest hook. A lieutenant or captain would be better, and someone above these ranks, like an inspector or a chief, would be ideal. But he just didn't know any such officers well enough.

He thanked Heffernan and went back to work.

In a spacious office whose walls were adorned with plaques, Joseph Heffernan sat across from Deputy Inspector Charles R. Prestia, the commanding officer of Brooklyn North detectives.

"Inspector," Heffernan said, "I'd like to make a recommendation for one of my more active and reliable young RIP detectives. He's asked me for consideration to be assigned to the Seven-Five squad. His name is David Carbone, and he's an excellent worker. He's solved a lot of cases, made a lot of collars. I personally believe he's up to the challenge and would be an asset to the squad."

The inspector sat upright in his chair and listened attentively. Sergeant Heffernan had an impeccable reputation in the department. With twenty-three years on the job, he was known as a first-rate supervisor and a demanding boss, not to mention a no-nonsense officer. Detectives who lacked the appropriate skills, drive, and industriousness didn't last long in his squad.

"Coming from you," Inspector Prestia said, "that carries a great deal of weight. I'll see what I can do."

High-ranking officers never said an unequivocal yes to such requests, because even they didn't know how their appeals would go up the chain of command.

Heffernan nodded approvingly, gratified by the inspector's response. He rose and extended his hand. "I appreciate it, inspector," he said.

Five months passed with no word. It was already two months beyond the time that transfers had been promised, and Dave was beside himself. What was taking so long?

A month later, Dave got instructions to report to Lefrak City. Transfers were finally being effected, and there were forms to fill out. He sat in a large room with other young cops; the nervousness of the men and women in the audience was tangible.

Papers were handed out, instructions given. Then a captain started calling out the assignments. It wasn't long before he got to Dave's name. Dave stood up.

Over the past several months, Dave had run through numerous scenarios of this moment, in each one of which he was dispatched to a different precinct and detective squad in the city. NYPD cops knew all the city's police precincts, whether they were crime-ridden and dangerous or placid and calm. A precinct was not only a cop's workplace, but for a cop embarking on a new facet of his career, it was, along with his coworkers, a major component in the tapestry of his education. Where a cop was trained could make a substantial difference in the kind of officer he or she turned out to be, and young officers vied for choice assignments.

But Dave had suddenly gone emotionally numb. Too much rode on the words the captain was about to utter.

"Carbone, Seven-Five squad."

Dave nodded and sat down, his mind temporarily blank. It took several minutes for him to assimilate that he'd really gotten the plum he'd asked for. And it wasn't until half an hour later, after all the assignments had been called and all the speeches had concluded, that he realized he was the only one in the group of 150 white shields to have been transferred to the 75th Precinct.

As the others milled about, offering congratulations or sympathy, Dave remained sitting quietly for a moment, savoring the thought of his new assignment. Then he leaped up and shouldered his way through the throng, making for the nearest pay phone. He couldn't wait to tell Luciann.

3

Twirling a cocktail shaker, Dave deftly returned the bantering insults with which his assembled friends clothed their genuine pleasure at his new assignment. Luciann, ecstatic at the news, had insisted on throwing a party to celebrate. But in the last few days, Dave had found his thoughts repeatedly turning to his past rather than to his future, and again this March evening he was preoccupied with memories of his childhood and unable to fully connect with the ongoing conviviality. His rise in the NYPD had been remarkably smooth—not that he hadn't deserved it, but his youth had been so devoid of ease that he was suddenly feeling a lack of continuity.

A dozen people were gathered in the Carbone home, a seven-room ranch nestled in the middle of a long quiet block on the south shore of Nassau County, Long Island. Part of a sprawling bedroom community that featured half-million-dollar waterfront homes and elegant split-levels, this side of town was lined with modest houses owned by blue- and white-collar workers.

Several cars were parked in the Carbones' driveway and in front of the house. Inside, on the dining-room table, a six-foot deli hero was surrounded by hot plates of baked ziti, stuffed shells, lasagna, sausage and peppers, and barbecued chicken; dishes of macaroni salad, potato salad, cole slaw, and pickles; and soda, orange and tomato juice, and liquor. The Carbones' friends stood chatting around the table or hunkered down on the velvety couches arranged around the modern fireplace in the sunken den.

The harried pace of life with a newborn child had prevented Luci Carbone from celebrating Dave's appointment to the NYPD five years earlier, but this time around the occasion couldn't be neglected. With all the tragedies and gloom of life, Luci felt, the happy times needed festive acknowledgment. And she was inordinately proud of her husband.

Dave was having trouble squaring his own pride in his accomplishments with the persistently intruding memories of his early years; the disparity was too great. From a family where money was so scarce that all its members had to go to work once they were old enough, and college was out of the question for any of the eight children, Dave's rise to professional status seemed a small miracle. He tried to trace the patterns that had led to the present moment.

The Carbones' strong work ethic was the contribution of Dave's father, Joseph, who for many years hadn't even owned a car—he chose not to drive ever since several of his buddies in the Marines were killed in a fiery car accident—and he had walked twenty-two miles to and from work almost every day, regardless of the weather. His salary at Grumman's, where he worked as a maintenance man, wouldn't support a family of ten, so he also painted houses in the neighborhood.

Dave had carried ladders and cans of paint with his brothers and sisters as they accompanied their father on his jobs. These were a family venture, and when a child was old enough, he or she was always recruited; there was never any choice in the matter. Playtime was a luxury to be enjoyed by other, more fortunate children. Dave's father painted ten to fifteen houses a year, ranches to two-story colonials, and the kids were there to carry supplies through the streets, scrape the outside walls, hold the ladder when he was painting the roofs or ledges, and lend a hand in any other way they could.

The austere work ethic of the father filtered down to the children. When he was nine or ten, Dave, the fourth-eldest, began taking on his own jobs around the neighborhood, dutifully turning all his earnings over to his parents, as did his brothers and sisters. When it snowed, he shoveled as many sidewalks and driveways as he could. In the warm weather, he mowed lawns with the family's push mower. He began his first formal job as a stock boy in a supermarket at sixteen, adding a second job as a part-time mechanic in a gas station the next year. The after-school and weekend jobs made a gruesome schedule for the high school student. Three days a week, he was employed in the supermarket, working as fast as he could in his eleven-to-seven shift so he could grab a little sleep before shuffling off to school. After school and on Saturdays, he fixed cars at Pugliese's Service Station.

School had never meant much to Dave. His grades had been poor, he had rarely done his homework, and he was prone to fighting with his classmates. One memory was particularly harrowing.

By the middle of his fourth-grade year, Dave had felt certain he was going to be left back. His academic problems were exacerbated by a teacher who seemed to delight in picking on him. He especially hated her habit of grabbing his arm and shaking it.

One day, as his teacher was scolding him shrilly in front of the class, he lost it. Wriggling his arm loose from the teacher's grip, he punched her in the stomach. As she doubled over, gasping, his classmates let out shrieks, and he stared at her for an instant, not believing what he had done. Then he bolted to the opposite side of the room and vaulted out the open first-floor window.

After sulking for three hours at a nearby store, Dave returned home at three o'clock. His mother seemed happy to see him, and Dave decided it would be prudent not to upset her with the troubles of his day. With eight kids and a husband, Mom had enough on her mind.

"How was school today?" she asked pleasantly.

"Fine," he responded, avoiding her eyes.

"Anything new?"

"No."

He sensed an edge creeping into his mother's last question, and he glanced up to see her mouth tightening ominously. Then she began to yell at him. The principal had called to tell her what had happened. His mother's face grew more and more livid, the veins pulsing at the side of her neck, as she read him the riot act. Dave stood silently, head down. If she wanted to scream, he could take it. If she wanted to hit him, he could take that too. But please, he prayed to himself, please, don't let her tell his father. His father meted out discipline like Captain Bligh.

Dave was up in his room when his father returned home from work late in the afternoon. After a brief conversation with Dave's mother, his father mounted the stairs and lumbered through the bedroom door, hardwood paddle in hand. A large man with a strapping upper chest, he seemed to fill the room, his menace radiating to every corner. As his father administered one powerful whack after another, Dave gritted his teeth. He told himself he'd show his father he was strong and could endure whatever he inflicted. By the end he was raw, but as always, he had stood it—physically. Emotionally was where it really hurt.

Dave nursed his wounds in his room while the family ate dinner. When his father had finished his meal, he stretched out on the couch as usual, a bottle of beer by his side. Eventually he fell asleep. Then Dave's mother quietly brought a tray of food up to his room.

She set the tray down on his bed. Dave leaned over to survey its contents as she pulled a chair up to the bed and sat down.

"Are you hungry?" she asked.

"Yes, Mom."

"Look." She reached out and cupped his cheek with her hand. "Davey, stay in line, do your work. Everything'll be okay."

Dave was reassured. When things went wrong, his mother would always help him through. He could depend on her. And he needed that. As much as he loved his father, Dave could expect from him nothing but anger and criticism.

Dave smiled and gazed up at his mother. Her eyes had become

moist. That scared him; more than anything, he didn't want to see her cry.

"I'm sorry," she said softly, tears beginning to stream down her face.

As she tried to get out a few words, a lump burst in Dave's throat and he turned away, unable to look. This was the one thing he couldn't deal with. He felt a burning sensation shoot down his body, and his stomach tied into a knot.

"Daddy," she sobbed, "did more than I thought."

Doris Carbone, a slight, brown-haired woman, was the sixth of ten children. Her father had been a first-generation American, the son of an Irish bobby and a Canadian woman who had settled in New Jersey. Doris's parents had lived in Brooklyn and Long Island, where they taught their four children staunch values and habits of personal integrity.

In 1947, after one failed marriage, Doris married Joseph Carbone, then a handsome former Marine, the son of immigrants from Naples. The marriage produced eight children. The oldest child, Joseph Edward, had once confided to Dave that it had seemed to him as if their mother was always pregnant. The children were all named with a J or D after the mother or father, and Joey was followed by James Severino, Jeanne Madeline, David William, Diane Marie, Dale Michael, John Patrick, and Debra Ann. In between Jimmy and Jeanne, a set of twins and a single were lost.

The parents ran a highly regimented household. One of the prime routines was dinner at four-thirty when Joseph came home from work. All the children would be seated at the table ready to eat. With ten mouths to feed, meals were cooked on a grand scale. Doris loved especially to prepare Italian dishes. But dinners were usually sullen affairs. The children weren't allowed to speak unless spoken to by Mom or Dad, and they couldn't leave the table until Dad did.

Doris was much more intuitive than Joseph, with an uncanny knack for knowing when the boys were up to something. There was, for instance, the time when Dave was in junior high school and a beginning smoker. Smoking, of course, was a no-no for any of the Carbone children. They knew that if caught they'd be in for a beating. Mischievous Dave figured he'd lay a double whammy by hiding his pack of cigarettes a couple houses away, in the bushes of the neighborhood "witch," Mrs. Denston, who owed her reputation to her ferocious temper, her scraggly silver-brown hair, and her pointy nose, not to mention her habit of confiscating all balls hit onto her property.

On his way to school one morning, Dave stuck his hand in the bushes to grope for the pack of cigarettes he had deposited there the day before. No cigarettes. Dave stood there, puzzled, his hand amid the twigs, wondering what in the world could have happened to his smokes. Suddenly, his mother popped out from behind the bushes. "Is this what you're looking for?" she shrieked, delivering a few hearty wallops before sending him off to school sans his stash.

At the height of the Vietnam War, when Dave was ten, an overwhelming desire to get out of the house moved eighteen-year-old Joey Carbone to enlist in the Marine Corps. As a private first class with the 2d Battalion, 3d Marines, Joseph fought in Quang Nam Province during the Tet Offensive of '68. In February, his company ran into an ambush, and Joey was badly wounded. At a military hospital, three priests read last rites to him within a twenty-four-hour period, but, miraculously, he was able to gather enough strength to call home.

Dave remembered hearing his mother's sudden wail after she took her son's call. Shortly, Joseph summoned all the children downstairs to tell them what had happened. Dave was terrified; Joey was his favorite sibling, the older brother whom he revered.

It wasn't until Joey returned stateside and was sent to St. Albans Naval Hospital in nearby Queens that Joseph Carbone bought the first car he had ever owned, a station wagon, so he and Doris could visit Joey. The children never accompanied their parents on hospital visits but eagerly awaited their reports. Joey eventually recovered; young Dave was impressed by his brother's courage and aspired to emulate him in every way he could.

In addition to a strong work ethic, Joseph Carbone had imparted to his children the value of good citizenship. He was a volunteer fireman, and when his sons turned old enough, they too joined. On his eighteenth birthday, Dave put in his papers at the firehouse, and a week later was a fireman, joining his father and his older brothers Joey and Jimmy.

Then when Dave was nineteen, his father got him a job at Grumman's fixing trucks. Dave was still undecided about what he wanted to do with his life, but the salary was good while he was making up his mind. A year after he started with the company, he switched from mechanic to truck driver, making runs between the company's different offices in Nassau County.

In 1977 the town of Merrick, Long Island, crowned Doris Carbone its Mother of the Year. It was a title she proudly bore and richly deserved. But before she could relinquish the title the next year, she suffered a heart attack and died. The loss affected the Carbone family deeply. Doris had been the glue that had kept the family together, something that became more evident as time passed.

But for a few years the male Carbones preserved a degree of family solidarity by their joint service at the firehouse. For Dave, it was a chance to put into action qualities that he had internalized from exposure to the contrasting personalities of his parents. His gratitude for Doris Carbone's sensitivity and compassion had inspired in Dave a desire to help people in distress; and his powerlessness before his domineering father as a child had nurtured in him a need to be in a position of command. Within a few years, he became company engineer of the twenty-member hook-and-ladder company. A popular leader who shouldered his share of the scut work, he exercised his authority well, his firmness tempered by fairness and understanding.

A few years after Doris's death, when Dave was in his early twenties, his brother Joey joined the Nassau County Police Department. Dave, who still idolized Joey, began to contemplate a new direction for his own life. As a boy, Dave had at times thought about becoming a cop, and a detective in particular, but it had seemed just too far-fetched. What he knew of detectives was mostly from the world of film and television. They were supersleuths who matched wits with the most brilliant criminals, or tough guys who used their muscle and the threat of intimidation to get things done. It was all very appealing and most entertaining, but not the sort of career he realistically expected to have. With Dave's success as a leader of the volunteer fire department, however, the idea no longer seemed so unrealistic. Not only would becoming a cop enable him to emulate his older brother, but it would also provide him with security, decent pay, and retirement benefits.

Appealing as it was, the notion did not blossom into action until a couple of years later, when Dave and several of his fire department buddies were talking one evening and one of them suggested taking the police department test together. In the twinkling of an eye, the possibility was transformed in Dave's mind into a goal. They all took the test; one by one he and his friends were summoned for follow-up interviews, and then Dave was called.

"It's something I really want," Dave told Luci after he was accepted, "but I don't know if I should take it."

Sitting in their kitchen, Dave explained his concerns to his wife. If he joined the police department, Dave would have to take a cut in pay from his job at Grumman's. With an eight-month-old baby and wife to support and mortgage payments to make, Dave didn't know whether they'd be able to survive financially. In addition, school had never been one of his strong points, and he was unsure whether the police academy, with its courses in law, police science, and social science, would be too much for him.

"Whatever you choose to do," Luci said, "I'll support you one hundred percent."

Gazing at the wall, Dave had reflected for a moment, then turned to his wife. "I want more for my family than what my father could give us," he said softly.

Luci nodded, understanding Dave had just made his decision.

From that point on, Dave's desire to become a professional took precedence over his financial concerns. He began to think of the choice not so much as a risk but as an opportunity to do something he thought he'd really enjoy, to help people, to exercise his leadership abilities, and to make something of himself. But even with the decision made, he was, he had to admit to Luci, terrified.

Although he lived in the backyard of New York City, in Long Island, Dave had been to the city only once in his life; when he was a child, his twin aunts Lillian and Helen had taken him and some of his brothers and sisters to see the Statue of Liberty. Because the Carbones hadn't owned a car until Joey returned wounded from Vietnam and they needed to visit him at the naval hospital in Queens, the family had never traveled any farther than they could walk.

Consequently, Dave's view of New York City came through a television tube. The frightening TV news reports made the city appear to Dave to be a a huge, violent metropolis plagued by incessant crime. Now here he was on his way to becoming a subway cop—it would be eight months before he could roll over to the city police force from Transit—and he had never even set foot in a New York City subway. He felt odd about becoming "the law" in the subway, when he couldn't even tell uptown from downtown.

But he was also savvy enough to realize that training would adequately prepare him for the job, and that, in fulfilling a major ambition, he would be a quick learner.

As Dave embarked on his career in law enforcement, his relationship with his father and brothers took a disastrous turn. Waging a campaign at the firehouse against three contenders in 1983, he became the second assistant chief of the fire department, and two years later won the election for first assistant chief. The next year, he decided to run for chief. But there was a problem. His brother Jimmy was the current chief, and Jimmy announced his intention to run again. Dave had thought Jimmy would step aside and let his brother take a turn—Dave would, after all, have done the same for him—but Jimmy was unwilling to give up the position. The two brothers engaged in a heated battle for the job, and Dave was surprised and hurt when his father wouldn't intercede on his behalf or even attempt to mediate, passively allowing the campaign battle to escalate into a feud.

Shortly before the election, just after Dave had entered the police department's RIP unit in 1986, word began to circulate among the firemen that the New York City rookie detective was spending most of his time at his job and was neglecting the firehouse. Dave acknowledged this to be the case; his career was blossoming and he was moving quickly toward realizing his goal of becoming a homicide detective. Dave still felt he could be a terrific chief, but when the election was held, he lost.

Dave was devastated, not so much by the defeat itself as by the hard feelings engendered by the fraternal contest. He eventually drifted away from the fire department, becoming essentially estranged from his father and all his siblings but his brother Joey, who himself had left the family circle for good some years before.

Dave stood in the doorway of the den, watching his friends enjoy themselves. How proud Mom would be, Dave reflected, if she could be here to share his achievement. How delighted Doris Carbone would be to see what her son had made of himself, and where he was going. Maudlin sentiments always seemed to fill Dave's heart when he thought of his mother. In contrast, his father's cold neutrality in Dave's fire department contest with Jimmy made Dave unsure whether Joseph Carbone would be pleased at his younger son's success, and Dave acknowledged to himself that he didn't really want to find out.

The memories were becoming too painful. With an effort, Dave shook them off and joined a knot of his friends who were telling each other cop stories.

By nine o'clock, the last of the guests had departed, and Dave and Luci put their daughter, Danielle, to bed and began to clean up. The party had taken Dave's mind off his transfer to the Seven-Five detective squad, where he would not only embark on a new phase of his law enforcement career but become enmeshed in a new world.

As he collected overflowing ashtrays and sticky glasses, his mind returned to his future, and it made him apprehensive. The world of a detective was dark, depressing, sordid, filled with cruelly dispatched corpses, grieving families, depraved criminals. He knew that. He knew his work would be a lot different from what it had been in patrol, and even in RIP. A patrol cop went on jobs, and those jobs were over when the shift was over. In RIP, he had hunted robbers, but not murderers or other kinds of criminals. Now it would be different. Different crimes, different kinds of bad guys. The investigations would be different; they might exact a personal toll on him if a criminal continued to elude him over time. A robbery victim told you as much as he or she could, but with murder it was different. Dead people couldn't talk.

He was confident he could do the job, but he was concerned that he might lose some of his humanity. As a patrol officer he had often presided over crime scenes, guarding them till the detectives arrived. The corpses lay off to the side, marred by the ugly, raw penetrations of bullets or blades. Their eyes had that glazed death look, the "zombie stare," as the cops called it. Puddles of blood covered the floor. The walls were splattered red. Friends or family of the victim were apt to run around screaming, throwing themselves against the furniture. It was almost enough to make him sick.

But then the detectives in their silk suits and gold pinky rings would parade in, nonchalant, and look around. Step over the body, move it around indifferently as if it were a mannequin. It could even be a little kid lying there, and they'd be chewing gum and talking about what they wanted to eat later. Part of Dave could understand that and part couldn't, but he knew he didn't want to become like them, callous, uncaring.

Luci crept into bed an hour after Dave. He was still awake. Out of habit he wrapped his arms around her, but his mind was adrift. His eyes closed, he was nervously anticipating the beginning of a new professional journey, a journey that would take him into one of America's worst killing grounds. He would need to call on every bit of training and experience he had ever had and stretch his faculties to the fullest. As he felt his way through cases, learning how to find and read clues, work out conflicts, play hunches, target a suspect, Dave wondered how this would affect him. How would it affect his family? What would become of him in a world populated by the worst elements of society? Perhaps he would be able to ease into it, he mused hopefully, and his apprenticeship would be a deliberate, circumspect process.

Dave's mind unrolled a montage of imagined crime scenes as he fought to let himself fall into slumber.

Inside a car stopped at a light in East New York, Brooklyn, the driver
peered across the intersection. Up ahead, he and his woman passenger
could see a scattered group of men along the roadway. Several stood in
the center of the road, gesticulating, flanked on each side by others.
The men in the center could have been involved in some type of dispute, but it was hazy and dark out and difficult to see.

The light changed. Whatever was happening ahead seemed to
have run its course, and the driver tapped his horn slightly, wishing the
people blocking his path would move so he could drive through.

What happened next was surrealistic, horrifying, and swift.

One of the figures spun around, angered by the stranger's inter-
ruption. He raised his arm to chest level, focusing briefly. His fingers
coiled and squeezed, and a bullet rocketed straight through the windshield of the car and into the forehead of the driver, right between the
eyes. It was a good shot, wonderfully placed considering the light conditions, distance, and haste. A high-pitched, strident scream evapo-
rated into the predawn dusk as the car rolled aimlessly forward and up
onto the sidewalk, coming to a halt upon impact with a building.

Blasts of cold, dank March wind hissed loudly. Residents of the
community were getting their last winks of sleep. The first rays of the
sun would soon be penetrating the darkness and ushering in a new
day.

"Whatever you want, we got here. You want a pound of weed, a
bundle of crack, a brick of hash, a key of cocaine, a key of heroin, a
hand job, a blow job, a tittie fuck, a cunt fuck, anal sex, a fairy, two
queers, two queers and a pross—we got it all. East New York, man, it's a
drug and sex junkie's candy store."

A veteran detective was waxing rhetorical about the commercial
highlights of the 75th Precinct to David Carbone, the squad's new
white-shield investigator. The DT seemed to take a wicked pride in the
area whose murders Dave was to help solve.

The area was considered one of the most ominous and deadly

pieces of real estate in America. In its 5.6 square miles, gangs and drug-dealing were rampant, and the projects were so dangerous that the cops themselves avoided them after dark unless they *had* to go in.

At night, East New York sometimes sounded like a war zone. A quick succession of eight shots would ring out, then two, then six, four, or ten, just like in the movies—except that it was real. One of seventy-five precincts in New York City, the Seven-Five often led the city in robberies and shootings, and with some one hundred murders annually, it owned the dubious distinction of having either the highest or second-highest number of homicides of any precinct.

Trying to maintain order were the precinct's more than 315 uniformed cops and thirty-five sergeants, lieutenants, and captains. On any given tour, the patrol cops flew all over the precinct on gun runs, drug sales in progress, shots fired, family disputes, auto accidents, aided cases (heart attacks and other sudden illnesses or injuries), robberies, assaults in progress, and rapes in progress. RMP units typically went on more than twenty-five radio runs a tour—at least twice as many as in the average New York City precinct.

Patrol handled jobs—assignments—as Central dispatched 911 calls, or as the officers saw crimes unfolding in front of them. Investigations followed the commission of crimes and were handled by the precinct detective squads, which were part of the Detective Bureau. There were twenty-one detectives in the Seven-Five squad, who handled everything from burglaries and assaults to kidnappings and murders, and ten detectives in the RIP unit across the hall, who just did robberies.

"If you see anybody here with a finger cut off, that's a low-level drug dealer," said another detective to Dave. "Some of the gangs here punish their dealers when they come up short or smoke the product they're supposed to sell. But it's not all that bad for the sellers." He paused a moment like a comedian getting ready to deliver a punch line. "They get a choice of which finger they want severed."

"Or if the sellers do something else wrong," another detective interjected, "their suppliers pull out their teeth with a pair of pliers, break their legs with a baseball bat, or go over their bodies with an ice pick."

The new kid in the squad stared intently as some of the detectives, enjoying their fresh bait, laughed raucously at his serious countenance. David Carbone was getting the welcome treatment from his fellow workers.

Unlike squads in some other big-city police departments, the detectives in the Seven-Five and many other NYPD precinct squads didn't regard newcomers with suspicion or fear. There were no furtive glances or backroom huddles or prying questions. Dave was glad about that, and relieved he wouldn't have to undergo the kind of scrutiny other rookie detectives do.

"Who are your hooks?" they'd ask in other cities. "How long are you on the job? What kind of cop were you? Why did you want to come here? What do you want out of this place?" Question after question, all to elicit whether the newcomer, if he happened to see the rules being bent, could be trusted. It wasn't until the rookie had demonstrated to everyone's satisfaction that he wasn't out to snitch on them or show them up that his new colleagues would relax around him.

But it wasn't solely because the Seven-Five detectives were such nice guys, so secure about themselves, and so confident about their work that they were so nice to the outsider. They had an ace up their sleeves. They made telephone calls.

They called the rookie's former bosses to check him out. They sniffed out his friends. They asked around. By the time a rookie came to the precinct, they knew more about him than they needed to know. Checking out Dave, the Seven-Five detectives had found he was an okay guy, and a good cop.

"Dis the wrong person here by accidentally stepping on his sneaker or brushing his shoulder and you're in for big trouble," one detective warned. "Look at him or his girlfriend for longer than two seconds and he'll stick a gun in your mouth and blow your brains out."

"These guys laugh at the Mafia here—you know, the way the mob puts out a contract on you if you betray them," added the first detective. "A contract? Hah. That's for pussies. They don't need a reason to kill you here. There's no need for any red tape or bureaucracy. They just shoot you on the spot."

"Yeah," another voice interrupted, "but they're afraid of the Colombians. I mean, the regulars here, they'll just shoot you. A clean, quick death. The Colombians are into torture. It's an aesthetic thing. They *like* it. And they'll take out everyone they find in the room along with the guy they're gunning for."

A different detective took up the litany. "If they're after a guy who's in his car with his baby, they'll lay the baby out flat on the ground and shoot it before they whack the guy. If they're after somebody who's at home when they look for him, they'll kill everybody there—the grandma, aunt, uncle, the kids, the dog, the goldfish. They'll shoot his pregnant wife twice—once in the head and once in the stomach. And the guy they're after? They'll give him the Colombian necktie. They'll be sawing his throat while they're literally ripping out his tongue. Then for good measure they'll shoot him in the head five or ten times."

"Give us twenty-two minutes, we'll give you a homicide," offered a middle-aged detective, lampooning the slogan of a popular local all-news radio station.

The detectives laughed. They liked a good slogan. On their calling cards, above the lines where their name and number appeared, the detectives had printed on different cards "Our day begins when your day ends" and "If you don't die, we don't try."

Dave was beginning to feel a little queasy, but he hoped he was able to keep it from showing on his face. He figured ruefully that he must be succeeding when the first detective continued relentlessly, seemingly determined to get a rise out of him.

"They kidnap kids off the street here and throw them into abandoned buildings, where they force them to sell drugs. Nice kids, twelve, thirteen years old. They seal them into a corner of the building with cinder blocks and make them sell through a little hole. Every seven hours or so they'll shove a Big Mac into the hole. In the projects, they force kids to sell drugs by threatening to kill them or their families. Sometimes the gangs'll just come in and take over some old lady's apartment. By the time the undercovers make their buys and get a warrant, the drug dealers have moved out and taken over somebody else's apartment."

"Take a picture of yourself tonight," another advised. "Then give it to your wife so she'll remember what you look like." The detectives roared while Dave grinned wryly.

The animated mood in the squad room changed quickly a minute or two later when Detective Sergeant Michael Race, a burly, six-foot ex-Marine and one of the supervisors of the squad, emerged from his office.

"All right, men," he barked. "Night watch picked up three homicides this morning." The supervisor of the borough's night watch unit, which handles all homicides in Brooklyn after 1:00 A.M., when precinct detectives go off duty unless they're working overtime, had awakened him at home with a phone call at 5:55 A.M. to tell him what was going down.

"One guy was killed because he was gay," continued Race. "Another because he was in a room full of drunken people and when he put on somebody else's pants, they thought he was stealing their wallet. And a third because he beeped his horn."

Race glanced over the detectives gathered around. Two of them—

Mike Redmond, a second-grade detective with a quarter of a century on the job, and Joe Hall, another twenty-year-plus veteran—assisted the others present only on their homicide cases. The other detectives composed Team One, one of the three teams in the squad that worked all kinds of cases. The teams were on a four-by-two chart, working four days, then off two days, then back for four days and off another two, and so on. The first two tours of any set were from 4:00 P.M. to 1:00 A.M., the second two from 8:00 A.M. to 4:00 P.M. Team One consisted of Jerry Roman, Jack Cutrone, and the newest member, David Carbone. Al Smith, another member of the team, was out this day.

"Jerry, you take the gay case. Jack, you've got the pants case. And Dave, I want you to catch the car homicide."

David Carbone was stunned. It was his first day in the squad, and here he was the detective in charge of a homicide investigation.

"Are you fucking kidding me, or what?"

Race laughed. "Don't worry, we're not throwing you to the wolves. We all help each other here on the cases. I'll go over the nuts and bolts of a homicide investigation with you and walk you through the case step by step."

Race gestured for Dave to follow him. As he turned to leave, he waved a hand at the other detectives. "All right, everybody, let's go. Gentlemen, we'll catch you back at the barn later." Jack was going to go over to his crime scene with Joe Hall, Jerry with Mike Redmond.

As they left the room, Race explained to Dave that normally all the members of a team would go out together to start an investigation with one member designated the catching detective, but there were three homicides to start investigating at once and one detective was out, so the team had to split up. Dave knew from his time in RIP that every case that came into a squad, whether a petit larceny or a murder, was assigned a catching detective. This was the person who oversaw it and was ultimately responsible for everything from the paperwork, to reporting on it to the squad CO, to working with the DA's office in pressing charges or bringing it to trial. The other members helped out with the many facets of the investigation.

Race and Carbone walked briskly through a maze of corridors to a staircase down to the first floor and past a legion of uniformed cops who were beginning their day tour. Exiting through the rear door into a parking lot, the sergeant and his new pupil slid into an unmarked Plymouth Fury. Mike Race stepped on the gas and commenced his minicourse in Homicide 101.

"One of the most important things you have to learn is how to read a crime scene," said Race, his left hand resting lightly on the wheel as he maneuvered skillfully through traffic, his right hand punctuating his lecture with angular gestures. "You should be able to scan a scene and pick up things the untrained observer wouldn't. Train yourself to be observant and ask why something is the way it is. Look for anything out of the ordinary and make a note of it.

"You walk into a home where someone was murdered. How is the body lying? What's the victim wearing? Are his garments ripped? Does he have any scratches? In what position are the victim's arms? His hands?" Race took his eyes off the traffic for an instant to glance at Dave.

Dave knew that as a detective he'd have to search corpses for personal papers and effects. But he also knew no one was allowed to touch a body, or anything else where a murder took place, until the Crime Scene Unit had processed the scene. He nodded to show he was taking in the lecture.

Race continued, his eyes back on the traffic. "Was the front door open or closed? Locked or unlocked? Are the windows open? If so, how much? Walk into every room of the house and take notes. What stations are the TV and radio turned to? Is the stove on? What's being cooked? A couple lives there, but dinner is set for three people. Who's the third person? How many toothbrushes are there? A woman says she lives alone, so why is her toilet seat up? Why is a man's clothing in her closet?" He stopped talking momentarily to maneuver the car deftly around a slowing bus, then had to slow down himself as the light ahead turned red.

He eased the car to a halt and turned to face Dave as they waited. "Look for impressions on the carpet. Maybe someone moved around the furniture to throw you off or tried to recreate the scene like it was before the crime. You can never make a crime scene exactly the way it was before, even if you know how it must have been, but you look closely for clues. A crooked picture, for instance, might indicate a violent fight." He paused, and Dave nodded again.

The sergeant looked up at the light and put the car in gear. "There's a knack to reading a crime scene, and it takes time to develop," he said, as the car moved forward again.

Dave was paying attention with only half his mind. The other half was focused on what would happen when they got to the crime scene. Where the fuck do I start? he wondered, befuddled.

In RIP, he had learned the basic structure of an investigation, but that didn't tell him anything specific about what was involved when the crime was a homicide. Sergeant Race must know that, he thought. So what do I do when I get there? How do I start without looking stupid?

"The canvass is also important," Race continued imperturbably, not noticing his rookie's perplexity. "You did canvasses in RIP, so you know how to do these. But it's more complicated with homicides. Knock on doors and find out who might have heard or seen anything. Be sure to maintain control and do the interviews on your terms, not theirs. You'll be doing canvasses all hours of the day, but don't worry about the time. If you're up, they're up.

"And of course never take anything for granted," he added, glancing again at Dave for emphasis. "Just because someone says 'I came home from work and found a body so I called the police' doesn't mean it's true. Also, some people in jail will say they have information on a murder. Guys who are locked up will say anything to cut a deal, but sometimes they're telling the truth. Just remember they don't make credible witnesses."

He chuckled dryly. "Anyone can say he committed a murder. We try and prove it. Not only prove that he did it, but prove that someone else didn't do it."

Race was talking quickly but driving slowly, and this was making Dave jumpy. He was impatient to get to the scene, but he knew Race was trying to cover a lot of territory in the brief ride. He sat back and tried to concentrate on what Race was saying.

"One of the other most important things is to learn your victim," the sergeant continued. "Where did he work? What was he doing over the past week? Who were his friends? His enemies? If the victim was killed at a location other than his home, what was he doing there? Was he with anyone? Who might want to kill him?

"The victim's family may play a major part in helping you, but in the ghetto sometimes they won't tell you things. They may get a phone call from an acquaintance letting them know who did it. But they may not tell you. They may be afraid. Or they might want to take care of it themselves."

Race thought for a moment, then resumed. "Ask the family to see the victim's telephone book and telephone bills. Run the names and locations. Flags may pop on certain locations, and you'll find out that Narcotics or the DEA is working cases there. Get the investigator's name and call him and tell him what you've got. There could be surveillance on the location already, unbeknownst to you.

"Who did the victim call? You might see on a phone bill that in the month of April he called Cali, Colombia, twelve times. Does he have an aunt there, or does he have a drug situation going?

"Look at his credit card statements. What did he spend money on? Go through photograph albums with the family. Ask who everyone is. Maybe someone will call anonymously and say JJ did it, and you'll remember the family has a picture of JJ. If not, and JJ, whose real name might be Johnny Jones, has any priors, we can run him through BCI and get his criminal history, and then we can get a department photo of him."

Race was finally winding down. "So you go around a crime scene and look through every nook and cranny. Basically, you go in and be a scavenger, because you've got to learn as much about the victim as you possibly can."

They stopped at another light, and the sergeant again swung round to face Dave. "Do you think the investigation of the murder of President Kennedy was done differently from any other investigation?" he asked.

Dave was quiet, pondering what he thought was a trick question.

"It would seem so, but it wasn't," said Race, answering himself. "Some homicides create more press. There's more pressure to solve the case, you're awed by the fact that it's the President, but murder is murder and they're all done basically the same way, except that some are more detailed and there may be more angles to investigate. You find your ballistics evidence, conduct interviews, analyze the medical examiner's report, come up with theories, and investigate them."

Dave considered where the killer he was about to start looking for could be. He was probably a neighborhood skel, so chances were he was holed up in some local crack den. Dave would have to return later to the vicinity with the other detectives to do a thorough canvass, maybe push a little strongarm if necessary.

Race had another question. "Would you treat the victim of this homicide like President Kennedy?"

Again, Race spoke before Dave could answer. "There's an old saying that I believe: 'A drunk man deserves a safe street just as much as a sober man.'" The light changed, and Race sent the car forward, but he kept darting quick glances at Dave as he drove.

The sergeant finally seemed to have tuned in on Dave's increasing tension. "Don't worry about solving the case," he said. "A captain in the Two-Five squad once told me that the most important thing in working a case is just to take detailed, chronological notes so when a defense attorney cross-examines you in court a year down the line, you'll be able to answer him. Or if something happens to you or you're off on a particular day that someone phones in important information, or if you're transferred, someone else can take your notes and pick up the case."

Dave saw radio cars up ahead and knew they were approaching the crime scene. He willed the butterflies in his belly to still their wings.

A minute later, on the service road of Linden Boulevard by Fountain Avenue, they were out of the car, and Race spoke to the first officer quietly for a few moments. Dave had his notebook out and wrote down the time they arrived and what the lighting and weather conditions were. The officer, Edward Serocki, then gave Dave pedigree information on the homicide and the victim: Frederick Stager, male white, age thirty-five. Lived upstate in Garnerville, New York, with his wife and three kids but worked and lived with his sister Irene during the week in Brooklyn.

The victim and his sister had been on their way to buy milk at the Sunnydale Farms store. At 4:10 A.M. they were stopped at a light. On the other side of the light in the middle of the street were three men who seemed to be arguing. When the light turned green, Stager moved up a little and waited, but the men continued to stand in the street, in the vehicle's way. Stager finally tapped his horn. One of the men approached the vehicle, took out a .45 from his waistband, and shot him through the windshield in the face. The car, out of control but moving slowly, crumpled gently into a building wall. The first officers on the scene found the sister hiding under the dashboard. The victim was taken to Brookdale Hospital, where he died at 7:50 A.M. Dave wrote as Serocki spoke, then he went over to have a look at the car.

He entered more observations in his notebook. Zigzag skid marks. Dodge Aries, four-door, tan. Rented. Right front end smashed into a wall. Gear in drive. Key in the ignition. Windows closed. Bullet hole ten inches from the base of the windshield.

About a half hour after they arrived, Race told Dave it was time to head back for the precinct. Dave was thinking he should canvass the area, find out what stores were open early in the morning, if there were any bus routes along the street, what car services were in the area, and who might have been walking a dog early in the morning, but Race said the victim's sister was back at the precinct, and he wanted Dave to interview her and get her statement.

On the way back, Race went over the interview. "The first and most important thing is to calm your witness," he said. "Not only was her brother shot, but it happened right in front of her. It probably traumatized her. Talk to her, get her coffee, calm her down. There are dozens of people running around at the precinct, and she doesn't know who's who, what's going on. Explain to her what's going to happen."

Dave knew some of the basics, but he wasn't looking forward to talking to the victim's sister.

"She'll have to go to the morgue to identify the body," Race continued. "She'll talk to the DA. Tell her about lineups, what the alleged perp will be doing, that he won't be allowed to talk to her. Explain everything she's going to do. Gain her trust."

A few minutes later, with Dave in tow, Race turned the heavy round silver knob and opened the thick blue door marked "Detectives." As Dave strode into the squad room, he felt a sudden rush, a reaffirmation that he was a detective, an important person, working on a serious case.

As Dave went to the movement log book to sign in, he looked around. His first impression of the room had been its size. He'd been in a fair share of squad rooms before, but this was by far the largest one he had ever seen. It was huge. If they needed such a big room, he thought, they must *really* be swamped with cases.

Around the room were more than a dozen desks, placed back to back in pairs or in clumps of three or four. There were fans and wastebaskets scattered about, large green and gray filing cabinets lining the walls, piles of telephone books marked "75 Squad," stacks of police forms, reports and other paperwork, mounted plaques, hanging chalkboards, a wall on which were printed the phone numbers of special police units, precincts, DA offices, federal agencies, and hospitals. The front center of the room was a holding cell; to the right were the bosses' offices; to the left was a lounge, an interview room with a one-way mirror, and a bunkroom. The walls were pale blue cinder blocks, the floor was scuffed and dirty, and the room looked drab and worn— just like a squad room should look, Dave thought. After signing in, Dave hung his outer coat and sport jacket on a rack. Then, bracing himself, he walked through a short hallway on the far side of the room and into the lounge.

Dave scanned the room. Sitting on the edge of one of the hard chairs, arms resting on the table, was a very thin, almost scrawny, woman in a shapeless drab green coat who looked to be in her middle thirties, although her face was so hollow it was hard to tell. She had looked up when he entered and was staring at him, her eyes wide, her mouth parted. As Dave crossed the room toward her, she ran her fingers hastily through her scraggly blond hair in a futile primping gesture. Dave could see her hand was shaking badly.

"Hello, I'm Detective David Carbone," he said to her as he approached. "I've been assigned to handle your case." She nodded quickly, then shook her head as if confused. She's not in great shape, he thought. "I'm sorry about what happened," he said softly.

Her mouth began to tremble, and she pursed her lips. Then she said hoarsely, "How's my brother?"

Dave stared uncomfortably at the floor. "I don't know," he said. He knew the rules of the game. Get the information first, then tell the loved one of the victim's death. A distraught witness makes a poor supplier of information. "We're waiting to hear from the doctor," he added.

When he was investigating robberies, Dave had sometimes played dumb, but this was the first time he had had to lie, and he felt guilty. But he also realized that while it was cruel, maybe unfair, to lie to this wretched woman, it was in the interest of solving her brother's murder. She was on the edge as it was; if she became hysterical, he wouldn't be able to get any coherent information.

Dave asked her to tell him what had happened. She sobbed intermittently as she related what she remembered. She didn't appear to know more than Dave had learned already. This wasn't surprising; she had been sure, as she now repeated over and over, that she was going to be shot as well and didn't recall much else but her terror.

Dave was patient, but speed was essential, and he tried delicately to prod her for details. As the minutes went by, when he asked her a question her head would begin to nod, and when he paused for her answer he would see that she had dozed off. When he touched her shoulder to wake her up, it would bring on another fit of sobs. He brought her coffee and asked if he could get her some food, but she was in no condition to eat; she could barely hold the coffee without spilling it.

After twenty-five futile minutes, Dave excused himself and asked her to wait for him.

Mike Race was working on some papers in the squad room, and Dave headed to his desk.

Race looked up as Dave approached. "Did you see how skinny she is?" he asked.

"Yeah," said Dave. "She must be on the Jenny Crack diet."

Race shook his head and went back to flipping sheets of paper on his clipboard.

"I'm not getting much out of her," Dave continued. "I'll give it another few minutes, then explain about her brother, give her a run-down on what we're likely to need her for, arrange for her to go to the morgue. Then I'd better get some of the paperwork out of the way, clear the decks. There isn't a lot to go on, but I have a few ideas. I want to get back to the site; there's a deli halfway up the block, and it may have been open at the time, but I'm not sure—"

"Carbone." Race cut him off. "We have the killer. He's downstairs. Patrol picked him up seventeen minutes after the murder."

Dave looked at the sergeant blankly. "You have him? But I thought—"

"I didn't tell you because I wanted to take you through the initial process, from step one. I thought this would be a good training case, broken down in basic steps for you. Plus an arrest was made, so you don't need to feel pressured. I could have given you a horror case that would have buried you, but I figured it would be better to hand you a ground-ball job first time out so you could get familiar with the basics."

Dave felt deflated. "How did patrol find him?"

"David DeGeorge, a patrol officer in the precinct, noticed someone sitting on a bench across the street from the shooting who fit the description of the perp that was broadcast. DeGeorge and his partner started toward him, but he got up and ran. They chased him into the Cypress housing project and out onto Fountain and Hegeman avenues. It was put over the air, and a patrol car coming south from Sutter Avenue cut him off and grabbed him. During the chase the perp dropped a .45 under a car and put his hat over it." Race rose from his chair and clapped Dave on the shoulder. "So all you've really got to do now is follow through, take care of the paperwork, see if the sister can pick him out of a lineup. Oh, and you'd better tell her about her brother. When you come back, I'll get you started on the paperwork."

A short while later, Dave sat working his way through the Fives, the basic paperwork of an investigation in which every detective described each thing he had done on a separate form. The neophyte was upset with himself. The dead man's sister had taken the news about her brother with surprising calm and had not shown much emotion when she heard a suspect was in custody; she seemed to have withdrawn into herself, far away from the turmoil of the past few hours. She hadn't asked Dave when he had found out her brother had died. That, at least, was a relief. But how could he not have figured out that the perp had been caught? The clues were there; Race had practically thrown them into his lap. Where was the canvass? The trip to the hospital to talk to the emergency-room doctors or see the body? A follow-up with Crime Scene? And everything seemed to have been taken at a snail's pace. Dave prided himself on his intuition, his powers of observation, but now he felt like a fool. He hoped this wasn't indicative of the kind of detective he'd make.

Other things hit him too. Were Stager and his sister really going out to buy milk at four in the morning? Stager was probably a crack addict on a mission to buy drugs. Dave felt sorry for Stager, but then ran his name with BCI and found that Stager had had an arrest record himself.

His first budding mystery had come to a rather fizzled climax. While he was glad the perp had been caught, Dave had been relishing his first chance to track down a killer and was disappointed there'd be no hunt.

Not to worry. In the 75th Precinct that opportunity would present itself more often than he could ever imagine.

5

At eight o'clock the next morning, Al Smith and Mike Redmond took Dave down to the front desk on the first floor to show him the squad basket. This contained the paperwork on new cases that had come in since midnight. It was a daily ritual for the cases to be broken down and assigned to the squad. Several trips were made during the tour to pick up new paperwork as it accumulated, and it was done by the detectives on a rotating basis. Even though he was new, it was Dave's turn up, and time for him to learn how to do what the detectives called "redlining."

Dave was preoccupied not so much with the technique he was about to learn—paperwork was always a drag—but with the imminent challenge of actually doing cases—shootings, homicides, burglaries, missing persons, grand larcenies, stolen cars, bank frauds, embezzlements, any felony crime, actually, which was what the squad investigated. He'd have to start in right away. The two basic detective courses, CIC, or the Criminal Investigation Course, and Homicide, probably wouldn't come until a year or two later. He'd learn as he went along, on-the-job training, so to speak, but he didn't want to come off as slow. New as he was to the squad, he had a solid foundation of street smarts from his years on the beat and in RIP, and he was determined the rest of the squad would quickly find that out.

Coming from Long Island to New York City as a rookie cop had been a drastic change for Dave. His lily-white suburban enclave featured tidy homes and manicured lawns, pristine streets and placid surroundings. There was crime, to be sure, as there was in any modern suburban neighborhood, but it was infrequent and virtually invisible—a burglary here, a stolen car there. And, yes, there was drug use in the local schools, but it was for the most part dealt privately, not out in the open on corners or in front of stores as it was in the city.

In that environment, Dave had had very little interaction with blacks and Hispanics. There had been only a few minority students in all the schools he had attended, and his view of them came primarily from the media—which gave him mixed feelings. It seemed to him a disproportionate number of blacks and Hispanics were involved in committing crimes, on the one hand; but on the other, the conditions under which those in the inner city lived were distressing. These perceptions were combined into a mixture of fear and sympathy, and he realized both stemmed from ignorance. When he became a cop, he had resolved to get to know these people better, to confront his preconceived notions. He hoped both would prove to be exaggerated.

But hitting the streets of New York City as a cop was a rude awakening. Seeing images on television was one thing, coming face to face with the conditions was another. They were far worse than he had ever imagined. He found nice families living pitifully in abandoned buildings, in apartments with floors missing entire boards or completely rotted away, cockroaches scrambling everywhere, a wretched stench permeating the premises. In the winter these subhuman dwellings were unbearably cold, in the summer intolerably hot. He went into homes where a mother and four kids slept in a single bed, or where newspapers were laid out on the floor as beds and blankets and the only light at night came from the moon. Instead of recoiling from these unfortunates, he befriended them, tried to learn as much about them as he could. Before long, he subconsciously began adopting the lingo of the inner city, even the cool gait and hand expressions.

Out on patrol, Dave watched people closely, got a feel for the neighborhood. He began to learn about the street-urchin criminals the cops called mutts—what they did and how they did it, how they acted and where they ran to after they struck. He began to think like a cop.

Then in Anticrime, where he dressed as a street denizen himself, he searched for these mutts, waited for them to strike. He drove around in beat-up old cars, loitered in subways, staggered down the street holding a beer bottle filled with soda, slumped on park benches looking strung out. In the darkness he conducted rooftop surveillances, targeting through a night scope locations that were constantly being hit. He watched the mutts and remembered they were creatures of habit.

He made collars and heightened his cop senses. In debriefing his prisoners, he asked them how they carried out certain crimes, why they did this or that, where they hid. He fine-tuned his instincts, developed a keen awareness of what was happening on the streets, a feel for the criminal mind. To catch criminals, a detective had to think like them.

In RIP, Dave learned the mind of a robber. He also learned how to use the system to track a robber down. And he was bowled over by what a well-equipped, well-tuned police department could do.

If he supplied a name and approximate age, BCI responded with that person's complete criminal history. If he provided a location, CARS (the Computer Assisted Robbery System unit) told him all the arrests made at that location, as well as the criminal history of everyone arrested there. The name and NYSIIS number of somebody who had been arrested produced, from the borough CATCH (Computer Assisted Terminal Criminal Hunt) unit or the NYPD Photo Unit, the person's photograph. There were other units to call to find out if a person was on parole, had any outstanding warrants, had received any automobile summonses. There was an almost endless number of places he could call to obtain information about one aspect or another of the person he was tracking. For that one investigation, Dave found out, he might do myriad mini-investigations.

Now he had to apply the basics of conducting an investigation to a different world. He was going to have to keep up with the other detectives in the squad and meet the approval of the bosses. A heterogeneous bunch, these guys were crackerjack detectives and demanding supervisors, among the very best in the Bureau. Technically, they all knew the job well, but with their diverse personalities, they each brought something special to their work.

Endowed with a charm that could soften the edges of the most hard-assed human garbage, Al Smith—known to his fellow cops as Smitty—was a detective one couldn't help but cotton to. Slightly portly, with a skin tone of rich mahogany and short-cropped hair, he was suave and an immaculate dresser, and he oozed confidence. He was the quintessence of cool, an ambassador of hip and affability, and he was often the detective brought into an interrogation to outslick a suspect who was not cooperating.

Alexander Francis Smith had been born in the West Indies and had come to the United States with his family when he was seven. He attended Xaverian High School in Bay Ridge, Brooklyn, and New York University on a scholarship, majoring in sociology. Smitty was working as an admitting clerk in a Queens hospital when he took the police civil service test. His ambition when he was in college had been to become a lawyer, but lawyers were a glut on the market at the time he graduated; being a cop seemed a good alternative. Before coming to the squad, Smith, the only black member of Team One, had worked in Manhattan North Narcotics, a unit that busted drug dealers, from small-time hustlers to large organizations. The unit worked out of the

Two-Six in west Harlem and covered the Three-Oh in north Harlem and the Three-Four in Washington Heights, both highly dangerous, drug-infested areas.

Jack Cutrone was Smitty's polar opposite: intense, deadly serious, intimidating. Tuning in to a situation on the street, staring sharply, he could read a person's eyes with uncanny precision to determine if he or she was lying. When a case lacked anything solid, his pride prohibited him from giving up. He worked doggedly until he found a lead and ran with it until he broke the case.

Cutrone had found his calling in law enforcement. One of eleven children from a working-class family, he grew up in the Flatbush section of Brooklyn and enlisted at seventeen, finishing high school in Maine under a Navy program. In the service he worked as a diesel mechanic, and later he drove a truck and loaded trailers in a supermarket warehouse. But he scored a ninety-eight on the police civil service exam and found he had a natural talent for police work after graduating from the academy.

Of the four Team One detectives, Jerry Roman was the only one over forty. A meticulous worker and dresser who sported a thick mane of silver hair combed straight back, Roman was one of the first undercover cops in the department to infiltrate major drug organizations. Unlike most narcotics officers, who are part of teams that make buys and then bust the sellers, Roman had gone underground and infiltrated drug gangs so deeply that he became intimately knowledgeable about their activities and was able to supply information that led to many arrests. Because many of the gangs had roots in South America, his Hispanic background was an asset in his work.

Each of the squad's three teams was assisted by homicide detectives who worked only murders. They didn't actually catch homicides but worked with the catching detective on new homicides and helped work unsolved old ones. It was only after years of successful experience that one became a homicide detective, and that was something every regular detective aspired to be. Team One's homicide detectives were Joe Hall and Mike Redmond.

With his mild, soft-spoken manner, wire-rimmed glasses, and benign, cherubic face framed by short, wavy black hair, Joe Hall was a ringer for a priest. Indeed, his colleagues often joked that he should don a collar. While not the physical paradigm of most people's image of a detective, he just happened to be one of the best in the NYPD Detective Bureau.

People readily talked to Hall: witnesses, perps, people on the street. They felt secure, they trusted him. He had a bevy of informants, and his information led him to make scores of arrests. And he was good to the people who were good to him. He'd go out of his way for an informant and be true to his word in helping perps who came through for him.

Hall started out in the NYPD working for the now defunct Bureau of Special Services, an undercover unit that investigated subversive groups. He had become a detective in 1982 and was assigned to the 46th Precinct squad in the Bronx, one of the busiest in the city at the time. Three years later he became a homicide investigator in the Seven-Five.

Mike Redmond was already a legend in the Detective Bureau, known for his vast experience and lightning-quick and perspicacious assessment of situations. A cop since 1965, Redmond had spent years working in the South Bronx, when it was essentially anarchic, ruled by outlaw gangs.

Redmond was the father figure of the squad, sometimes called the "old man" or "old-timer." His appearance and personality helped him out on the street, where people tended to trust him over the younger guys. He had that old-fashioned detective style and commanded respect wherever he went. He knew about as much as one could know about detective work and the NYPD. Neophyte detectives yearned to come to the Seven-Five just for the privilege of learning from him.

The Seven-Five squad had traditionally been filled with seasoned detectives. If there was an opening, a veteran from another precinct or unit was invited to grab the spot; experienced detectives were most desirable for the ever-busy squad. But in recent years, as the NYPD became younger, so had the Seven-Five squad.

The younger detectives, of whom Dave was one, cut a stark contrast to the older ones. They might sport a ponytail or wear an earring. They dressed hip, they were easygoing, they bore a different image altogether from their predecessors.

Detectives of the seventies and earlier were typically war veterans and older, staunchly conservative men. They wore fedora hats, smoked pipes or cigars, and avoided making fashion statements.

But this is not to say that because they were straitlaced, they were not good detectives. Quite the opposite. They were revered on the job, as if they were at the top rung of a caste system. Mike Redmond, who came into the Seven-Five squad at the tail end of that era, told each new investigator in the precinct detective unit about the respect the old-timers commanded, both on the street and in the precinct.

"When detectives came on the scene," he said, "they were like gods. Whatever they said was like God's chosen words. They were the entire show, and they were consummate professionals.

"Years ago, patrol wasn't even allowed into the squad room. They had to stop at the front gate and couldn't enter unless they had a reason and a detective invited them in. The squad room was the detectives' domain, and even patrol cops were outsiders there.

"And certainly the detectives had a way about them. Their demeanor and the way they carried themselves set them apart from the other cops. They knew the right way to talk to people, to handle them. Whether it was a reluctant witness or a hardened criminal, they knew just how to get the most out of that person."

Perhaps to some extent the reputation of the old detectives was a myth, but they solved a high percentage of their cases and were so well respected on the job that they established the tradition of detectives in the NYPD as a breed apart from the rest of the force. One tangible factor that distinguished them from their modern counterparts was age. It usually took about ten years before a police officer could get into the Detective Bureau back then. During the 1970s, perhaps this was due to the financial difficulties New York was suffering at the time. But it was also a reasonable period for a budding detective to develop the necessary instincts and street smarts. By the time a cop became a detective, he needed to be able to manipulate to some degree the uncooperative people he'd encounter in his investigations.

To get into the Detective Bureau, a cop always had to show good activity. Many of today's old-timers came out of TPF, the Tactical Patrol Force, a specialized unit of cops that was put into any area of the city that needed police assistance. It could mobilize a lot of officers quickly in the event of a riot or disaster. As a general rule, a cop had to make fifty collars in three years to get into the Bureau. And that would be as a white-shield investigator. From date of appointment, it would normally be at least nine or ten years before a police officer could get a detective's gold shield.

That changed through the efforts of the Detectives' Endowment Association, the union for New York City detectives. The DEA sponsored bills regulating the length of time that a cop working in an investigatory unit such as RIP or OCCB could get his gold shield, reducing it to twenty-seven months. (It was later reduced to eighteen months.) Hence there had been a younger class of detective in recent years.

Old-timers, like Mike Redmond, remembered that when they were new to a squad, the veterans would train them, but the rookies didn't speak with the veterans. For chitchat, rookies spoke to the other rookies. Only if you wanted to ask questions about how to do things would you speak to an old-timer. Each had a distinct personality—some were rough, others gentle—but they were all special, every one of them, and they meshed fluidly when they were working on a case.

Technically, detective was a promotion from police officer. It was the same rank as police officer, but the detective enjoyed a higher base salary and more prestige. And unlike a promotion to the higher ranks of sergeant, lieutenant, or captain, promotion from police officer to detective did not require a civil service examination. The elevation to detective was based on merit—a reward for good work and making a lot of collars.

Within the rank of detective in the NYPD were three grades: first, second, and third. The highest grade was first, and accordingly had the highest pay scale.

Perhaps as a reflection of the changing mores and fashions of society, the new detectives were different in other ways from their predecessors. In the past, for example, if a cop, except perhaps for an undercover officer, wore an earring, he was branded a homosexual. Many modern cops wore earrings not as a sign of sexual orientation but just in the style of the times. Such was the case with Dave.

Dave had gotten his earring on a dare. One day he was in the Roosevelt Field shopping center on Long Island with his wife and daughter when they passed an earring booth. "You know, I really should get my ear pierced," he said to Luci. "I've always wanted to."

Luci raised her eyebrows. "You always talk a good story, but you never do it," she said.

A half hour later, Dave and his family continued their shopping jaunt, a discreet gold stud embedded in Dave's earlobe.

The police department's quasi-military organization required cops to conform to conventions, but some personal expression did manifest itself, straining the toleration limits of the department to the maximum.

Back in the squad room, Redmond, Dave, and Smitty sat around a desk with other detectives nearby. A pile of Sixty and Sixty-One sheets from the squad basket now sat on Dave's desk.

"Read through all the Sixty-ones," said Mike Redmond, "and separate the open cases from the closed ones."

Sixty-ones were complaint reports that police officers filled out based on the jobs they got, or from people who came into the precinct to file complaints. Copies of all the Sixty-ones went to the squad, except for robberies, which went to the precinct's RIP unit; the squad determined what cases it would or would not investigate based on Detective Bureau guidelines. The Sixty-one spelled out the crime. Sixty-ones were indexed chronologically by patrol on what were called the Sixty sheets.

Paperwork occupied a large part of police work. In patrol, Dave filled out Sixty-ones—reports were often referred to by numbers, letters, or both—as well as accident reports, aided reports, missing person reports, and On-Line Booking System arrest worksheets. In RIP he worked mainly with Complaint Follow-Up Informationals, known universally in the department by their anachronistic abbreviations, DD Fives, or Fives, for Detective Division Form Five. Detectives worked with basically the same reports, just in different ways.

"Patrol indicates on the Sixty-one whether a case is open to the squad or closed," said Redmond, "depending on the crime." Some cases closed out rapidly. For a grand larceny auto, for instance, patrol transmitted an alarm on the stolen car, and there was usually no investigation by the detectives unless further evidence popped up. For an act of criminal mischief such as a broken window or slashed tires, patrol filled out a Sixty-one and closed the case unless a witness came forward or other information surfaced that could be investigated.

"But ultimately we decide whether a case should be investigated," continued Redmond. "Patrol may close it, but we may choose to keep it open. Maybe we're looking for someone for murder who lives in the same building or area as a woman whose car was stolen. We only know the guy's first name, Walter. So we talk to the woman, inquire about her car. Ask her if she knows the bad guys in the area. Maybe she does. Maybe she knows Walter lives in apartment 5F. We act nice to her, get her to talk. It's all in how you use your authority, not how you abuse it.

"After you've read through and separated the cases, you break down the open cases into times, separating cases for the day team and the night team, depending on when they hit the sheets." He pointed to the Sixty sheets, which listed the times the cases were entered on them.

"Anything from midnight to two P.M. goes to the day tour, anything from two P.M. to midnight goes to the night tour. When you're on a turnaround, going from your second night tour to your first day tour, you catch both tours. You're responsible for the whole twenty-four hours."

Smitty chimed in. "We're the catching slime," he said, "because we catch all the cases. The homicide guys don't catch cases. They couldn't catch a cold." There was always a bit of envy between the regular squad detectives and the homicide detectives, and the regulars never failed to take an opportunity to needle them. Redmond gave Smitty a withering glance.

"Gotcha," said Smitty, smirking. Dave tried to keep his mouth from twitching.

"Now you assign the cases to the detectives," continued Redmond doggedly. "We call this red-lining, because with a red pencil, on the Sixty sheets you box in the cases on the sheets that you'll assign to the detectives."

The Sixty sheets were a running order of the police reports taken in the precinct. Each Sixty sheet held ten cases. With seventy to a hundred complaints coming in daily to the precinct, there might be as many as ten or more Sixty sheets each day. The cases were reviewed, and those that were taken by the squad were given a PDU (precinct detective unit) number from what was called the Four-ninety-four sheet, which was a running order of the cases that the squad investigated.

"Let me go through sorting the cases for the day with you," said Redmond, picking up a stack of Sixty-ones. "You'll get the hang of it quickly."

With the stack resting in his left hand, Redmond lifted the top sheet with his right and scanned the filled-in information on the paper, settling on a typewritten paragraph near the bottom. This was the space in which the patrol officer tersely described the offenses, using abbreviations throughout, such as "t/p/o" for time and place of occurrence, "comp." for complainant, "GLA" for grand larceny auto.

"At t/p/o boyfriend punches girlfriend in face with fist, causing minor injuries. She's being referred to court for an order of protection." Redmond explained that although this was an assault, the woman had refused medical aid, so she could not document her injuries. "Case closed," he said, slapping the sheet facedown on the desk and peeling the next from the top of the pile.

"At t/p/o reporter states unknown person or persons did lift metal shutter, enter premises, and remove above-listed property without permission or authority to do so." After reading the list of items taken and their value, Redmond outlined the criteria for the squad to take a burglary case: if there was a witness, if the monetary value of the burglary was over $5,000, if the location had been burglarized at least once before within the previous six months. "Since none of the criteria was met with regard to this burglary," said Redmond, "the case is closed, although a fingerprint team will dust the premises. If they get a print and there's a hit, we'll reopen the case."

Dave listened attentively as Redmond continued to read the offenses and pronounce whether or not the squad would take the cases. He was struck by the rapidity and decisiveness with which Redmond rendered the dispositions. To become adept at this himself, Dave knew, he would have to become intimately familiar with the Bureau guidelines and the squad's own procedures. Redmond quietly surveyed each sheet, then summarized aloud.

"Family order of protection . . . gotta take it.

"Menacing with a gun . . . gotta take it.

"Rape . . . notify Sex Crimes.

"Criminal mischief . . . complainant does not want to prosecute . . . case closed.

"Fire . . . notify Arson Squad.

"Missing person . . . gotta take it.

"Assault . . . complainant wants to press charges . . . gotta take it."

Over the next half hour, Redmond reviewed all the Sixty-ones. Then he demonstrated the red-lining on the Sixty sheets, noting the order of assigned cases for catching detectives in the squad. At intervals Smitty interrupted with caveats.

"You have to do your first Five—such as Interview of the Complainant, Response to the Scene, Response to the Hospital, Interview of the First Officer on the Scene, Canvass, or Notification of the Family— within three days of getting a case," he said. "You do your second Five within seven days after that, a third Five within the next twenty-one days, and a Five for every twenty-one days after that for as long as the case remains open. That might not sound like too much work, but we get so many cases here that it's easy to get backed up."

After they finished—only twenty-four of the seventy-one cases listed were assigned—Dave filed the paperwork on the open cases into the coops, or mailboxes, of the detectives to whom they were assigned.

Then, because the complainants on Dave and Smitty's cases didn't have telephones, the two, along with Mike Redmond, went out to interview them at their homes. The first, a woman who claimed she had been hit in the face, had given a bogus address. "Ain't no Lenore here," said an old man who came to the door. The second address didn't exist.

"Feel like Chinese food for lunch?" Smitty asked as they cruised the street looking for the address.

Dave hesitated a moment, recalling the shrimp and Chinese vegetables he had eaten yesterday. "Sure," he said. Redmond nodded his assent.

On the way to the restaurant, Central blared a message over the portable: "Man shot at the corner of Newport and Williams. EMS is already eighty-four, removing him to Brookdale."

Since they were near the hospital, Smitty responded that he and the two other detectives would go directly there, and they would meet the rest of the team afterward at the crime scene. It was too bad somebody had to get shot, but it couldn't have come at a better time for Dave. Maybe in a few hours Chinese food wouldn't seem so unwelcome.

A few minutes later, they pulled up at the Linden Boulevard entrance of Brookdale Hospital and walked through the sliding glass doors, where a security guard nodded to them. The corridors were lined with people lying prone on gurneys and gazing hopelessly at the ceiling. The waiting room diagonally across was filled to capacity; people were sitting on the floor in the vestibules. One elderly and apparently homeless man, Dave noted with some distress, had no feet.

"EMS took the victim to the ER," Smitty said to Dave. "You'll get to know that room. You'll be there plenty of times. Probably just as well you missed lunch."

As they crossed the nurses' bay, a young Latino woman in a white uniform cheerfully said hello to Smitty and Redmond.

"Meet the new guy," Smitty answered, extending his arm. "Detective Carbone." The two exchanged smiles.

A half-minute later, the three detectives were in the emergency room. Doctors, nurses, and technicians were huddled over a body.

Sprawled naked on the table was a young black man, muscular and lean, about twenty. A technician had just cut off his clothes with a pair of scissors, and a doctor was inserting a tube down his throat. A foam-like substance dribbled out of his mouth.

His eyes were closed, and his face was covered with blood. Blood oozed out the holes in his chest onto the table. There didn't seem to be much life in him.

"I've seen victims actually fight on the table," Smitty said. "They're in shock and they think they're still fighting some bad guy. The doctors have to tie them down."

Smitty walked over to the man and bent down to his right ear. "Did you see who shot you?" he asked loudly. The detectives always tried to elicit a dying declaration from victims in the ER. A technician said it didn't look too good. Smitty repeated the question, but the young man was unresponsive. Smitty dragged a chair over to the table, mounted it, and snapped a picture of the young man's face with a Polaroid, for use in the investigation if the victim had no criminal record and the detectives couldn't obtain a photograph of him. Then Smitty joined Dave at the foot of the table.

"Fucking cold in here," Dave said.

Next to the victim a nurse was greasing the end of a catheter. With the catheter in her right hand, the nurse grabbed the man's penis with her left and used her first right finger and thumb to separate the lips on the organ's head.

Dave couldn't believe what seemed to be about to happen. Was the woman going to insert the rubber hose, maybe a half inch in diameter, into the man's dick? Can't be, he thought. A dick is meant to go into something, not for something to go into *it!*

The woman was having difficulty introducing the end of the catheter into the victim's urethra. She stretched the lips farther apart and tried to wedge the catheter in.

Smitty saw the look on Dave's face and guffawed. "In the squad, this is what we call the Johnson Tube Sit-up Test," he said. "She's going to shove that tube up his Johnson, right? If the guy bolts up or screams, it means he feels it and he's going to live. If there's no reaction, then it's the pearly gates for him. Or maybe purgatory."

Veteran detectives knew this procedure was part of the medical management of shock when a person suffered a major trauma such as a motor vehicle accident or gunshot wound. Massive blood loss was rapidly replaced with fluids, but because of the risk of overloading the heart and lungs with fluid, a catheter was introduced directly into the bladder to measure urine output precisely so doctors could meet the body's fluid demands properly. But it looked like some insanely barbaric method of torture to Dave.

The nurse finally managed to insert the catheter into the victim's penis, then worked the tube in deeper and deeper.

"I guess he's a DOA," Dave remarked, wincing with each motion of the nurse's hands. There was no reaction from the man.

All of a sudden, the man's hand moved toward his penis, and he groaned. Dave wished he had remained insensible. He thought he'd almost rather die himself than wake up to such a sensation.

"He'll live," Smitty pronounced. "No way he's gonna croak if he felt that. Okay, so if he talks, we'll take the case. If not, and these gunshot victims sometimes say they'll take care of what happened themselves—they're not all that much different from the perps—we'll close it out.''

Just as Smitty spoke, urine began gushing from the catheter into a calibrated plastic bag. The man on the gurney began moaning and wriggling.

"Doctors say there's no medical basis to the Johnson Tube Sit-up Test," Smitty continued, thoroughly enjoying the sick expression on Dave's face, "but we've found that ninety percent of the time we can use it to predict whether someone will live or die. We know whether to stick around and interview the victim or not."

Dave continued to stare at the man, pondering the excruciating notion of having a long rubber tube ramrodded into one's schlong.

Smitty laughed. "Say, how's your stomach?"

"Don't ask," Dave grunted.

Smitty grinned. "Mine's sending out an APB for food."

Redmond reached into the man's trousers, which were draped over a chair. He withdrew a wallet and fanned through the papers inside, searching for identification.

"Here's an address," he said. "Let's check it out."

"Damn," said Smitty. "I guess I'll have to wait for that moo goo gai pan.''

6

The woman at the door of the third-floor apartment seemed alarmed when she saw the salt-and-pepper combination of suits before her. Dressed in a pink sweatsuit, she appeared to be in her early forties, with a glowing brown complexion.

"Come in," she said hesitantly, after seeing the flash of the shield.

Sensing her deep apprehension, Redmond began by saying that her son Henry was all right, but he had been hurt and was being treated at Brookdale. He circumvented her questions as best he could, making light of her son's condition and telling her they'd send a police car around soon to take her to Brookdale.

"We'd just like to ask you a few questions," Smitty said, "if you wouldn't mind."

The woman settled reluctantly in her chair, and Dave looked around. Across the room was a sleek-lined modern leather sofa next to a gilt-trimmed glass étagère. The room had a stylish look, with an antique desk and chair in the opposite corner.

"What time did Henry leave the house today?" Smitty asked.

"I don't remember exactly. Seven hours ago, I guess. Early in the morning."

"Did he say where he was going?"

"No, but I think he was going to meet his friend Ink. That's his nickname. I don't know his real name." She twirled a finger nervously in her hair.

"Do you know where he lives?"

"I don't know his exact address, but it's somewhere around New Lots and New Jersey."

"What's Henry like? I mean, what is he into?"

She answered quickly. "He likes music and sports, he plays basketball a lot. He's never been in trouble before, detective. He's a good boy."

"Yes, I know. We just have to ask."

"Anybody might want to hurt him?" Dave asked.

"No, not that I know of. No."

After a few more minutes of conversation, the detectives thanked the woman for her time and assured her a radio car would be coming soon to pick her up.

"New Lots and New Jersey," said Smitty in the car. "That's a heavy drug location. Do you think he's into the scene?"

"His mother said he's clean," answered Redmond. "She seemed pretty together."

"Maybe he's just starting to get into the business," Dave said. "She probably doesn't know what's going on yet."

Redmond picked up the radio. "Five squad, Central." Five squad was the designation for the 75th Precinct detectives. "Send a radio car to Wyona and Riverdale, and raise the Five squad unit at the shooting on Newport and Williams."

Seconds later a voice sounded. "On the air, Central." It was Detective Cutrone.

"Jack," Redmond said, "the guy in Brookdale's in stable condition. We just spoke to his mother. We're going to check out New Jersey and New Lots."

"Okay. We're at the dirt lot at Newport and Williams. Nothing much here except the usual garbage—crack vials, needles, empty beer bottles, rags. Crime Scene's finishing up, and then we'll do our canvass. We'll meet you back at the office later."

After traveling one block south to New Lots Avenue and turning left, the threesome drove several blocks east to New Jersey Avenue and parked their unmarked car. It was a typical bland East New York landscape. Some stores, some apartment buildings, no trees, no grass. Dirty and dismal-looking.

The detectives got out and looked around. It was an overcast day, the sky charcoal gray. The sun had yet to penetrate the blanket of somber clouds ushered in with the previous day's rainstorm. Normally, groups of young men hung out on the corners, watching people who passed by with eager faces, but today there were few drug dealers to be seen.

Three young men were leaning against a car in animated conversation. They were all clean-shaven and looked fresh and energetic.

"Yo, whassup?" Dave said, as the detectives approached the men. "Any of you guys know Henry Pressman?"

A chorus of yeses echoed back.

"Anyone here know his friend Ink?"

Blank stares and head shakes greeted the question.

"How do you know him?" Dave asked, looking at the largest teen.

He was thin, at least six-one, and wore ripped blue jeans, an open black bomber jacket over a T-shirt, and a black-and-yellow cap.

"We hang out together sometimes. Shoot a little hoops, know the same girls." The tall teen hesitated a moment. "What's this all about?"

"He's been hurt. Were you with him today?"

"No," he said, as did one of the others. The third said he had been with him briefly earlier. He had short hair and wore thick glasses. He was dressed in jeans, a windbreaker, and muddied sneakers.

"What time did you leave him?" Dave continued.

"I don't know. A few hours ago."

"Do you know where he went after you left him?"

The guy shrugged, saying he didn't keep tabs on his friends. Mike Redmond intervened. "Say, would you mind coming with us to the station house? We can talk better there."

Dave shot a look of surprise over to Smitty. Why bring him in so quickly? He'd been taught that you don't bring anybody in until you've got something on him, you don't shoot your load until you can prove the person was guilty. Jesus, this guy wasn't even a suspect yet!

Ten minutes later, the unmarked car parked in the back parking lot of the precinct, and the three detectives escorted their visitor upstairs to the squad room. Dave always felt exhilarated there. The ambience of the squad room appealed to him: the phones clanging away, the police band crackling with the voices of Central and patrol, plainclothes cops shuffling prisoners into the room's holding cell, bosses constantly walking out of their offices with papers they set down on desks and asked the detectives questions about. But for now the animated buzz was gone. Everybody was out at the crime scene. Only Sergeant Schurr remained to man the squad room.

The detectives took the visitor to the interview room and told him to wait for them there. It was a plain, dismal room with a pockmarked wooden bench, a few chairs, a table, and cinder-block walls. He declined Smitty's offer of a soda.

Redmond immediately called BCI to see if the young man they'd brought in had any previous arrests in the city, and the response came back negative.

"Hey, Mike," Dave said softly to Redmond a minute later in the lounge. "Why'd you bring him in?"

"Didn't you see his feet?"

Dave thought a moment, then slapped his forehead with the palm of his right hand. "Oh, shit, yeah."

A few minutes later, Jack Cutrone, Jerry Roman, and Joe Hall returned from the crime scene. They had just finished their canvass.

"Did you guys collar somebody?" Cutrone asked.

"No, why?" Dave responded.

"The people on the street said the DTs just arrested Ink for the shooting."

"That's Ink? What a fucking liar. Said he didn't have a street name."

Joe Hall was holding a clear plastic bag containing a gun that had been recovered at the crime scene.

Dave picked it up and carried it into the interrogation room. Smitty and Cutrone followed him.

"Okay, young fella," Dave began. "Why don't you tell us what happened?"

"Nothing. I left Henry and that was it."

"Does the name Ink ring a bell?"

"No. Should it?"

"I think so," Dave said, holding up the bag with the gun. "See this?" He paused, staring his subject straight in the eyes. "We got your fingerprints on this gun. Now look at your sneakers."

Everyone looked down. Crusts of dried mud were adhered to the sides. "We extracted a footprint from the lot at Newport and Williams. We're going to compare it to your soles. And I bet the mud on your sneakers matches the mud in the lot."

No prints had yet been taken on the gun, nor footprints in the mud at the crime scene. Dave was lying. He thought he was just starting to become good at that, and it pleased him. He knew that an integral part of his job as a detective would be to prevaricate.

In talking to suspects, detectives could lie, but they could lie only up to a point. They could say they had the suspect's fingerprints on a gun or on a glass when they didn't, but they couldn't show the suspect a particular set of fingerprints and say they were his. They could deceive people, but they could not change the facts of a case.

"Some people may not like the idea that we lie," Mike Redmond had told Dave when explaining the basics of detective fabrications, "but our job is to solve shootings and murders. Someone does a crime, someone has to answer to it. We do what we can legally to get a suspect to confess.

"And when you lie, people will believe you. You know why? Because you're the law. People think you have to tell the truth, but you don't. You just got to be able to convince people that what you're saying is fact, even though it may be a load of bullshit."

Confronted with the detectives' apparently overwhelming evidence, the young man lowered his head and began talking. He and Henry had been playing with the gun in the lot. Ink had pulled the hammer back, and the gun had accidentally gone off. Henry started screaming he was shot, and in a panic Ink dropped the gun and ran home.

"Is he alive?" he asked, his eyes glassy and moist. "I thought I killed him."

"He'll probably make it," Dave said. "Look, we're going to have to arrest you and put you through the system. You can either have your own lawyer or a court-appointed lawyer represent you."

As the tour was drawing to a close, some Team One detectives drove the prisoner to Central Booking, where he would be held until arraignment, while others began to make phone calls and hit the typewriters.

Two hours later, Dave popped open a can of Mountain Dew in the lounge. It was his first break of the day, and he had forgotten how hungry he was. He searched the refrigerator and beamed when he spied a large red apple. Munching it, he sat down to relax.

Shortly thereafter, Jimmy Owens of Team Two strolled in. "Yo, Dave," he murmured. He poured himself a cup of coffee from the urn and slumped down in the chair next to Dave with a sigh.

"You know, Jimmy," Dave said, "I've got to tell you, I'm really impressed with Mike Redmond. He saw the dried mud on this guy's sneakers and put it together with the crime scene, the dirt lot with the mud from the rain yesterday. It seems obvious, but it didn't click with me right away. I didn't even notice the mud on the sneakers."

Owens, a gold-shield detective in the squad for two years, chuckled. "I know," he said. "The old-timers here—Jerry Rupprecht, Al Kennedy, Joe Hall—they're all terrific. But if there's one person you should watch real closely, it's Mike Redmond."

With his gravelly voice and occasionally cantankerous manner, Redmond had been christened Grumpy. But the old-timer had an impeccable reputation in the Detective Bureau, and in his squad he was looked up to, even revered, for his brilliance and quick thinking. And in the Seven-Five, with some of the inflated egos bouncing around, he was unofficially regarded as the glue that kept the squad together.

"The guy's a legend in his own time," Owens said, sipping his coffee. "He may look like an old sleeping dog, but he's a real smart old sleeping dog."

Large, husky, and with thinning brown hair turning silver on the sides, Redmond had a perpetually tired look. He had dark circles under his eyes and fit the image of a seasoned Irish cop. Redmond often sat quietly in the office and watched the other detectives, observing like a father figure, not saying anything, just taking it all in. Later, perhaps, he'd approach a detective and talk to him about a particular remark he had made and proffer some advice.

Dave was reminded of what he had been told at RIP: keep your ears open and your mouth shut, and watch how things are done. It was the old-timers like Redmond and Joe Torres from whom he learned the most.

"I'd been a cop for thirteen years before I came into the Bureau," Owens said, "and I thought I knew it all. But then I met Mike Redmond, and one day he really opened my eyes. I found out he's just one hell of a fucking good detective. He made me realize I have a lot to learn. Wanna hear?"

"Sure," Dave said, sitting back to listen.

"It was an early-morning homicide, a stabbing in the north end of the precinct. So I go to the crime scene and as I walk up the front stoop I see thick shards of glass, the first indication of violence. In the vestibule are larger pieces of broken glass, and right in front of the second door and into the hallway are these huge pools of coagulated blood. Bloody handprints are on the outside of an exterior door to the first-floor apartment, and on the floor is blood, lots of blood." He shook his head, remembering.

"Just off to the left is a staircase leading to a second floor where the body is. I climb up the stairs, and as I get to the top landing I turn right. Directly in front of me is a bedroom. The door's ajar, and on the floor next to the bed is the victim, a man. There's a large bloodstain on the rug." Owens spoke with intensity. His nostrils flared and his eyes narrowed sharply.

"The bedroom is, like, unkempt, but not filthy," he continued. "Just to the left of the bedroom is a kitchen area. It's bright and clean, and it strikes me that it doesn't quite fit the situation. I notice in the kitchen a bloody palm print on the windowsill, and the window is open.

"There are two other bedrooms and a bathroom on the same level. The owner of the property rented the rooms, probably to illegal aliens." He swallowed a mouthful of coffee and made a face.

"After looking around for about twenty minutes, I go downstairs to check with EMS and the first officer. Then I hear a car roaring up the block, coming to a screeching halt in front of the location. It's Mike Redmond, and he walks that slow, deliberate walk of his to the steps. He asks me what happened, but he's not looking at me. His eyes are already going, looking at the broken glass on the steps as he's walking toward me. As he breaks through the front gate, his hands slip into his pockets." Seeing Dave's raised eyebrows, Owens explained, "You know, when you walk into a crime scene, one of the things you don't want to do is start touching everything, and it's automatic with Mike that he puts his hands away."

Dave nodded, picturing Redmond.

"So Mike looks at the broken glass, the blood on the door. He just stands there, head turning, not saying a thing. Then he goes upstairs and looks around—in the bedroom, the kitchen, the hallway. It's all only a couple of minutes.

"Then he turns to me and says, 'Hey, Jimmy, do you know what happened here?'

" 'Yeah,' " I answer.

" 'What?' he says.

" 'The guy got stabbed to death.'

"Mike purses his lips and gives me one of those 'You dipshit' looks. 'You notice anything that would give you any ideas?' he says.

" 'Yeah. The partially open prophylactic.' There was a ripped-open prophylactic lying on the floor next to the bed.

" 'What do you think that is?' he says.

" 'Probably that they were homosexuals and they had some sort of dispute.'

" 'Do you know how it happened, Jimmy?' This time, I knew he wasn't looking for me to say that the guy was stabbed.

" 'It probably started downstairs and ended here in the bedroom.'

" 'Nope. That guy died right here where he was standing when he got stabbed.' He gives me this jarring look. Then he says, 'Can you tell me why there's all that blood downstairs?'

"Now, I'm stumped," Owens admitted. "There's a lot of blood downstairs. 'No, I don't know why the blood is downstairs,' I tell him. 'If you tell me that this guy was stabbed and killed up here, and there was no confrontation downstairs, then I don't know how it got there.'

"Mike looks at the body on the floor in the bedroom. 'Apparently,' he says, 'the guy put up his hand in defense as the knife came down at him, and the knife passed his arm and went deeply into his chest, lodged in his heart, and he dropped back from where he was standing.' He pauses a moment. 'Now what about the blood downstairs?' "

Owens shook his head, grinning at the memory of his own befuddlement. "I told him I didn't know.

" 'Take a good look around,' he said.

"So I look, but don't see anything.

"Mike points his finger up, staring me straight in the eyes.

"I look up, and on the ceiling outside the bedroom where the victim is lying are blood spatterings across it continuing about a foot or so down the wall opposite the bedroom.

" 'Now you notice, there's no blood on the stairs,' Mike says.

" 'Right. The blood is in two separate locations, upstairs and downstairs, but there's no blood on the staircase connecting the two.'

" 'How's that?' he asks.

"I can't answer. I'm pretty much baffled at this point, thinking it could be a whole range of things, or none of them. I tell him I don't know why there's no blood on the staircase. So he reconstructs the whole crime for me.

" 'We're looking for a murderer who wounded himself,' he begins. No weapon had been found at this point. 'You noticed the prophylactic.'

" 'Yes.'

" 'There's a book of matches on the night table with the name of a nightclub in Queens. It's a good bet the victim was out partying last night and met his murderer at this club, or one like it, came back in the early-morning hours to his apartment, where they engaged in some sort of sexual activity, or were about to, when an argument broke out.

" 'The victim attempted to throw the murderer out of his bedroom, and in fact had gotten him to the threshold in the hallway, when the murderer decided he was going to assault him.' "

Owens glanced at Dave to make sure he was following the intricacies. Dave, totally fascinated, gestured to him to continue.

"Now me, as a rookie, I see the victim by the bed and a large amount of blood next to his body, and I can't see how this detective is telling me the murderer was standing out in the hallway at the time he stabbed the victim.

" 'Look up, again,' Mike says.

"I do, and I see the blood.

" 'Now, how did the blood get there?' he asks. 'There's no blood in the hallway, no blood on the staircase, but there is blood on the ceiling and the wall opposite the door of the bedroom. So tell me, how did that happen?'

"I give him a blank stare.

"He shakes his head and says, 'Judging from the size of the wound in the guy's chest, a very large butcher knife was probably used. These knives don't have blood grooves in them, which makes it extremely difficult to extract a knife that's deeply embedded in the body. Hence, the explanation for the blood on the ceiling and wall directly opposite the bedroom door.'

"I'm still a little starry-eyed, so he explains.

" 'The murderer was out in the hallway facing the victim and the open door to his bedroom. He stabbed him in the chest and had to use extreme force to extract the knife. As he removed the knife from the chest, he snapped his arm up, and blood sprinkled off the knife and spattered across the ceiling and onto the wall.

" 'Look at the blood droplets,' he says. Now, here he goes into a discourse about blood spray. How every blood droplet has a tail that points to the direction it came from. So you follow the tail, and you can tell the blood came from a particular point and what its trail was.

" 'The victim, from the thrust,' Mike continues, 'fell backward into his room. The murderer now turned and ran down the staircase. He reached for the door and pulled on it, but it didn't open because—unknown to him—the door was locked with a key, which you need even to exit the location. So he went into a panic because he just stabbed this guy, there was all that screaming, and he wants to get out.

" 'Working on the theory that most people are right-handed, he probably had the murder weapon in his right hand as he attempted to open the door. The more he panicked, the harder he tried to open the door. But his subconscious took over, and he transferred the knife to his left hand and used his strong right hand to pull open the door. Not being able to get the door open, he now went into a complete funk and started thrashing at the glass with his left hand in an effort to break it.'

"The door had three panes of glass—a center pane in the door and two strips of glass on either side of the door enclosed in wood paneling, about six inches wide and coming down about halfway from the top, to about the center level of the door." Owens described the door with his hands, drawing rectangles in the air.

" 'In all probability,' Mike continued, 'because it was an old house with thick beveled glass, the first time he thrashed the glass he didn't realize how hard it was going to be to break it. He used an overhead stroke, the knife bounced off the glass, and he accidentally wounded himself with the thrust. He finally succeeded in breaking the glass and then went into another stage of panic realizing he couldn't fit through the six-inch opening he'd created. Then he completely freaked.

" 'That's the reason for the massive amount of coagulated blood directly in front of the door.

" 'Now he realized he was bleeding. He turned and saw the door behind him on the first floor, which is a possible exit from the building. In a dead panic, he pounded on the door to have somebody open it, but he didn't succeed in getting it open.

" 'At this point he realized the only way he'd be able to escape was through a window on the second floor. He was bleeding badly, so he grabbed the wound in an attempt to stop the bleeding as he ran back up the staircase. He got back up to the second floor but didn't want to go back to the room where the body was. He then turned and saw his first hope of escape, which was daylight through that kitchen window.

" 'He had to let go of his wound in order to get the window open. He put his left hand down on the windowsill as he was climbing through the window. Below the window, he saw there was an awning that jutted out, and below that he saw an old vehicle he could jump onto.' " Owens paused for emphasis.

"We looked out to the rear yard, and Mike says, 'There's your escape route.' I look out and see an old vehicle in excellent condition—except for one thing. It's got a dent in the roof."

"No shit!" muttered Dave.

Owens rolled his eyes. "It all fit together so perfectly, and I realized then I had a helluva lot to learn. But after he tells all this to me, I say to myself, 'I'm still gonna get this old fuck.'

"So I say to him, 'But one thing's sticking in my craw, and I just have to have an answer. If your theory about the blood is correct, then why did this guy decide not to take out the bigger piece of glass in the center door, which he could have fit through?'

"He points to the door and says, 'That's why. He hacked the glass on the left side, and he did it with his left hand.'

" 'That doesn't make sense,' I protest.

" 'Sure it does. The fact that he didn't take out the center pane of glass on the door indicates that he was in an extreme state of panic. He used his left hand to take out the left pane of glass while he was tugging on the doorknob with his right hand. That was for two reasons. Number one, because the wall runs alongside the left side of that door, and he wouldn't have been able to use any kind of power thrust with his right hand on that left pane of glass. Number two, because the doorknob is on the left side of the door.'

"I look at him and said, 'You fucking hump!'

"Then Mike looks down at the floor by the door and says, 'His blood is coagulating, and that's a sign of a very severe wound. We're going to find this guy in a hospital.'

"Sure enough, we get a call that a cab driver drove a bleeding madman to the hospital earlier in the day. Someone a block away from the house was getting into a cab, and the man jumped in the other door and ordered the driver to take him to the hospital.

"We met the guy in Brookdale Hospital. When we finally got his confession, he admitted that he and the victim met at a club in Manhattan, hung out with each other, went to a club in Queens, and then the guy invited him home. He wouldn't go into the particulars of the homo stuff, but he easily confessed to the murder.

"After we saw the guy in Brookdale Hospital, we found the murder weapon to the right side of the door behind the refrigerator.

"And I said to myself, 'Mike Redmond is some piece of work.' He put this whole thing together in just a few minutes and completely lit up my brain."

Dave was slouched down, arms hanging at his sides. As Owens was recounting the story, Dave had subconsciously slid lower and lower into the chair until his arms were practically scraping the floor.

"Wait a second," he said slowly. "I'm still trying to figure out the part about how he knew the perp switched the knife from his right hand to his left and smashed the window with his off hand."

7

Late one night near the end of March 1988, Captain John Finn, the CO of the 13th Division of Detective Borough Brooklyn, in charge of the 73rd, 75th, and 81st precincts, emerged from his office jingling a silver bell.

Dave was sitting at his desk typing a Five on a missing person when the bell sounded. "What's going on?" Dave asked, turning around to Smitty.

"That's the homicide bell," Smitty replied, grinning. "Whenever the captain takes the call for a homicide, he comes out ringing the bell. Got quite a sense of humor for an old buzzard."

An erudite veteran with thirty-four years on the job who was fluent in five languages, and to whom the commanders of the precinct detective squads that composed his division reported, Captain Finn was a soft-spoken, genial man who didn't feel his position of authority elevated him above such mundane tasks as answering the precinct phone occasionally, along with his official duties, which included maintaining division statistics and overall responsibility for all the detectives in the division. He personally took an interest in young criminals who had been arrested and brought into the squad room. He bought them food, summoned their families and counseled them, and took the youths under his wing in any way he could to set them on a straight path. Frustrated and angered by the massacre of people in his precinct, Finn had even begun composing sardonic ditties about it. His first, based on a verse of Tennyson's "Charge of the Light Brigade," was inspired when the precinct broke its homicide record:

> The people of East New York
> Have been volleyed and thundered
> At last the number slaughtered
> Has reached one hundred.

Dressed in a suit—the captain never took his jacket off—Finn announced solemnly to the detectives, "You've got a male black DOA shot in the head at Fountain Avenue under the Belt Parkway.''

Dave felt a wave of excitement surge through his body. Not that he was waiting for somebody to be murdered, but he was up to catch the next homicide, and he was anxious to prove himself. The detectives put on their coats and filed out, departing the station house in two cars: Dave, Smitty, and Mike Race in one, Mike Redmond, Joe Hall, and Jack Cutrone in the other.

"Lucky you," said Smitty as they headed east on Sutter Avenue.

Dave pondered the words a few seconds before responding. "Lucky me? Why lucky me?"

"You've got a dump job. The area is known for dump jobs and bones.''

Mike Race, behind the wheel, chortled in confirmation. Dump jobs were tough to solve. There were usually no witnesses, the areas where the bodies were deposited were isolated, the killers had usually removed all identification of the victims. There simply wasn't much to go on.

"Go ahead, you guys, fuck with the rookie," Dave shot back. "No problem. I can handle it." Actually, he didn't feel so confident.

When the cars came to Fountain, they made a right. The drive south was long, to the farthest sector of the precinct. They passed the Cypress Hills projects on the left, then, after Linden Boulevard, a factory area where prostitutes approached cars as they drove by. The buildings lining the streets later gave way to patches of wild grass and weeds. The area was largely deserted except for the occasional junkie shooting up. Finally the stretch of wild growth was halted by a metal-fence enclosure of mounds and mounds of garbage, the sanitation department's local dumping grounds.

Powder-blue-and-white patrol cars were up ahead at the end of the road, and several cops were standing around talking. The unmarked cars pulled up to the concrete overpass of the Belt Parkway. The detectives got out and spoke with the officers briefly before walking over to the body to take a look. The air reeked of garbage, the foul odor piercing even in the cold night. The area was completely desolate, and no one other than the officers was to be seen.

"Look!" Dave said as he approached the body. "Fucking steam's coming out of his brain." He turned to Smitty, his eyes wide. 'Musta been a real hotheaded dude.''

A cacophony of laughter erupted from the cops. Smitty responded, "Or maybe he watched too much MTV.''

Gallows humor, classic detective repartee. It was a protective measure, helping the cops maintain an emotional distance between themselves and the brutality they had to deal with.

The scene was even more ghastly than Dave had imagined. The man's skull was half blown off, leaving a gaping hole on the left side with much of his brain spilled out on the concrete beside him.

The victim, a black man who looked to be in his early twenties, was lying faceup with a handcuff dangling from his right hand. Apparently there had been a struggle, and the assailant or assailants couldn't cuff the other wrist. The blast had caused the victim's left eye to retract deeply into his head, while the other eye stared vacantly ahead. Behind and above the body was a guardrail splattered with blood.

Although it was obviously a dump job and the victim was probably not one of the community's model citizens, Dave was still exhilarated. The crime scene was his; he owned the case lock, stock, and barrel. All the uniformed cops and seasoned detectives milling about were waiting for him to take the initiative.

And no one was standing over him as on his first day with the Stager car-beep murder. Although that had happened only a few weeks before, he had been assigned so many cases in the interim—eighty, including eleven nonfatal shootings—that he was no longer considered a neophyte who had to have his hand held as he worked through a case. He had much more to learn—cops are always learning, no matter how long they've been on the job—and the detectives were there to assist him every step of the way as he needed it. But he was catching cases now just like everybody else in the squad and was regarded as a peer. And he was holding up well. Some guys came in and found after a week or so that they couldn't take the pressure of the volume of violent cases in the Seven-Five. They requested transfer. One seasoned detective Dave had heard about had transferred out after the third homicide on his very first day.

Dave felt he was just hitting his stride. But this case was a natural loser. How was he going to solve it? His mind drifted back to RIP. It was so much different with robbery victims; they were alive to tell you what happened and probably give you a description of their assailant. Not so with homicides. Dead people don't talk.

The detectives snooped around, but there wasn't much to see. There didn't seem to be any clues on the ground. The perp or perps probably had left nothing behind.

There was nothing to do until Crime Scene arrived. Whenever there was a murder, a two-man team from the department's Crime Scene Unit, headquartered out in the Bronx, came to process the scene. On a busy day, they sometimes took hours to arrive. This day the detectives were lucky; a half hour later, a blue station wagon pulled up and two men got out.

"I can't believe you got here so soon," said Dave, relieved. "If you hurry up, maybe you can get your pictures before the guy's head stops smoking."

"I once waited so long for you guys," Smitty added, "that rats were lapping up the stiff's brain matter."

The crime scene detectives responded with wan grins and went immediately to work.

The function of the Crime Scene Unit was basically threefold: to record the scene, to collect all the physical evidence, and to reconstruct the crime scene.

Recording the scene was done with photographs, notes, and sketches—investigative tools that allowed the detectives to see at a later date how the crime scene had looked and who had been there, and to help witnesses remember what they could. In trial, the photographs and sketches became the "eyes" of the court.

There might be physical evidence, or clues, at a crime scene, and this all had to be collected and logged. Physical evidence included ballistics, blood, semen, body fluids, latent fingerprints, hairs, fibers, glass fragments, footprints, tire marks, clothing, objects—almost anything at all.

The most difficult task for the crime scene investigator was to reconstruct the scene. The reconstruction of events came from the physical evidence observed and collected. The crime scene investigator put it all together and was expected to determine just what had happened, so that when a witness or suspect was telling a story, the interrogating detective would know whether the physical evidence supported the story or not.

By the time the crime scene investigator got to the location, the officers present would already have at least a little information about what had happened from speaking with witnesses or conducting a canvass. A witness might have told them what he saw—for instance, there was a dispute, and then one of the individuals grabbed an automatic and fired from the bathroom. The crime scene investigator gathered from the officers present whatever they had learned. Then—and this was the key to any good crime scene investigation—he would disregard it all, or rather, put it on the back burner. Because now he began his own investigation. He recorded the scene, collected the physical evidence, and then reconstructed the scene.

He examined what physical evidence there was and where it was located. If he found discharged shells by the kitchen at the other end of the hallway, he knew the shooter hadn't been in or near the bathroom when he fired—an automatic ejects shells no more than a few feet away—and that the witness was either lying or had an unreliable memory.

He looked at the shed blood to tell where the victim had been sitting or standing when shot. If there was little blood by the body, or if there were drag marks on the carpet, the body had probably been picked up and moved. The investigator examined the victim's hands for defensive wounds, such as cuts or scrapes; skin and hair under the fingernails also indicated a struggle. He examined the bullet wounds on the body. The suspect might say, "He pulled the gun on me, and we wrestled for it, and I shot him." But if the crime scene investigator saw no stippling (burn marks on the skin) around the bullet wound, he knew there couldn't have been a struggle in which the two were close together and the shooter shot at very close range; the shooter had to have been at least two feet away. Or the suspect might claim the victim had been coming toward him with a knife when he shot him from three feet away. But then if the crime scene investigator observed on the victim's body either a star effect (a ripping apart of the skin leaving five or six tears, resembling a star, that resulted from a contact wound) or a distinct stippling, he knew the shooter either had the gun pressed against the victim (causing a contact wound) or had been less than a foot away when he had pulled the trigger.

If the victim was lying facedown and the skin on the back of his legs was purplish-red, the investigator knew the body had been turned over or moved. As a body lies on a surface and goes into rigor mortis, blood drains down through the body, settling at the bottom, or lowest point, and becoming fixed, a phenomenon called lividity. Even if the body is later turned over or moved, the purplish-red color remains.

Each crime scene was different, but the clues could spell out what had happened and enabled the investigator to put everything together and come up with a reconstruction. Having completed a comprehensive evaluation, the investigator went back to all the information he had initially collected and determined whether what he had come up with matched what he had been told.

The importance of the work of the crime scene investigator could not be overstated. Suppose a detective had told the investigator that a husband and wife had been arguing in the kitchen when the husband pulled a gun out on the spot and shot and killed her. But when the investigator photographed the scene and collected the evidence, he determined that the husband had gotten up from his chair, walked to his bedroom, opened a drawer of his dresser, taken out the gun, and returned to the kitchen—having time, in other words, to think about his actions—and then had shot his wife. That would add an element of premeditation.

A search through the victim's pockets revealed no identification, so for now he would be listed as a John Doe M/B/20s. The crime scene didn't appear to be a nest of hidden clues. In fact, no evidence of the killer was left behind, and the area was so desolate there wasn't really much that could be done with a canvass. Before he became a detective, Dave had often pondered a similar scenario in his mind.

You find a body on a corner. You knock on every door in the area, but no one claims to have heard or seen anything, so you don't have any witnesses. The Crime Scene Unit comes and combs the scene but finds no clues. The medical examiner performs an autopsy and finds nothing that can help you with your investigation. One .38 to the head and another to the chest, but that's all he can tell you. You check to see if the victim had any previous arrests but find he's clean. Indeed, you've got nothing but a corpse, a roaming murderer, and a case crying out to be solved. How do you find the killer? Where do you begin your investigation? You have to be some kind of magician, it seemed. The allure of the power that magic represented was what had so compellingly drawn Dave to detective work.

It was Mike Redmond who had given Dave the rundown on these sorts of cases, and it was simple—on the surface. Redmond, possessed of unquenchable zeal and enthusiasm for the job, had engaged Dave in conversation almost every spare moment each of them had had since Dave had arrived at the precinct. That was his style. He helped everyone, but more often detectives came to him for advice. Redmond dispensed as much information and wisdom as he could, compliments of his quarter century on the job, but he also recognized potential when he saw it. He had taken Dave under his wing because he believed Dave had a special quality. Dave had become his sorcerer's apprentice.

With little to go on at the scene, Dave contemplated Redmond's simple but sagacious advice: Learn your victim.

Learning the victim opened up a world of investigatory potential. Who did he know? Where did he go? Who might want to harm him, and why? You delved into the world of a stranger and exhaustively examined his life, traced his steps over the past week or so, and followed them, you hoped, to a rendezvous with the killer. Each piece of information could lead to a separate investigation, so there might be numerous investigations within the overall case. And the payoff, of course, was the construction of a big picture. What was the victim into? Who would have reason to kill him? What was the victim doing at the scene? What had brought the killer to the scene? Finding the answers to these and other questions might help the detective solve the case.

Dave's first step was to interview the security guard at the sanitation dump. He had heard a loud shot, probably as a result of the echo under the bridge, but that was it. He was so terrified Dave had to interview him through the gate.

"Didn't you see anything?" Dave asked.

"Shit, I ain't no cop. I called the police. I'm locked behind this gate and that's where I stay. I don't go out for nothing. That's your job."

Back at the precinct later, the detectives sat down to begin their paperwork. Most typed the first Fives required for a case: Response to the Scene, Interview of the First Officer, Report of EMS, Notification and Response of Crime Scene Unit, ME Investigator at the Scene. Dave began with the Detective Bureau Unusual Occurrence Report. Anytime there is a newsworthy or out-of-the-ordinary occurrence, such as a murder, reports providing all the known details have to be dispatched to everyone in the detective's chain of command all the way up to the highest level of the Bureau. In this case, that meant the 13th Division commander, the CO of Brooklyn North Detective Operations, the deputy chief of Detective Borough Brooklyn, and the chief of detectives.

The next day, Dave and Joe Hall went to the Kings County Hospital Center, where NYPD detectives assigned to the morgue fingerprint all unidentified DOAs. Detective Joe Tully gave Dave a print card with all of his victim's fingerprints on them.

Dave's olfactory senses were offended. "You smell this shit all day?" he said to the morgue detective.

"Yeah," responded the detective. "But after a while you get used to it, and everything smells like it. Every morning I put on my special cologne, 'OD Toilette.' "

From the morgue, Dave and Hall drove to police headquarters at One PP in Manhattan. Inside police headquarters were various units that were open to cops twenty-four hours a day.

On the sixth floor was the DOA Desk, which received from the morgues in New York City copies of fingerprints of all murder victims and unidentified corpses, whatever the cause of death.

"Detectives sometimes bring prints of unknown DOAs here to try to get them identified quickly," Hall explained to Dave. "If there is trouble identifying a DOA, detectives in the Missing Persons Unit also catch the case with us to get the DOAs identified and claimed by their families. Unidentified DOAs are buried in Potter's Field.'' Dave couldn't imagine a worse end to a human life than an anonymous burial.

The so-called DOA Desk was actually a large room filled with desks and computers and rows and rows of cabinets containing the print cards of some six million criminals and New York City civilian employees, including police officers, going back to 1910.

Dave handed the fingerprint card to a technician at the DOA Desk to see if he could match the prints with those of anyone who had ever been arrested in the city of New York.

Because every person has a unique pattern of ridges on his or her fingertips, it was possible to determine whether a set of prints from a deceased person matched those of someone who had previously been arrested. A match yielded not only the victim's name but all the details about that person collected by the police.

Sitting at a desk, the technician placed a magnifying glass over the right thumbprint. The card contained the prints of each finger in two rows of five squares, with the right thumb on top and the left thumb on the bottom. He was using the so-called Henry system to come up with a classification: the letters A, T, U, R, and W denoted patterns of arches, projections, loops, and whorls; and numbers, or values, for the different fingers indicated where the whorls fell on the little squares on the print card.

After examining the thumbprint for several minutes, the technician rose from his desk and disappeared into a forest of filing cabinets. In the middle of one row, he opened the top drawer and flipped through a batch of fingerprint cards. He stopped at one, comparing the classification numbers, and made a notation on the card he had examined. Back at the reception area, he extended the card to Dave with a faint smile of satisfaction. Dave took the card. He gazed at the top, where the name of his victim was now written: Mizell Harris.

Dave sighed, relieved he had something solid to go on. But along with the ID came the confirmation that the man was a bad guy, or at least had been in the past. He might have been an innocent victim of murder, but he wasn't exactly a pillar of the community. Too bad, but that's the way if often went. What goes around comes around. But you solved their murders just as you would that of an upstanding citizen. We're all equal citizens in death, Dave thought. At least the corpse now had a name.

On the fingerprint card, the technician had written Harris's NYS-IIS number: 4988763L. Dave grinned. He loved these babies. Once someone was arrested, he or she was permanently branded with these digits. Just pop them in the computer and you got a printout of the person's criminal history; his wretched life became an open book.

Dave filled out a Ninety, a request form used for a variety of department materials. Then he went to another desk and gave the form to someone who worked in the BCI Unit.

The technician put Mizell Harris's name into a computer, and out of the printer flowed Harris's rap sheets and On-Line Booking System arrest worksheets. Rap sheets contained the charges and dispositions of a person's arrests—his or her criminal history. An OLBS arrest worksheet was filled out every time the person was collared. It was the arresting officer's report, in which he spelled out the crime the person was locked up for.

To the untrained eye, an OLBS arrest worksheet was a confusing mass of data. To the detective, it represented a wealth of information waiting to be decoded. As Dave had filled out numerous arrest sheets in patrol, Anticrime, and RIP, he was very familiar with this form. But interpreting its data to pursue an investigation was a different story.

Detectives had to sort through the information on arrest sheets to see what was of value. If the arresting officer had asked the perp his name and address and he had responded, "Santa Claus, One North Pole," Santa Claus would go down on his record as an alias. Whatever information the perp gave was recorded.

Joe Hall and Dave studied Mizell Harris's arrest sheets.

"There are three things of special importance," Hall said. "Phone numbers, arrest locations, and names of associates.

"Whenever somebody is arrested, he's entitled to make a phone call. Many of these mutts don't make calls, because they know the cops'll take down the numbers. But the arresting officer should dial the numbers for them if they call and note them on his report. These are people you may want to contact.

"The locations are important, because you can call Narcotics or NITRO"—Narcotics Investigative Tracking Recidivists Offenders—"and see what they have on them. You can call the precinct and ask the arresting officer about the location and the perp. You can call CARS and get all the arrests made at that location. The point is, you'll gather information on the locations where the victim was arrested and build a profile on him.

"As far as the people somebody's been arrested with are concerned, their arrest numbers go on each other's On-Line Booking System arrest worksheets, so you'll have to pull those reports to get the information on who they are and where they live. People who get locked up together hang together. They might tell you what you need to know—with a little persuasion, if necessary.

"Look at the raps of the victim's associates. Maybe one of them's got a case pending or there's a warrant out on him. Or maybe he's done other shit that he'll think you're there for. If the raps say he was locked up ten times, does that mean he's only done ten crimes? How many times do you think he did something and didn't get collared for it? You don't know what he's thinking and he doesn't know what you're thinking, but you're the *po*-lice and you can play with him."

Dave was learning how complex a homicide investigation was. It could be filled with endless tributaries that had to be explored. "While we're here, let's go get a photo of Mr. Harris," Hall said.

The two went down to the basement, and Dave filled out another Ninety, this one a picture request. He gave the form to a clerk, who, after looking at the subject's NYSIIS number, riffled through endless cards in a filing cabinet and pulled out a negative with a matching NYSIIS number. He put the negative into a large photo duplication machine, and several minutes later, front and side mug shots emerged.

Back at the station house, Dave sat down to call the numbers on the arrest report. Starting with the last arrest sheet, he dialed the first number on it. To his amazement, luck struck again when the number turned out to be that of his victim's family.

"Is this the residence of Mizell Harris?" he asked.

"Yes, why?" came a voice.

"This is Detective Carbone from the 75th Precinct. I'd like to come over and talk to you about Mizell. Are you going to be home for a while?"

"What's this in regard to Mizell?" The voice now sounded alarmed.

"I'd rather discuss it in person," said Dave.

Forty minutes later, Dave and Joe Hall were in the living room of the apartment where Mizell's mother and brother lived.

"Please sit down," Dave began. Then he made his inquiries: "Does Mizell live here? When was the last time you saw him?" The mother and brother answered warily.

"I hate to bring you bad news," Dave said softly, "but Mizell was shot and killed yesterday in the 75th Precinct."

The mother, whose apprehension had been building, let out a

shriek and then collapsed to the floor. The brother shook his head in disbelief. "I thought something was up," he finally managed.

In making a death notification, detectives have to decide whether family members are capable of talking about their deceased loved one at the time. Often the detective will give them a few days to recover, and return when they're more composed.

"Mizell was into some stuff," Dave said, hinting that he knew about Mizell's previous arrests. "May have gotten him killed."

As the conversation dwindled to an end, it became apparent that the brother knew something but didn't want to talk in front of his mother. He said he would call the detectives in a few days.

A feeling of sympathy for Mizell's mother and brother began to creep through Dave, but he quickly stifled it. He had learned early on to have compassion but also to build a wall of resistance; emotional involvement could get in the way of his investigation. The mother and brother seemed genuinely nice, but too often, he had been warned, the victim likely got killed because he was into shit, his mother may have taken a few collars herself, his brother had probably served time, and his father could be in jail for murder. Maybe not in this case, but Dave didn't want to allow the wall to weaken.

When he returned to the precinct, Dave called NITRO to run Mizell's arrest locations and learned they were all drug spots. He then called Brooklyn North Narcotics to get further information on the spots. He called cops who had arrested Mizell in the past. Out on the streets every day, cops can often provide a lot more information than what's been fed into a computer. And true to his word, a few days later Mizell's brother called. He said Mizell had been a seller in a drug gang, and that he had frequently come up short. The gang had issued several warnings to him and had threatened to kill him if he didn't mend his ways. "I'm sure this is why they wasted him," he said sadly.

"What gang was it?" Dave asked.

"The Unknowns," said the victim's brother.

The name immediately struck a chord with Dave. A multitude of homicides and assaults in the Seven-Five had already been tied into the gang. Indeed, a joint investigation by the squad and the feds was well under way.

The Unknowns was one of the biggest heroin and cocaine organizations in Brooklyn. It employed 150 people and sold approximately $100 million a year in drugs throughout Brooklyn and in the Bronx. Most of the heroin came from China, Hong Kong, and Thailand, the

so-called Golden Triangle in Southeast Asia. The operation was efficient, and gang leaders used ruthless violence to keep their workers in
line.

The Seven-Five squad had first become interested in the Unknowns when an investigation of a murder revealed that the gang was
behind it; at least eight murders had been linked to the Unknowns
since 1986.

Because the gang's crimes extended into international jurisdic-
tions, Sergeant Race had contacted the feds, and a federal task force
conducted through the Eastern District of the United States Attorney's
Office was assembled. A joint investigation of the DEA, New York City
Police Department, and New York State Police had to date resulted in
the confiscation of almost $5 million in cash, twenty-five vehicles worth
in excess of $356,000, jewelry valued at over $300,000, and an assort-
ment of weapons and kilos of heroin.

Drugs were big business in East New York and were sold under a
system in which corners—or locations, or spots, as the jargon goes—
were owned by an individual or group, or leased to others. The owner
of a spot would never stand outside and sell drugs. Sellers faced being
arrested by the cops or held up by street thugs. What better target of
robbery than a drug location? The bounty would include abundant
cash and drugs, and the heist would be very unlikely to be reported.
Drug spots were guarded by men who waited nearby with guns to protect the sellers from stickups. Owners (sometimes through others who
worked for them) hired sellers to peddle their wares, and the sellers
usually didn't even know who they were working for. They were the
ones who got beat up or arrested. While some of the sellers were regular working people who just needed money, most were crackheads and
dope addicts.

Sellers earned $5 for every bundle of drugs they sold, and at the
end of a shift they had to turn in the money they collected or their
unsold drugs. If the gang gave a seller a hundred bundles that he was
to sell at $10 apiece, at the end of his shift he had better have $1,000 or
whatever amount less in bundles. With one's life at risk for dishonest
behavior, it would seem that sellers would have to be insane to try to
cheat their bosses. But sellers who were drug addicts often smoked the
very product they sold—sometimes substituting their own inferior
product for the organization's—while they worked. When their shift
ended, if they couldn't account for all the drugs they had been given to
sell, or the substitution was discovered, they incurred punishment.
Such had apparently been the case with Mizell Harris.

Carrying the BCI photo of Mizell Harris, Dave, with Smitty and Mike Redmond, drove to the Nine-Oh Precinct in Williamsburg, where Mizell had sold drugs. They canvassed the area around Broadway and Lorimer, which was a spot for the Unknowns, but to no avail. Everyone was obviously afraid to talk or to become a witness in the case. Frustration enveloped the detectives as they sat in the car appraising the situation.

"I'm going to harass the drug location," Dave announced suddenly. "They won't talk to us, so we'll let them know we're going to hound them until we solve the murder."

Smitty and Redmond followed Dave out of the car. Aware of the presence of cops in the area, the sellers were out but not dealing. A bunch were gathered around the corner waiting for the detectives to leave.

Dave ambled over to a short, stocky, powerfully built man with curly brown hair and a trim mustache and wrapped his arm around his shoulders.

"Everything okay?" Dave asked. "Having any problems?"

Smitty and Redmond shuffled close behind. They belched out hellos and walked over to the other drug dealers, echoing choruses of "How ya doin'?"

Dave continued busting the chops of the man he held his arm around. "Listen, we just want to make sure that you're safe and that your neighborhood is safe," Dave said with a bland grin. "We'll hang out with you guys to make sure everything is okay. *Okay?*"

Dave's attempt to harass the spot was short-lived. The dealers didn't say anything; they just looked at each other guardedly. Less than ten minutes later they dispersed.

"These mutts are not *that* stupid," said Smitty. "They know we don't have anything on them. Let's hope they don't drop a dime on us."

When cops harassed drug dealers, the drug dealers had ways of harassing the cops in return. They'd go to a nearby phone, call the police department's Internal Affairs Division, and make some kind of allegation about a cop: he was dealing drugs, taking drugs, working for a drug dealer, taking bribes. They'd give damaging information about the cop, as well as a good description of him. And, of course, IAD would investigate it, whether it was true or not. Anytime an allegation was made about a cop, it received the utmost attention of the unit, no matter who had made the allegation. And this usually proved a great annoyance to the cop—it could make his life completely miserable for the period it took to complete the investigation.

There were other things drug dealers did to stick it to the cops. A favorite ploy was to dial 911 and report a cop shot at the other end of the precinct. This would bring every available police unit to the area as fast as it could possibly get there.

Dave knew the antics of drug dealers from his patrol, Anticrime, and RIP days. He had always made it his business to learn whatever he could about the areas he worked in. He'd go to drug spots and memorize faces, write down license plate numbers, study how business was carried on. Knowledge, he believed, was half the battle of being a good cop, so he would go one step further.

"They'll be back soon," Redmond said.

"I know," Dave answered, his eyes exploring the streets, "and so will we. In the meantime, let's canvass the area."

The neighborhood was fairly bustling on this early afternoon— mothers out with small children, old ladies pushing light metal carts piled with supermarket bags, girls playing double Dutch on the sidewalk to a rap beat. Occasionally, disheveled men in frayed clothing would straggle by.

Holding a photograph of Mizell Harris, the detectives asked the pedestrians if they knew or had seen him. Mostly they were greeted by blank stares and shakes of the head. Finally, a frail, filthy-looking prostitute displayed instant recognition. She asked the detectives to meet her in half an hour a few blocks away, where the drug dealers would not see them.

At the allotted place and time, the woman joined the detectives. She had known Mizell Harris, she told the men. She had a soft spot in her heart for him. Dave found it hard to imagine this pitiful creature could have any room for concern for anyone else; she looked as though it was all she could do just to keep on breathing.

"We're poor and we're all crackheads," she said, her voice low and hoarse. "I was Mizell's friend. I liked him. We partied together, smoked together, you know?" She broke into a fit of harsh coughing, then wiped her dripping nose on her sleeve. "They shouldn't just go ahead and kill people. It was wrong what they did."

Although the woman's credibility would be a problem, Dave knew he had a cooperative witness. The street people hated the drug dealers because the dealers seemed to rake in money effortlessly while they struggled to make a living by peddling their flesh.

"He was pushed into a car," the prostitute continued. "Two men came and spoke to him for a minute, then they pushed him into a car." She gave the day and time, and it was about six to eight hours before Mizell's body was discovered in the Seven-Five. She couldn't give a good description of the car, but she recognized the abductors from the area and thought they were from the gang Mizell worked for.

The detectives thanked her, got into their car, and drove away.

An hour later the drug dealers were back selling at Broadway and Lorimer. Business was slow now, word having filtered out that the cops were about. The drug dealers were waiting for people to regain their confidence in the spot and make their purchases.

Another hour passed. Then the dealers watched with disgust as a car pulled up and the three detectives jumped out again. They approached the dealers energetically. "How ya doing?" Dave asked loudly, his arm enveloping a dealer. "Hey, we just want to make sure that you're all still safe here, so we're gonna hang out with you for a while. A long while. That okay with you?"

While the drug dealers had to put up with the antics of the detectives, who they knew were just busting their chops, they also knew they were fairly safe from being arrested. It was common knowledge in drug organizations that the police department discouraged precinct squad detectives from making arrests for narcotics because of the potential for corruption. Busts had to be tightly controlled and monitored, the philosophy went, because the amount of money and drugs the arresting officers would encounter could be tempting. Street cops would collar those they saw selling drugs, but busts of large operations were usually conducted by the Organized Crime Control Bureau, with a supervisor always present.

After ten minutes the dealers dispersed again. "We'll be seeing you," Dave called after them with a leer, wondering how successful his attempt at frightening them had been. The three detectives then piled back into their car and headed for the precinct.

As Dave delved deeper into the case, he spoke with Mizell's friends and other people who worked for the Unknowns. For some reason, no one would talk about Mizell. He even asked detectives at the Nine-Oh, who were investigating members of the Unknowns and who had locked up several of them, for assistance, but none of the people they knew would talk about it either. Why would somebody want to put his life and the lives of his family in danger by giving up information and testifying? It would only make sense if an individual was facing a long jail sentence and wanted to cut a deal with the DA. Unfortunately,

Dave could find no one who was in that situation. It was also possible, of course, that no one except the main dealers knew who had killed Mizell.

The case growing older and going nowhere, Dave became more and more anguished. He had a dump job in a secluded area and no witnesses. Even though the victim had been a drug seller and perp himself, Dave was putting 100 percent into the case. The problem was, Mizell's friends and associates weren't giving 100 percent back.

And so it was with great regret that Dave had to stop actively working on the case, temporarily at least. With the volume of murders in the Seven-Five, he didn't have the luxury of actively working on a homicide for six months or longer, as do many other squads around the country. And with all the leads exhausted, there was nothing else to do. Perhaps sometime down the line somebody who knew something would be arrested and willing to cut a deal.

"Don't be too upset," consoled Mike Redmond. "This is reality. You're not going to solve every case, because people aren't going to talk."

As Dave nodded, acknowledging Redmond's assessment, deep down he was questioning his adeptness at his craft. If he weren't a novice at the game, he mused, he would have found some way to discover who had killed Mizell Harris. Still, with new cases barraging him, he had to move on.

And so he left it. Homicide number 19 for the year in the 75th Precinct: open case.

8

Mired in frustration, Dave set himself with renewed zealousness over the next few months to learn as much as he could about detective work. In a whirlwind of tours and cases, he catechized his team members and the homicide detectives, beseeched them for information, and carefully observed them in action. Picking and choosing what he thought were the best work habits and techniques, he began to put together his own individual style in conducting investigations.

To his surprise, he discovered that many popular conceptions about detectives had their roots in nothing more than fiction and fantasy. The scientific wizardry of Sherlock Holmes often enabled the fictional detective to perceive some arcane clue that was invisible to everybody else and ingeniously, if not effortlessly (Hollywood drama notwithstanding), crack the case. But real-life detectives, he found, needn't be terribly adept in science, forensics, or ballistics to solve cases.

In a large metropolitan police department, there were specialists who handled the myriad duties of an investigation: forensic pathologists, ballistics experts, fingerprint technicians, to name a few. The catching detective was more like the captain of the team, responsible for collecting the results of these people's work and directing them to pursue any particular angles that seemed promising. It was then up to the detective to take all this information and run with it as he chose in the course of his investigation.

Above and beyond a fundamental grasp of technical knowledge, the qualities in a detective that counted most toward success at apprehending a perp and obtaining a confession were curiosity, aggressiveness, confidence, and perseverance, a bundle of attributes that might broadly be defined as personality. Many police officers aspired to become detectives, Sergeant Race told Dave, but not everyone could go in and get a confession. "If you have the technique to track down a perp and get a confession, then you've really become a detective," he said. "Often it's just you against the suspect. You don't have a witness who'll testify, and you need to get the suspect to confess, otherwise you have no case. Get him to confess, and you've solved the case. You can even become a star.'' Dave was determined to become a star.

Attempting to elicit a confession came at the end of what was often a long series of investigative steps. Each one could be vital. Building a case was, Dave had learned, like erecting a building. You started with or created a foundation, however flimsy, and painstakingly fit every brick in place. There was no precise order of steps; often intuition, attained through years of experience, guided the process. It might be that not all the pieces would fit, and if that was the case, the detective had to determine why. Some just might not belong, but perhaps some other little piece was missing that goes between the bricks already in place. If a case was built properly—and that might take a lot of diligent investigation—by the time the top floor was under construction, the detective would have figured out the overall blueprint of the structure. If the suspect was in custody, that blueprint might make it possible to obtain a confession.

One thing that made Dave's job easier was learning the precinct. He knew from his experience as a cop that if you didn't know the area you worked, you might as well just let the bad guys run over you. To be an effective cop, to think like the people who commit crimes, the patrol cop or detective had to know the neighborhood, its infrastructure, ethnic and racial tapestry, personalities and economics, idiosyncrasies and quirks.

Although detectives in the Seven-Five squad didn't have individual partners—all their teammates were their partners—Dave forged a friendship with Al Smith that helped him with his work. Every chance they had, Smitty and Dave toured the precinct, which was bordered by Van Sinderen Avenue on the west, Drew Street on the east, the Belt Parkway on the south, and Highland Park on the north. They'd cruise by drug locations, heavy homicide areas, the projects, junkyards, pross beats. They'd pass the methadone clinic and the women's shelter. They observed who was hanging out, standing on the corner, sitting in the middle of the block on a milk crate. They studied faces and tried to register an indelible imprint of them in their minds. Street people were often witnesses to crimes or heard information about them and could be vital assets in investigations.

The detectives observed the heavy drug locations: Milford and Pitkin, Livonia and Pennsylvania, Ashford and Dumont, Blake and Ashford, Norwood and Fulton, Wyona and Fulton, Miller and Hegeman, New Lots and Alabama. They watched the dealers in action, how they operated, who was buying, what they sold.

Dave and Smitty drove around day and night. The street inhabitants varied at different times, as did the street activity. Before long, Dave came to know the 75th Precinct well, and if it wasn't always unsightly, it was full of stark contrasts.

Abandoned buildings stood adjacent to well-kept homes, litter-strewn lots between tidy yards, rotting row houses in the center of tree-lined blocks, burned-out storefronts next to shops protected by steel roll-down gates. Late at night, people straggled down busy avenues, and the multicolored bulbs outside bodegas lit up in rapid succession like Christmas lights as trains thundered overhead on the elevated tracks. In the pitch black, young adolescents roamed around in twos and threes, fifteen-year-old girls wheeled baby carriages, clusters of young men stood on corners and in front of houses waiting for consumers of drugs, large bands of teenagers roved the streets, greasy-faced psychotics wandered about in putrid rags, desperate drug addicts huddled in the cold, homeless people shivered by outdoor stoves or burrowed inside burned-out buildings, toothless whores loitered outside the women's shelter where they lived, eager to do tricks for $5 or $10 a pop. This was the ghetto.

In fact, the area wasn't completely poverty-stricken. Certain segments actually thrived, thanks to the booming drug trade. Clothing stores, jewelry stores, shoe stores, and car dealers all did brisk business, not to mention funeral parlors, florists, headstone makers, and coffin companies.

In East New York, drugs were a large and deadly business. Gangs functioned like corporations, with a hierarchy of positions. They killed ruthlessly when their turf was encroached on or when something went awry internally. Drug organizations from other areas sometimes came to East New York to make a score, and East New York gangs often branched out to other cities to enlarge their power base. Street-level selling in the area was done by young people, and there was no problem recruiting members. Where else could a sixteen-year-old make $1,500 a week? And the youth was protected from stickups by enforcers around the corner who brandished semiautomatic pistols and submachine guns.

Growing up in East New York, young people acquired their NYSIIS numbers as youths in other areas got their first Nintendos. By the time a kid was sixteen or seventeen, having been shot three or four times was no big deal; it was akin to getting flu shots. Dave thought Sergeant Race's description of East New York summed it up best: "It's a planet within a planet."

Up until the early 1960s, East New York was predominantly a quiet Jewish and Italian neighborhood. This mix began its ascent around the turn of the century, with the tide of immigrants from Central and Eastern Europe. Originally part of a Dutch settlement extending back to the seventeenth century, East New York always maintained some flavor of its heritage, with street names like Van Siclen, Hendrix, Schenck, and Van Sinderen; many of the eighteenth-century Dutch pioneers were buried in the cemetery at New Lots Avenue and Schenck, which still exists today. And the area also had some historical significance: George Washington and the Duke of Wellington had passed through it during the Revolutionary War.

While other New York neighborhoods became associated with crime and celebrated mobsters, throughout the twentieth century East New York remained relatively quiet. There was Murder, Incorporated, in the 1930s, and the hoods who in the 1950s operated out of the cabstand at Pitkin and Crescent made famous by Nicholas Pileggi in his book *Wiseguy,* but the area historically never achieved the ill fame of such New York City bastions of crime or spawning grounds for gangsters as Hell's Kitchen, the Lower East Side, Little Italy, Bensonhurst, and the South Bronx.

Instead, East New York was just one of Brooklyn's many placid neighborhoods, where during the summer festive block parties were held, kids played stoopball and stickball, and people hung out or slept on the fire escapes. With the area's proximity to main thoroughfares and highways, people from throughout the metropolitan area flocked to East New York to shop. Blake and Pitkin avenues were famous for the wooden pushcarts that lined them. There were painted spots for the pushcarts to be parked; early in the morning the vendors filled the spots and assembled their wares—clothing, household items, food, whatever you wanted, they had it—and people haggled with the vendors as if it were an Arabian market.

The stores also enjoyed prosperity, one notable example being the Fortunoff department store, which occupied more than two blocks on Livonia Avenue at the western border of the precinct. Actually a series of small stores, rather than a large building with one roof, Fortunoff was founded by Max and Clava Fortunoff, who had initially sold pots and pans from a pushcart.

A sociological phenomenon of New York City in the post–World War II era was the mass migration of longtime residents to the suburbs, where the surroundings were more peaceful and the homes not too expensive, promising the chance for a better life. This exodus continued through the end of the sixties, simultaneously with the arrival of minorities who had fled the slums for more palatable neighborhoods with affordable housing.

During the fifties and sixties, at the height of the transition, whites and blacks and Puerto Ricans lived side by side. But around the mid-sixties, peaceful coexistence eventually gave way to racial unrest and sometimes civil disturbance. Racial tensions flared and fighting erupted occasionally, escalating to riots along with the rest of the city in the summer of 1966, when turmoil raged through many American cities, and following the assassination of Martin Luther King, Jr., in 1968.

With the potential for violence to explode at any time in East New York, by the middle of the decade the NYPD had to establish a special temporary command. A mobile van was set up at the triangle of Ashford, New Lots, and Livonia, and Tactical Patrol Force (TPF) cops from around the city reported there around the clock.

Because of all the crime in East New York, the precinct was known by the seventies as an A house, according to the NYPD scheme of delineating activity in precincts by letters, with A at the top and C at the bottom rung of the crime spectrum. Around the early 1970s, when the 75th Precinct moved from Miller and Liberty to 1000 Sutter Avenue, it became a popular choice for cops to work. It especially appealed to NYPD cops who lived on Long Island; it was either the closest A house to their homes or the easiest to commute to. In 1974, some two thousand police officers were on the waiting list to come to the Seven-Five.

With urban blight spreading over East New York since the fifties, by now the precinct was quickly evolving into a ghetto. Many of the old shops had closed up or moved elsewhere; the pushcarts were largely ancient history. Empty fields became desolate dumping grounds. Once-comfortable residential blocks sprouted dilapidated homes and abandoned buildings. Instead of kids playing on the streets with balls and bats, filling the air with jubilant shrieks, drug dealers now congregated on corners, and the sound of gunfire was routine.

By the seventies, East New York was predominantly black and Spanish, the housing projects by then the exclusive domain of these groups. As the decade drew to a close, an influx of South American groups—Dominicans, Colombians, Jamaicans, Hondurans, Guatemalans, and Salvadorans—continued the transformation of the neighborhood to virtually total minority status.

Some white cops found the stress of working in a ghetto too overwhelming, too disorienting. There was Police Officer Bobby Torsney, for instance, who with his partner one Thanksgiving Day in the mid-seventies drove into the Cypress Hills housing project in their radio car. Torsney got out of the car and without any provocation whatsoever nonchalantly walked over to a fifteen-year-old black boy, drew his revolver, and shot him point-blank, killing him instantly. Torsney then walked back to his car and sat down. The officer, a Vietnam vet who suffered from post-traumatic stress disorder, was later found incompetent to stand trial.

In the 1970s a few gangs existed in East New York, but their names—the Nomads, the Crazy Homicides, and the Sex Boys—were often more colorful than their crimes. The Sex Boys, for instance, who derived their name from their clubhouse in an abandoned building on Essex Street, were mostly into robberies and drug selling. But they also had a misguided habit of annoying the precinct cops and firemen, and early one morning they found their clubhouse roaring in flames. The gang members angrily stormed the station house, demanding to know who had torched their hangout. Soon after, the gang dissolved, its members sent to jail, murdered, or moving on in other directions with their lives.

Of all the crime ever to hit East New York, of all the robbery sprees and drive-by shootings and stabbings and murders, everything paled in comparison to a legendary incident that took place a few years later, on April 18, 1984. The details were engraved in the mind of every detective who had worked on the case, and one night in an after-hours session Joe Hall and Mike Redmond regaled Dave with their memories. Hall, who was new in the Seven-Five at the time, had been the detective to catch the case, but because of its importance he had been pulled from it and replaced by a more seasoned detective.

There was a championship hockey game on when the desk officer first notified the squad, and the detectives figured the desk officer was just trying to break their balls, so high was the body count.

The first call announced five bodies. As the detectives were getting ready, another call came in. "Seven dead," the desk officer reported as the men were putting on their jackets. "Nine down," came a third call half a minute later. When the detectives arrived at the crime scene, they almost went into shock. Corpses were strewn all over the home like litter. The place looked like a horror house at an amusement park, except that all the bodies were real. The final tally: ten dead. The incident, dubbed the Palm Sunday Massacre, was the worst single mass homicide to date in the history of New York City.

The Seven-Five squad supervisor working that day called all the detectives who were on an RDO, or regular day off. "Pack your clothes and come in," he barked.

The crime scene was at 1080 Liberty Avenue, the ground-floor apartment of a two-family house. Bodies sprawled on the floor, reclined in chairs, lay in beds. The worst part was the age of the victims. They were mostly children, from four different families but all related. The victims' ages were three, four, four, five, ten, ten, fourteen, fourteen, twenty, and twenty-four. Many were seated around a table, like wax dummies. The youngest was found coiled in a crib. There was one survivor, an infant, missed because it had been lying under a blanket.

Several hours after the gruesome discovery, the Seven-Five squad room was a madhouse. At least fifty detectives and bosses packed the room. The NYPD's chief of detectives was there, inspectors, chiefs, the mayor. So much brass came in that the captains, joked the detectives, were virtually relegated to gofer status.

A task force formed that worked the case systematically and painstakingly. What hit everybody was the tender ages of the victims. Three- and four-year-olds murdered? The detectives were enraged. Normally, these seasoned veterans banter a lot during investigations. But for a long time following the murders, a somber mood pervaded the squad room.

Two months and one week after the discovery of the ten bodies, the detectives collared the murderer. The homicides were the work of one man using two guns, a .38 and a .22. It was a crime of passion; the perpetrator, a heavy freebase cocaine user who was prone to violence, had suspected the owner of the house of having lured his wife to leave him. Thinking she was being hidden in the house, the murderer arrived to get her, and when the inhabitants could not produce her, the crazed man began shooting. He later said he had killed the children for fear they would be able to identify him.

The arrest of the killer offered satisfaction to the detectives but could never erase the vivid memory of the crime scene, nor of the wake. The funeral home was mobbed with weeping people. Dozens of uniformed cops guarded the premises. And worst of all, said Joe Hall, were the ten open coffins stretched out across the room—the victims, the poor innocent children, dressed for death in white.

The NYPD addressed narcotics selling primarily through the division called the Organized Crime Control Bureau. OCCB was also a spawning ground for the city's detectives, and it was from this unit that Al Smith came to the Seven-Five squad.

Working out of the Manhattan North Narcotics Unit in the Three-Oh precinct, Smitty was part of a team that made "buy-and-busts" in Harlem and Washington Heights. The team consisted of a sergeant and five or six investigators and one or two undercovers. They used three cars; Smitty was one of the investigators.

A simple buy-and-bust usually went down in the following manner. The team would go into an area where they knew drugs were being sold—they would previously have made buys and done a "recon," or surveillance and study of the scene. In a couple of cars, the team would park a block or two away in opposite directions while the undercover went in to make a buy. He would be backed up by an investigator, acting as a "ghost," who would hang around the location, or "set," and keep the undercover in visual range.

After the buy was made—sometimes sellers would give the drugs to steerers to do the hand-to-hand if they didn't feel comfortable with the buyer—the undercover would walk around the corner to his vehicle and transmit over the radio that he had made the buy, along with a description of the seller. A conversation might go as follows:

"Cobra Sixteen, Five to Cobra Sixteen, leader. The buy is good. Are you ready for the description?"

"Ten-four."

"All right, boss, we got two subjects. Subject number one is a steerer, male black, dressed in a white T-shirt, blue jeans, white sneakers, and a Yankees baseball cap. Number two is the seller, a male Hispanic. He's got the stash under his blue baseball jacket, and he's wearing black jeans and black sneakers. He's selling blue caps."

When the team moved in to arrest the pair, the seller's drugs would, they hoped, match the description. In this case they would be crack, and the top of the vial would be blue.

Buys inside locations were much more complicated and dangerous. A couple of buys would have to be made by an undercover, not carrying a gun, and out of sight of his backups. Then a warrant was obtained from a judge. While they were waiting for it to be issued, recons were made with the cops dressed as housepainters or deliverymen. They'd study the layout of the entire location, searching for back windows and fire escapes to determine escape routes and places where drugs could be thrown out. How many windows were there, where were they, and how did one get to them? When the team executed its warrant, each person knew his specific function. There would be cops outside with bolt cutters to cut chains to get to the side or rear of the building, and cops stationed on every floor securing those floors. Two cops would freeze the hallway outside the apartment that was being hit. Having carried a 150-pound steel ram up several flights of stairs, another team would break down the door, watched carefully by a supervisor aiming a double-barreled shotgun.

Having worked extensively in ghettos and areas of high crime and major drug trafficking, Smitty understood the problems faced by young cops just coming in from their comfortable suburban backgrounds. They spoke to him about it. It was almost like a ritual, these confessionals of new detectives.

While his skills were progressing after only a few months in the Seven-Five, Dave's enthusiasm was waning. "It wasn't like I expected it would be," he said of detective work to Smitty after several frustrating canvasses in which witnesses refused to testify.

"You go in thinking you're gonna be a blockbuster detective," Dave continued, "but the ghetto zaps your idealism and enthusiasm. People just don't give a fuck. You may see yourself as the white knight, but to the black folk you're the oppressor, just another honkie. In a bad precinct like East New York, even the good people won't cooperate. They'll tell you information, but they won't testify. So you know what happened, you know who did it, but you can't prove it, because you don't have a witness. It's not like you don't try. You try, but it's like shoveling shit against the tide. You get burned out after a while."

Smitty remembered his own discouragement as a white shield after only a short time. Witnesses told him, "I didn't know him. It's a shame he got killed, but why should I risk my life? So when the killer gets out of jail—that is, if he ever gets put away in the first place—he can come after me or my family?"

"Sometimes it's harder to get a witness than it is the perp," Smitty said.

"And there's a problem with a lot of the drug murders here," Dave complained. "Look at who your witnesses are: crackheads, prostitutes, and drug dealers. Who else is going to be at a drug location at three o'clock in the fucking morning? Who in the jury is going to believe them when they're trying to figure out whether to send somebody away for life?"

"A witness is a witness is a witness," Smitty answered, knowing his words wouldn't provide much solace. "All you can do is put together the best case you can and hope the jury believes you. Will they believe a prostitute on the stand who's been arrested fifteen or twenty times herself? She's your witness. She's all you've got. You have to get a jury to believe you. Yeah, it's a tough way to solve murders. We have to convince twelve people that the guy's guilty. The defense attorney only has to convince one that he's not.''

Adding to Dave's disillusionment was the reluctance of even victims to talk. He'd been in the emergency room at Brookdale too many times when a conversation like this had taken place:

"Who shot you?''

"I don't know.''

"Who were you with?''

"I don't know.''

"You don't know? How could you not know who you were with?''

"I don't remember.''

"Why would someone want to shoot you?''

"It must have been an accident.''

"Oh, yeah? Nine times is an accident?''

The philosophy was either "I'm alive, forget about it," or "I'll take care of it myself.''

So what do you do? Let the victim become judge and jury? Hell, no, Dave thought, I'm the law here. He would run the victim's name and invariably find out that that person was a perp. Then he'd tell the victim he'd better talk or Dave would find something to arrest him for. When victims were determined to exact retribution themselves, they were loath to help cops with their investigation. "If somebody shoots me and doesn't kill me," they'd say, "shame on them. I'll kill the motherfucker myself.'' But it wore on Dave having to go through this almost every time.

It was when Dave sat back and reflected on his career, on why he became a detective to begin with, that he was finally able to put things in perspective. He hadn't been so naive as to think all his victims would be paragons of the community. He had known he would be required to break his tail solving cases in which bad guys were the victims. It hadn't bothered him much then.

He thought about Mizell Harris, his unsolved dump job. Here was a guy dealing drugs—and most likely into more stuff besides—who had been savagely slain by other drug dealers. In that sense, his murder had been a public service. But Harris had come from a good family, at least as far as Dave could discern. Had he grown up elsewhere, his life might have taken a different course. But this was the ghetto, and the forces that guided the currents here were often too strong to overcome. Bad guys aren't born that way, he told himself. Somewhere in their souls were seeds of innocence and kindness, gentleness and goodness, whose growth and flowering had been choked off by the brutality of the ghetto environment. It was not up to him to absolve those whose perverted street justice had guaranteed such seeds would never have the chance to sprout again.

A thought effervesced out of his subconscious, one that would motivate him in the future when any doubt he harbored worked its way to the surface: Every life is worth something, and no one who takes even the meanest life should escape responsibility.

It was this sentiment that motivated David Carbone to buckle up and renew his mission, his sense of purpose.

9

After a few months in the Seven-Five Squad, Dave was getting the hang of being a detective. Although he hadn't yet collared his first killer, he understood well the mechanics of investigating homicides, having verified the truth of Sergeant Race's maxim—all homicides were worked basically alike. You get the call and respond to the scene. If the victim is at the hospital because he was alive when the police responded, the team splits up, half going to the hospital, half to the crime scene. At the crime scene you make personal observations and interview the first officer and other uniformed personnel. You notify the Crime Scene Unit and the ME and confer with them when they arrive and throughout their investigation. You do a canvass, interview witnesses, discuss the case with other detectives, and come up with theories. You follow your strongest lead or hunches and work the case.

In theory, this sounded easy, but in practice it involved a lot of work. Early on, Dave caught a few grounders, easy cases in which a witness spelled out the murder for the cops and identified the killer. But the first real homicide he caught that required him to hunt down the killer or killers came a few months after his arrival, during the summer.

"This could be your cherry," Redmond had told him. Dave chuckled at the sexual metaphor for a detective's first successfully resolved homicide, but he didn't need any additional incentive. This murder had raised his ire like no case he had ever worked on before.

It happened in the projects. Throughout New York City were public housing developments, clusters of grimy concrete buildings connected by arteries of walkways that set them off from the rest of the community. Insular and homogeneous, the projects offered low, stabilized rents, but the perils of living in them were often severe. Miscreants found a haven in these anonymous buildings, ruthlessly and unpityingly preying on their own—and indeed, the pool of potential quarry was huge. Some 600,000 people were registered in the city housing projects; an additional 400,000 lived there illegitimately.

In East New York, the projects included the Linden Houses, Unity Plaza, the Cypress Hills Houses, and the Louis H. Pink Houses. In some, gangs one or two hundred strong waged campaigns of terror, virtually controlling the area. They usurped apartments, shot people from the roofs, knifed, robbed, stole, dealt drugs, kidnapped, murdered. They established codes: If a person didn't live in the project, he couldn't come in. If he did, someone whose presence he would never even detect would kill him.

The call came in around eight-thirty in the evening of August 13, 1989, for the squad to respond to the rear of 1250 Sutter Avenue. Patrol cops were already there; when the detectives arrived, they were greeted by the spinning turret lights atop the RMPs. A telescopic light pole was rising out of a police Emergency Service Unit truck to illuminate the scene with its bright halogen light.

The detectives got out of their cars and walked several feet over to where a bunch of uniforms were standing, raising the yellow tape over their heads as they reached the cordoned-off area. They were in a parking lot of the Cypress Hills Houses. EMS technicians were rolling a stretcher to an ambulance. As they lifted the stretcher into the back, Dave took a quick look at the victim. It was a young girl with a pretty face, a porcelain brown complexion, tender-looking, baby-fat chunky. Her eyes open but expressionless, she lay quietly as blood seeped from a gunshot wound in her chest.

Dave followed the victim into the ambulance and crouched down next to her. He put his head close to her ear.

"Honey, can you hear me?"

There was no response. A few seconds later he tried again. She's too young for this to happen, Dave thought. She's too young to die.

"We gotta go," a technician said.

"Whaddya think?" Dave could not suppress the catch in his voice.

The EMS technician shook his head. Without saying a word, he held up his hand, curled his fingers tightly, and pivoted his thumb down.

Dave hopped out. The technician closed the rear door and the ambulance sped away, its blaring siren dissolving seconds later as the vehicle melted into the night. The detectives, flanked by rings of cops and civilians, stood by the spot where minutes earlier the girl had fallen, leaving a puddle of thick crimson glittering now under the artificial light.

Dave stared down at the pool of blood.

"Doesn't look too good," said Smitty. "I don't think she's going to make it."

Dave didn't answer. He just stood there flexing his jaw, unaware he was even doing so.

Several NYPD and New York City Housing Police detectives had arrived in a parking lot of the Cypress Hills projects. If the girl died, the case would be investigated jointly by both agencies. Every homicide in New York City was investigated by the NYPD. If it happened in a New York City housing project, the NYPD investigated it together with the Housing Police; if in the subway, with the Transit Police. Otherwise, Housing and Transit had full jurisdiction in their respective locales, and any crime that happened anywhere else in the city became the sole property of the NYPD.

There was a lot to be done. All the buildings surrounding the crime scene had to be canvassed. The area had to be searched for witnesses. Clues and leads needed to be ferreted out. A couple of detectives stayed behind to wait for the Crime Scene Unit while the rest split up. Some fanned out to the buildings, others went to the hospital where the victim had been taken.

Mike Redmond took the parking lot. He recorded the time, 8:35 P.M., and then approached the people standing around. One by one he interviewed them, getting nothing but several different versions of "Came after the police arrived" and "Saw and heard nothing."

Housing Detective Eddie Rosado of the Police Service Area 2 Detective Squad took down the license plate numbers of the cars in the lot. Sometimes perps stole cars and left them, complete with their fingerprints, at a murder scene. Sometimes people from outside the area were there at the time of the murder but were reluctant to come forward—somebody buying drugs, or a married person with his or her lover. Or perhaps a car belonged to somebody who lived in the area but was in potential trouble with the police. All this gave detectives another tool to pressure people who might be able to help the investigation. All the plates would be run.

When he finished recording plate numbers, Rosado interviewed the first officer on the scene, Peter Murray, a housing cop from PSA 4. Murray told Rosado he had been with officers Kissane, Meehan, and Jackson in their RMP, which was parked by the sidewalk about two buildings north of the crime scene.

"At about twenty hundred hours we heard a shot come from the rear of 1250 Sutter Avenue," he said, "and then a male black ran over to us and said someone was shot. We responded to the scene and found a female black lying in the parking lot with blood spots on the left side of her chest and blood coming out of her mouth. I tried to speak with her, but she was unable to respond. I spoke to a female on the scene who said she was the victim's stepsister." He turned his head to a girl standing nearby, and Rosado followed with his eyes. The girl had her head buried in her hands and was weeping.

In the emergency room of Brookdale Hospital, doctors were trying frantically to revive the victim as Dave, Smitty, Joe Hall, and Eddie Feit, a housing detective, arrived. A respirator was connected to her mouth, a heart monitor to her chest; intravenous tubes ran from long poles down to her arms. The girl lay motionless on the table as the staff swirled around her. Twenty minutes after she had been brought in, a young doctor, a dejected expression on his face, shook his head and pulled a curtain around the bed.

"I think she was DOA when we got there," Smitty said tonelessly. Dave turned on his heel and strode out the door, his stomach clenched like a fist.

In a grim mood, the detectives drove back to the crime scene to assist with the canvass. Now a homicide, the case would officially be jointly investigated by NYPD and Housing. The two catching detectives were Dave and Eddie Feit.

Born and raised in Brooklyn, Feit was a third-generation cop. Both his father and grandfather had worked in the NYPD, not a very unusual circumstance except that the family was Jewish. Not many Jews had served on the force back in the 1920s, and not many of their children came on the job after them.

The detectives piled out of their car. A monolithic mass of buildings loomed before them, like mountains in some vast range. The detectives had their work cut out for them. The basic scope of a canvass, the initial fact-finding mission, covered every window facing the crime scene.

Dave, Feit, Smitty, and Hall entered the building at 395 Fountain Avenue a little after eleven to begin their canvass. As they opened the door, a fetid odor assaulted them. Ascending the stairs and moving through the corridors, they sidestepped puddles of urine and clumps of dried feces. Roaches crawled on the walls in the dim hallways.

By now the detectives knew the identity of the victim. The girl at the crime scene who had been crying was her stepsister, and she had identified the murder victim as Racquel Cannon, age thirteen.

The detectives split up into pairs and took the floors one at a time. They knocked on the doors, and a minute or two later, the occupants opened the doors circumspectly, as far as the bolted chain would permit. The detectives explained they were investigating the murder of a girl in the parking lot. Had they seen or heard anything? Some said they had heard gunshots but had seen nothing. All were apprehensive and anxious to close the door.

On the fifth floor, Dave and Feit spoke through an apartment door with a boy named Matt, who had known Racquel casually. He had not seen her since the previous Friday, but he called his sister to the door.

"At about nine-thirty," she told them, "two girls knocked on the door and asked if Matt was home. He was sleeping, and my mother said to tell the girls to come back later. They asked me to tell Matt they were going back to Far Rockaway and would catch him another time. No, I never saw the girls before."

The detectives thanked the girl and went on to the next apartment.

As they left the building later, Feit said to Dave, "They knew she was an outsider. It's dangerous to enter the projects if you don't live here. What a fucking shame she had to die because she didn't know that."

The refrigerated drawers in the morgue at Kings County Hospital were kept at a constant forty-degree temperature, which warded off decomposition in bodies stored there for as long as several weeks. Most corpses brought there were autopsied rather quickly, but for one reason or another there was sometimes a delay.

The morgue was a small area at the back of the hospital off Winthrop Street, an autopsy room across from a room of drawers. The body of Racquel Cannon now lay in a drawer in the crypt, enveloped in the body bag in which she had been brought over from Brookdale shortly after she died.

At one-thirty in the afternoon, Racquel Cannon's mother, Geraldine, arrived at the morgue and in an upstairs room identified her daughter's body from a photograph.

Earlier in the day, a forensic pathologist had weighed and measured the body. Then he had inspected it, while it was still completely clothed. He had matched the hole in the clothing to where the bullet had entered on the left side of the chest and lodged in the upper right shoulder. If the holes hadn't matched up, the ME and detectives would have had a puzzle to solve. He had removed the clothing and had the body X-rayed. While this was being done, Racquel's clothing was labeled as evidence to go to the police lab.

At about two o'clock, Detectives Carbone, Redmond, and Feit came through the double doors of the autopsy room. As a rush of bittersweet odor struck his nostrils, Dave's attention was immediately drawn to the body lying directly in front of him. The chest had been cut and was drawn open like the panels of a door. The inside of the chest was hollow, all the organs and guts having been removed. The body reminded Dave of a hollowed-out canoe. A visit to the morgue never ceased to prompt him to question the meaning of life. Why were we here, and why did we take matters so seriously, if we were nothing but walking, breathing, flesh-covered shells of unsightly organs, if we were all to end up as rotting carcasses that would be dumped into some small hole in the ground where we would lie for all eternity?

There were two empty tables to the left of the corpse, and two occupied tables to the right. On the first adjacent table was the body of Racquel Cannon. An ME stood nearby.

The pathologist conferred briefly with the detectives, who now stood at the base of the table, ready to observe. Even detectives, inured to the worst of humanity, found autopsies unpleasant to watch, but they learned something from the examination often enough to make their reluctant presence mandatory.

The ME inspected Racquel Cannon's X-rays. One bullet had lodged inside the body, corresponding to the single bullet hole. Then he inspected the body for any evidence that might be present on the skin, such as bruises, lacerations, and scratches, in addition to the main wound. He looked for gunshot residue, to see if the girl had been shot at close range. If the identity of the victim wasn't known, or if the body was decomposed, the ME would note any identifying features such as birthmarks, scars, and tattoos; dental X-rays would also be requested.

Next he took a photograph of the wound, which would be preserved as evidence if the case went to trial. Then he did a complete external inspection of the body, noting the color of hair and eyes and details of the girl's other features. No rape examination—which involved taking swabs of the mouth, vagina, and rectum to be tested for sperm, and examining the anogenital area for injuries—was done, since it was known that the victim had been shot after a brief conversation with her assailant. Had her body been found somewhere, without witnesses to the assault, such an examination would have been routine.

Forty-five minutes later, he was ready to cut.

The doctor placed the tip of a sharp knife between the girl's small breasts and began to make a Y-shaped incision: to the tip of the left shoulder, then the tip of the right shoulder, then straight down the middle of the abdomen to the pubic bone. He pulled back the three skin flaps he had created to expose the ribs and the abdominal organs.

The detectives watched without saying a word. Dave tried to will his stomach not to crawl up into his esophagus.

The ME took some notes, then picked up an instrument that looked like a pair of pruning shears and cut off the chest plate and ribs, exposing the heart and lungs; there was a great deal of blood in the chest because of the gunshot wounds. With his scalpel, the ME meticulously dissected out the organs: heart, lungs, liver, spleen, intestinal tract, pancreas, kidneys, bladder, uterus, ovaries. He inspected each one, weighing and examining it for injuries or the presence of any natural disease. The doctor examined the uterus as well; pregnancy is sometimes a motive for murder or suicide. The ME established the path of the bullet, recovering it from inside the body to be submitted as evidence for ballistics examination.

Now that the body had been divested of all its organs, it looked like an empty shell.

Dave had learned to deal with the sight of murder victims. He hoped someday he would become as resigned to observing autopsies, to seeing human beings cut open as though they were frogs in a high school biology class.

Because the shoulder flaps were folded all the way back, the neck was exposed, from the root all the way up to the jawbone. The doctor dissected each of the layers of tissue down to the windpipe and voice box, looking for injuries. Then he removed them. He left the tongue intact, since it would not be needed for any specific purpose. The MEs tried not to be any more invasive than absolutely necessary.

The head was last. Doing the rest of the body first removed most of the blood, and the ME had a pretty clean field to work with while examining this area.

The ME touched the knife to the skin behind the tip of the right ear. He pressed down sharply and drew the blade around the top of the head to the skin behind the other ear. With the scalp essentially split in the center, he pulled the skin at the top and peeled it down to the level of the eyebrows, folding it over the face. To Dave, the girl's face looked like a mask hanging upside down and inside out.

Dave gazed on this unveiling in a stupor. That's just what our faces are, he thought, masks. All human flesh is just a costume.

The ME peeled back the skin remaining over the skull. The skin of the head was now severed and folded back in opposite directions. As a technician opened the skull with a heavy saw and the ME lifted the cap off in preparation for removing the brain, Dave imagined the physical substance and structure of his own brain inside its inviolate cranium, his thoughts flickering across the mass of tissue like beams of moonlight playing on the surface of a lake. The girl's brain, he reflected, had been similarly illuminated until a mere twenty-four hours ago.

Exposed now was the dura mater, the tissue covering the girl's brain. The ME cut that away, exposing the brain itself. Dave had to close his eyes as the ME lifted the brain out of the cranial cavity, then weighed and inspected it.

The girl's corpse was to be spared further violation; the ME did not feel it necessary to cut out the spinal cord. Save for the tissues taken for samples, the ME put the extracted body parts in a plastic bag. He tied the bag and put it in the body cavity, and a technician sewed the body up. The autopsy was now over. The corpse would be taken to the funeral parlor.

The depressing exercise of observing the autopsy confirmed for the detectives that the victim had been shot cold-bloodedly at close range, and that there had been no struggle. The three walked out of the morgue and into the bright day. The sun was baking down, and the humidity was high.

"I'm glad to get the hell out of that place," Dave said with relief, taking deep breaths of air. "Gave me the fucking heebie-jeebies."

At a quarter after one on the morning of August 14, Monique Rivera, the murder victim's stepsister, arrived in the squad room, her face pale and strained. "We can talk in there," Dave said, taking her elbow and pointing across the squad room.

In the interview room, Dave pulled a chair out for the girl to sit down, and then sat down himself in one next to her. Feit sat on a bench several feet back.

"We're sorry about what happened, Monique," Dave told her, his hands clasped. She had been too upset to speak with the detectives after the murder. "Anything you can let us know now will help."

The girl sighed as if to gain her strength, then spoke. "Me and Racquel left Far Rockaway about seven o'clock and took the subway to Euclid Avenue." Her voice was soft and fragile, and Dave inwardly willed her not to break down.

"When we got off the train," she continued, "I followed Racquel into the Cypress projects. We went to Matt's house. I knocked on the door, and Matt's sister said he was sleeping. She said we could come back later." This was encouraging; it was what Matt's sister had told them the night of the murder.

"We decided to leave," Monique said. "We walked to the parking lot. Racquel walked along the sidewalk, and I went through the parking lot." She faltered, then composed herself, dealing with a mixture of guilt and relief, Dave guessed. Had she been walking next to Racquel, perhaps she would have been shot instead of Racquel, or with her.

"I looked over to my left," Monique continued, "and there was Racquel with two black kids. One kid went up to her. He said, 'Bitch, gimme your earrings!' She turned around and saw he had a gun. She said, 'That's a fake gun.' He was aiming it at her chest. She started walking toward the parking lot, and I heard a sound like a firecracker. Then she screamed and fell down. The two kids ran toward the bleachers on the ball field."

"What did the boy with the gun look like?" asked Detective Feit.

"He was about thirteen years old. He was short and thin. He had short black hair. He was wearing a white T-shirt, or maybe it was gray. He had on black or dark blue jeans."

"Anything else?" Dave asked.

The girl shook her head. It was dark, and everything had happened so fast she hadn't gotten a good look at the boy's face.

"You were terrific," Dave said to her. "This'll be very helpful to us. You're a brave girl." He took her hand briefly, and she looked up at him, her eyes brimming. "We'll be in touch," he said.

Sleep was a luxury in the aftermath of a homicide, and the detectives were on a roll. Dave had worked through his turnaround, done the day tour, and was now on overtime well into the night. He had been up twenty-two consecutive hours checking out possible leads, doing interviews, and banging out Fives.

Dave, Eddie Feit, and Eddie Rosado, the housing detective, returned to 1250 Sutter Avenue to continue the canvass of floors four through seven. Other detectives had been there previously, but a number of people hadn't been home or hadn't come to their doors. On the sixth floor they found a woman who had some information.

"I was home," she said hesitantly. "I heard what sounded like a shot. I looked out the window and saw several Spanish guys trying to help a girl who was lying in the parking lot. My daughter told me later she heard it was a boy who shot the girl and that he was about thirteen or fourteen. He got a gun from a guy named Jeff. This Jeff told the boy to scare the girl and get the earrings.''

"Any idea where Jeff lives?'' Rosado asked.

The woman went to the window and studied the view for a few seconds. Then she pointed. "That building over there.''

Felt and Rosado moved up beside her and followed the direction of her finger. "That's 385 Fountain,'' said Rosado.

The woman remembered something. "Oh, and my daughter also heard the gang that gave the boy the gun is going to send him down South,'' she said.

The detectives looked at each other. Dave asked, "What gang is that?''

"You know, the one from the projects here. They cause a lot of trouble.'' She began to look nervous.

"Where's your daughter?'' Dave asked. "We'd like to talk to her directly.'' Anxious now to get the detectives out of her apartment, the woman told them she'd have her daughter get in touch with them when she came home.

As they ambled down the corridor, Eddie Feit muttered a scatological expletive to Dave. "The A Team,'' he groused. "That's all we need.'' The participation of the A Team would add to the complexity—and danger—of the investigation.

Having participated in a joint Housing–city police investigation of the A Team, Eddie Feit knew the gang was one of the most notorious in all Brooklyn. Numbering about a hundred members and associates, the A Team controlled about half the Cypress project, which occupied thirty buildings on twenty-nine acres. During the investigation, a city police officer, Ed Byrnes, was murdered in a police car. One of the leaders of the A Team was a top lieutenant in the gang that had ordered the hit; Brian "Glaze'' Gibbs allegedly had committed at least ten murders himself.

Most of the residents of the Cypress Hills projects were decent, hardworking people. Gang members terrorized them with robberies and beatings until they were so intimidated that few would ever testify against the gang, even when they were the victims.

The A Team employed whatever tactics were necessary to fulfill its criminal objectives. Heavily involved in the drug trade, for example, the gang members needed indoor locations from which to peddle their wares. The gang's MO was to send someone to hook a young mother on crack and then move her out to a tenement, threatening harm to either her or her child. Gang members would then use the apartment to sell narcotics or to store drugs, weapons, or cash, while continuing to pay rent. As time wore on and the potential to be caught increased, they'd abandon the apartment and move on to another.

The A Team members didn't limit themselves to the Cypress projects. They committed robberies in Manhattan, especially around Times Square, but their power base was narcotics in the Cypress projects and the surrounding area.

After Feit, Rosado, and Dave finished canvassing the floors at shortly before midnight, Dave suggested they pay another visit to Matt. The boy was still up, and again they interviewed him through the apartment door.

"Don't hold anything back," Dave told him. "Even if you think it's stupid or just a rumor, let us decide what's valid and what's not." People often knew more than they realized.

"Well, I did find out something," Matt said hesitantly. "I was on my way home when I heard some kids talking about the girl who was shot last night. They were saying the guy who shot her tried to take the girl's earrings and that she said something back, and that's why he shot her. They said he was about twelve or thirteen. I heard them say the name Mel."

The Cypress Houses management office maintained files on every registered tenant of the project. "We're looking for a boy twelve to fourteen named Mel," Eddie Feit said to the manager, Kenneth Reisberg.

Reisberg retrieved a stack of files. Dividing the stack in four parts, he and the three detectives combed through each file for someone with the name Mel, or any variation of it, who fit the general description. Every building in Cypress had to be covered, some fourteen hundred apartments in all. And there was no guarantee the search would be fruitful; many who lived in the projects were not registered. But after several hours and hundreds of files, Reisberg finally found a name: Melson McNeal, described as a male black twelve years of age.

The detectives finally had not only the name but the address of a possible perp in the Racquel Cannon murder. But there was no immediate rush to pick him up. Before he was questioned, there was homework to be done.

Back at the office later, the file open in front of him, Dave called the Waldbaum's Supermarket at Cross Bay Boulevard in Howard Beach, Queens, and asked for Mrs. McNeal.

"She's off today," a woman said. "Would you like to leave a message?"

"Oh, that's okay. I'm family, I'll call her at home."

The last thing Dave would do would be to identify himself as a police officer. He just wanted to verify that Melson's mother worked there. During an investigation, it was important to know as much as possible about the people being interviewed. If the detective dropped his load at the right time and with the right force, the interviewee might think the detective knew more than he really did.

Next Dave called the Kings County morgue for the results of Racquel Cannon's autopsy. The official cause of death was a single gunshot wound to the left side of the chest, penetrating the heart and lung. No surprise there.

Team One was into heavy overtime again, working into the night on their day tour on this second day following the Racquel Cannon murder. Mike Redmond and Richie Brew were out canvassing 1240 Sutter. Smitty and Joe Hall got pulled away from the investigation to work on some new cases that had come in.

Dave called Racquel Cannon's stepsister, Monique Rivera, to come in for yet another interview. She elaborated a little further on her previous story, but Dave doubted she would have anything else of substance to add. It was time to document her recollections. Dave called the DA's office to request a riding assistant district attorney. Witnesses to crimes in the borough were brought to the DA's office in downtown Brooklyn to tape their statements, but at night the ADAs would travel to tape the witnesses for certain crimes—homicides, shootings, sex crimes such as forcible rape and sodomy, senior-citizen crimes. Whenever the trial or trial hearings were held, the tapes could refresh the witnesses' memories, but the tapes themselves were not used in a court of law.

When Monique's taping was finished, Dave turned to Eddie Feit. "What a great witness she'd be," he said, "if only she could identify the perp."

The next morning at nine forty-five, Dave, Mike Redmond, and Eddie Feit paid a visit to the P.S. 36 Annex, Melson McNeal's school in East New York. It was a school for slow learners, currently in summer session.

"Melson hasn't been in school since Friday," the principal told them. He had tried calling Melson's home, but there was no answer.

"What about a photograph?" Redmond asked.

The principal picked up a mimeographed program for the class that had just graduated on June 23 and opened it to the class photograph. He handed it to Redmond, pointing out Melson's face. But the picture wasn't clear enough for them to use; they'd have to get the original from the photographer.

For the first time since Racquel Cannon had been murdered three days ago, Dave felt a tinge of optimism. Soon he'd have a picture of the possible killer of Racquel Cannon. But the A Team gang from Cypress was planning to move the shooter out. Whether the kid in the picture was the killer or not, one thing was clear: The good guys had better move fast.

On the wall above Detective Sergeant George Hohenstein's desk in the boss's office adjacent to the Seven-Five squad room was the Precinct Detective Homicide Chart, listing the year's homicide victims to date. Each of the two tally sheets contained spaces for up to forty-eight victims. As he and Eddie Feit stepped into the office to confer with Hohenstein, Dave noticed Racquel Cannon's name had been inscribed on the chart.

With his suspenders and bow tie, a revolver at his waist, Sergeant Hohenstein was the quintessential image of a 1950s New York City detective. But his full mane of straight blond hair gave him a youthful appearance, and he bore a faint resemblance to Robert Redford.

"Here it is, sarge," Dave said, as he handed a crisp color photograph of Melson McNeal's class to Hohenstein, seated behind his desk. "Should we go get him?"

"You'll have to bring him in with his parents," the sergeant said as he scanned the photo, "because he's underage. If you brought him in by himself and he confessed to the murder, the confession would be thrown out. But remember, if you bring everybody in and the kid wants to talk but his parents don't, or if the parents want him to talk but the kid refuses, you can't talk to him."

Hohenstein hooked his thumbs through his suspenders and leaned back in his chair. "If they request an attorney, you're going to end up having to either let him go or arrest him. And without a witness, you're going to have to let him go, because what are you going to lock him up on? On hearsay?"

Dave shook his head. "Even if we did have a witness, they probably wouldn't testify."

"If you don't have any witnesses down the road, you can bring him in and hope he chokes his chicken. But it's too early in the investigation to blow your load. If you grab him now without a witness, you'll just have to cut him loose, and he'll know you want him for murder. So leave him out there now and continue canvassing until you find a witness. Take another shot at it."

Dave and Feit reluctantly agreed, but one thought bore heavily on their minds: Finding a witness would be a race against time.

Over the next week, Dave and Eddie Feit relentlessly canvassed and recanvassed the Cypress projects and the area around them within a five-block radius.

"So what do we have so far?" Dave fretted to Feit one afternoon. "We've got the name and picture of a suspect, but we're not really sure if he even did the fucking murder."

The two were standing on a sidewalk near the spot where Racquel Cannon had been gunned down. Weary after days of fruitless canvassing, they stood in silence, trying to determine if there was some small detail they had missed, some other path they could pursue.

"Hey, you guys detectives?"

The detectives looked up, startled, to see a wiry boy about eleven or twelve standing just a few feet away. The detectives smiled.

Even though many young kids living in the projects got swept up in the other side of the law, there were always a few who were fascinated by cops. And the cops wanted to be good role models for them; as fleeting as any interaction might be, it might well be something they would remember for the rest of their lives. So they tried to provide inspiration and encouragement.

"Are you here about that girl who was killed?" said the boy, his voice thin and piping.

"Yeah," said Feit, a little surprised. "You know anything about it?"

"Yeah, I saw it. I saw the whole thing."

Dave and Feit looked at each other in astonishment. Did they finally have a witness to the Racquel Cannon murder?

The detectives quizzed the boy for a minute to see if he was on the level. He was. Down deep they had been convinced no witness would ever come forward. Everyone knew talking to the cops could get a person killed. He was just a kid, Dave thought, but he was either incredibly brave or incredibly stupid.

There were steps to be taken immediately. The first was to get out of there; the A Team had eyes all around the project. The second was to talk to the boy's mother. The witness was just a boy, and without his mother's permission they wouldn't be able to use what he said.

"Is your mother home?" Dave asked. "We'll need to talk to her also."

The three repaired to the boy's apartment at 740 Euclid, the boy first, the detectives shortly afterward. A woman in the room registered an expression of alarm when she saw two detectives on her son's heels. Dave reassured her that the boy wasn't in trouble and explained why they had come. With the mother's reluctant consent, Dave asked the boy to repeat what he had told them in the playground minutes earlier.

"It was getting dark and I was in the playground playing on the swing," said the boy. "I heard someone saying, 'Give me your jewelry, give me your jewelry.' I saw Jamel standing with a girl, and Jamel was pointing a gun at her. The girl turned to run, and he shot her. I saw him run away, but I didn't see where. I kept swinging."

"How do you know Jamel?" Feit asked.

"From school."

"Do you know Jamel's last name?"

The boy shook his head slowly from side to side.

Dave was perplexed. "You say Jamel, but we heard it was a Melson who shot the girl. Jamel and Melson, they both have a *mel* sound. Could they be the same?"

"I don't know no Melson," the boy responded. "But I do know Jamel. His name is Jamel. Ja-mel."

"Would you be willing to tell the assistant district attorney what you told us?" Feit asked.

"Sure," said the boy, his eyes widening as if someone had offered him tickets to a Knicks game.

Dave knew the next part was delicate, and crucial. He turned to the boy's mother. "He's our only witness in the murder," he said. "Without him, we may not be able to put the killers away. They'll be free to shoot somebody else." He looked meaningfully at the boy.

The mother was understandably conflicted about her son's welfare. "We'll look out for him, and you too," Dave reassured her, contemplating the options. The kid's identity could be kept secret until he had to testify, which probably wouldn't be for another year. Even in testifying before the grand jury, his name would not be revealed. And if the suspect pled guilty, there would be no trial. If worse came to worst and the kid had to testify publicly, he and his family could be relocated out of harm's way. "We'll do whatever it takes to protect you both," he told her, and paused a moment, wondering whether she comprehended the risk.

Feit spoke up. "May we take him to the DA to get his statement taped?'' The mother, biting down on her lower lip and staring at the floor, assented.

Feit immediately called the Brooklyn DA's office to arrange for a taping of the witness.

"Listen," Dave said to the mother and son. "You know you can't tell anybody about this." He turned to the boy. "Don't go around bragging about what you're doing. Keep your mouth shut. Understand?"

The boy nodded his head absently. His mother rose from her chair, grabbed his arm, and yanked him in front of Dave, a heavy hand on each shoulder. "You listen to the detective, now," she hissed to her son, as her eyes, full of worry, met Dave's over the boy's head. Dave took the boy's hands in his and repeated his warning as forcefully as he could. The boy's eyes widened again, and Dave glanced up at his mother. She nodded slightly, and Dave released the boy's hands, hoping he had gotten through.

Feit strode back into the room, having finished his phone conversation. He explained to the boy what would happen next, for safety's sake.

Dave and Feit proffered their cards to the mother and walked out the door. They went to the roof, crossed over to the next building, and exited on the ground floor, meeting their witness around the corner.

At the DA's office, the boy handled the taping like a pro, receiving profuse congratulations from everyone present.

An hour later, Dave and Eddie Feit were back at the Housing Authority management office, requesting a search for a boy named Jamel approximately twelve years of age. It took the office manager fifteen minutes to compile a short list of names, addresses, and descriptions. The first one seemed the best bet.

At dinner hour, Dave and Feit again knocked on the door of their witness. After they were invited in, Dave withdrew from an envelope the class photograph picturing Melson McNeal. "Do you see Jamel here?" Dave said to the boy.

The boy scanned the picture for a minute, then shook his head.

Feit eyeballed Dave. "We're talking two different kids here."

Dave, Feit, and Housing Detective Romagnoli drove to 395 Fountain Avenue and took the elevator to the seventh floor. One of the detectives rapped on the door. They all stood to the side, their hands on their revolvers.

The door opened slowly and a woman's face appeared in the crack.

The detectives clamped the handles of their revolvers tighter.

"Mrs. Strong?" Dave inquired.

"Yes," she said, after a moment's hesitation.

"We're detectives. Do you know why we're here?"

The woman's eyes began to well with tears, and the detectives knew they were in the right place. Jamel Strong had shot and killed Racquel Cannon.

The woman broke into tears as a man came into view behind her, his face grave. "He was scared of Jeff," she declared between sobs. "Jeff had warned them not to talk to the police." The detectives exchanged glances; Jeff was apparently a member of the A Team. "Jamel's at his aunt's house in Coney Island," she continued. "Let me call over there." Her husband, silent up to that point, offered to take the men to pick up his son.

Encouraged by the parents' willingness to help, the detectives accepted. Twenty minutes later, the three detectives and the boy's father pulled up in an unmarked squad car to a building in Coney Island. At an apartment on the fifth floor, the father asked if he could speak with the boy's aunt, and a minute later the woman appeared out of a back room with the boy.

At last the detectives were face to face with the object of their intense search. The boy moved slowly, his steps measured. His eyes were lit up and his small, thin body seemed fragile and weak. How was it possible, Dave asked himself, for this thirteen-year-old to brandish a real gun and squeeze the trigger and snuff out the life of someone his own age? Dave glanced at the boy's father and was instantly sorry he had done so. The father's look of agony was unbearable.

"Jamel?" Feit demanded.

"Yes," the boy said softly.

"We have to talk to you. We'll go back to the 75th Precinct."

"Welcome to the big leagues," Dave muttered grimly as he slapped handcuffs on the boy's bony wrists.

At the station house, Jamel's father called his wife to come down. When she arrived, her eyes red and swollen, Jamel, his parents, and Dave and Feit gathered in the Juvenile Room of the RIP office, down the hall from the squad room.

"If you don't talk to me now," Dave said to Jamel, "our witness will do the talking."

No, Jamel said, he would answer the detectives' questions. His parents consented, and Dave read the Miranda rights to Jamel and his father, Roy Strong. If either the father or the boy said no to any of the questions or declined to waive his rights, all communication regarding the case would have to cease, and an attorney would have to be obtained.

If Jamel didn't confess to the murder of Racquel Cannon, it was important that he put himself at the crime scene at the time of the murder. If the witness picked him out as the shooter, he couldn't say he wasn't there. The detectives already had enough to arrest Jamel. A confession would just be icing on the cake.

"We don't know what happened that day because we weren't there," Dave said. "Why don't you tell us?"

The boy squirmed in his seat. He was looking down. A moment later he began to talk in flat monotone, his voice barely audible at first.

"I was sitting on the bench in front of 385 Fountain Avenue with Tony. We saw two girls walk into the building. Then Tony left, and I was by myself. Jeff called me over.

"He said, 'Jamel, go rob them girls.' I asked why, and he said, 'Because they got earrings.' Melson came out of his building, and Jeff told him to go with me to rob them girls. Jeff said, 'If you don't do it, something's going to happen,' and he handed me a gun.

"Me and Melson started to walk towards the girls, and I gave the gun to Melson. When we got to the girls, I said, 'Give me the earrings,' and the girl looked back. Melson handed me the gun, and it went off. The girl started to walk funny, and we ran. We ran up to Jeff's friend, and he said, 'Jeff said to give me the gun.' I gave him the gun and ran home. I left about nine o'clock with my friend Yu-Yu. We went to Yu-Yu's uncle, and he gave him twenty dollars. Yu-Yu gave me the twenty dollars, and I took a cab to my aunt's apartment in Coney Island."

The boy stopped, breathing quickly, and looked up at his father, who turned his head away.

The detectives weren't sure whether their young subject realized he had just put the nails into his own coffin. Dave excused himself, returning a few minutes later with a DD Five on which Jamel's statement had been typed. The boy and his mother read it over and signed it.

Dave then retrieved a RIP photo book that had shots of members of the A Team at Cypress and laid it on a table for Jamel to look through for Jeff. After only a few minutes he put his finger down on a picture. "That's him," he said. He lowered his head and pulled his shoulders forward, seeming to sink into himself.

The photograph showed a husky man with short hair, a goatee, and a cold stare. Printed on a board that was hanging around his neck was his NYSIIS number. In the photo reference book, which contained information on the perps in the photos, Dave found the name: Jeffrey Sykes.

Dave filled out a Wanted Card stating that Jeffrey Sykes was wanted for murder. Even though Sykes hadn't pulled the trigger, he had told Jamel to take Racquel Cannon's earrings, so Dave reasoned that he had acted in concert and was a co-conspirator to murder. The Wanted Card would be dispatched to One PP and given an ID number; anyone who was arrested in the city of New York would be checked against the information on the card, and Dave would be notified of a match.

"You're being charged with the murder of Racquel Cannon," Dave informed Jamel quietly. "We'll be taking you up to Spofford later, and tomorrow you'll be arraigned on the charges." Spofford was a holding facility for juveniles in the Bronx.

Dave escorted the boy and his parents to the interview room, where they sat silently on a bench, not looking at one another.

Six hours later, an ADA arrived to videotape Jamel. Before a camera, Jamel repeated his story and made a full confession. If in the trial the defense claimed the police had beaten the confession out of the defendant, the video would be an important piece of evidence to refute the allegation.

A short while later, 6:20 A.M. now, the kid who had witnessed the murder peered sleepily through a one-way mirror. No lineup was necessary, since the witness knew the alleged perp. This was just a one-on-one viewing, a show-up, as the detectives called it.

"That's Jamel," he said, looking into the interview room, his voice husky with sleep. "He's the one who shot the girl." An ID by the witness. The case was virtually ironclad now.

As the sun was rising on what promised to be a bright, steamy day, Jamel bid his parents goodbye. Dave sensed leaden relief on the part of all members of the family. The whole episode was a damn, horrible shame, Dave thought, in which everybody lost. One thirteen-year-old dead, another to wither away in jail. And for what? For a $3 pair of imitation gold earrings?

When Dave and Feit returned to duty the next morning, they learned that late the previous afternoon, after their day tour was over, Cheryl McNeal and her son, Melson, had turned up at the squad room. She had heard the police had arrested Jamel Strong for the murder of Racquel Cannon and were looking for her son. Detectives Tony Simione and Tommy O'Donnell read the boy and his mother the Miranda warning and obtained their agreement that Melson would answer questions about his role in Racquel Cannon's murder.

Dave read through the Five containing the transcript of the boy's remarks; it corroborated the other accounts. Melson had reported Jeff Sykes's instructions to Jamel: "Stick the girls for the earrings. I don't like them, they're not from the projects. If she don't take them off, shoot her." With a shudder, Dave remembered the icy stare on Sykes's face in his mug shot.

After hearing the boy's story, the ADA decided it couldn't be proved that Melson McNeal had been a participant in the murder of Racquel Cannon and ordered his release. The boy had never said or done anything that would make him a conspirator to robbery or murder, the ADA reasoned; he had only watched another boy rob and shoot the victim.

Dave was furious. He protested to the ADA, but he was shot down. "That's fucking Brooklyn justice for you," he fumed to Eddie Feit.

There was still the unfinished business of collaring Jeffrey Sykes. During whatever time he could find, Dave grabbed Feit, Smitty, Redmond, Cutrone, or Hall to search the projects and the streets for any trace of Sykes, coming up empty on each attempt. It's just a matter of time before I nab the scumbucket, Dave promised himself, remembering Racquel Cannon lying unresponsive in the ambulance and the autopsy that had coldly dismembered the girl's adolescent body.

Five months later, a phone call came in to Carbone in the squad room.

"Detective," came the voice over the line, "this is the Wanted Desk. I am responding to the Wanted Card you put out on Jeffrey Sykes. He was arrested yesterday in Manhattan South for robbery two. He's presently being lodged at the Two-Five."

Elated, Dave immediately called Eddie Feit. A little before nine that evening, Dave and Feit interviewed Jeffrey Sykes in the 25th Precinct squad room. Feit read the Miranda warning to Sykes, who waived his rights and signed the rights card. Then he made a statement, in which he admitted the gun that had killed Racquel Cannon was his.

At one-thirty the next morning, a lineup was held in the Seven-Five. Melson McNeal stood behind the one-way glass mirror and after a few seconds announced, "Number three is Jeffrey Sykes. That's the person who gave the gun to Jamel and told us to rob the girl.''

It was a hit. Dave was delighted. He had finally nailed Sykes! But his triumph was ephemeral. To his extreme disgust, when he called the ADA who had ordered the release of Melson McNeal, she told him they needed somebody to corroborate the witness independently, that a perp could not be identified by another perp. The DA's office would not take the word of one perp over another.

"You wouldn't authorize McNeal's arrest when we had him in custody," Dave sputtered incredulously, "so what does that make him? A witness. And a witness *can* identify a perp."

The ADA was adamant. "I will not authorize the arrest of Jeffrey Sykes."

Dave exploded. "You gotta be fucking kidding me! I'll do what I gotta fucking do anyway." Dave slammed down the phone, one of the few times on the job that he had ever really lost it. "Let's lock him up anyhow," he said to Feit.

Later in the morning, Dave heard from a cop he knew. She had been processing an arrest at the Brooklyn Early Case Assessment Bureau and had happened to see a memo on the ECAB supervisor's desk that read: "Do not process any arrest by Detective Carbone under any circumstances." It was signed by the ADA who had refused to authorize the arrest of Jeffrey Sykes.

That afternoon Dave called the ADA. "Why did you write the memo?" he demanded.

"What memo?"

"You sent a memo down to ECAB not to authorize my arrest of Jeffrey Sykes. Why did you do that?"

She paused a moment, then said calmly, "Because I know you, Carbone."

Dave and the ADA had become acquainted when Jamel Strong was arrested; she had been the prosecutor. Dave's reputation in the DA's office had preceded him. ADAs had to authorize a felony arrest before a suspect was incarcerated, but Dave sometimes put perps in the system without calling the DA's office for approval. As she had worked with him, this ADA had found Dave a bit ornery. She had several times had occasion to ask him to come to her office to discuss the case, but if he had been too busy with other investigations, he had put her off. He did things too much according to his own convenience, she felt.

Dave thought Sykes should have been arrested, but he also understood how the DA's office saw it. The DA looks at a case in terms of its potential to be prosecuted. It didn't matter whether a detective thought someone had committed a crime, or whether some of the evidence showed that he probably had committed it. If the DA thought the evidence was not good enough to prosecute the individual and obtain a conviction, or if the suspect refused to cop a guilty plea before going to trial, the DA wouldn't go with it. The detective would be required to obtain more evidence—and in the meantime, to release the suspect.

Still, it was difficult enough to arrest criminal suspects even without opposition from the DA's office, Dave thought, especially when there weren't many witnesses. Sometimes there were none, or the witness was a crackhead prostitute with a long arrest record herself. You grabbed the murderer and brought him in, only to have the ADA tell you there would be no arrest authorization. You knew your collar had done it, but just because your witness wasn't upstanding enough in the eyes of the ADA, the suspect went scot-free. But now the suspect knew you knew he had done the murder, and he was free to go anywhere he pleased. In the meantime, your witness wouldn't testify anymore because she had already put her life on the line only to see the suspect released. The family of the victim was upset, and you were back to ground zero. It all put the detective in a bad predicament.

When Dave turned Jeffrey Sykes back over to officers in the Two-Five for the robbery charge on which he had been locked up, he walked out of the precinct, and that was the last he saw of Sykes. The man who had proffered the murder weapon and told young Jamel to steal the earrings was never charged in connection with the murder of Racquel Cannon.

It was quiet in the squad room on that frigid morning of December 20, 1989, the detectives buried in case folders or murmuring into telephones, slightly fatigued from their turnaround. Only seven hours separated the transition from their last night tour to their first day tour—seven hours, that is, assuming no late jobs came in or they didn't go out for a nightcap. Seven hours to go home, get to bed, sleep, awake, wash, dress, eat, fight traffic, and make it back in again. Some detectives made the journey home, while others slept in the bunkroom at a far corner of the squad room or found soft places nearby to stay the night.

Mike Redmond looked over at Dave, who was doing the morning red-lining. He debated whether he should say something to him. Although still relatively new in the squad, Dave was already stretching the detective dress protocol. The top button of his expensive shirt was open; his Italian silk tie was draped about his neck, both ends hanging loosely on his chest. His sleeves were rolled up with precision. At the back of his neck rested a budding ponytail, drawn back carefully from his expertly coiffed head. A diamond earring sparkled from his left lobe, and masses of solid gold jewelry adorned his neck and fingers. A study in flashy elegance, but not quite the image he had posted his first day.

Dave's wife, Luci, had also noticed the drastic change in her husband's sartorial habits. Whereas clothes previously had been almost inconsequential to him, ever since becoming a detective Dave had taken conspicuous pride in his appearance. He demanded his suits fit impeccably, be fashionable in style and material, and be neatly pressed and spotless. Accessories had to match perfectly, and his hair had to be sculpted to perfection. Dave's burgeoning interest in gold jewelry further surprised her. But all this pride and meticulousness, she figured, was just part of being a detective.

Such transformations weren't that unusual, Redmond reflected. It's just that the incubation period was normally longer. From the beginning, Carbone had struck Redmond as a bit of a maverick—his extensive wardrobe of fancy cowboy boots was a statement of sorts—but he was a hard worker and a damn good one at that. In his brief tenure he had solved seven of ten homicides: Billy Curtis, M/B/32, shot twice in the chest; Raymond Rios, M/H/34, shot multiple times; Glenn Rodriguez, M/H/24, shot multiple times; Yvonne Harris, F/B/34, stabbed multiple times; Edward Scott, M/B/55, hit on the head with a bat; Racquel Cannon, F/B/13, shot in the chest; David Morrison, M/B/22, shot in the neck. But no matter how effective he was, a detective had to beware of how much he flouted the unwritten rules of style. For now, Redmond decided, he would keep quiet.

The bright afternoon sun did little to warm the freezing air that had pitilessly descended on New York. It was ten degrees outside, but the windchill made it feel like five below zero.

"Can't you finish the work today?" asked the man, a bit of anxiety in his voice.

"No can do," said the mechanic dressed in greasy green overalls.

The two men were standing next to a car parked behind a Dumpster overflowing with garbage in the rear lot of the Pit Stop, a grease and lube joint whose front was on Pennsylvania Avenue in East New York. The hood of the car, an '87 Chrysler Conquest, was open.

"But I have to leave for Massachusetts later today. Can't you do it?"

"Sorry, bud," said the mechanic, walking back into the shop.

The driver pursed his lips in frustration, closed the hood, and got back into the car. He turned to the passenger sitting next to him and began to speak.

A minute later, two armed men approached the car, coming up on opposite sides. The man on the driver's side tried the door and swung it open, thrusting in an automatic. The gunman who crept up on the passenger found the door on his side locked, so he had to step back and take aim at the window.

As the occupants of the car realized what was happening, their eyes widened, and they became paralyzed with fear. But it was fleeting. A series of loud, hollow cracks erupted as the two men were sprayed with bullets. The reverberating sound broke the stillness of the cold and previously tranquil afternoon.

"Five John. Ten thirty-four. Male shot in the rear of 832 Pennsylvania Avenue crossing Linden Boulevard and Stanley Avenue."

Police Officer Dennis Lane and his partner, Robert Yeager, were about a mile away in their radio car when the call came over.

"Ten-four, Central," Lane said.

They put on their lights and siren and sped to the location. A crowd of people had gathered around the car. "Over here, over here!'' people shouted as the officers pulled up. Lane and Yeager ran up to the car. "Oh, shit!" Lane said, as he pulled his radio out of his back pocket.

"Five John eighty-four Central." The officer had to speak loudly to make himself heard over the yelling and commotion. "Have two males shot in a car at the location. Going DOA. Rush a bus to the scene. Have the patrol supervisor and the squad respond."

The transmission was listened to attentively in the squad room.

Dave picked up a portable. "Five squad Central, be advised we read and are on our way." The homicide was his. As he radioed Central, everyone in the room was on his way to get his coat and sign out in the logbook. The detectives moved quickly, serious expressions on their faces. Whenever a job came in, the mood in the office changed quickly. A minute later the squad room was empty.

Police Officer Janet Barry was one of the Seven-Five's SP9 operators, manning the precinct's Finest and Sprint computers. The Finest machine was used to run checks on motor vehicles, warrants, stolen guns, and missing persons and was linked to police lines around the country. The Sprint computer was essentially the station house's lifeline to the city. Every call made to 911 was input to the system, and the SP9 operator could in seconds pull up information on any job in any precinct in the city. By punching in a location, the operator could obtain all jobs around it within the past twenty-four hours.

On the way to the parking lot in the rear of the station house, Dave and Al Smith stopped in front of the twenty-foot desk where Barry sat. She handed Smitty a Finest computer printout, which he folded and carried out to the car with him.

"Says here there were two males shot, not one," said Smitty, who perused the printout as Dave squeezed out of a spot and navigated the unmarked car through the parking lot glutted with RMPs. "The caller was a male." The Finest computer printout gave the basic facts of a job. As information came in, the Central operator fed it into a computer. Because Central was so busy, its operators might not have time to give additional information over the air.

"That's an industrial area, isn't it?" Dave asked.

"Yeah," said Smitty. "I wonder what the hell could be down there. It's not a drug spot or a residential area. It's a beat where prosses walk."

"A setup robbery?"

"Doesn't sound like it to me."

Six blue-and-white radio cars and two EMS ambulances had converged on the back lot of the Pit Stop. People standing behind the police line were pushing forward to get a look, and the cops had their arms stretched out trying to hold them back. Two other unmarked cars pulled up at the same time as Dave and Smitty's.

The thrill of uniformed cops parting like the Red Sea to let the detectives through hadn't yet worn off on Dave. A cluster of blue opened up as he moved into the cordoned-off area. "Who's the first officer?" he asked a cop standing nearby.

"Yo, Lane," the officer shouted.

A mustachioed young cop, who was standing next to an RMP scratching out a Sixty-one, looked up, nodded, and walked over.

"Whaddya got?" Dave inquired.

"It came over as a ten thirty-four, male shot," Dennis Lane said. "We responded, and when we pulled up there was a big crowd around the car. We looked in and saw two guys shot."

Lane added that some people who hadn't witnessed the shooting had reported seeing two men run to a small red car on Sheffield Avenue and drive south. "I radioed it to Central," he said. Dave nodded his thanks.

With the preliminaries out of the way, Dave went over to the car, a two-door silver Conquest, and stood between the open car door and the driver's seat, peering at the first body, which was slumped forward between the steering column and the console. Blood was still trickling from the head, and there was a pool of thick, viscous crimson on the floor below. Dave stared at the man, who was probably in his early twenties, for a minute or two, moving in close but being careful not to touch him. He was trying to detect the presence of powder around the gunshot wounds, which would mean the man had been shot at close range. Then he walked around the front of the car to the other side and stood outside the closed door, looking through the fist-sized hole in the tinted window. The body of a teenager reclined in the passenger's seat, head tilted back to the right, eyes slightly open, spidery streaks of red dripping down his green jacket and another puddle of blood on the floor directly in back of him.

"Can you believe it?" said Smitty, who had come up behind Dave. "A double in broad daylight."

"Brazen perps," Dave answered casually. His own composure bothered him a little.

A few of the squad's "floaters"—Jerry Rupprecht, Richie Brew, and Hank Mathes, detectives who rotated weeks of steady days and nights and assisted in old and new homicide investigations—came over to look in the car. After making brief but thorough observations, careful not to step on any ballistics that might be on the ground, they fanned out for the canvass.

With notebooks and pens in hand, the detectives started their search for anyone who might have heard or seen something. Dave continued to examine the car and the concrete just around it as Smitty clicked away with a Polaroid. A few minutes later, Smitty looked over to Dave. "Fuckin' freezing," he said. "I hope Crime Scene gets here soon." It was the middle of a bitter-cold spell, and it was difficult to concentrate on anything but keeping warm.

Sergeant George Hohenstein stood nearby and called the detective duty captain on a portable phone, standard procedure when anything heavy went down. The duty captain passed word up the chain of command so all were informed. With a double murder, the media would be asking a lot of questions.

"Balls!" Dave said under his breath, launching a small steamy cloud into the cold air. He had been a white shield in the Seven-Five PDU for nine months now and had caught or assisted in fifty homicides—already more than many detectives see in a lifetime—and it still never ceased to amaze him that people killed in the open in the middle of the day.

Lane came over with another bit of information. "EMS pronounced them both dead at thirteen-nineteen hours," he said. Dave nodded grimly.

Dave retrieved the radio from Smitty. "Central, get an ETA for Crime Scene." He was anxious to have a closer examination of the corpses and go through their wallets, but no one was allowed to do this until Crime Scene had arrived and processed the scene. Dave stood by, and thirty seconds later the operator informed him Crime Scene had already left, but traffic was heavy and the estimated time of arrival was uncertain.

Mike Redmond pulled Dave aside. "Dave," he said, "this looks like a hit, a planned assassination, you know? Whoever did it came just to kill these guys."

"You think so?" It was a plausible theory, but Dave thought it could also have been an attempted robbery, and he didn't want to rule anything out yet.

He surveyed the scene. Some of the other detectives were talking to the people behind the police line, the others were on the street. As the detectives spoke, their eyes shifted around constantly, with one ear on the conversation, the other on everything else around them.

Dave gestured to Smitty with his head, and the two strolled over

unobtrusively to the people behind the police line. It was good practice for detectives at the crime scene to back into the crowd and listen
to people talking. As they stood there, they heard some guys call out to
them, "Hey, DT," or "Look, it's Crocker and Tubbs," the latter a reference to the salt-and-pepper detective partners of the *Miami Vice* television show. Smitty laughed. He was used to this sort of thing. But he
also knew that although cops didn't get treated with much respect in
the area, the detectives had an unsettling effect on the bad guys.

A few minutes later, leaving Smitty to see what he could pick up
from the crowd, Dave moved on to the garage, speaking to a mechanic.
The mechanic knew the driver as Shaun; the man had occasionally
brought his car in for repair. Shaun had come in earlier that day and
had been very anxious for him to do some work on his car on the spot,
and he had done a few things, but he had had to get back to some
other work he was in the middle of. "I told him to come back tomorrow," said the mechanic. "He said he couldn't, he was leaving today to
go to Massachusetts."

"Did you see who did it?"

"No. I didn't."

Dave opened the door of the garage, and a burst of cold air hit his
face; the wind resisted him as he returned to the car. Leaning over the
driver's side of the windshield, he jotted down the car's Vehicle Identification Number under the registration stickers on the dashboard and
pulled out his radio.

"Five squad, Central."

"Go ahead, Five squad."

"Give me the registered owner of Massachusetts license plate seven
four four Thomas Nancy Adam. Also, run VIN number John John
three Charlie Charlie five four Nancy four Henry Zebra zero two two
two seven."

Trailed by Smitty, Sergeant Race came over to the car, a grin on his
face. "They waited eleven minutes for a ten-minute lube job and got
themselves greased instead," he lamented.

Smitty let out his patented guffaw.

Some of the other detectives were returning now from their canvasses.

"Whaddya have?" Dave asked.

"The usual," Richie Brew answered. "Nothing. They heard shots,
they ran outside, and that was it."

Hank Mathes joined in. "One guy said, 'Witnesses get killed
around here. I didn't see nothing.'"

Dave frowned. The reluctance of people to speak to detectives at crime scenes was virtually written in stone. The detectives understood this, but they also had faith in the people of the community, faith in them as honest, caring people who wanted the violence stopped and who would come through for them in the only way they could without fear of reprisals. That was why detectives gave out cards at scenes in bulk quantities. The calls, usually anonymous, would come in later.

"We'll wait and let the street do the talking," Dave said.

A minute later a voice sounded from Dave's radio.

"Five squad," came a woman's voice.

"Five squad, Central," Dave answered.

"The car is registered to an Oliver Brown of 8 Fessenden Street, Mattapan, Massachusetts." The VIN was for the same person at the same address.

Dave sighed with relief; he'd been hoping the two numbers would come back to the same registered owner. If they didn't, he would have to investigate why the plate and VIN didn't match. But here was Central giving the name Oliver Brown, and the mechanic had said the name of the driver was Shaun. Had Oliver Brown lent his car to Shaun? Could Shaun be an alias for Oliver Brown, or vice versa? Could the other victim be Oliver Brown?

Where the hell was Crime Scene?

Just then, Detective Jerry Rupprecht came over to Dave. With twenty-four years on the job, he was the senior member of the squad. Rupprecht had once been a decoy cop, dressing as a Hasidic rabbi to attract muggers as backup units hovered around him incognito. Even though Rupprecht stood a towering six-five, he had been constantly attacked.

"Dave, can I talk to you a moment?"

Rupprecht led Dave to an area off to the side, where he leaned in closely and spoke in hushed tones.

"I found someone in the Pit Stop who said he saw what happened, but he was really scared to talk about it. I managed to get him to spill it. He said he was standing at the rear of the garage when he saw two male blacks shooting into the car. One opened the door and fired straight at the driver. The other tried the passenger door and it was locked, so he shot through the window. Both were husky and over six feet. One was wearing brown pants and a red-and-blue-checkered jacket, the other was wearing a mud-colored jacket."

A cloud seemed to lift from Dave's mind, and a thought suddenly sprang to his awareness. The owner. Where was the owner of the shop? Returning inside the garage, he approached a group of workers and inquired.

"He went to pick up some parts," one said.

"When did he leave?"

"Just after the shooting." That struck Dave as peculiar, but for now he let it hang. Outside again, the wind howled and whistled and blew cans into scraping frenzies along the streets. The crowd began to thin out, and soon it would be quiet save for the winter wind.

The wait promised to be protracted, what with Crime Scene's arrival to process the scene delayed. The canvass completed, the other detectives could return to the station house, check out some leads, knock out a few Fives. Dave stayed behind for Crime Scene, and Smitty and Sergeant Race waited with him.

A catching detective frequently played back a homicide in his mind, searching its recesses for some detail that hadn't registered at the time. Dave wanted the crime scene indelibly imprinted in his brain and decided to have another look inside the car. By now the bodies looked hard and stiff. It wasn't rigor mortis, because that didn't set in for about twelve hours. It was the temperature. Dave's attention was again drawn to the floor in the front. The puddles were now formed into frozen islets of red. Human liquid, coagulated solid, about an inch thick.

"Bloodsickles," he shouted suddenly to Smitty and Race, who were standing about twenty yards away. "Fuckin' bloodsickles."

"Hey," yelled Race, "it's too cold to wait outside. Let's go in the car and turn up the heat."

More than two hours after the call had come in for the shootings, a powder-blue station wagon marked "CSU" on both sides pulled up on Sheffield Avenue. Crime scene detectives Bonan and Rinaldi alighted. After a brief conversation with Dave, they got down to business. They photographed everything—the victims, the car, objects on the ground—exactly where it was, in its undisturbed state.

Next, the two crime scene detectives scoured the area for ballistics, making sketches showing where they recovered spent shells and rounds. The ballistics told a story. When detectives arrived at a crime scene after a murder, all they had was a body, bloodstains, and the ballistics. They needed to reconstruct exactly what had happened, and the ballistics helped them do that.

Bullet tracking showed approximately where the gunman had been standing and in which direction he had fired. Automatic weapons eject their shells, so recovering those shells could indicate where the shots had been fired from. Anyone who entered a crime scene had to be careful not to kick or touch any ballistics before the scene had been processed. The ballistics could also reveal the type of weapon used.

Ballistics also helped detectives verify or discredit the stories of witnesses and alleged perps. People sometimes spuriously claimed they had been witnesses to crimes, for reasons ranging from a desire to collect reward money to mental problems, and ballistics made it possible for the detectives to verify or discount some of the details of their descriptions of the event. Likewise, if someone confessed to a crime, the detective had to be sure the confession was valid. The confessor's story had to match the evidence.

After finishing with the area around the car, crime scene detectives Bonan and Rinaldi reached into the car, pulled the two bodies out, and laid them flat on the ground. As the remaining crowd gawked and murmured, the detectives opened the victims' jackets and pulled up their shirts, exposing their chests. The ME at the morgue would determine which of the holes in the heads and chests of the corpses were entrance wounds and which were exit wounds. But Bonan and Rinaldi examined the holes to help them account for all the ballistics. If fourteen shells were found at a crime scene, it was important to find fourteen rounds, or be able to account for them. Rounds might pass through a body or lodge in it. If someone had been shot in the left side, there should be a hole in the right side. If there was no hole, it meant the bullet was still in the body.

Bonan and Rinaldi ran their fingers along the victims' bodies; they separated strands of hair searching for holes in the head. In the passenger's corpse they counted two ins and outs in the head, one in and out in the chest, and one in and out in the right thigh. The driver had been hit once in the head. The bullet had entered the lower left back of his head and exited at the top on the right side. With a surplus of shells, it appeared some of the rounds were embedded inside the car. If so, these would be recovered after the car was impounded and stripped. The bullets appeared to have come from a 9mm.

Dave watched the crime scene detectives, noting where they recovered the ballistics and their count of the ins and outs. He observed with distaste the lewd fascination of the crowd with this grisly tableau. Yeah, you wanta see a show, we'll give you a show, he thought. Why would anybody want to stand outside in this freezing weather to see dead bodies? I'm getting paid for it; what's your excuse?

After Bonan and Rinaldi finished with the bodies, Dennis Lane, the first officer, who had been given all the evidence recovered and marked by the crime scene detectives, removed all the possessions on the corpses—wallets, change, keys, a small telephone book, and more—and put them in a bag for vouchering with the rest of the evidence back at the precinct. Finally, the processing was complete, and it was time to go. Two EMS workers put the bodies in bags and loaded them in an ambulance for delivery to the morgue.

With the sun starting to set and the air turning even more frigid, everyone was glad to get the hell out of there.

As he drove back to the precinct, Dave mulled over the information he had acquired, eliminating some possibilities, selecting the direction he wanted to take the investigation. Of course, this early he might be heading down the wrong track, but he had to start somewhere. The trap, Dave knew, was to have tunnel vision, thinking the chosen path was the correct one—only to discover down the road, when the leads were no longer hot, a left turn should have been taken early on. The detective made educated guesses based on his expertise, but he tried not to get locked into his initial reaction.

Detective Richie Brew had told Dave about a body that had been found one Super Bowl Sunday on Louisiana Avenue between Flatlands and Stanley, an abandoned factory area that was a dumping ground for murder victims. The victim's head had been split open, and he seemed to have been a homeless person. It was an apparent homicide.

But a toxicology analysis found the victim's alcohol content to be 0.29—well above the 0.1 intoxication indicator. After the victim was identified the next day through his fingerprints, Brew had gone to his family, who led him to the victim's girlfriend, with whom he had been living. Brew found out that the victim had become drunk and had fallen down a flight of steps, cracked his head, and died. The neighbors hadn't wanted the police harassing them, so they had packed the body in a car and dumped it at the location where it was found. "I thought it was a murder," Brew told Dave, "but he died from a fall. You make presumptions, but they're not always right. What you think you see might not actually be what happened."

With an open mind, Dave began to make initial assumptions about his double homicide. He ruled out a robbery; the victims still had their wallets, and there was no sign of a struggle. A random shooting? Given that there had been two murders and each victim had been shot several times, that was hardly likely.

"Mike Redmond was right," Dave announced suddenly to Race and Smitty. "It was a hit. There was no exchange of words. The victims weren't shot once or twice—the perps made sure they were dead. It was definitely an out-and-out execution, an assassination."

So why would two young men be assassinated? He suspected it was drugs, given the area and the victims' ages. Drug hits were usually for revenge, but it could be something else.

Dave considered what else he had. There was a description of possible perps, but it was so general it could fit many people in the area. There was a witness, but he was terrified, and it was questionable whether he would testify if there was a trial down the pike. And there was the all-points bulletin on the car, which had turned up nothing yet.

He had a few scant pieces, not much to go on, but more than he often got. Now it was time to try to come up with more pieces of this puzzle and fit it together.

Dave started to hum a jaunty tune under his breath. He was enjoying himself.

11

An early-winter darkness had settled in by the time Dave, Smitty, and Race returned to the office. The other members of Team One were at their desks banging out Fives in what would probably turn into heavy overtime, while the night team was commencing its tour.

As Dave sat down at his desk, he glanced over, as he did frequently during a tour, at the sign pinned on the far wall. The conversation piece of the squad room, the thing that always seemed to draw one's attention, it consisted of a large, boldface headline clipped from a newspaper that read "Death's Door," and two square placards underneath those words, each bearing a digit. Together, the digits represented the number of murders to date that year in the precinct.

Someone had already recorded the double homicide that Team One had just been out on, Dave noticed. The digits 9 and 0 blared from the wall. Unbelievable, Dave thought, that in this small quadrant of Brooklyn ninety lives would have been taken so far this year.

After poring over all the personal belongings removed from the victims at the crime scene and making photocopies of the little telephone book he thought belonged to Oliver Brown, Dave sat at his desk staring at the pages. There were several numbers listed; he picked up the phone and began running through the numbers. Each call went pretty much the same way.

"Hello, this is Detective David Carbone of the 75th Precinct. I'm calling to see if you know an Oliver Brown."

"Never heard of him."

"Well, do you know a guy who drives a gray Conquest with Massachusetts license plates? Maybe his name is Shaun."

"What's this about, detective?" The people seemed to get defensive at this point.

"You must know him, because he had your name in his phone book," Dave pointed out. "But maybe you know him by a different name. Anyway, he was shot today in East New York, and we're trying to notify his family. There was another person shot with him, and we don't know who he is either."

"I'm sorry. I can't help you."

"Listen, if you don't want to help me, would you take my number and forward it to the people who know him, who know his family, so they can call me?"

That's how the phone calls went.

Just before 8:00 P.M., two women walked into the squad room. The younger one was petite and had a magnificently sculpted face; she appeared to be in her early twenties. The other was twenty or thirty years older and had the same ebony complexion.

Cheryl Pough, the squad police aide, summoned Dave, who came over to greet them. He introduced himself and ushered the two women into the interview room.

The young one spoke up first. "My name is Monique Henry. I heard my husband may have been shot today in East New York." Dave detected annoyance in her voice.

"Is his name Oliver Brown?"

"No. I don't know any Oliver Brown."

Dave went back to his desk to retrieve some documents and pictures.

"Is this your husband's car?" He showed her a picture of the outside of the car in which the two men had been killed earlier.

The woman looked down for just a second. "Yes, that's his car, all right. How is he?"

"I just want to get some information first. You don't know him by any other name?"

"I said no!" she spat.

Holy shit! There's definitely an attitude problem here, Dave thought. Perhaps she was just defensive about cops, as many people in the area were. But after a long afternoon in the cold, fatigue was starting to set in, and he was in no mood to play games.

"Well, his name appears to be Oliver Brown." Dave set down on a desk a Massachusetts driver's license under the name of Oliver Brown with a photograph on it. "Is this your husband?"

The woman took a quick glance and registered a faint expression of surprise. "Yes. But his name's not Oliver Brown. It's Shaun Henry." She looked at Dave accusingly. "What's this all about, anyway?"

"We're not sure. There were two people shot in a car today, and only one had identification on him, and that said Oliver Brown. We want to make sure what we tell you is correct. We don't want to tell you something about your husband if he wasn't your husband."

Smitty came into the interview room and joined the circle. "What does your husband do for a living?" he asked.

"He's a carpet layer."

"Was he hanging around with anyone today?"

"I don't know. He left early this morning." She glanced briefly at the older woman.

"Did he say he was going to meet anyone today?"

"No. He just said he was going to Massachusetts."

"Why was he going?"

"I don't know."

"You mean he just comes and goes without telling you what he's doing? That's pretty nice of you. So where does your husband live?"

"I want to know what this is about!" the woman demanded. The older woman, who had been looking increasingly distressed, seemed on the verge of tears, but remained silent.

"Where does your husband live?"

"I'm not telling you."

This was the last straw for Dave. He was just doing his job, and he was being as cordial as he could. He was trying to get a few answers so he could solve this brutal double homicide. And what was he getting in return? An attitude, that's what. He fished through his hand for a picture of the victims seated in the front seat, a nice graphic picture showing blood coming from the holes in their heads.

"Is this your husband?" he asked, slapping down on the desk a 2×3 Polaroid. Monique Henry slowly turned her head and lowered her eyes to the picture of the two dead men. She focused first on the one on the right, the body reclined on the car seat and dressed in a silver jacket and a Chicago Bulls cap, a bullet hole in the right cheek, the teeth blown out. As her eyes moved to the other victim, they widened in recognition. The man was wearing a gold shirt with brown and blue stripes over an undershirt. He was a sight: eyes closed, lips parted, streaks of blood across his cheek, a thick band of blood across his forehead.

The woman seemed about to faint, but she composed herself.

"That's my husband," she said softly.

"Why don't you have a seat?" Dave said, compassionate for the first time.

Smitty rolled over two chairs, and the two women sat down. After a moment of grim silence, the younger woman, deeply shaken, asked what had happened.

Dave gave her the details of the murders. The killers were either after her husband or the other victim, he told her, or maybe even both. "We need to know if your husband was into anything. Drugs? Gambling? Loan-sharking?"

"No, none of those things."

"Did he have any arguments lately?"

"I'm not aware of any."

"Do you know of anyone who might want to kill him?"

Dave's questions were all met with the same response: a terse, blunt negative.

During the questioning, Dave stuck his head out of the interview room and looked over to Mike Redmond. "Hey, Mike," he said, "do a round robin on Shaun Henry."

Redmond dialed BCI and requested a name check on Shaun Henry. While he waited for BCI to get back to him, Redmond called NITRO. Narcotics said it would check on Henry and get back to him. Next, Redmond dialed the SP9 operator downstairs, who pulled up Henry's name on the computer. There were no outstanding warrants on Henry, and he had had no New York State driver's license.

A minute later, BCI called. "Shaun Henry had five priors," the BCI operator reported. His NYSIIS number was 5603573Q. In his previous arrests he had given his name as Shawn, Shaun, and Shaun A. Most of Henry's previous arrests had been for narcotics, including criminal possession and criminal intent to sell.

Next, NITRO checked in with similar information. Redmond called Dave and Smitty over to his desk and apprised them of the data he had collected. The two then returned to Henry's wife.

"I asked you before if your husband was into anything," Dave said, "and you said no. But he was into drugs."

"No. He wasn't into drugs," she protested fiercely.

"Was he ever arrested?"

"I'm not sure." Her face took on a sullen expression. Either she's pulling a number on me or she was on Pluto whenever her husband got arrested, Dave thought.

"Mrs. Henry," Dave said, raising his voice a notch, "we just ran your husband's name, and it came up five times for drug possession and sale. And you're telling me you don't know nothing?"

The woman stood up, her face livid, shouting now in the squad room. "What are you trying to say?" she screamed. "What are you trying to say?" Glaring wildly at the detectives, she grabbed her mother and walked out.

Detective Sergeant George Hohenstein emerged from the bosses' room. "Did she give you anything?" he asked.

"Yeah," said Dave, staring after the women in disgust. "She gave me a jerk job." He turned back to Hohenstein. "I think she'll come across in a few days, but she didn't want to tell me anything now. She didn't know who the passenger was."

There was just one more thing to do before calling it a day, and that was to prepare the Unusual—the Unusual Occurrence Report. The brass needed to have these reports on their desks in the morning, and tired as he was, Dave forced himself to slip the form into the typewriter and peck away.

A little after two the next afternoon, Dave and Smitty drove to the Kings County morgue to pick up the fingerprints of the two homicide victims. They waited impatiently through the morning; prints of murder victims weren't taken until after the autopsy, as fingerprinting could ruin possible evidence on the hands. When they finally got the prints, they headed to Manhattan and police headquarters.

"I'm looking to get an ID on these fingerprint cards," Dave said, holding up the two 8×8 cards to a young woman at the DOA Desk on the sixth floor. She called over a senior fingerprint technician, who took the cards from Dave. Dave explained that he had a tentative name and NYSIIS number on the first victim, but nothing on the other as yet. If the victims had any priors in the city, the tech would be able to determine who they were.

Sitting at a desk, the tech placed a magnifying glass over the right thumbprint and began his analysis. Five minutes later he got up, disappeared into the rows of filing cabinets, and came back with a NYSIIS number.

"Here's one," he said. "I'm going to go back and do the other set of prints now."

As the tech disappeared again, Dave looked at the card and saw Shaun Henry's name written across the top row. Five minutes later the tech returned.

"Sorry, Carbone," he said. "This guy's a John Doe. No hit on the prints. He was never arrested in New York City."

Dave thanked the technician, then gave Shaun Henry's NYSIIS number to a BCI clerk, and he and Smitty waited for a printout of Henry's priors. "Damn," he said to Smitty. "I'm going to have to get that woman to try to find out who her husband was with when the two of them got blasted. She's gotta know him. She's gotta know him by something."

Back at the precinct in the evening, Dave called Monique Henry. When she picked up the phone, Dave kept his voice calm and sincere.

"Have you changed your mind about talking?" Dave began. "Would you want to elaborate on any of your husband's arrests? Want to tell us who was in the car with him?"

"No," said Monique icily, "and I'm not in the mood to talk."

"Well," said Dave, struggling to keep his voice pleasant, "if you need anything, please call me." He replaced the phone gently in its cradle, then let out an obscene expletive. He was infuriated by her persistent cold attitude.

Glancing around the squad room, Dave observed most of the detectives hunting and pecking with their quick fingers. Too damn much paperwork, he said to himself peevishly, as he inserted a long pink form with a carbon set into the typewriter and began typing a Five.

Returning well after midnight from a fruitless canvass of local prostitutes, who were often tuned in to the area's grapevine, Dave and Smitty found the station house almost deserted. A lonely holdout, Sergeant Hohenstein emerged from his office. "We had two more," he announced. "Idris Britton, a male black, sixteen years old, was shot multiple times at the corner of Blake and Alabama avenues, and Gladys Copeland, eighty years old, was stabbed inside 559 Jerome Street."

"Four homicides in one day," said Smitty, sighing heavily. "Not quite a record, but up there."

Dave shook his head. Half of those were his.

When a detective caught a homicide, he had four days to work it before he went back into the rotating order. Returning to his double homicide investigation the next day, Dave had this in mind, thinking also that the more time passed, the colder the case got. So, with few leads to go on, he was delighted to receive an anonymous phone call in the office that morning, three days before Christmas, that was to shed some light.

"The guys that were killed at the Pit Stop, they were in a drug gang from Flatlands Avenue," a ragged male voice grunted.

Dave asked the caller his name, but the caller didn't want to give it. So he asked if the caller knew the victims.

"Yeah. One was a guy named Shaun. I knew the other guy as Frantic."

Frantic, Dave thought. How the hell did a guy get a name like Frantic? The caller was probably giving accurate information, however, since he had Shaun's name right.

"What can you tell me about Frantic?"

"I think his last name is Dudley and he's from Roxbury, Massachusetts," said the caller.

Dave felt a sudden rush of euphoria. Another tie to Massachusetts. "How old was he?"

"Fifteen, sixteen."

The caller didn't know anything more but promised to call back if he found anything further. Hanging up the phone, the rookie detective sighed with relief. There was satisfaction in receiving a new solid lead. Perhaps an even stronger gratification was the call's reinforcement of Dave's faith in the people of the community. Despite the apathies and fears that were all too apparent on canvasses, more often than not someone in the precinct came through for the police.

Dave immediately called the Roxbury Police Department and was connected to Kathy Johnston, a detective sergeant in Intelligence.

"Would you run the name Dudley from Roxbury?" Dave asked.

Johnston fed the name into a computer. Seconds later, data appeared on her screen. "A Robert Dudley was arrested on July 14, 1989, for cocaine sale to an undercover," Johnston reported. She gave him Dudley's DOB.

A drug-related collar. That would make sense. Just as he had thought all along. This case smelled of drugs.

"Thanks," Dave said. "I appreciate that."

"Wait, there's more," Johnston announced. "An address in Brooklyn."

The Flatbush home was a single-family brick house on a quiet residential street, not the kind readily found in violent East New York. A middle-aged woman came to the door and Dave flashed his shield, Smitty standing next to him. The woman, a look of consternation on her face, invited the two detectives in.

"Sit down, please," Dave said, "because I'm not sure if I have the right house."

"It sounds bad," the woman answered, her voice strained.

"It is. Do you know anybody by the name of Robert Dudley?"

The woman breathed heavily, and her face compressed momentarily in anguish. "Oh, my God," she said. "What did he do now?"

"Well, do you know him?"

"Yes, he's my nephew. He's been staying with me for a few years. I haven't seen him in several days—he just takes off from time to time. What did he do?"

"I've got bad news for you. He was shot and killed in East New York the other day."

The woman winced in anguish, and the detectives said nothing. Then Dave plunked a photo down on the table. "Is this Robert Dudley?"

Surprisingly, the woman did not fall apart on them. "I knew this was coming," she said with resignation, nodding yes. "He's been arrested many times for drugs, although not in New York. And he hangs out with drug gangs. I tried telling him, but . . ." The woman's voice trailed off. "He was uncontrollable."

"Well, you don't have to worry about that anymore," Dave answered reflexively, then was instantly chagrined at his poor choice of words.

At last the second victim of the double had been positively identified, and the case had a small infusion of fresh air. Back in the squad room, Dave notified Missing Persons. The unit wouldn't have to continue its search on the unidentified DOA, and Robert Dudley wouldn't be laid to eternal rest as a John Doe in Potter's Field.

The next day Dave called the Roxbury PD again to augment the information he had on Dudley's arrest and to see if his other double victim was connected to drug spots up there. He gave the names of Shaun Henry and Oliver Brown—who were one and the same—and the response came back negative. This person, in his real name or alias, had never been arrested there, and hence no connection could definitely be made.

Sitting at his desk, Dave analyzed what he had learned since the day of the double homicide. The victims' names were Shaun Henry and Robert Dudley. The ME had reported both had died of multiple gunshot wounds to the head and chest. Both victims had previous arrests for drugs, and their deaths were the apparent result of some sort of execution. Two male blacks had been seen fleeing from the scene, and an APB on their car had gone for naught. The wife of one of the victims, Monique Henry, had so far refused to talk to him. And that was it. The canvasses had basically turned up little. If Dave could ever produce the perps, there was a witness, although the man was old and frightened.

Dave reclined in his chair and put his feet up on the desk as he reflected on the crime scene: the two young men sprayed with bullets, the blood oozing out of their bodies, the layer of thick red frozen on the car floor. He had been in the squad for several months now, he thought, and had met many people, cultivated many contacts. It was time to reach out.

Cheryl Pough, the squad police aide, stood at the front of the lounge. It was a small room, taken up mostly by a long table that people always had to squeeze past to get a seat when the chairs closest to the door were occupied. Near the door was a refrigerator, a microwave, and a coffee urn, next to which stood a garbage can that always seemed to be heaped to the brim. A TV mounted high on the far corner wall played quietly, and on the wall across from it was a bulletin board on which were posted restaurant menus and notices of retirement parties, DEA meetings, and things for sale.

The room was full of detectives hunkered over their meals. Crumpled aluminum foil and soda cans and pizza boxes sat on the table; the men alternated wolfing down their food with talking or craning their necks to watch the TV. Dave was working on a platter of baked ziti.

"Someone here to see you," Cheryl said, smiling at Dave. Pough had a most pleasant manner about her; as the only woman in the squad room, she gave it a measure of warmth.

Dave furled his eyebrows and nodded in recognition. He had been expecting someone and was pleased the visitor was true to his word, not only showing up, but early to boot. Confidential informants were all too often undependable, like the Ice Man. The Ice Man was a young street hustler from the projects whom Dave had met a few months ago. He had been a witness to a crime but developed a sudden case of amnesia when the detectives came calling. Dave had taken Joe Hall's advice and run his name. Sure enough, the guy had a record. He was even on parole.

"Great," Joe had said. "Now, this is how you jerk him off." Hall proceeded to instruct Dave on the finessing of uncooperative witnesses. "You say, 'You do me a favor, and I'll do you a favor. You're out on parole on a drug charge, but you were at that drug location. That's four years in the hopper if I report it to your parole officer. But I'll make believe you weren't there if you tell me what I need to know.' Now, he doesn't know you can't arrest him for standing on a street corner, but he thinks you're doing him a favor, so he'll talk to you.

"You want to make sure he doesn't bullshit you or hold back information. So you tell him about all the collars he's taken. You say, 'Hey, didn't you get arrested last year with Felix? And six months ago with Scissors?'

"Now he's saying to himself, 'Holy shit, this motherfucker knows what he's talking about. I can't bullshit him.' He doesn't know you ran his raps and got half his life story. They try and act smart, but they're stupid. It's all a mind game and how well you're able to bullshit your way through it. That's what makes you a really good detective."

And that's how Dave got the Ice Man to become a CI. The two men developed a mutual trust and even a sort of friendship. The Ice Man thought he had a friend in law enforcement, and Dave had a valuable street source. He told the Ice Man he had been deputized, and the Ice Man got a big charge out of that. Now whenever the Ice Man heard something he thought could help, he called Dave. And when Dave needed something important, he reached out to the Ice Man.

Dave ushered the Ice Man into the interview room and offered him a choice of a bench or chair. He took the chair, Dave pulled over the bench, and the CI began to relay details of the gang to which Shaun Henry belonged.

Dealing crack and cocaine, the gang was known variably as either Poison or the Posse from Flatbush. It was headed by George Chang, a small-time felon who had previously served time for drug possession and sale. Chang, whose street name was Stretch, had two underbosses—someone with the nickname Tookey, and Charlie Brackett, who helped him run the organization and keep his men in line. Some twenty-five men worked for Chang, all attracted by the heady allure of working for a drug organization and the large sums to be made. The members, known mostly by their street names, included Kersha, Mikey, Orval, Plopa, Spike, Saacha, Squally, Tuff, Willey, Chubby, Caribbean, China, Skipper, Steel, Cash, Phil, Starsky, and Stumbles, whose real name was Shaun Henry.

Poison operated out of two spots in Queens and two in Brooklyn. The gang had been doing well until February or March 1987, when Chang had begun to stiff his workers. Shaun, Tuff, Starsky, and Edgar "the Horseman" McDonald, "cooks," runners, and packagers for Chang, decided to break away and form their own gang, making the Horseman the gang's leader. They were optimistic about their new venture and knew they could count on Caribbean, Phil, Willey, Skipper, and others to come with them.

Chang ostensibly gave his blessing to the new operation, but in September 1987 he shot Edgar seven times in the head and told the rest of Edgar's gang they could either come back to work for Chang or be killed themselves.

Edgar's gang had completely severed contact with Chang and the other Poison members, but the rival gang members were so frightened they were going to be executed that a few months later they started to fall apart as a gang themselves. There was no doubt in their minds that Chang would make good his threat.

In 1988, Shaun Henry decided he wanted to get out of the drug business altogether. No more gangs, no more dealing, even on a small scale. But before he could make his break, there was something he had to do: help his friends avenge Edgar's murder, killing Chang before he got to them. They set themselves to drawing up a plan.

First the gang members had to become legitimate entrepreneurs. They still had plenty of earnings from their drug activities. Tuff and some others opened a barbershop on Troy and Church. Shaun, a.k.a. Stumbles, went into the rug installation business.

As they were carving out a new life for themselves, their former leader was about to have a fatal encounter. In January 1989, while sitting in his Chevy Blazer in Flatbush, George Chang was shot several times. The police hadn't solved the case, and none of Chang's or Edgar's associates knew who had killed him—at least that's what the CI said.

As his informant spoke, Dave began to suspect that Shaun Henry had had a part in the killing. All the old gang members, the CI said, including Shaun, Starsky, and Phil, had attended Chang's funeral.

Soon after, Shaun got married and broke completely from his former crew. Occasionally he saw Starsky and Tuff, who were now selling crack in the Bronx, but for the most part he was settling into a new life with his bride. With the fear of reprisal by Chang removed and the excitement of new, legitimate ventures ahead of him, Shaun Henry felt he was getting a second lease on life.

Then came the double homicide. The CI said the other occupant of the car killed along with Shaun was Robert Dudley, who worked for Shaun, which Dave had already learned. Dave thanked the CI and walked him out of the squad room.

The next day Dave called DBQ, the Detective Borough Queens, to obtain information on the murder of Edgar McDonald. George Chang had purportedly placed McDonald's body in a car, which he had abandoned in the borough.

"Look in your Homicide Log," Dave said, "and see if somebody was found in a car with gunshot wounds to the head back in September of 1987."

A detective combed through the oversized ledger book to see who had been found that month who fit a description of the victim.

"We had a few killed around that time," said the detective, pausing as he read each entry down the page. "Oh, yeah. There was a guy found in a car that month who was shot multiple times in the head."

"Is that the only one?"

"That's the only one."

"What was the precinct?"

"The One-Oh-One."

"Read me what you got," Dave requested.

The detective pulled the case and read it, and Dave listened carefully to see if it matched what his CI had given him. It did. He wrote down the names of those who had been interviewed. Maybe some of the names would pop up later.

Dave thanked the Queens detective, hung up, and dialed the Six-Seven detective squad.

"In January 1989," Dave said to the detective who took his call, "was a guy named George Chang killed in your precinct?"

Dave held on while the detective went to look in the Homicide Log. A minute later he returned to the phone.

"A George Chang was killed on January 3, 1989, in front of 1488 New York Avenue. He was known on the streets as Stretch."

"Yeah, that's him," Dave said. He'd have to read the case folder. "I'll be over."

A few hours later, Dave was in the Six-Seven squad room perusing the DD Fives and other paperwork in the Chang homicide case folder. The case was unsolved. The names of dozens of suspects and witnesses had been noted, and Dave jotted each one down.

With all the names he had collected so far, the investigation promised to be much work. But Dave knew exactly how he was going to carry it out. He had the method firmly under his belt now.

"You know," Dave said to Smitty at One PP after they had received rap sheets from BCI and pictures from the Photo Unit, "first Edgar gets killed, then George, then Shaun Henry and Robert Dudley. There's got to be some sort of connection."

"If the same names keep popping," said Smitty, "then you're probably looking at the right players. It's probably all connected—you just have to put it together."

One of the names that continually popped was Charlie Brackett. Dave had a feeling about him. He remembered his CI giving that name as one of Chang's henchmen, and Brackett seemed to match the witness's description in the Shaun Henry–Robert Dudley murders of one of the men who had fired into the car and fled the scene. Dave read Brackett's raps and noticed he had outstanding warrants for drug and gun possession, parole violation, and other offenses. Could be him, he thought. Just might be.

Now all he had to do was prove it and come up with Charlie Brackett.

12

"Say, Carbone, I was wondering if I could borrow you for a while."

Dave was wading through the small pile of Fives that he and the other detectives had prepared on his double homicide, to see what had been typed up so far and what hadn't. There was Response to the Scene, Notification of Crime Scene, Interview of the First Officer, Interview of EMS, Canvass of the Area, Plates at the Scene, Interview with the Witness, and Response to KCH Morgue. Missing were a few more canvass Fives and a Reinterview with the Witness; they were in fact in the typewriters now. Dave rested the case folder on his desk and looked up. It was Jimmy Owens of Team Two.

"My team's shorthanded today, and I need someone to assist me on a call that just came in from Central about a baby not breathing. Housing Police responded, and EMS took the kid to the hospital."

Dave tilted his head down in thought. Although he was wrapped up in the investigation of his double, perhaps he might pick up a few things that could help him in his work. He was still new at the game and needed—welcomed—all the experience he could get.

"Yeah, I'd be happy to assist you, Jimmy."

Dave was glad also to have the opportunity to work with James Edward Patrick Owens, a highly decorated cop who not only had a reputation for being aggressive, street-smart, meticulous, and downright serious, but looked tough as all hell, which he indubitably was.

Owens wasn't tall, but what he lacked in height he more than made up for in raw physical power. He had a barrel chest and arms as thick and solid as timber logs. He was a second-degree black belt in Shotokan karate and had a commanding voice, but the thing that was most remarkable about him was his intensity. When he spoke, his nostrils flared, his jaws clamped down like a vise, and his eyes pierced you. He was said to have laser-beam eyes, because when he looked at you, he didn't just look at you, he cut right through you.

James Owens was the product of a life of confrontations and violence. When he was four, his mother had placed him in an orphanage, where a nun had later tried to drown him. The youth had yearned to tell his mother but kept quiet out of fear that the nun was testing his ability to maintain secrecy. Later, in the tough Red Hook section of Brooklyn, an area known for gangs and mobsters, he constantly had to defend himself from the omnipresent human vultures.

In the Vietnam War, Owens had served in the Long Range Reconnaissance Patrol, a highly specialized unit that scouted out enemy positions for advancing military divisions. It was a highly dangerous assignment, in which he was introduced to one of the more unpleasant tasks of combat: killing. He killed so often that he actually lost track of how many enemy soldiers he had cut down. But one memory always remained fresh in his mind. He had been the point man in a three-man mission to detect booby traps and enemy forces hiding in ambush. Owens and the two others had moved quietly through the brush until they came upon a dry gully, about twenty-five feet across and fifteen feet deep. On the other side were four black-pajamaed Vietcong soldiers, who were cooking. The three Americans crept up on the VC so quietly that their presence wasn't detected until they were just about on top of them. Three VC bolted in shock, but one picked up his rifle. Owens and the compass man opened fire on him. The image of the man gazing at them in horror as he was being riddled with bullets had always haunted Owens.

"We got a notification of a possible child abuse," Owens drawled. Whenever Owens was angry, he accentuated his words. "The child's over at Brookdale."

Owens and Dave drove to the hospital right away. In the emergency room, the baby was sprawled on a gurney. They looked down at her and were sickened by the sight. She lay naked and motionless, her face and abdomen battered blue.

"She's dead," a doctor said, the palms of his hands stretched out in front of him.

The two detectives had already surmised that. They also presumed that the baby had been dead by the time EMS got to her, although the mother probably hadn't been told this. EMS tended to let doctors or cops inform parents of these things because of their often uncontrollable reaction. Sometimes at DOA scenes, EMS would put on a show, ostensibly making every effort to save the person's life when, in fact, it was already too late.

"Her name was Sasha Long," the doctor continued. "Thirteen months old." The detectives remained transfixed, staring at the girl.

"It's very evident," Owens finally said, his face resembling a clenched fist now, "that somebody's going to jail."

Dave thought of his own young daughter and wondered how anyone could be so heartless. He and his wife were unable to have any more children, and the thought struck him like a knife as he stared at the dead baby.

The doctor gently rolled the girl's little body over so the detectives could see her additional injuries. Mounds of wine-purple flesh, some dime-sized, others massive puffs, littered her back. Along the tender line from the anus to the vagina the skin was perforated and covered with cakes of dried blood. It was appalling to see such severe damage on this tiny little body, and to imagine the suffering the child must have endured.

Fifteen minutes later, the two detectives strode into the squad room of Police Service Area 2 of the New York City Housing Police. They immediately went into a huddle with the housing detectives. "This is what we've got," said one. "The victim's mother is Patricia Long, twenty-five years old. She has two young sons and is on welfare. The children's father is in jail. Patricia Long lives with Levan Turner, age twenty, from Manhattan." The detective consulted his notes.

"Turner said he put the baby to sleep while her mother was out, and when the mother returned, she checked the baby and discovered she wasn't breathing. The mother screamed, and Turner said he told her to call an ambulance while he scooped the baby up to give her mouth-to-mouth resuscitation."

Dave rolled his eyes and bobbed his head, casting a he's-full-of-shit look. Turner was an obvious suspect.

"Turner's portraying himself as a doting, caring stepfather," the detective continued, "and if he hurt the child, he isn't giving an inch. In fact, he's cold as ice. And Patricia Long, the baby's mother, vehemently denies Turner hurt the child in any way. 'Nobody messes with my babies,' she said. 'I'm only out for a short time. I only leave them with him.' "

"Yeah, with him," Dave said. "That's why she's dead."

To the housing detectives, Patricia Long hadn't seemed possessed of a normal mother's emotions. She was too disconnected, and she had become extremely defensive about the possibility of her boyfriend's sexually abusing her child. The detectives said that although the mother had told them Sasha slept in a crib, there was no crib to be found in the apartment. Rather, they seemed to think the baby slept on a sheet on the floor with a naked lamp behind her.

"Someone had been doing something gross to this child," Owens interjected. "Even without an autopsy, it was obvious there was extreme sexual activity performed on the child. At the minimum, we have a sexual abuse case here.''

The detectives thought maybe a pen or some other type of object had been used to inflict damage on the child, but they didn't really know. It would be up to them now to find out how the damage had been done and who had done it. Housing Police brought Turner in for questioning.

There were many techniques of interrogation that detectives learned through courses and from detectives they worked with and developed on their own. What they used depended on their experience, personality, and training. But as each subject was different, with a complex set of emotions, attitudes, and values, the techniques employed by any single detective might vary. Detectives evaluated their subject as they went along and reacted accordingly, improvising an on-the-spot custom-designed examination.

Detectives often wanted to appraise how compliant their subject would be, and there was one simple method that gave them a good clue right from the start. When the detective shook hands with the subject at the time of introduction, in grasping the subject's hand, the detective pivoted his own around clockwise. If the subject's hand followed course easily, it could be interpreted to mean he would be tractable and forthcoming; if not, it was an indication he might be resistant and difficult.

The seating arrangement of the interrogator and his subject was another consideration and could symbolize the loss of the person's freedom. The detective sat between his subject and the door, blocking the subject's exit and giving him the idea that telling the truth was the only way out. To further instill in the subject the feeling that he was trapped, the detective could move in close at appropriate times during the interrogation. When the detective really meant business, he would loom within inches of the suspect; when he found the suspect cooperating, he would back off and give him room. It was like a sophisticated, delicate dance whose choreography was improvised anew at every interrogation.

Certain specific kinds of questions—referred to by such terms as open-ended, direct, closed, mirror, probing, and leading—were used to get a suspect to feel comfortable and start talking, to break him if he was a hard-ass, to encourage specific responses, to develop a common bond with the person, to make the subject feel as though the detective wanted to help him, to show professional concern. According to formal training in interrogation methods, there were sequences to these questions, designed to break the subject down and elicit specific kinds of responses or confessions. Detectives knew these techniques didn't work on everyone. Often the suspect was sizing them up while they were analyzing him, a two-way avenue on which they would have to proceed according to the reactions they got. They could mix up the formal techniques and match them to the person, as well as use their own.

The so-called scan technique involved asking the subject to describe his activities the day of the crime, covering a period from several hours before to several hours after. The detective would listen to the entire recital without interrupting, paying attention to the degree of detail. If the person provided explicit particulars of events up until the time of the actual crime, then glossed over what he was doing at the time of the crime and concluded with a detailed post-crime accounting of events, it was a signal to the detective that the subject was trying to conceal the criminal behavior that was the focus of the interview.

There were all sorts of methods a detective could use to break a subject's defenses and make him lose control. These might range from gently touching the person, to raising the tone of voice, to pointing to an object on the table and asking the subject, "Would you pass that to me?" (so he subconsciously felt he was assisting the investigator), to appealing to the subject's sense of values, religion, or civic duty. Deep down, a person who had committed a crime usually wanted to give it up, and the investigator was there to do whatever it took to help him.

Owens and Dave walked into the interview room to talk to Turner. He was seated on a wooden chair, looking calm and composed. Dave shook his hand and gently put his other arm around the man's shoulders.

"What's your first name?" Owens asked.

"Levan," said the man. His voice was high and melodious.

"Hi, Levan." Owens's tone was friendly. He wanted his subject to feel comfortable, so he would talk freely and not clam up or curse at his interrogators.

The detectives started out with routine comments and questions. "It's a terrible shame what happened to Sasha, isn't it? I'll say a prayer for her later," offered Owens sympathetically, his eyes half closed. "Tell me about yourself. What are you into?" Dave inquired with interest. They were trying to gain Turner's confidence and develop a common bond. Over the forty-minute period, they mentioned Sasha several times, but Turner would say only that he loved the child and would never hurt her.

Housing detectives followed. They found Turner more concerned about clearing himself than about the dead baby. They couldn't break through his icy shield either.

Over the next several hours, Owens and Dave alternated with the housing detectives in questioning the suspect. Owens used every psychological trick he knew to break Turner down. He appealed to his human feelings, he occasionally made gentle body contact, he tried to make Turner believe that, yes, people do make mistakes sometimes and that the detectives understood and wanted to help him. At times he feigned losing his temper, although Dave wasn't sure how much was actually pretense.

"Do you think I'm a clown?" Owens shouted, throwing down pictures of Sasha lying dead, covered with bruises and cuts, while Turner maintained his cool composure. Owens's ears were bright red and his neck stiffened, muscles popping out. "Look at her face and tell me how that happened!"

"Calm down, Jimmy," Dave said soothingly, pushing him out of the room. They were playing good guy–bad guy. Although perps were aware of this technique, it could be extremely convincing when used skillfully. But Owens was so emotional that Dave was actually afraid he was going to strike Turner, and that would end the case right there. With no justice for the baby.

Outside the room, both cooled off while housing detectives went in again to talk to Turner.

Dave also remembered what Mike Redmond had told him. Don't give your subject too much information. Let him tell the story, and you just listen. Some detectives had a tendency to interrupt a subject to show that they knew something or to ask questions. But what they did, in effect, was break the person's train of thought. Let the person go through his whole story, Redmond had said, and then go back and ask your questions. Be patient.

"How did you get her to stop crying?" Owens asked when they went in again. "What were you doing with her? How did you say you got her to stop crying?" Sometimes he prefaced a question by saying, "Levan, you will cooperate with me, won't you?" or "You want me to do a good job with this, don't you?" As he asked the questions, Owens changed his tone of voice, eased his posture, varied his facial expression. But Turner never gave a satisfactory answer to any of the questions.

Finally, there was a tiny movement in the right direction. "I tried to make the baby feel good," Turner said softly.

Owens didn't show any reaction, but he was elated. His subject was beginning to come around, beginning to lose that icy control.

Owens, sitting on a roller chair, moved close to Turner, inserting his left leg between Turner's legs. He contemplated his next question. If he asked, "What did you do to her?" that would imply guilt. He didn't want to do that. "Now, how do you go about making a little baby feel good?" he asked wonderingly. Turner seemed touched by Owens's gentle body contact.

"I rubbed the baby's thighs," Turner admitted.

Owens appeared fascinated. "Her thighs?" he said.

"Yes, you know, on the inner parts, close to the crotch." Turner demonstrated on his own leg.

The two detectives looked at each other sharply. The bastard was beginning to give it up.

Owens leaned back in his chair and lazily stretched his arms up and back, clasping his hands behind his head. "Oh, and how's your family?"

Dave understood this odd change of subject. Owens was trying to divert Turner's mind from the possibly incriminating statement he had just made.

You put your suspect on a rail, Owens had told Dave during one of their brief cooling-off periods. You push him forward, then back up a little. But once you get any kind of a statement, he is committed to that statement. You back off a little, but stay on the rail. If your suspect feels he's losing control, he'll back off. You let that aspect go for a while, go on to something else, then come back. And ask another question that will incriminate him. He'll finally put the pieces together and realize you've nailed him.

Still leaning back, Owens continued, "And by the way, when you rubbed the baby, exactly how far up her thigh did you touch her?"

Once Turner let himself go, it was classic textbook material. He confessed everything. He told them how over the past four months he had been having sexual contact with the baby, first by rubbing, then by penetration with his fingers.

As the detectives listened to Turner's odious recital, they both had to work hard to maintain an emotional distance from this man who had raped and killed a baby, to keep from leaping on him and beating him to a bloody pulp. It was crucial to maintain the pretense of friendly interest.

Shelving emotions during an interrogation was one of the essential rules of being a good investigator. Especially, as Dave knew, with the real bad-ass guys. If you came on macho, they'd say, "Okay, mother-

fucker, lock me up.'' When you had no witnesses and had to break
your suspect, you had to do everything you could to get him to talk, no
matter what it cost you in self-control. If you let your anger interfere
with your questions, you'd lose your subject. Instead you had to hold
on to your own emotions and play to his. You might ask him, ''Why are
we fighting each other?'' or ''If you've got a problem, isn't it better to
get it out in the open?''

Owens began picking up the pace now, hoping Turner would mess
up on his statements and give more truths than fabrications.

''So tell us, how did you get the baby to stop crying today?''

''I didn't rub the baby . . . well, I touched it only once. . . . Actually,
I put my finger into it.'' The suspect gradually began to reveal what
had happened.

''It's okay,'' Owens said. ''We understand.'' He rested his arm
gently on Turner's shoulder. ''We're your friends. We're going to help
you.''

''I took a bath with the baby,'' Turner finally said, after telling how
Sasha had been crying all day and he couldn't get her to stop. He had
been alone with the baby in the apartment.

''Why was the baby crying?''

Turner began to act out what he had done. Seated in his chair, he
pretended he was reclining in a bathtub with the baby in his arms. He
brought the pretend-baby's vagina to his groin area and then moved
the baby away, like a jerk-off doll.

''I bounced it up and down on my cock like this,'' he said, grinning, moving his hands back and forth. He kept on repeating the mo-
tions, picking up speed as he went along. ''I was fucking it like this.''

'' 'It'?'' Owens could no longer contain himself. ''What do you
mean, 'it'?''

''You know, the baby.'' Turner looked puzzled. What the hell else
would you call the baby?

Owens and Dave exchanged ''holy shit!'' looks. *It!* His girlfriend's
baby, whom he had raped and presumably killed, was an ''it''! Turner
had not the least bit of compassion for the baby he had ravaged and
cruelly destroyed. Nothing.

Turner's coldness was really getting to Owens now. ''This is one
heartless fuck,'' he whispered to Dave. Pictures of Sasha's battered
body lay before the two detectives, and they both were horribly
tempted to tear Turner apart.

''You may want to kill him, but that's not our job,'' Owens told
Dave outside the room. ''Our job is to solve the murder—find out who

did it, why it happened, and how it happened—and be able to prove it. We have to get a statement consistent with the victim's injuries. If Turner says he lacerated her ear with a hanger and there are no ear injuries, that is an inconsistent statement. So let's put our feelings aside and get the job done." Owens knew he was saying this as much for himself as for Dave.

They went back into the room to continue questioning Turner. The biggest job was still ahead: to get a full statement from their suspect.

After a few minutes of small talk, Owens rested his arm gently on Turner's shoulder again. He wanted to continue to gain Turner's confidence but was wary Turner might accuse him of using physical force to coerce him to make up lies.

"So, what else happened?" he asked.

"After the bath, the baby was annoying me, so I shook it," Turner said. "Then I threw it across the room, and it hit a wall. It was still screaming. I didn't know what else to do, so I kicked it." Turner demonstrated how he had done this, and Owens was amazed. It was exactly as if Sasha were a football and Turner had picked her up and drop-kicked her straight into the wall. "Then I put my foot on it."

Owens asked him to show what he meant exactly, so Turner stood up. Pretending Sasha was lying on the floor, he put one foot down. Turner, oblivious to the crime he had committed, was "performing" for the detectives. That was something detectives often strove for, to provoke the suspect's ego to take over so he acted out or described his crime as if it were an accomplishment.

"First I put my foot on the baby like this," Turner said, shifting his weight onto one foot. "It was still crying, so I stepped on it with both feet." Turner was a large man, weighing over two hundred pounds. Little Sasha weighed probably about a dozen pounds. "I stood on it until it stopped crying. Then I put it in bed and watched TV."

Turner's complete detachment from his crime was horrifying. He seemed to be saying, "What did I do wrong? It was no big deal." Owens was staring at Turner with his laser-beam eyes and thinking, You sick fucking bastard. In a way he felt sorry for him, but mostly he wanted to kill him. He knew he had to get out of the room.

Outside, Sergeant Race was talking with some housing detectives when Owens emerged, his head down.

"Are you okay?" Race asked. Owens looked up, his eyes brimming with moisture. He was shaking. Race had known Owens to get emotional occasionally, but he had never before seen him react this way.

Owens didn't answer. He walked straight into another room and slammed the door.

A few hours later, two assistant district attorneys, a young man and woman, and a video technician came to take Turner's statement. With the videotape running, it became a show again for Turner as he acted out how he had had sexual intercourse with the baby. In the middle of his recital, the woman ADA felt sick and had to leave the room.

As the proceedings were being videotaped, the video technician took close-ups of Turner's face to show he hadn't been beaten. During the initial interview with Owens and Dave, Turner had been hand-cuffed so he couldn't hurt himself and blame the detectives. After Turner gave his statement, the ADAs asked other questions: Were you threatened in any way? Were you beaten tonight? Were you coerced into making a statement by the detectives? Were you offered anything to say it?

Owens and Dave were afraid that Turner would deny saying what he had told them and make an accusation of physical coercion. If that happened, the videotape would be stopped and the case could be thrown out. The ADAs would have to call their supervisor to discuss the possibility of starting an investigation of the detectives based on the suspect's accusations.

Owens asked the ADAs to cooperate with him in prosecuting Patricia Long, the baby's mother, but they wouldn't comply. If you take away a mother from two children, one reasoned, then the state has two kids to take care of. Owens protested that based on what had happened, the mother was unfit to take care of her children and something horrible could happen again. Oh, no, said the ADA, the mother was just a victim of a man's violence. Owens muttered to Dave that she hadn't had a mark on her, and swore he'd have photographs taken to prove it. Not that this would change the ADAs' decision, but he wanted to rub their noses in it. The chances of being prosecuted as an accessory to a crime in Brooklyn were slim to none. There just weren't enough resources.

Owens expounded his philosophies on the legal system to Dave later that night at a watering hole, where strong beverages only partially tempered the awful memory of the day behind them.

Owens told Dave that even though Turner had made a statement, he would probably get a lawyer and try to fight the charges.

Dave was outraged. "How the hell can an SOB lawyer accept money to keep filth like Turner on the street?"

"Defense counsel can be absolutely ruthless trying to defend their clients," Owens responded heavily. "It's their job. 'Look at this officer,' " he said shrilly, impersonating a lawyer. " 'He's two hundred and twenty pounds. Now look at my client. He's only a hundred and forty. Of course the officer threatened him!' " Owens downed the last of his drink and signaled the waitress for another. "That sounds like fact. The jury hears all about police corruption and brutality, so they think, yes, of course the cop is guilty. The one percent of criminals who make it into uniform make the rest of us look bad."

Dave was feeling more and more depressed, but Owens was relentless. "Then we get hit by a lawsuit. We're accused of being bigots. We lose our constitutional rights, our wages, our sexual ability. Even the wives get in on it. They sue us for divorce when we can't get it up because we're too strung out trying to find a way to save our necks.

"Why do people sue?" he asked rhetorically, waving his fresh drink. "Because the city pays off. The city has a slush fund for nuisance suits. It's a lot cheaper to throw someone two or three grand and say get out of my face than drag the case through the courts."

Owens smiled humorlessly, then took another swallow from his glass and grimaced. "A lot of mutts out there are getting rich off the city. You just have to have a good enough story. One of their favorite sayings is 'Officer, if I wasn't doing it, somebody else would.' That's how they excuse being sleazebags."

Owens set down his drink. He ground the heels of his hands into his eyes, then slid his hands up his forehead and through his hair, arching his back and stretching his arms straight out. Then he leaned forward again and picked up his almost empty glass, a look of deep weariness on his face.

"When I was a young officer, I watched a case I had go down the tubes," Owens said. "I was really upset, and the defense attorney knew it. After the trial he came over to me and said, 'Don't take it personally, Jimmy. Don't take it to heart. The court legal system has nothing to do with the truth; it's only who's the best liar.' "

"Waitress," said Dave, "let's have another round here. Doubles, please."

During the last weeks of 1989, with increasing frequency patrol cops popped into the squad room to take a quick peek at the "Death's Door" sign on the wall across from the room's reception area.

The detectives smirked or laughed when the uniforms came up to check the number. Time was running short. The cops had purchased tickets for the precinct's Lucky Stiff Lotto, and the prize would soon be awarded. Whoever came closest to guessing the year-end number of murders in the Seven-Five would win the precinct's homicide pool.

With the 75th Precinct's notoriously high annual body count, many of the detectives and the patrol cops downstairs—and from other precincts, too—chipped in to the pool. At $5 a clip, it ran to several hundred dollars. "The uniforms always come into the squad room about this time to check out the number," Smitty told Dave. "If the number doesn't come close to what they put in at, they do weed canvasses in the precinct for undiscovered human bones. That's why the number goes up in late December."

A couple of uniformed officers entered the squad room and diffidently walked to the gate, looking across at the far wall. Smitty winked at Dave.

"Whaddya got?" Smitty shouted from his desk by the corner window at the opposite end of the room. "I'm ten over," one said ruefully, then left with the other.

Two days before Christmas, a twelve-year-old boy named Elford Verette was sitting by his apartment window getting a haircut when bullets blazed through the window and struck him in the head. He died hours later.

Team One gave up their Christmas to work the Elford Verette case. Forty-six straight hours into it, the Team One detectives were suffering from exhaustion. But on Christmas Day, before they could catch their breath, two more homicides came in.

James Simmons-Harris was gunned down in front of a liquor store by a man identified as "Freddy Krueger." An informant told them that the previous Christmas the gunman's friend had been murdered, and he had vowed to murder someone every year on Christmas Day. Rigoberto Rodriguez was shot by a bodega owner after he and three accomplices robbed and beat the owner and stole the store receipts.

"I'm frustrated," Dave told Smitty, expressing a desire to work on his double. "It happened only five days ago, but it seems much longer."

"Here homicides get stale faster than bread," said Smitty. "You get one, and before you settle in from the canvass, another comes in. And another and another. And these are all on top of the dozens of other cases that come in daily."

With all the killings, Dave had moved full circle to the top of Team One's homicide rotation order again. But he was backlogged with work and hoped the rest of the holiday season, through New Year's, at least, would be quiet and that no one would be murdered. Only six days, he thought. If only no one would be murdered for six days, I might be able to spend some time with my family. It didn't, on the face of it, seem like too much to ask.

Four days later, Dave's hope of a regular set of tours was dashed when a call of a "heavy bleeder" came over the radio. The Team One detectives were finishing up at a crime scene where four people had been shot and were only around the corner from the address given by Central, so they decided to coast over there even without confirmation that the victim was a DOA.

Since Dave was up, he spoke to the first officer when the detectives entered the three-story house. They were in a small ground-floor room, and a man whose clothes were drenched with blood was sitting on a sofa. EMS technicians were in another room working on the victim.

"The man over there," Officer Steven Russell said to Dave, "said that someone came into the house and stabbed the victim, and he ran to his rescue. He fought off the assailant, and the assailant ran out."

"What's the victim's name?"

"Jameeh Ash-Bright. He lives here. He's the super. He's thirty-five years old."

A minute later two EMS technicians carried the victim out on a stretcher. Another tech popped his head into the room.

"Detective, we're going to leave now."

Russell's partner, John McGann, asked how the victim was doing.

"Forget about it," the tech said. "He's a goner."

Patrol put up the yellow crime scene ribbon, and one RMP after another pulled up to the residence. The static of radios filled the air as detectives milled around the premises, looking at what was there. A uniformed officer whispered in Dave's ear, and Dave went into another room. He spoke to a man, tall and gaunt, who lived in the house. "Dennis did it," the man said, "but he's my friend, so I don't want him to know I told the cops."

Back in the squad room, the man with the bloody clothes, Dennis Cargill, sat in the interview room. Dave stood next to Smitty, who was on the phone with BCI. Before an interrogation, a detective wanted to know as much as possible about his victims and suspects, so Smitty was running names.

"Our victim, Jameeh Ash-Bright," Smitty announced to Dave, "had a long criminal history himself. He had eight pages of rap sheets for fucking drug arrests." Smitty referred to Ash-Bright in the past tense, since he had been pronounced dead on arrival at the hospital. "Whoever killed him just removed another drug dealer from the streets."

"Ah, yes," Dave hummed. "A community service murder!"

The two detectives walked to the interview room where Dennis Cargill was waiting. Dave shook his hand, then sat next to him, his knee wedged in slightly between the man's legs. Smitty stood nearby.

Cargill was visibly upset, saying he wished he could have helped his friend sooner, and Dave tried to comfort him. He asked Cargill how he felt, inquired about his family. He tried to calm him, take his mind off the horrible event that had just happened. Dave's sincere voice and manner seemed to mellow the man, whose arms and legs gradually relaxed.

Between topics in an animated but casual conversation, Dave said nonchalantly, "Oh, I almost forgot, I have to read you your rights."

"Yeah?"

"You know your rights? You've been arrested before, right?"

"Yeah." Cargill was out on parole for assault.

"I have to read you your rights because I've got to question you. I just want to make sure you understand. You didn't do anything wrong, did you?"

"No. You heard my story."

"You understand English?" Dave asked.

"Yeah."

"Good. Let me just read you your rights."

After reading the six Miranda rights, Dave proffered Cargill a rights card.

"Can you read? Did you go to school?"

"Yes, yes."

"Good."

The man read the rights card and signed it.

After a few minutes more of chitchat, Dave asked Cargill to tell him what had happened again.

Cargill repeated his story of rescuing his friend, Jameeh Ash-Bright, from an armed intruder.

"Listen, Dennis," Dave said. "We may have a problem here. Jameeh's alive, and he told us you stabbed him."

Cargill's laugh was strained. "That's pretty funny."

"No, really, he's alive," said Dave earnestly, eyes wide. "And he said the two of you are really good friends and that you didn't mean to do it, but he did say it was you."

Cargill's eyes narrowed. "He's dead. You can't tell me he's not dead."

"Listen, Dennis, I'll call him for you. You wanna talk to him?"

"Yeah." Cargill seemed a little tense now.

Dave walked out of the small room into the squad room and grabbed a phone. As he stretched the phone line back to Cargill, all eyes in the squad room watched.

Dave dialed the phone, and Mike Redmond, out of sight in the squad room, picked up. Dave asked for the emergency room doctor and inquired about Jameeh Ash-Bright. Dave listened for a moment, pressed his lips together tightly, said, "Thank you very much," and hung up.

"You can't talk to him now," Dave told Cargill. "The doctor said he's being repaired right now. But doctors and nurses are working on him, and as soon as they're done Jameeh's going to call back. You can talk to him then."

Cargill still wasn't convinced.

For the next ten minutes, Dave made light talk with the man, then he stood up. "Let me call the doctor again," he said, carrying the phone out of the room. "Maybe he's got an update."

Dave returned a minute later. It seemed Jameeh was still in surgery. "Maybe we can take a run over there later and you can talk to him. You want to write him a note?"

"No, but can I leave now?"

"No, you can't leave. That you can't do, not yet. When you leave, I'll be going with you."

Dave and Smitty exchanged faint smiles. The man didn't understand that meant going to jail.

A few minutes later, Dave excused himself to make a third phone call. When he returned, he said Jameeh might be able to talk with him soon.

"Are you kidding?"

"I'm not kidding. Why would I kid you? What the hell do I care? So do you want to get out of here, or go to jail for what you did? Are you sorry?"

"Yeah," said Cargill, eyes welling.

"What are you sorry for? I thought you just told me you didn't do it."

"Well . . . uh . . ."

"You did it. I know you did it. So don't lie to me."

"But I'm sorry, I'm sorry. I'm really sorry."

"Okay. Now tell me what really happened."

Cargill, his voice unsteady, said he and Ash-Bright had been arguing the past few days. Cargill kept turning the oil burner on, and Jameeh, the super, kept telling him not to.

"I came home after working all night," Cargill said. "When I got
home, Ash-Bright came to my room and asked me for a drink. I told
him I had enough already. Then he asked me for two dollars. He
started getting into my face about an argument from the other day. He
told me he had something for me, and he punched me in the face.
During the fight, I pulled out a knife and stabbed him."

Cargill interspersed his words with sobs. "I didn't mean to hurt
him," he blubbered.

A doctor at the hospital where the homicide victim had been taken
had told Dave that Jameeh had been stabbed about twenty-five times.
You call that an accident? Dave thought.

"When can we go see Jameeh?" Cargill asked.

"I'm sorry to tell you this, but he's in another world now," Dave
said. "He didn't get a chance to say goodbye. He died a little while
ago."

Cargill put his hands over his face, and his shoulders heaved. Dave
gave him a minute, then interrupted.

"Listen, Dennis, the DA wants to come here and take your statement. Will you tell him what happened while they videotape you?"

"Yeah, yeah," he sobbed.

Two hours later, an assistant district attorney arrived at the precinct with a video technician in tow. Cargill repeated his story for the
ADA, and it was all inscribed on tape.

"He's as good as gone," Smitty said to Dave afterward. "You know,
you're a pretty good jerkologist, I have to say."

"Nah!" Dave brushed the compliment aside, then thought better
of it. "Well, I guess I'm all right. But my goal is to be a master jerkologist. This guy is small potatoes. I want to be able to trip up some of
them real bad-ass motherfuckers."

He was thinking of Charlie Brackett; the unsolved double murder
loomed in his mind. I've got to find that guy, he told himself. I've got
to find him, because if I don't, he's going to kill somebody else.

PART TWO

If a man is burdened with the blood
of another, let him be a fugitive
until death. Let no one help him.

—*Proverbs 28:17*

13

There was a mix of suits and uniforms in the dimly lit basement room of the Knights of Columbus hall on Hale Street and Jamaica Avenue in East New York. A line snaked around the kitchen at one end, men and women eager for servings of the night's roast beef, while others were gathered around the jukebox at the other end bopping languidly to the music. In between, the bar was crowded with cops propped on stools or wedged between them, or sitting at nearby tables scarfing down the dinner.

In a small area behind this room, the Seven-Five Precinct held its monthly club meeting. These meetings were forums to discuss internal problems and working conditions at the precinct: cops who didn't pick up their jobs or back others up on patrol, parking difficulties around the station house, unclean bathrooms, the need for more equipment in the weight room, sending flowers to officers who'd had a death in the family. Just as important, the club meetings were social outlets to eat, drink, and shoot the shit.

Three small tables were pulled together at the center of the room. Seated around them were Dave, Cutrone, Smitty, Race, Redmond, and Hall. They were drinking beer and demolishing the mounds of food on the platters before them.

Jack Cutrone, puffing on a cigarette, was making small talk. "This job is like an eight-hour movie," he proclaimed. "A movie that changes every tour because every case, regardless of the crime, is different. Different bodies, different reasons, different people."

"You know," Dave commented, "the first day I got here I had the Stager homicide. Remember the guy who honked and got whacked? In the Homicide Log, in the Remarks column, some joker had written, 'The fine just went up in New York City for honking your horn.' " He shook his head. "No disrespect to Mr. Stager, but I thought that was kind of funny."

A wide grin came across Smitty's face. He took a healthy sip of his beer, then set down his glass. "I once had a case in which a thousand-dollar drug deal went sour," he said. "The dealer shot his associate on behalf of the customer. I put a punch line to that: 'The Customer Is Always Right.' "

A burst of laughter rose from the table.

"I got a better one," said Cutrone, pouring himself another beer. "Remember that case with that guy who walked down Blake Avenue past the school? There was a whole bunch of people sitting on the project steps, and the guy decided to take out his wiener and piss on the telephone pole. During the investigation, we found out one of the girls sitting there didn't like that—like she never saw a dick before, you know?—and she told her boyfriend to take care of him. So the boyfriend walked across the street, and just as the guy was pulling up his zipper, he pulled out a gun and shot him five times."

Cutrone paused, then delivered the punch line: " 'Paid his fine at location.' "

The laughter at the table was raucous, and the detectives dosed themselves with more beer.

Smitty made another contribution. "Remember when Modell's up on Pennsylvania and Cozine first opened, and we got that call for the three people shot? We started interviewing that one guy who told us his friend had bumped into this guy and the guy turned around and said, 'Don't you got something to say?' And nobody said anything, so the guy pulled out a gun and started shooting everybody and killed the guy who had bumped into him." Smitty raised his hands, palms out, and looked around at the detectives. "Now, can you blame him? I mean, what happened to manners? That's why we called that one, 'Courtesy—Your Life Could Depend on It.' "

"What about the Peekaboo Homicide?" Redmond asked.

Dave hadn't heard of that one. "What the fuck was that, Mike?"

"The McDonald's on Atlantic and Hendrix was being robbed. It went bad. The security guard ran and hid in a back room. He crouched down under the small window on the door. But then he decided to take a peek at what was going on, and the minute he raised his head and looked out, the perp put a twelve-gauge shotgun to the window and blew his head off." Redmond paused a moment, then said demurely, "Peekaboo!"

Tears were coming to the detectives' eyes now, more from the laughter than the smoke. The food was gone, but the detectives continued to wash down the beer.

"My turn," Dave said. "I had a case not too long ago involving another East New York entrepreneur, Chino. He'd robbed a drug spot. His best friend called him up later and told him the guys at the spot, the Colombians, wanted to pay him a weekly salary not to rob them. Nice job, huh? Anyway, they met later in the evening at Pitkin and Berriman, and Chino realized it was a setup. He jumped back into his car, and his best friend fired at him and missed.

"So Chino raced down Pitkin Avenue, and a few blocks later the dumb fuck ran out of gas. He got out and went to buy gas in a can. Word got back to Chino's friend, so when Chino was walking back to his car with a gallon of gasoline in an antifreeze can, his best friend drove by and lit him up."

" 'Don't forget to fill your car up before you meet the bad guys'?" suggested Cutrone.

"Nope," Dave said. " 'Good friends are hard to find nowadays.' "

Now Joe Hall spoke up. "Remember the one with that ongoing drug war? And one of the guys thought he'd be smart and wear a bulletproof vest? I guess he never thought about getting shot in the head. The punch line for that was 'Damn, the vest worked fine, but I forgot to duck.' "

"How about the Request Homicide?" Race asked. "Two neighbors lived in a three-story walkup. One thing led to another, and one guy came carrying a butcher's knife to his neighbor's door and threatened to kill him. 'Go ahead and kill me,' the neighbor said. 'Go ahead.' He died later of multiple stab wounds."

"I've got that one beat," Smitty said. "Remember they put that guy underneath the cross on the church wall on Hegeman Avenue and sprayed him with an automatic? The quote of the day for that one was 'Don't forget to say your prayers.' "

The noise at the table grew even louder.

Redmond said, "What about Jimmy Owens's case, where two guys were arguing? One called the other a motherfucker, and the other one said, 'I wouldn't be a motherfucker if you kept your mama off the street.' Then bang, he killed him. The punch line for that was 'Things I Wish I'd Never Said.' "

The room was abuzz now, thick clouds of smoke drifting above the detectives' heads. The bar was congested like Friday-afternoon rush hour on the Long Island Expressway.

At the detectives' table, joke after joke tumbled out as the men recalled their cases. To the casual observer this morbid comedy would seem grossly insensitive, but the detectives desperately needed to blow off steam. What they saw in the precinct was so overwhelmingly ghastly that they couldn't assimilate it into their psyches unfiltered. A kid blown away because he didn't say "Excuse me"? A security guard shot through the eyes for peeking? It was beyond nightmare.

The detectives were well aware they were venting a profound but unspoken inner distress. It was almost a job requirement, these occasional sessions of gallows humor. They didn't inflict it on their families at home. They knew it sounded cruel, but they also knew they weren't heartless; they needed to make light of the horror exactly because they felt it so acutely. To let it out in this manner from time to time was the healthy thing to do. If they kept it bottled up, they'd go mad.

Luci Carbone had been pacing the floor for hours, her irritation now having mushroomed to anger. Where was Dave? Why was she always the one home taking care of the baby? It wasn't as if she didn't have to get up in the morning too, for her job as a medical technician.

It was 4:30 A.M., and Luci had been up all night, tending to her daughter, Danielle. Plagued by chronic ear infections, Danielle required constant attention—trips to the doctor, medication, the extra loving care and comfort a child needed when she was ill.

Dave should have been home a long time ago, Luci fumed. He hadn't even called to let her know he wasn't coming home after his tour ended.

Luci had expected Dave home right after work, since he had been on a turnaround and hadn't gotten much sleep the night before. He liked to catch up on his sleep, if he wasn't working on a heavy case, on the night of the day tour following the turnaround.

She assumed he had stopped off to have a couple of beers with Smitty and Jack Cutrone. The trio were becoming increasingly tight-knit, and occasionally, on their turnarounds, had stayed up all the hours between the night tour and the following day tour.

Dave's behavior was bothering her a lot lately. If anything went wrong as far as the job was concerned, she would stand by him no matter what. But she wouldn't tolerate his coming home and telling her they took pay away or transferred him because he had been drinking. When he had been in the Nine-Four and his partners were caught drinking on the job, they were put on modified duty and dumped from Anticrime back into uniform. Such behavior, she had told Dave, was inexcusable.

"Where the hell is he?" Luci wondered aloud this time. The words echoed in her mind until another thought struck her. Why was she doing this alone? She asked herself reproachful questions, then chastised herself. Thought upon thought ate away at her, as on too many nights over the past several months. Luci's and Dave's schedules just didn't seem to coincide, and she felt lonely, almost unmarried.

Luci Carbone understood as well as any other spouse what it meant to be a cop's wife—the anxiety from worrying all day whether he was in danger, the long hours of waiting while he was on overtime, which might amount to an entire day or even two. But cop or not, Dave was married, and she believed marriage was a partnership. It was only fair that her husband make every effort to share in the responsibilities. This was one of the principles she had set for herself and her husband. They were rooted in a childhood in which she had never known her father, and she had vowed, as she listened to her mother's endless disparaging comments about him, that her own marriage would not suffer the same fate.

Luciann Knox was the only child born to parents who had divorced when she was two. Although her mother had remarried when Luci was seventeen, Luci had grown up without a normal family life and felt the crushing pangs of loneliness that can often overwhelm a young person.

As she grew older, Luci developed a deep, serious side, becoming almost too introspective for her own good. Not a runaround sort of person, Luci didn't date widely, tending instead to stick with the guys she had developed some sort of relationship with. In fact, before Dave, there had been only two—a fellow she had dated on and off for ten years beginning when she was sixteen, and a mortician.

Luciann was working in the Syosset office of Long Island's largest employer, the Grumman Corp., when she first met David Carbone. At the time, she was engaged to the mortician.

Dave was a driver then for Grumman, delivering mail and internal correspondence to the company's different plants. When he saw Luciann Knox for the first time, he was knocked out by her sensuous lips, dreamy almond eyes, and flowing brown hair that framed a beautiful pear-shaped face. Indeed, Luci attracted scores of men, but she had a strong personality, blunt and assertive, as well as a firm, no-nonsense voice, and this often intimidated men once they began to converse with her.

Engrossed in a telephone conversation, Luci perfunctorily pointed to a spot for Dave to set down the package he was delivering. He obeyed, his mind racing to devise a way to attract her attention. In fact, Luci could hardly fail to notice Dave—in his leather cowboy hat, brown leather cowboy boots, and tight-fitting jeans, he struck her as rather cute—but it never occurred to her to act on her attraction, as it did Dave.

Two years after he and Luci first saw each other, Dave made a delivery to Grumman's Bethpage office, where she was now working. Although Dave himself was engaged by this time, he felt irresistibly attracted to this woman, and he contrived to be assigned as many of the Bethpage delivery runs as he could. Playing for her attention, he'd pretend to trip, or he'd sing "Getting to Know You" to her with exaggerated gestures, but Luci was unreceptive. She smiled but never encouraged any kind of association.

During this time, Dave didn't let his engagement stop him from sleeping around, often enjoying nocturnal trysts at the firehouse where he expected one day to be chief. He confided his behavior to Luci, who had at last begun to let down some of her reserve. Luci was not amused. "If you were my husband, I'd kick your ass," she told him. Marriage carried no guarantees of eternal happiness, she felt, but on the other hand, if you were going to do it in the first place, you ought to try your best to make it work.

But she was beginning to wonder about the depth of her own commitment to her longtime fiancé, the mortician. He seemed to think the bond of marriage by itself ensured permanence, obviating any need for mutual effort at developing the partnership. The week before the wedding, she broke off the engagement and the relationship.

Dave married his fiancée, and only a short time later came to the unpleasant realization that he didn't love his wife. Life at home became almost unbearable for him, and he shared his problems with Luci, who was now feeling lonely and unmoored. To her, he was like a forlorn puppy, and she supported him through this rough time. Their relationship was strictly platonic, and they would often see each other at "Grumman Grabbers," company parties at local pubs held after work on paydays, Thursdays.

When Dave separated from his wife six months later, he thought he would be free to woo the woman he really wanted. But Luci had doubts about pursuing a serious relationship with him. She distrusted his flirtatious ways and figured he only wanted to party and have a good time. He was young, with an ego and an unrestrained desire to enjoy life to the fullest. But when Dave told Luci for the first time that he loved her, despite her doubts, something inside told her he meant it. She told him to get his life in order, then come back, if he wanted.

Dave came back. He persisted and persisted with Luci, and before long she was hooked on his sweet, earthy personality, not to mention his shimmering blue eyes and rough good looks.

Their romance bloomed fully now, and three months later, Luci consented to Dave's entreaties for marriage, with one caveat—she knew all his secrets, so there would be nothing he could do that she wouldn't know about. Resigned to pursuing a course of faithfulness in marriage, Dave accepted the warning put to him.

With Dave's father and his many brothers and sisters, Luci eagerly looked forward to enjoying the closeness of the large family she had never had. But she was rudely awakened by the cold shoulder she received. Despite Luci's efforts to endear herself to the Carbones, Dave's family remained loyal to his first wife and refused to warm up to Luci.

Around the time Danielle was born, a crucial event took place in Dave's life: he was appointed to the New York City Police Department. Luci was overjoyed. It was the chance Dave was waiting for, a chance to make something of himself. He carpooled to the police academy in Manhattan with a bunch of recruits each day, and Luci was amazed by the transformation she was witnessing. Dave became diligent and serious, and she believed he had finally found his niche.

After Dave graduated and had spent just a short time on the street, another transformation occurred. The sweetness and carefreeness that had seemed to characterize him in earlier days gave way to a pungent cynicism. As time passed, he became more inward, more drawn into himself. He stopped telling her everything about his tours of duty when he came home. Instead, he withdrew to the front yard or basement to work on the house. In the beginning, he had always come home with a smile, eager to share his day; but since RIP, he didn't seem to want to talk about his work anymore.

Luci understood this and accepted it. Being a cop in the big city was not like being a cop in suburbia, and the tales she heard about what a cop had to put up with on the city streets made the urge to erect a wall, some kind of barrier, more than understandable. She came to realize that the things cops see in their daily work change them forever. And while she imagined these changes were more pronounced while he was working, at home Dave was still quite gentle, and Luci continued to have a wifely upper hand in their marriage.

If she found it hard to get used to his rigorous new hours, when Dave was assigned to the Seven-Five detective squad the adjustment became more difficult. On his turnarounds he often slept at the precinct, so she might not see him for two days. She began to resent the fact that he had such a full life, topped off with carousing at bars after work, while she was a slave to the pressing responsibilities of her own work and home.

Dave was cognizant of this and felt bad about it, but at the same time was wrapped up in his career aspirations. His dream finally come true of making detective, he wanted to fit in again and felt obliged to follow his partners after work to local haunts. Once Luci smelled perfume on his jacket. He swore the scent had been in the air at the bar he'd been at, and that he had done nothing wrong.

Luci's patience was tested. She tried to consider the emotional toll that stress takes on a cop, telling herself Dave was only reacting normally. She recalled the time when, as a patrol officer, Dave had come home late one night after he had been shot at. He and his partner had responded to the call of a man with a gun, and when they had pulled up to the location, a bullet had blazed right over the roof of their RMP, narrowly missing Dave in the driver's seat. He had tried to make light of it, but she could see he was spooked. He had tossed and turned in bed, agonizing for hours in the darkness. He finally said, "I can't close my eyes. I saw it coming at me."

But despite her deep understanding of what a cop goes through, even compassion, she told herself as time passed, has its limits.

Luci Carbone was sitting silently on the couch in the darkened living room when Dave walked in at five in the morning. He tiptoed into the bedroom, and when he saw Luci wasn't there, he knew the problems they were having must have gotten to her. She must be waiting for him somewhere else. I'm fucked! he thought as he went to find her.

"Don't even think about going to sleep," said Luci as Dave slunk into the living room. "If you think I'm going to sit here while you're out with your buddies drinking every night, you've got another think coming."

Dave was drunk, and he had hoped he could get an hour or two of sleep before having to arise again for work, but he knew it was hopeless now. He could tell by the tone of Luci's voice that there was a serious problem.

Luci's teeth were gritted. "I've been up with Danielle for hours. And not even a phone call from you. Where were you?"

Dave tried to sober up quickly. "I worked some overtime, and then we decided to stop off before we came home."

"This is not the marriage I expected. I don't need to be married to be alone. I could be out partying too." Luci paused, then bit her lip. She looked up at Dave, and he saw tears were streaming down her face. "If this is the way things are going to be, I want a divorce."

Her words hit Dave like a slap in the face. He no longer felt drunk. He sat down heavily in the chair facing the couch.

"You're right," he said, realizing he had become complacent.

"There isn't anything more important to me than you and the baby. I don't want to be without you. I love you, and if I lost you, everything I've been working for would have been for nothing." He gazed at her pleadingly, real fear in his eyes.

Luci dabbed at her face and tried to hold her voice steady. "It's either going out with the guys or coming home to your family," she told him. "Once in a while would be fine, but not this every-night stuff. And you can't go for hours without calling. Give me the courtesy of a phone call to let me know you're going out. And to see what's going on here, to find out if everybody is okay. You didn't even know Danielle was sick."

Dave knew Luci was right. And if he wanted to say one bad thing about her, pick one shortcoming, he couldn't. His wife was a paragon of virtue, he thought, an angel, better than he ever deserved.

"I lost sight of what I've been doing," he said, his voice husky. "Please don't leave me. Please forgive me."

He got up and stood before her. Extending his hand, he gently pulled her up from the couch and embraced her tightly. He whispered in her ear, "I love you. I'll love you always. I promise I'll change."

Although he had hardly slept for two days, Dave barely noticed the throbbing in his head. He showered, ate breakfast with Luci, then got dressed, feeling entirely sober. Caught up in the conflicting demands of two different worlds, he had not achieved the proper balance for a family man, and he had to make an important decision. He could be a cop twenty-four hours a day, or assign an appropriate portion of those hours to fulfilling the requirements of being a husband and father. Always ready to have a good time, Dave had never quite made the transition from being single to a settled-down home life, and he had to admit he enjoyed the late-night carousing, the beers and the jokes and the smoky, raunchy aura. But when it came down to it, the choice was obvious. He knew where his priorities lay.

And so his habits changed. He regularly called home to make sure his wife and child were okay. He made sure that if he went out with the guys after work, he told Luci where he'd be and what time he'd be home—and Luci really appreciated Dave's renewed efforts of communication. More often, Dave forsook these social events and went home to his family. A lot of responsibility came with being a cop, but he realized he hadn't yet accepted a commensurate degree of responsibility for his personal life.

In a very short time, he grew up.

14

Several months into his investigation of the Shaun Henry and Robert Dudley murders, Dave received an interesting phone call. It came from a Detective Joe Howard of the New Haven Police Department. Howard was looking into a local homicide, and he thought the two of them might be of some help to each other.

"Whaddya got?" Dave asked.

Howard went into detail about the murder one year earlier of a small-time drug dealer and cocaine addict named Kevin Moody.

Moody was selling B-bags, or burn bags, stamped with the "Crazy Eddie" trademark (one of the typically whimsical names given to various brands of crack). Moody would smoke some of the coke, then would replace what he'd used with baking powder or some other bogus substance and pass it off as the authentic Crazy Eddie brand, diminishing, of course, the reputation of the real thing. The dealers got wind of this and decided to make an example of Moody.

Late one night, three men went to the Eastern Circle housing project in New Haven where Moody lived. Finding him outside, they chased him around the project's semicircular drive, which was set on a hillside. People from all over the project gathered around and watched as the men pistol-whipped Moody. Then the men picked him up and threw him into their trunk.

Despite the severe beating, Moody thrashed around in the trunk, begging to be freed. The dealers made a quick stop to purchase a flashlight, then drove to a large municipal park, where they dragged him out. With the beam of the flashlight cutting a path through the pitch-black darkness, two of the drug dealers marched Moody into the woods.

All the way through, Moody cried and pleaded for mercy. He begged his captors for forgiveness, pleading with them to show a morsel of compassion. When they were deep in the woods, one of the men held up a gun while Moody closed his eyes and scrunched up his face, his trembling lips moving in an incoherent prayer for mercy. In the few seconds before the gunman pumped four bullets at close range into Moody's head, a large damp stain spread across the front of his pants.

From Howard's tone and description, Dave could feel the terror the eighteen-year-old Moody must have felt.

Residents of Eastern Circle were initially unwilling to provide any information on the murder, so New Haven detectives had little more than the barest descriptions and nicknames. But they also knew the dealers used two apartments in the project as their base of operations. With a subpoena, they obtained phone records for both apartments and found telephone calls to New York City and other places.

At the same time, in another part of town, a street dealer was arrested. He had a telephone book with a nickname in it, the same as one of the suspects in the Kevin Moody murder. The detectives were able to trace the nickname to an apartment in New Haven. From the lease and telephone records, they identified the tenants, now suspected of killing Moody.

One of the suspects had been dumb enough to use his real name as a secondary lessee on the apartment. When New Haven detectives went to the apartment building, the people identified him as one of the residents and one of the drug dealers responsible for some violence in the neighborhood and at the project that night. But no one would pursue a complaint or give the police sufficient probable cause to pursue any warrants.

"So who were they?" Dave asked Howard.

"Charlie Brackett and George Chang," Howard said. "Now up until recently, about fourteen months after the homicide, we could not get a single eyewitness to come forward and help us with the investigation. People were that terrified of these guys.

"But finally an eyewitness did come forward and described what he'd seen at the scene of the beating. He identified Brackett and Chang and a local kid, the third guy in the car. We arrested the local kid, and he filled in the blanks—driving out of the park, Brackett and Chang had joked about Moody begging for mercy and wetting his pants. By the time we got the kid, as you may know, Chang had already been murdered. The local kid went on trial, and the jury found him not guilty. They believed he wasn't an active participant in the kidnapping and the murder—he'd stayed by the car when Brackett and Chang executed Moody in the woods. The jury felt the kid was more or less under duress."

Detective Howard went on to explain that he had learned Charlie Brackett had a record with the NYPD. Chang didn't become known to him until after he was dead. Through the New York City Corrections Department, New Haven detectives had contacted the Bureau of Alcohol, Tobacco and Firearms—which had started a nationwide computer base of Jamaican criminals, who were operating criminal organizations in just about every major urban center around—and found out that an associate of Chang's had been murdered in Texas. There were already inquiries on Chang, and a red flag popped. The ATF referred the New Haven police to the NYPD's 67th Precinct, where Chang had been killed.

"They said, 'You'd better call Carbone from the Seven-Five Precinct, because he's got Brackett as a suspect.' "

Dave grunted assent, and Howard continued.

"I got pretty familiar with the Brooklyn Jamaicans who had come up here to New Haven. They had no desire to go back to East New York. These were hard guys, but even they couldn't handle the indiscriminate violence in your area. They were afraid if they stayed down there, they'd die.

"When I finally got hold of a couple of them and showed them the picture of Brackett and Chang, they shuddered. One of them said, 'These are evil guys. All they do is kill people.'

"That's the one thing about this case that's always kept me going," admitted Howard. "I'm not going to say it was so much my concern for the victim, although he went through hell. But to premeditate and act out this murder as coldly as they did—you go all out to solve it. You want to get these guys off the street, because wherever they go, there's going to be bodies."

Dave detected regret in the caller's voice. If Howard had arrested Brackett, he wouldn't have been able to kill Shaun Henry and Robert Dudley.

"We're an urban center, and I've seen a lot of violence," Howard said, "but this has to be the single worst premeditated, cold-blooded murder I've seen."

The two detectives spoke at length and agreed to stay in touch.

"Nothing on any of the plates," Janet Barry informed Dave at the front desk.

Dave was pissed. It had been a good try, but to no avail. Having gleaned the addresses and phone numbers from Brackett's rap sheets, he had ordered lugs and tolls—cop jargon for telephone records—on Charlie Brackett's house, Brackett's mother's house, and Brackett's wife's business, a hair salon. Dozens of pages had come back from the telephone company. Each of the numbers called from or received at these three places had to be checked out. Dave had looked up their addresses in Cole's directories, then given them to CARS to run to see whether any location had had any arrests. Zippo. So he and Smitty had spent the day staking out a number of the locations, watching who went in and out, and jotting down the license plate numbers of cars in the driveways and around the residences and businesses. Now here was Janet Barry saying that nothing checked out.

Exasperated, Dave turned to Smitty. "He's got to be *somewhere.* I don't think he's in Connecticut. It doesn't look like he's in Brooklyn. And not in Florida either."

An informant had told Dave that one of Brackett's cars had Florida license plates. Dave had already called the Dade County police to have them run a complete check in Florida, but they, too, came up empty.

And Dave and New Haven detective Joe Howard had mailed and faxed each other numerous reports and notes from their files. Dave ran the locations of all the 718, 212, and 516 phone numbers, and nothing popped there either. He had put massive efforts into tracking down Brackett, but so far nothing was panning out.

"If you had an arrest warrant on him," Smitty responded, "you could have him on NCIC."

The National Crime Information Center was the FBI's national computer network of people wanted by local law enforcement. If a person on NCIC was stopped anywhere in the country by a cop and the cop ran his name, a flag would pop. To get a name in the computer, there had to be an arrest warrant out on the subject. To obtain the warrant, Dave would have to go to the Brooklyn DA to have it drawn up and then signed by a judge.

"Nah," Dave said. "Then he'd have an automatic right to counsel, and if he has that, you know he's not going to talk. I need to talk to him. If I talk to him, I think I can jerk him off to get a confession out of him. Besides, Detective Howard in Connecticut already has an arrest warrant on him. He is in NCIC, so why should I have to put one out? Then I'd have to expose my witness, which I'd rather not do."

Smitty leaned back in his chair. "I hear ya," he said.

Sitting at his desk, Dave stared at the "Death's Door" placards on the wall to his right. It was early May of 1990, and the number was swiftly approaching the middle double digits; at this rate, he reflected sadly, the precinct would surely break one hundred murders this year. He thought of the poignantly whimsical little poem Captain Finn had composed after one recent massacre:

> *Amazing grace,*
> *How sweet the sound*
> *That saved a wretch like me.*

I was once alive
In the Seven-Five
But now I'm thirty-three.

He was wondering how so many people could be killed in such a small area when Jerry Rupprecht told him he had a phone call.

Dave picked up the phone. "Carbone."

"Hi, Dave, Joe Howard."

"Yo, Joe, whassup?"

"There doesn't appear to be too much more we can do to help each other find Brackett," Howard said to Dave resignedly. "I'd think if he's back in Brooklyn, you're going to hear about it."

"Probably," Dave said.

"In my case," Howard continued, "I think I've gotten as much as I'm going to get here unless some other people come forward and help me out. But I don't think that's going to happen, because even though they know the other guy is dead, there are folks here who just hate the sight of me because they know I'm going to start talking about it again and try to recruit them, and they don't want any part of it."

Howard thought Brackett was a real morose, inscrutable kind of guy, the type who inspired instinctive fear.

Sometimes Detective Howard seemed discouraged, Dave noticed.

"No one wants to talk to you," Howard continued. "People are unreliable sources of information to begin with—that's even if they're trying to help you. You're wandering on in the dark with a little torch trying to find your way to the truth, and even then you have to find it in such a way that you can present it in court in front of a judge and a jury."

"Joe." Dave interrupted Howard's dark train of thought. "You've been working too hard. What you need is a little stakeout work. And I don't mean the work kind. I'm talking stakeout. You know, like taking your *steak out*. That's what you need, Joe. Don't let that meat loaf."

One day, Dave received a call from a disgruntled East New York resident. His apartment had been burglarized, and a print team had come out to dust his place. The prints were run but nothing popped, and there were no witnesses to the crime. The man was upset because he felt "violated" by the burglary—cash, jewelry, and electronic equipment had being taken, a window had been broken, drawers and closets had been emptied, and clothes had been thrown all over the place—and he was also indignant because the detectives seemed to be doing nothing about the case.

Dave listened sympathetically to the man. Then he said, "So what would you like me to do about it? I don't mean to be smart, but if no one saw anybody do the crime, and the burglar didn't leave any finger-prints or evidence behind, what can I do?"

The man snorted derisively. "What are you asking me for? You're the detective. It's your job to figure out what to do. You seem to have forgotten, we pay your salary. So get busy!"

There was a loud click as the man slammed down the receiver.

Dave sighed. People had unrealistic expectations of what detec-tives could accomplish, most of it from television and movies. Detec-tives could only work with what they had, and if they had nothing, there was simply nothing they could do. Detectives weren't magicians who could conjure up evidence out of thin air. The only time they could break a case like this, barring a confession down the line from an apprehended perp, was when they had a witness or some evidence, such as a fingerprint, was recovered.

Dave had had some burglaries for which witnesses had been found, but there was a problem: They weren't willing to tell the story in court. "Why should I testify against some psycho drug dealer or addict?" they wanted to know. "So they can be released after a few months and come looking for me or my family?" Dave was forced to concede they had a point.

In other instances, although the witnesses might have solid infor-mation and be willing to testify, their reliability would not be likely to impress the court. "The court wants to hear testimony from three nuns and a priest," Smitty had observed, "but your witness at a drug location isn't usually going to be an upstanding citizen. It's going to be some mutt. That's who's going to take the stand. You might not be happy about it, but you take what you can get."

Dave had found that many complainants wouldn't press him or other detectives for progress on catching the perp. Often they didn't seem to care. With people being killed on every other street corner in the community, he thought, why get carried away over a burglary? Why would anyone put his life at risk for the sake of some possessions? All too frequently, a witness wouldn't testify to having witnessed his best friend's murder.

Dave understood this was the reality of life in the ghetto. Burglary victims sometimes didn't want to pursue a case in court even when the detectives found the alleged perp. "You got the guy?" they'd say in-credulously. "Oh, let him go. I can't take two days off from work to go to court." Or, "You got my car back? I don't want to press charges. We'd spend more time in court than the guy would get." Of course, when that happened, it was all over. If there was no complainant, there wasn't any case.

Dave had even had a case in which the complainant had gone to court, but after waiting several hours for an ADA, had said disgustedly, "I'm not waiting no more," and left. The suspect had been released from jail, and Dave was open to a lawsuit. Fortunately for him, the suspect never sued.

The bulk of the cases that came into the Seven-Five squad fell into three categories: homicides, assaults, and burglaries. Homicide was in a class by itself. It was the only crime in which the victim couldn't talk to the detectives. "We speak for the dead person," Redmond had told Dave. "We file the charges for the victim. We're the complainant for them." All the other crimes had a complainant, but if the complainant or a witness wasn't willing to testify, the case was closed.

There were also larcenies and other types of crimes, but many of these were referred to specialized units. Robberies, of course, went to the RIP unit. Rapes, sexual assaults, and related crimes went to the Sex Crimes unit. At one point early in his career, Dave had considered requesting assignment to that unit, but he had decided it wouldn't be challenging enough for him. Most sex crime victims, he believed, knew their assailants, so it was simply a matter of tracking a known perp down.

With the high volume of crime in the 75th Precinct, there often simply wasn't enough time or manpower to investigate cases in which no one had been seriously injured or killed, especially when all the work involved so often came to naught. While Dave lamented this, there wasn't much choice; most of his time was spent on murders.

Over the next few months, as scores of people continued to get whacked in the Seven-Five, Dave worked his cases in anticipation of a very special moment that was approaching, one every white-shield detective looked forward to: getting his gold police detective shield.

At seven o'clock on the morning of June 27, 1990, fifty white shields being promoted reported to One Police Plaza. On the tenth floor, they assembled into a line, and one by one they turned in their silver police officer shields. Another officer threw the silver shields into a box and handed them their gold shields. They exchanged their police officer identification cards for detective ID cards. As they trooped into the auditorium a short while later, Dave realized that when he had turned in his white shield, he had forgotten to remove from it the good-luck charm he had taped onto the back—an oval gold medallion bearing the image of the Blessed Mother, arms outstretched in blessing.

By the time the ceremony was to begin at eleven o'clock, the auditorium was filled. Luci and Danielle were there, having taken a cab into the city from Long Island. Luci was holding a videocamera to tape the event. Dave and the other officers were seated at the front of the room in their blue dress police uniforms.

This occasion marked the first time in years that Dave had worn his police uniform. But since he was now fifty pounds heavier than the 135 pounds he'd come on the job with, he had to borrow all the different parts of the uniform from other officers. He also had to cut off his ponytail. He'd instructed his barber to save and braid the nine-inch section of hair to give to his daughter. For the ceremony, Dave sported a military-style haircut.

Numerous dignitaries attended the promotion ceremony, including Police Commissioner H. Lee Brown and Chief of Detectives Joseph Borelli. Tom Scotto, Jack Healy, and Al Marini, the top executives of the Detectives' Endowment Association, the union for NYPD detectives, were also there. The fifty new gold shields stood up, and the PC swore them all in together. Then, one at a time, they walked to the podium to receive their detective certificates.

After the ceremony, Danielle begged to put on her dad's police cap and gloves. Then it was Dave's turn to have his picture taken with Chief Borelli. As Dave bent down to have Danielle replace the hat on his head, a photographer snapped a picture, which appeared the next day in the *New York Daily News*.

Luci and Danielle were proud of this moment. For Dave, it was an official confirmation of his new status. No longer a white shield, he had earned the rank of detective and would no longer have to put the initials P.O., for police officer, before his signature. Although he would still be doing the same work he had done as an investigator in RIP and the Seven-Five squad, he was now officially a detective in the New York City Police Department, a full member of the Detective Bureau. He could now sign his name *"Det.* David Carbone.''

Over a background of menacing, discordant woodwinds, the camera focused first on a painted sign bearing the words "The Pit Stop," then drew back for a long shot of a grubby-looking auto repair shop. As the camera tracked around to the rear of the shop, a parked car occupied by two passengers came into view. For a moment nothing happened, then all of a sudden two men brandishing guns glided silently into the camera frame from either side, swiftly approaching the car. The background music rose to an agitated climax as the gunmen raised their weapons and spewed a rain of bullets on the men seated in the car. The gunmen then turned and ran, disappearing around the side of the shop. The camera moved in for a close-up through the shattered car window of the passengers, now awkwardly sprawled across the seats, motionless, their faces and bodies covered with blood. A mournful, sustained minor chord swelled briefly, diminishing into silence as the camera withdrew slowly and the scene faded to black.

Thousands of people in the New York City metropolitan area would see this reenactment of the Shaun Henry–Robert Dudley murders, which was run on Channel 5's *New York's Most Wanted* television program in conjunction with the NYPD's Crime Stoppers Unit. Having exhausted almost all his leads, Dave had decided he needed the public's assistance in locating Charlie Brackett and had requested the Crime Stoppers Unit to highlight the double murder on television. When a criminal was on the loose, it was often difficult to find him unless he messed up and revealed himself or somebody turned him in. So far, Brackett hadn't been careless, and no one had called the police.

In addition to the reenactment, the segment featured an interview with Dave, who identified Charles Brackett as one of the suspects. The program's host asked viewers to call 577-TIPS if they could provide any information that would help police find the killer.

One of the first calls to come to the station was from Charlie Brackett himself. His voice was stone cold, his message brief. "I'm going to get Carbone before he gets me," he decreed.

The next day Brackett issued a second threat, this time more explicit, to a 911 operator. "I'm going to kill Detective Carbone," he averred. The operator immediately called police headquarters and relayed the threat, which was referred to the NYPD's Intelligence Division.

A short time later, the phone rang at the Carbone home. Luci took the call; Dave was out picking up dinner at Galleria Pizza, a nearby Italian restaurant. When he returned, Luci appeared very upset.

"What's the matter?" he asked.

"Some detective called, and he wants you to call him immediately. It sounded important." Luci looked Dave straight in the eyes. "I'm worried," she said.

Dave called the Intelligence Division detective back right away.

"Are you having trouble with anybody lately?" the voice over the phone asked.

"No, not to my knowledge."

"Did you just do a case with somebody on TV?"

"Yes. I'm looking for a guy named Charlie Brackett. I want him for a double murder in the Seven-Five, and he's also wanted for murder in New Haven."

"Well, he called the station and nine-one-one and said he's going to kill you." The intelligence detective paused a moment. "How real a threat do you think it is?"

"Brackett's a major drug dealer, and he's killed three people that we know of so far. The threat doesn't bother me personally, but because of my family it does mean something."

"Do you want any extra protection?"

"For my family, I'd appreciate it."

Luci, sitting in the living room, was reading her husband's face. "What was it?" she asked when he hung up.

"That asshole I put on TV the other day said he's going to kill me. Don't worry about it."

"Does he know where we live?"

"No, I don't think so. The house will be monitored for a while, but I don't think he'll come after you or Danielle. If he wants me, he knows where he can get me. But just for the time being, don't answer the phone. Let the machine take the calls. And if you see anybody suspicious on the street, call nine-one-one."

Brackett's calls weren't the first death threats Dave had received. Just a few months earlier, someone had called the station house and said, "We're going to kill Detective Carbone." Because Dave had locked up a number of perps, he didn't know who the call had come from. The leader of a Dominican gang being investigated by Dave and Joe Hall had issued threats on both detectives' lives also. And when he was in RIP, he and Billy Ciorciari used to mess with the drug dealers on the street so relentlessly that calls constantly came into the precinct from rough-sounding men threatening to kill Starsky and Hutch, the street nicknames of the two detectives.

Dave was used to death threats and understood they came with the turf. They really didn't bother him, but he always worried about his family. To make sure he wasn't being followed home from work, he never stopped at a red light in East New York, he regularly changed his route home, and he drove as fast as he safely could. These were precautionary measures active detectives sometimes took.

Dave considered his conversation with the Intelligence Division detective a moment. Somehow Brackett's calls worried him more than any of the others he had received. Brackett was cold-blooded, ruthless, and cunning, no doubt about it, and there was no telling where he might stop. So it was prudent, Dave concluded, to accept police protection.

Nassau County police, at the request of the NYPD, began special surveillance of the Carbone home. Both patrol units and detectives were assigned to watch and safeguard the house.

Brackett's death threats prompted one other change in Dave's life. When he was not working, he had separated himself from the job as much as he could, and he usually didn't carry an off-duty revolver because it was cumbersome under the shorts, T-shirts, and sneakers or jogging suits he favored for casual wear. But from that time on, he never left his house without his gun.

But Dave also resolved he wouldn't let his job interfere with his personal life. He would continue to hunt down criminals without worrying that the repercussions of a chase or arrest might affect him personally. He believed the potential risk to his family was minimal; in any case, he was in the kind of job in which it was just an occupational hazard. Luci and Danielle knew it too, and they accepted it. Their pride in Dave overshadowed any fear.

15

Although Brackett had made no attempt to carry out his death threat, the Carbones never dropped their guard, even at home. Dave checked out the occasional lead on Brackett when it came in, but he spent most of his time immersed in his new cases, which continued to pour in at a merciless rate. Sometimes payoffs turned up in unusual ways.

When the phone call came in one morning from the Warrant Division about the release of Derrick Vaughn from Sing Sing Prison, Dave felt an immediate charge. He'd have to work quickly, do some fast talking, but it would all be worth it if he could claim his bounty: a murderer.

"We were told to notify your squad when Derrick Vaughn was released," the caller stated, "and he's being released later today."

Dave speedily obtained permission to go to the correction facility in Ossining, New York. With Jerry Roman, he immediately set out on the three-hour journey upstate.

Judicious planning was behind the trip. Sergeant Race had asked Dave to investigate some unsolved murders. This one involved the case of Harold Bartlett, a twenty-five-year-old who had been shot down on Miller Avenue. A witness had identified the killer as Derrick Vaughn, but efforts to find Vaughn had failed.

Everybody's gotta be someplace, Dave had reminded himself as he began his investigation. It was the kind of very basic logic that detectives once in a while had to use on themselves when a criminal eluded them.

The first thing to determine was whether the subject was dead or in jail. Dave had called BCI and found out that Vaughn had recently been arrested on a gun possession charge and was serving time in Sing Sing. How fortunate, Dave thought, but he soon realized he had a problem. The witness could not be located to charge Vaughn with Harold Bartlett's murder, and without a witness, there simply was no case.

A master jerkologist shouldn't have to worry about a minor technicality like a witness, Dave mused. An idea popped into his head, and he picked up the phone. Calling the CARS unit, he obtained the date Derrick Vaughn was going to be released. The timing was nearly perfect. Vaughn would get out of Sing Sing in just a few months. Arms folded, Dave had reclined in his chair and smiled. He would be waiting.

That afternoon, to any uninformed observer, Dave was casually hanging out in the release processing area of Sing Sing. He spotted a man finishing up some paperwork at one of the desks and approached him. "Say, aren't you from East New York?" he said brightly.

The man looked up. "Yeah. So?"

"Oh, man, what a fucking coincidence. I'm Detective Carbone. From East New York! I was just up here visiting somebody. Hey, man, what's your name?"

"Derrick Vaughn," said the man, unsmiling.

"Derrick Vaughn? Yo, man, I know you." Dave rubbed his jaw and thought a moment. "Hey, ya know, there was something I wanted to discuss with you back at the precinct. You getting out now?"

"Yeah, man. I done my time."

"Good for you." Dave slapped him on the shoulder. "Why don't you let me give you a ride back home?"

"That'd be great, man," said Vaughn, unsuspecting. "I'm going home to see my girl. She was just up here. Yeah, she bought me this brand-new Fila outfit and these brand-new sneakers. I can't wait to see her." Vaughn let out a whooping laugh. "I'm gonna be slamming ham tonight." His eyes were lit up.

"Outta *sight*, man," said Dave fervently. "Let's get the fuck outta here."

The ride back to East New York was filled with mirthful banter. Sitting in the backseat, Vaughn rattled on about how happy he was to be out of jail and to be reuniting with his girlfriend, and the detectives up front chatted about their jobs. It was all small talk, but they were enjoying themselves, having a good time.

"Yeah, I did my time, man," Vaughn said as they arrived in East New York. "Can't wait to go home and see my girl. Gonna take her out to dinner tonight, then get me a slice."

The unmarked squad car pulled into the rear parking lot of the 75th Precinct. "Here we are," Dave said. "Home of the bone. Yo, man, this won't take long."

In the squad room, Dave asked Vaughn to sit down.

"A few months ago, weren't you in some kind of shootout with a guy in East New York?"

Vaughn scratched his head. "When?"

"A few months ago. You got into an argument with some guy and had a shootout."

Vaughn thought a moment. "Oh, yeah," he said, laughing.

"Listen, before we get into it, it's just procedure, but I have to read you your rights. Don't worry, the guy's still alive. He's in Pennsylvania in a rehab program. But he told us everything, that you two had a fight, that you pulled out a gun and shot him. I have to take care of this case because it's still open." Dave shook his head and blew a frustrated sigh, as if to say what a pain in the ass this whole thing was.

"Yeah, man, I understand. It's okay."

So Dave read him his rights.

"Say," queried Vaughn, "you *sure* he's still alive?"

"Yeah, he's just in rehab. Don't worry about it."

Vaughn was anxious to see his girlfriend. "How long is this going to take?"

"As long as it takes you to tell me what happened."

"Okay, because I'm running out of time here. You know, I really gotta go."

"You're going to go, man, I promise you. Now, why don't you tell me what happened?"

"Well, me and Harold got into an argument over money I lent him. I said, 'Yo, when you going to pay my money?' He told me he ain't giving me my money, and then he stepped back a little bit, and then I backed up a little bit. He pulled out a gun and fired a shot at me and missed. I fired a shot at him, and then I ran."

"What kind of gun did you have?"

"A revolver."

"And Harold?"

"I think he had a revolver too."

"How many times did you shoot him?"

"Once."

"After you shot at him, what happened?"

"I ran."

"Do you remember where you ran?"

"Up Miller."

"What happened to your gun?"

"I was running. I dropped it, and I didn't bother picking it up. I just kept running."

"Do you remember where you dropped it?"

"No, it just fell out of my pocket."

"You never went back?"

"After I pulled my gun and shot, I took the fuck off. I ran away and never went back there."

"You never went back there to find out what happened?"

"No, man. That ain't my thing. I did my shooting and off I went."

"No kidding?"

"That's it." He paused. "Are you sure the guy's alive?"

Dave spread his hands, his eyes wide. "The guy's alive! How do you think I know you did it?"

"Well . . . uh . . . I guess so."

"That's how. That's how I know." Dave nodded earnestly.

"Can I go now?"

"Well, wait a second. I gotta call the district attorney's office and tell them you're saying the other guy had a gun. You're kinda like saying it was self-defense. And then we'll leave it at that. Let me call the DA, because we gotta take care of this problem now."

Vaughn was visibly upset that he would be delayed getting to his girlfriend. Maybe he shouldn't have accepted the ride with the detectives after all.

"Yo, man, gotta go."

"I know you gotta go, I understand that. You are going to go."

"Okay, good."

"I'm going to call the DA, so sit down and relax." Vaughn sat in the interview room, and Dave brought him a soda. Soon Vaughn was telling other detectives who came in how he was going to go home and take his girl out to dinner in his brand-new Fila outfit tonight.

After calling the DA's office, Dave returned to the lounge, shaking his head. Vaughn looked at him with alarm.

"We've got a problem," said Dave sadly.

"Oh, man," Vaughn whined in frustration. "What the fuck's the problem?"

"The DA wants to come down and talk to you about this."

"Yo, man. How long's that gonna take?"

"As long as it takes you to tell him the same thing you told me."

"All right. Get him down here now, man. I'm in a talking mood. I wanna go."

A short while later an ADA arrived. "Listen," he said to Vaughn. "I have to read you your rights."

"I know my rights."

"No, no. I have to read you your rights on video before I talk with you."

"Okay, okay, no problem. Let's hurry, because I've gotta go."

With the videotape running, Vaughn gave his story again, exactly as he had told it to Dave.

As Vaughn acted the whole story out, Dave laughed to himself. This is great, he thought. The guy's doing acrobatics for the ADA.

After Vaughn finished telling his story, he looked at Dave. "Yo, can I go now?"

"You're gonna go, but not just yet. It's up to the man here."

Vaughn turned to the ADA. "Yo, man, can't I go now?"

"Listen, I can't talk to you," said the ADA. "If it's not on record I can't talk to you, so I'm going to leave the room."

Dave shrugged at Vaughn. "That's the DA's thing. They can't talk to you unless it's on record."

"Yeah, yeah, I understand."

Dave excused himself to take care of some business. A half an hour later, he stuck his head in the room.

"How you doing?"

"Yo, man, is it time to go? I been here a long time. I helped you out. The guy's alive, right?"

"Yeah, I told you the guy's alive. But I have to see what the DA wants to do with the case. If he's going to let you go, he's going to let you go. Not a big deal."

"Okay." Vaughn sighed in frustration and buried his head in his hands.

In another area of the squad room, the ADA, pending authorization from his boss, was writing up the charge: murder two, just as Dave had known he would. He shook his head. Vaughn didn't even know yet that he had murdered Harold Bartlett. A short time later, the ADA received authorization to lock up Vaughn on the murder charge.

Dave sauntered back to the lounge. Before he could speak, Vaughn exclaimed, "Yo, man, could I go?"

"Got a problem," Dave said, like he was really sorry.

"Oh, man, another problem?"

"It's a small problem, but you can't go home just yet. I'm gonna have to put you into the system real quick. The ADA is upset. You had a gun, and he wants to charge you with it."

"How long will this be now?"

"I don't know. How long is arraignments? Ten, twelve hours? It's still early enough. You should be able to make night court."

"Night court?"

"Yeah, you ever watch that show on TV?"

"Oh yeah, night court."

"You'll make night court. No problem."

Vaughn asked if he could call his girlfriend, and Dave said sure.

"Yo, baby," Vaughn said into the phone. "I'm not going to be home soon. Maybe later tonight or tomorrow. I gotta take care of this little problem from an old case that I have."

Dave and Roman escorted Vaughn back to the squad car. During the trip, Vaughn expressed his gratitude to Carbone for expediting his case. Dave was gracious.

"No problem, man."

"I'm really pissed I didn't get to go home right away, though. You think I still might get to go home tonight?"

"You might. Are you going to be able to get there?"

"Yeah, man, my girl gave me some money. I'll take a cab. I'm good to go." Vaughn glanced out the window, then turned to Dave. "Yeah, I don't mind going to court. No problem. Because the guy had a gun."

Twenty minutes later they arrived at Brooklyn Central Booking. After Vaughn was processed, Dave clapped him on the shoulder. "Yo, man, I'll see you tomorrow."

"What you mean, *tomorrow?*"

"Oh, I'm sorry. I mean later on, maybe. I may come back to night court tonight just to see if you get arraigned or not." Dave knew he wouldn't, but he did intend to come back in the morning.

The next morning, Dave was sitting in the rear of the courtroom when Vaughn was brought before the judge for his arraignment. He stood in his white Fila outfit, now limp and wrinkled, and his brand-new sneakers. His hands, uncuffed, were behind his back, and he was bopping back and forth. He appeared antsy. Dave could see he was anxious as ever to get out of there and go home. His girlfriend was sitting near the front of the room.

The prosecutor began reading the charges. Vaughn was looking around the room as if to say, "Who the hell is this dude talking about?"

The judge said, "You've been charged with murder in the second degree. How does your client plead?"

Derrick Vaughn looked behind him to see who the judge was talking to. Murder? Someone in the courtroom had done a murder? He twisted his neck and swept the room with his eyes, looking for the murderer.

Then it hit him. "Murder who?" Vaughn shouted. He turned to the judge, who was staring at him. Vaughn's head snapped back. "Yo, I didn't murder nobody."

"You're being charged with murder in the second degree," the judge said.

Vaughn's girlfriend stood up and screamed in protest.

Vaughn suddenly thought of Carbone. "Yo, man, the mother-fucker fucked me. He *fucked* me!"

The judge peered at the court-appointed lawyer. "How does your client plead?"

"My client pleads not guilty, your honor."

"No bail. Remanded at this time." The judge looked down at the papers before him and assigned a future court date.

Dave sat in the back trying to stifle his laughter. Vaughn had been nice to him, but he didn't feel guilty about putting a stroke job over on him. Vaughn's crime had been ruthless. He thought about the statement of the witness to the murder of Harold Bartlett, which he had read in the case folder.

The witness had been standing in the front hall of a crack spot waiting to buy drugs from Bartlett when the manager of the spot, whom she knew as Devon, entered. She heard the two arguing over a shortage of money.

"This better be right or I'm going to kill your ass," Devon had shouted. When he had finished counting he said, "You're forty dollars short. Where is it?"

"Eason said I could smoke two vials," Bartlett explained, referring to another manager of the spot.

"Yeah, fine, but what about the rest, you little fuck?"

Devon then attacked Harold. "I'll work off the money, I'll work it off," Harold cried, as Devon slammed him again and again.

At this point the witness realized the situation was growing serious, and she left, going across the street. A minute later she saw Harold Bartlett come outside with Devon right behind him.

"You better not run," Devon had shouted.

The witness reported that Bartlett had turned to run. "Then Devon pulled out a black Western-type revolver and fired a shot. Bartlett went back into the crack spot, then immediately came out and staggered into a grocery store on the corner, where he collapsed on the floor."

Dave acknowledged that Bartlett wasn't a model citizen himself. He was a drug dealer, and he hadn't even cooperated in the investigation of his assailant.

In the hospital, twelve hours before he died, Bartlett was interviewed by a detective.

"Who shot you?"

"Nobody."

"How did it happen?"

"I did it myself."

Harold Bartlett's brother, Andre, said he knew Devon, and identified him by his real name, Derrick Vaughn. After a mug shot of
Vaughn, who had a previous arrest record, was obtained from the
NYPD's Photo Unit, detectives displayed a photo array before Andre,
and he picked out Derrick Vaughn, the man he also knew as Devon.
Two weeks later, the witness to the killing of Harold Bartlett came to
the squad room and viewed another photo array. Pointing to Vaughn's
picture, she said, "That's him. That's the man who shot Bartlett.
That's Devon." She said she had known Devon for two years and had
seen him nearly every day.

In the courtroom, as Vaughn was being led away by armed court
officers, he cast a reproachful glance at Dave. Dave muttered under his
breath, "See, I told you you were going to go."

And go he did. He was sent to the correctional facility at Riker's
Island, where he was imprisoned while he awaited trial. About a year
later, Derrick Vaughn was convicted of murder and sentenced to
twenty-three years to life in prison.

16

A great many of the murders in East New York, Dave had observed, fell into one of two categories: drugs or disses. Dissing—being disrespect-ful—could be a capital crime on the streets of the ghetto. Dis murders were usually quick shootings over something nonsensical, an imagined insult or imposition, as in the case of the unfortunate man who had had the temerity to tap his car's horn when his way was blocked by an informal gathering on the road. Drug homicides, in contrast, could be for anything from a dealer stealing money from the organization he worked for to all-out gang warfare. With drugs a multimillion-dollar industry in the area, the players were often ruthless, stopping at noth-ing to keep their organizations going.

On a late-October evening in 1990, Team One was in the squad room on a four-to-one. The night was clear and bright, and cool breezes presaged the wintry weather to come. There was only an hour and fifteen minutes to go on the tour, and, blessedly, not much was happening.

From a window, Dave and Smitty surveyed the street. They spotted a figure with cut-up arms, blood dripping from his face, and a knife embedded in his neck. "Not many kids out tonight," Dave said, ex-pecting to see more ghoulish creatures. It was Halloween.

The two women were leaving the three-story house on the north side of the precinct, across from Highland Park. Just as they opened the door, three gunmen bum-rushed them—pushed them inside—and, pressing the barrels of guns to their heads, ordered them to carry out their instructions. Seconds later the women knocked on the door of the second-floor apartment, the home of a friend. When the friend opened the door, the gunmen burst in, shepherding their two prison-ers.

The first 911 call came in shortly before midnight. The voice was the Spanish-accented raspy whisper of an old lady.

"They broke into the house, on my girlfriend's floor. They're look-ing for drugs." A reel-to-reel tape recorder next to the Central opera-tor was spinning. "It sounds like somebody's getting beat up inside the apartment." The raspy whisper was edged with panic.

"What's the address?"

"672 Jamaica Avenue, in Brooklyn."

"The police will be there as soon as possible," said the operator reassuringly.

Inside the second-floor apartment was a woman and her two-year-old son. As the woman registered an expression of exasperation one of the intruders whacked her on the side of her head with his gun. For the next few minutes the three men pistol-whipped the three women, who fell to the ground and cried out in anguish. Then, while one of the men trained a .357 magnum on the captives, another tied everyone up with duct tape. The third man was shouting, "Where's the drugs? Where's the money?"

Three minutes after the first call, another came in to 911. This time the caller was a young woman, also with a Spanish accent. Her voice was urgent. "I was taking a shower, and when I came out, my mother was all upset, and she says, 'I don't know what's going on downstairs, but some people just walked in and there was screaming and bang-ing.' "

"Do you know if they have any weapons?"

"I don't know. But it sounds like people are getting hurt."

"All right, the police will be there, ma'am."

The woman resident of the apartment pleaded she didn't know anything about drugs or money, and a man thrashed her over and over again. As she lay on the floor, hysterical now, the man said, "Okay, if you don't tell me I'm going to kill your baby."

The woman screamed, "No, no!" She crawled to a back bedroom and pulled out a large black duffel bag filled with drugs.

"Now where's the money?" he demanded.

"I don't know, I don't know!" the woman cried, straining to see her baby.

Two police officers entered the Jamaica Avenue building by the front door and were greeted by the young woman who had made the second 911 call. Wide-eyed, she pointed to the second floor.

Police Officer Joel Goldberg, an eighteen-year veteran, knocked on the apartment door; Officer Fred Bonhag, a rookie, stood off to the side.

A few seconds later, Goldberg tried again. The door snapped open, and the report of a shotgun echoed deafeningly in the hallway.

The third 911 call came through a minute later. A woman was shrieking frantically. "A cop got shot. Somebody come quick. Hurry up. Quick!"

"Where at?"

"672 Jamaica. They shot the cops! They shot the cops!" The woman was hysterical.

"What are the cross streets?"

"Jamaica between Logan and Norwood. They shot a cop! Hurry up, please." Then the woman screamed to her mother in Spanish, and the mother screamed back in Spanish.

"What apartment?"

"Second floor."

"Hold on, hold on, let me get the cars going."

"Lock the door. Ma! Lock the door!"

Then the line went dead, and the operator heard a dial tone.

The detectives in the Seven-Five squad room were doing paperwork or perusing case folders and listening to the police band with half an ear. The voices on the radio were calm, even bored, exchanging routine bits of information. The Central operator, sector cops, the Central operator again, now maybe the burglary unit. Routine stuff. All of a sudden the leisurely rhythm of voices was interrupted. "Tenthirteen, ten-thirteen!" a cop screamed over the radio at the top of his lungs. Chairs clattered backward to the floor, coffee cups overturned, and papers scattered as every man in the room leaped to his feet as if shot through with a jolt of electricity.

One of a few radio codes in the NYPD that means an officer needs assistance, a 10-13 is the very worst one, the absolute horror signal, the one cops don't use unless their lives are on the line.

"Ten-thirteen!" came another voice, quick and sharp. "672 Jamaica Avenue. 672 Jamaica." There was shouting in the background, the sound of hysteria.

A series of rapid beeping tones was suddenly emitted over all the radios in the precinct. The alarm had been sounded; the Central operator was sending the cavalry into action.

"Ten-thirteen, I'm shot," the first voice cried out again.

The Central operators empathized deeply with the cops out on the street. The operators were the officers' lifeline, their support system. Safe in the fortress that is One Police Plaza, the Central operators did all they could to assist the men and women police officers risking their lives on the streets.

"Okay. 672 Jamaica, units . . ."

Another cop's voice interrupted harshly. "Ten-thirteen, cop shot, cop down."

The tones sounded rapidly in succession again.

By this time all available police units in the Seven-Five and adjoining precincts had begun blazing a path to the scene.

New voices sounded on the radio, asking Central for cross streets, descriptions of the gunmen, the best routes to the crime scene. It was up to the operators to get all the units to the scene as quickly as possible.

The radio was a babble of confusion—static, cops' voices, the Central operators, police sirens, the beeping tones, telephones being dialed.

At One Police Plaza, one Central operator was pounding the computer. Another was stomping her foot pedal to activate voice communication over the line. She stood up, pumping her foot, bending her knees, flexing her arms, talking quickly, gyrating, an agonized expression on her face. The Central operators for each of the other boroughs, in separate rooms partitioned by glass windows, watched her, feeling her anxiety as their own.

Sector cars, Anticrime and Street Crime units, Emergency Service Unit trucks, detectives, housing cops, transit cops—all were in motion now. The previously quiet darkness exploded with the wail of sirens and the furious flash of turret lights.

The wounded officer came on the radio again. "Get me to a hospital," he pleaded. "I'm shot!"

A robbery car was the first to arrive at the scene. The wounded officer was slumped against a streetlight outside the location, barely able to stand. Two cops scooped him up and raced into the night.

"Five robbery, one," the recorder transmitted. "We've got the officer. On our way to Brookdale."

The Central operator alerted Brookdale Hospital. Central was also communicating with the robbery car to coordinate with patrol officers closing the streets along the route. "They're going down Jamaica Avenue," the operator said. "Block the road for them." In seconds there was virtually a straight path to the hospital, impermeable by any civilian vehicle.

One by one, in quick succession, police units converged on the crime scene, until it was a mass of blue, radiating an undulating stream of radio noises. There had been information that some of the perps had fled the location, and several cops were already in pursuit.

Dave and Sergeant Race took the crime scene, and Smitty and Cutrone went to the hospital to interview the wounded officer. When Dave and Race pulled up to 672 Jamaica Avenue, the first thing they observed was a man lying faceup on the ground. They got out of the car and crouched down. The man looked Hispanic, and there was no life in him. Whatever had happened to the wounded officer, the case was now a homicide. Dave was up on the rotation order, so the case was his.

"What's in here?" Dave asked, eyeballing a large black sack next to the body. He picked it up and inside found three bags of white powder wrapped in clear plastic.

"Hey, Yeager," Dave shouted to the uniformed officer standing by the doorway. "Guard the drugs and body here while we go upstairs."

Large drops of blood dotted the pavement in front of the door. Dave and Race entered the house and clattered up the stairs parallel to the thick trail of blood, which grew denser as they ascended.

Uniformed cops thronged the vicinity of the apartment, their radios turned up; Dave could hear patrol officers informing Central of their pursuit of at least one of the perps. When he and Race got to the second floor, Dave directed a cop to seal off the building. Other officers were searching inside the building for any perps who had fled the crime scene.

"Are there any witnesses?" Dave demanded of one, looking around the hallway. The walls and floor were splattered with blood. Stuck to one wall was a ragged mass of body tissue, hair, and pieces of a jacket.

"Yeah, they're on the third floor."

The three women, shaken, disheveled, and bleeding, sat in the third-floor apartment; the child curled crying softly on his mother's lap.

"It was a robbery," said a uniformed cop. "These women were all tied up and beaten."

Dave spoke to each of the women privately while the uniformed cop watched over the others. The conversations were brief; he just wanted to get a quick sense of what had happened. They were twenty-one, twenty-two, and thirty-one years old. Two were Puerto Ricans, one was Dominican. They were bruised, but their demeanor was tough. The Dominican said she lived with her husband and their child in the second-floor apartment below. Of the other two, one was from the third floor and the other was her cousin who was visiting.

The women accompanied Dave to the second floor. The apartment was sparsely furnished—just a couple of beds, a portable stereo, and a small TV. While Dave engaged in quiet conversation with the women, the radio continued to broadcast the manhunt.

"We're in pursuit in the rear of the building."

"Okay."

"Anybody eighty-four yet?" There were dozens of cops in front of the building and inside it.

"Yeah, yeah."

Another cop interrupted. "Slow down, slow down, we got him, K." There was deep satisfaction in his voice.

"You have him, K." The relief was audible.

"Do you think you could identify one of the gunmen?" Dave asked the three women. They all nodded.

Dave spoke into his own radio. "Central, have that unit bring the perpetrator around to the front of the building." He was going to do a show-up, a one-on-one viewing by a witness of an alleged perp. He brought the three women down to the first-floor apartment. While the suspect stood on the other side of the front door, the women came one at a time to look through the glass peephole in the door. The lights in the hallway were off, and it was dark. Each woman identified the suspect as one of the men who had beaten and robbed them at gunpoint.

Going outside, Dave told one of the officers holding the suspect to take him to the precinct squad room. "Put him in the interview room," Dave said. "He's not to be touched or moved till I get there."

Next, Dave went over to the DOA lying in front of the house and had a patrol officer escort the women one at a time out to where he was standing. The body on the ground was covered with blood, an expression of anguish on the face. Patrol had informed Dave that the cops who had been at the door had gotten off some shots; presumably one, at least, had hit its target.

"Can you identify this man?" Dave asked.

All three women said he was one of the gunmen.

Dave wasn't sure to what extent the other two women were involved in the drug trade, if at all. "Take them in separate cars to the precinct," he said brusquely to another uniform. "Put them in separate rooms."

Crime Scene came right away, and Dave asked the two detectives to try to lift as many fingerprints as possible, since one of the perps was still missing.

Back at the precinct later, Dave conducted exhaustive interviews with each of the three female victims separately. Their stories matched, but they professed innocence when it came to the drugs.

Dave asked the Dominican woman how many times she had moved over the past year.

"Four times," she said warily.

"Why were there drugs in your apartment?"

"I don't know."

"Let me repeat the question. Why were there drugs in your apartment?"

"I don't know," she insisted. "Really, I don't know!"

"There's only two ways I do an interview," Dave snapped back. "My way, or my way. Now, it's obvious you live in a stash house. You say you moved four times over the past year. You know I know what that means. People who live in a stash house are on the go, because if you stay in one place too long, people in the area are going to find out and rip you off. And what are you going to do? Call the cops and say somebody stole your drugs?" He bent down and put his face close to hers. "As soon as I stepped into your apartment and saw nothing there, I knew you were a fucking drug dealer." Straightening up, he said, "Now, I could care less about pieces of shit like you and your husband, but I do care about your baby. So I'm going to put you and your husband in jail and take your baby."

The woman's tough pose collapsed, and she began to weep. It was her husband, she said, sobbing. He transported drugs at Norwood and Fulton.

Dave knew the location. It was a heavy drug spot, run by the violent drug organization known as La Compañía.

"Where is your husband now?"

"Making a delivery."

"All right. We'll get him later. For now, I'm charging you with criminal possession of a controlled substance."

"Why?" she wailed.

"Because the drugs were in your apartment."

The woman became hysterical, begging Dave not to take away her baby. Dave contemplated turning the baby over to the Bureau of Child

Welfare, trying to resist the soft spot in his heart for little ones.

As a police officer, he had the authority to take the baby away, because his drug-dealing parents were endangering his welfare, a violation of the penal law. Further, guidelines of the NYPD *Patrol Guide,* pursuant to the Family Court Act and the Social Services Law, permitted police officers to remove a child when the officer believed he or she was being abused, neglected, or maltreated. This baby was being raised in a drug den and both his parents were about to be arrested.

Anyone could call BCW and claim a child was being beaten or starved or hurt, and BCW would check it out. But a police officer who had reasonable cause, by his own observations, to believe a child's welfare was being threatened could take the child away immediately and start an investigation. If the child in the squad room had had bruises on his body, Dave would not only have taken him away but would also have been obligated to report the case to the New York State Child Abuse and Maltreatment Center. But the baby did not seem to have been physically injured, and Dave pondered a few moments.

He relented partially. "I'll let the baby stay in the family," he finally said with some reluctance, "but it has to be with your mother or aunt, somebody responsible and stable. No sister or cousins."

The woman, her chest heaving, thanked Dave profusely, promising that her mother would take care of her son.

"I'll let you make your phone call in a little while," Dave told her.

The man patrol had captured near the crime scene, whom the three women had identified as one of their assailants, sat sullenly in the interview room. He was stocky and rugged, with a large chest and thick arms. His eyes were coal-black.

The man spoke only Spanish. Dave summoned a RIP detective to act as an interpreter, and the man, surprisingly, told his story willingly.

His name was Artemio Cedano, and he was a police officer in the Dominican Republic. He had come to New York City about ten days ago, and some men in Manhattan had asked him to help them pull a robbery in East New York.

When they arrived at the location, one of the accomplices had given him a gun. He took it, thinking he'd be the lookout.

Cedano was guarding the women and boy in the bedroom with the other gunman when he heard a shotgun blast, followed by gunfire. He and the other gunman, whom he didn't know, ran into the kitchen, jumped out the window to the fire escape, ran down the stairs to the ground, and split up.

The third partner, apparently hit by return gunfire, became disoriented and tried to escape. He thought the window nearest him led to a fire escape, but he was wrong. When he went out, he went down. There was no fire escape at the front of the building.

"And I'm very sorry," Cedano finished up, an expression of sincere regret on his face. "They didn't tell me we were going to shoot a cop tonight. I knew we were going to a robbery of a drug location, but I had nothing to do with that cop being shot. If they had told me that was going to happen, I never would have done it, because I'm a cop. I would never hurt another cop."

Dave considered the possibility that Cedano had come to New York to do a hit. You don't fly two thousand miles to do a robbery, he thought.

Cedano repeated that he knew only the DOA; the escaped perp was unknown to him.

The police tape was still up, but only a couple of RMPs remained at 672 Jamaica Avenue. A man barged through, his eyes wide.

"What are you doing here?" the cop asked.

"I fucking live here. What the fuck are you doing here?"

Dave had instructed the patrol officers that if anyone showed up at the crime scene, they were to bring him in.

Ten minutes later, a uniform escorted the man into the squad room. The man was the husband of the Dominican woman and the father of the baby. Responding to Dave's questions, he claimed he was innocent, but that his wife was a drug dealer.

Dave shook his head. Drug dealers were truly among the scum of the earth. They'd sell out their mothers or wives or even their children just to save their own asses. Unfortunately for the husband, his wife and the two other victims of the robbery had identified him as the person in charge of the stash house. As far as Dave was concerned, no matter what he said, this man was going into the system.

Hours later, Dave finished his last Five. At the bottom he typed, "Case closed with four arrested, one outstanding."

The names of those arrested were printed above. They were the Dominican cop, the wife, the husband, and the dead man. Somebody could be DOA but still technically charged with crimes.

Reclining in his chair, Dave didn't feel very satisfied. One guy was still out there. No one shoots a cop and fucking gets away with it, he thought.

17

Joe Hall was off the next day, but Dave had asked him to come in. After he arrived, the two detectives, with Cutrone, Smitty, and Redmond, gathered in the lounge to have a sit-down—a discussion of the case to come up with a direction. The facts were these:

Three men had tried to rip off a stash house on the second floor of 672 Jamaica Avenue. The drugs and money belonged to La Compañía, one of the most ruthless and notorious drug gangs in New York City, with locations in Brooklyn, Manhattan, and the Bronx. Because the location of a stash house was usually known only to the members of the organization it belonged to, the ripoff was most likely an inside job. Of the three men who had tried to pull it, one was dead; another, the cop from the Dominican Republic, was in jail; and the third was missing. The NYPD cop who had been shot would live, but with a mangled arm. The detectives had to track down the third gunman.

Joe Hall, as it happened, was in the middle of an intensive investigation of La Compañía. The gang was selling large quantities of drugs on the street; on one night alone, a quarter of a million dollars had been taken in at the spot on Norwood and Fulton. But there was another reason for the urgency of the investigation. Hall had tied almost twenty murders in the city over the past few years to La Compañía. It had all begun with a Colombian who was found shot in the back of his head, with a piece of his chin missing. The ME attributed the latter wound to a human bite.

Dissension within the gang had enabled Hall to infiltrate it. He had developed informants, learned nicknames, ordered photos and rap sheets from NITRO, BCI, and other NYPD units, and assembled a profile on the gang. With the shooting of Officer Goldberg, however, he was stumped. Why would members of the gang try to rip it off? Why rip it off so carelessly that they'd have to shoot a cop? Hall told the detectives he would reach out to one of his more reliable confidential informants.

The lanky, curly-haired young man sat in the interview room, eyes averted from the detectives gathered around him, the same men who had attended yesterday's sit-down meeting. The young man's hands were clasped, his intertwined fingers rising and falling one by one, like restless waves in the ocean. Since the age of sixteen, he had worked for the gang, climbing his way up the organizational ladder. Now he wanted to break free, but he was scared. "You end up in either of two places," he asserted. "Jail or a cemetery." The CI had already spent a year in jail; he knew a number of gang members, himself included, were about to be arrested for selling drugs. Now he wanted out, and he was willing to give up almost anything to avoid another jail sentence. He told the detectives about the inner workings of La Compañía.

La Compañía was a $20-million-a-year New York City drug gang, made up mostly of Dominicans. It was run like a legitimate corporation, with business records and a full hierarchy of positions. The law of La Compañía was enforced by hit men who beat, shot, or killed anyone in or out of the organization who got out of hand or tried to rob any of the drug spots.

La Compañía ran three spots in East New York: Norwood and Fulton, Pitkin and Pine, and Atlantic and Crescent. The spots were run efficiently, with three shifts at each, midnight to eight, eight to four, and four to twelve, just like the patrol cops. A single spot on a four-to-twelve shift on a Friday night typically grossed at least $40,000. Gang members regularly switched shifts, and new combinations of people at the spots were constantly being devised so the cops didn't get to know faces or see the same people on the corner all the time. In contrast, the gang members knew the cops' faces well. They hid or hung out near the precinct during shift changes to see who was coming in and leaving.

The big boss of the gang was José Montalbo, known to everybody as Chelo. Handsome in an Al Pacino mold, Chelo owned condos and boats and had a collection of flashy cars that included a Mercedes and a Porsche.

The gang never hesitated to kill their own. One hit, said the CI, had particularly upset him.

The CI had had a friend named Ralphie, who was a seller for the gang. Ralphie had developed the habit of splitting one packet of cocaine in two and selling each half for the regular price, pocketing the difference.

One night, young Ralphie, on his way home, was kidnapped by some men in a van. The next day, neighborhood children discovered a bag dumped on the street. It contained Ralphie's body, in pieces. Before he had been carved up, he had been beaten to a pulp, then shot in the head.

"Charming story," remarked Detective Joe Hall as the CI finally fell silent. "Now let's get to the stash-house robbery. What about the guy who got away? Where is he now?"

"Dorian Rosario left the country," the informant said. "After the shooting he fled to Washington Heights, then he took a plane to the Dominican Republic."

"Where is he there?"

"I don't know. Probably hiding out with family. When I hear something, I'll let you know." A short while later, the CI left the station house the same way he had come in—out the back door with his sweatshirt over his head.

One week later, during a Team One night tour, a call came in reporting three men shot on Miller Avenue just north of Pitkin.

"That's a heavy drug location," Dave noted to Smitty as they signed out at the logbook.

"Yeah. And three down sounds to me more like a fucking drug war than a stickup."

When Dave and Smitty got out of the unmarked squad car, raindrops blew into their faces like a spray of pellets. It was a cool night, November 7, 1990, and raining heavily. They stood a moment on the corner looking up the block, where several uniformed officers were standing. Miller Avenue sloped upward from the corner, and the wind was pushing against them.

"Look," Dave said, staring at the glistening red water flowing down Miller to the intersection below. "A river of blood."

The detectives walked up to the yellow crime scene tape. To their right, three bodies were sprawled in the middle of the street several feet from each other. One body was face up, the other two face down. Raindrops danced on the water-and-blood-drenched bodies, which lay motionless.

There was a revolver lying next to the faceup body. "We'd better get this gun off the street," Dave said to Smitty. "When patrol vouchers it, they'll probably dry it and wipe off the fingerprints."

Dave knelt down, inserted a pen in the barrel, and carefully picked up the revolver. Holding it up to the moonlight, he peered into the cylinder. His eyes widened.

"Hey, Smitty," he said, "no wonder this motherfucker is dead. He came to a gunfight with an empty gun."

"You've got to be kidding. Let me see."

Smitty looked at the weapon Dave was holding up. Revolvers don't eject their shells, as automatics do; there were no shells in this gun's cylinder. "I don't believe it," he exclaimed. Sometimes guys carried empty guns because they wanted to look tough but didn't want to be charged with a felony possession of a deadly weapon—as opposed to a misdemeanor for an empty gun—but Smitty dismissed that possibility. "There's something strange about this," he muttered.

Dave shrugged. "Well, I'll put the gun in the car."

When Dave returned, Smitty was frowning. "You'll never believe the names of the victims," he said. Not wanting the victims' identification and the other contents of their wallets to get soaked in the downpour before Crime Scene arrived, Smitty had searched the bodies while Dave propped the recovered gun on the floor of the squad car.

"Don't tell me. Huey, Dewey, and Louie."

"No, you jerk. Two of them have the last name of Lugo."

Dave grimaced. "Oh, shit," he murmured.

Just yesterday, Dave had caught the shooting of a Roberto Lugo at a poolroom at Norwood and Fulton. When the detectives arrived at the crime scene, Lugo told them he had been minding his own business when some kid had burst in and begun shooting. The kid's aim hadn't been too good; he'd only managed to hit Lugo's hand. The shooting was entirely unremarkable for East New York except for one thing: Roberto Lugo, the detectives knew, belonged to La Compañía.

"Something *is* going on," Dave whispered, gazing down the incline, where the three bloody tributaries continued to merge into one rapidly moving stream of crimson.

Soon after, another one of Joe Hall's informants came through with a rundown of what had happened.

There was a rift in La Compañía between Chelo, the gang's founder, and a supplier, Maximo Reyes, to whom Chelo had turned over his spots when he began having problems with a rival Colombian gang. Several murders had resulted. Feeling the situation had become too hot, Chelo went to the Dominican Republic, where he owned hotels and nightclubs, and waited for things to cool down. When he returned and wanted back in, he found there were now two factions in the gang—those still loyal to him, and those now loyal to Reyes. The two factions held sit-downs, but they only ended in greater acrimony.

And now all hell was breaking loose.

According to Joe Hall's informant, three managers in Chelo's faction had set up the previous week's stash-house rip-off in which the cop, Joel Goldberg, had been shot. The three managers, Hispanic men

in their twenties and early thirties, were Roberto "Cabo" Lugo, Fran-
cisco "Rico" Lugo, and Rafael Lugo, all brothers. The Lugos found
the location of the stash house, then tipped off some stickup artists
from the Bronx. They weren't looking to profit from the enterprise,
just to do some damage to Maximo Reyes's faction. But the rip-off had
crossed the line; now it was all-out war. Reyes and his people knew it
had been Chelo's faction because of threats made during the sit-
downs.

In retaliation, Maximo Reyes and Victor "Muela" ("the Mouth")
Paulino hired a Puerto Rican kid from Washington Heights to go to
the poolroom at Fulton and Norwood, where Chelo's men hung out,
and kill Cabo. A member of Reyes's faction drove him to the poolroom. But in carrying out the hit, the kid had panicked. He opened
fire with a MAC-10 but only succeeded in shredding Cabo's hand.

This debacle resulted in an even more insidious conspiracy that
was hatched early the next day. Three of Maximo Reyes's men, Odalis
"La Ceta" ("the Z") Perez, Luis "Polova" ("Gunpowder") Nunez,
and Ramone "Colita" ("Ponytail") Bueno, met Rafael and Rico Lugo
and their cousin, Esmeraldo Reyes (no relation to Maximo), at the corner of Miller and Pitkin. One of the men in Maximo's contingent told
the Lugos who had shot their brother: a kid who hailed from the projects down on Miller Avenue.

The Lugos and their cousin had accepted this as a genuine gesture
to help them exact revenge on the would-be assassin. They believed
Maximo Reyes really didn't know they were behind the stash-house rip-
off and that Maximo was still trying to hold things together as one organization.

At nine o'clock in the evening, the two groups of men met at the
Pichardo Restaurant in East New York to plan how to find the Puerto
Rican kid in the projects and kill him. Rico brought a gun with him.
After making their plan, one of the men suggested they stop off at a
bodega to get some beer before heading over to Miller Avenue. As they
were about to get into their cars, Ramone Colita told Rico to leave his
gun out of sight in the car; the neighborhood, he said, was too hot to
carry it. Rico willingly complied.

When they arrived at the bodega, Colita stayed in the car while the
others went to buy the beer. While everybody was inside, he removed
Rico's revolver from its hiding place, unloaded it, and put it back.

A short while later, the cars parked on Miller Avenue between
Glenmore and Pitkin, near the project where the assassin was (falsely)
said to live. The men got out of the cars, and Colita returned Rico's

weapon. As the rest of the group strolled toward Pitkin Avenue, Colita put his hand under the front seat and withdrew a machine gun, then caught up with the others.

"It's over, boys," Colita said as he drew near. "We're wise to what you're doing."

The Lugos and Reyes froze, and Rico reached into his pocket for his revolver.

The other three laughed. "Go ahead," one of them said. "Shoot us." Rico aimed the gun at Colita and squeezed the trigger, but the gun only made a clicking sound. Then Colita, steely-eyed, repeated, "It's over."

Rico Lugo, Rafael Lugo, and Esmeraldo Reyes turned to run as Colita raised his machine gun and began spraying bullets. All three men fell to the street. Then La Ceta shot each one in the head just to make sure they were dead.

The CI had relayed this story plaintively to Joe Hall, who by that time had penetrated the inner core of La Compañía. Hall had a number of informants in the gang. One, a high-up member, had planted a recording device inside a VCR that sat in a video library in the room in which members conducted business. Before meetings and discussions, he casually passed the VCR and removed a tiny magnet on it, activating the hidden recording device. He had taped many important conversations and meetings, encompassing topics ranging from drug importation to planned assassinations. The CI then delivered the tapes directly to Detective Hall. If the other members of the gang found out, it would mean the CI's almost immediate death.

In the beginning, the CI had provided Hall with information in bits and pieces, but as time passed and the detectives' intelligence and cases against La Compañía improved, the CI came in totally. As all the Seven-Five detectives knew, people involved in criminal activities "flipped," or turned confidential informant, for various reasons.

For some, it was revenge: Someone from the gang had shot or beaten up a family member years previously, and now they wanted to get even. Morality was another reason. Somewhere along the line, a guilty conscience began to prickle. They began to want to put an end to the violence perpetrated by their fellow gang members and see them punished.

Some became CIs simply because they were police buffs. Although they operated on the other side of the law, as kids they had admired cops, perhaps had even wanted to become cops, and they got a vicarious thrill out of helping the police with their investigations. Others were merely interested in saving their own skins. Cooperation with law enforcement might result in less severe punishment than if they were arrested, went to trial, and fought the charges.

There were also gang members who lived in constant fear of getting whacked by their criminal colleagues. They hoped that if they provided the police with information, they would receive police protection and have a better chance of avoiding being harmed by the gang. Finally, there was money. Some CIs were paid handsomely by a government agency, police department, or prosecutor's office for their dangerous and covert work, earning well up into six figures.

After the triple, Seven-Five detectives began developing a number of anxious informants from La Compañía. There were anonymous phone calls, and several gang members even came into the squad room. Chelo's people were willing to talk to the cops now because they wanted revenge, because they feared for their own lives, and for just about all the other reasons criminals turn informant.

The detectives obtained photos of Colita, La Ceta, and Polova, and informants and witnesses separately identified all three perps in the triple. The detectives finally felt certain they had the right Colita, La Ceta, and Polova. It was now only a matter of finding them.

"Rosario's coming back!" a CI told Joe Hall over the phone.

Two months after the shooting of Police Officer Joel Goldberg at the stash house at 672 Jamaica Avenue, Joe Hall's confidential informant found out that Dorian Rosario, the one outstanding gunman of the botched stickup, was returning from the Dominican Republic. He planned to hide out in his girlfriend's apartment for a while.

Team One had the address of Rosario's girlfriend in the Seven-Seven precinct. Grabbing Rosario, if he showed up, could be dangerous. He might shoot it out with the cops, and he might be traveling with armed associates.

"Hope I never have to see if this thing really works," Smitty remarked, slipping the white armored vest over his head. It was late in the afternoon, and the detectives in the squad room were putting on their bulletproof vests—everybody, that is, except Carbone. Dave had never got into the habit of wearing one, even after he was first shot at in the street as a patrol officer. It wasn't a macho thing with him; he just never wore vests, and he had no intention of breaking the custom.

It ran against all common sense and all he had been taught as a cop, but he indulged himself in this one eccentricity. When asked about it, his response was, "Look, there are two vital organs a vest doesn't protect: your big head and your little head. Now if I get shot in the brain, I'm dead. And if I can't fuck anymore, I might as well be dead anyhow."

"Can't forget this face," Cutrone said a half hour later, holding the color BCI mug shot. Rosario had a long record.

Cutrone and Dave, sporting mirrored shades, were crouched down in the front seat of the Buick. "I wish this scumbag would get here soon," Dave said, straightening up a bit. "My fucking back's starting to hurt."

"Anything yet?" asked Mike Redmond, sitting in another car, over the radio.

"Negative, Grumpy," Cutrone answered.

The detectives waited patiently, but still there was no sign of Rosario. In each car the detectives conversed about their family or golf game or house and gossiped about other detectives in the squad.

Hours passed. The time always dragged during stakeouts, and the conversation grew steadily more desultory.

Finally, through the tilted rearview mirror, Dave spotted a small red car. That was the kind of car the CI had said the perp would be driving. Two men were in the front seat. "Check out the passenger," Dave hissed.

The car slowed down as it came up parallel to the unmarked car and proceeded to turn left. The detectives shot a quick look, and Cutrone, in the passenger seat, keyed his radio. "He just turned onto the block now. Let's get him."

As the red car pulled up to the house, Dave came up tightly on its bumper, while Smitty and Redmond shot up the one-way street and wedged in the car from the front. While the other detectives got out and trained their guns on the two men, Dave bolted from his car, jumped over the hood of the red car, and yanked open the passenger door. Grabbing Rosario by his jacket collar, Dave pulled him out of the car and threw him to the ground, then slipped cuffs on him.

They took Rosario back to the squad room and interviewed him. By this time it was too late at night to ask the witnesses to come in, so they were told to get there first thing in the morning to view a lineup.

The lineups were productive: two hits. Dave called the DA's office to have someone ride the case. After the suspect confessed on videotape to an ADA, he was fingerprinted. Several hours later, he was taken to Brooklyn Central Booking.

Team One's night tour would be beginning shortly, and the detectives, having worked straight through, never went home when their tour was scheduled to end at one o'clock in the morning. It was now two o'clock in the afternoon, and the prospects for sleep were dim. The second four-to-one would begin in two hours, and that tour was a turnaround, so there'd be only a handful of hours in the sack before they were scheduled to report for their day tour tomorrow at eight in the morning.

Sitting at his desk, Dave sipped a can of iced tea and nibbled on peanuts from a little bag. He wasn't feeling that tired yet, but he wondered what kind of shape he'd be in twelve hours from now if something heavy came down. Thank God for adrenaline, he mused.

On the bottom of a blue Five, Dave typed, "Case closed with an arrest (no outstanding perps)," and deposited the original top sheet in a basket for dispatch through interdepartmental mail to police headquarters for microfilming. He put copies in the P.O. Goldberg case folder.

Then he thought about Rosario's escaping a couple of months ago after Goldberg was shot, probably figuring he would never be caught even if he returned to this country. Dave nodded slowly. We did good, he told himself. We upheld the tradition that when you shoot an NYPD cop, you go to jail.

It was with deep exasperation near the end of 1990 that the Seven-Five detectives observed the number of homicides continuing to rise in East New York. It looked like a bleak fact of life that the body count in the precinct would break one hundred annually and set records in the city for the most homicides. But the detectives were showing the strain of their workload. After the triple murder Smitty had caught, six additional homicides were caught by Team One, but only one was solved. There were various reasons for this, primarily investigative snafus, but the bottom line was that Team One, as well as the whole investigative staff, was simply being overwhelmed by the incredible number of cases—nonhomicide as well as homicide—that were pouring in.

The internecine rampage of La Compañía was affecting the whole Seven-Five squad. The gang were out of control, and something had to be done to stop them. They were even shooting cops now, Officer Goldberg being the most recent example. And some detectives—like Smitty, whose clearance record was weighed down by the open triple

murder of Rico and Rafael Lugo and their cousin, Esmeraldo Reyes—
were especially anxious to see the demise of the gang and uncover information that could lead to solving any of the related open homicides.

A major turn of events was in the offing.

Having accumulated huge amounts of damaging information
about the criminal operations of La Compañía while investigating its
homicides in East New York, the Seven-Five detectives realized that
with the vast resources required for a case of this magnitude—as well as
the fact that the case would be easier to prosecute in federal than in
state court—the assistance of various federal agencies would be invaluable in taking down the organization and closing out their cases. Because the gang was importing drugs from outside the country and
transporting them up the Eastern Seaboard, numerous federal crimes
could be thrown into the whole prosecutorial package.

The need for federal agency participation had become apparent
when Sergeant Race and Detectives Joe Hall and Hank Mathes, who
were investigating La Compañía murders, approached the NYPD's
Brooklyn North Narcotics District, which investigated major drug operations in the borough's northern section, for help. Because assisting
in the investigation of La Compañía promised to be a long-term endeavor and the unit couldn't afford to pull its officers from their regular assignments, BNND regretfully but firmly declined to participate.

Various federal agencies were able to join the investigation, however, and were only too happy to do so. First in was the Drug Enforcement Administration, which would go after the gang for narcotics trafficking. Others were the Bureau of Alcohol, Tobacco, and Firearms,
which would go after the gang for running unlicensed guns across
state borders; the Immigration and Naturalization Service, which had
an interest in phony passports and other immigration fraud; and the
IRS, for the gang's income tax evasion. Even the Coast Guard was enlisted after it intercepted a boat tied to the organization that was carrying narcotics.

For a few months the detectives and investigators worked inten-
sively to build a case so a federal indictment could be drawn up by the
U.S. Attorney for the Southern District of New York. As more and
more people were murdered, some of the killers were captured and
locked up along the way. But the situation had so seriously escalated
that the massive planned takedown of the organization had to be
moved ahead, before more people on the indictment list were killed

and to protect any innocent bystanders who might be hit by stray bullets. Arrest and search warrants were obtained and plans for the takedown were set in motion.

At three o'clock on the morning of March 26, 1991, almost one hundred federal agents, along with Seven-Five squad members Race, Hall, and Mathes, gathered at DEA headquarters at 555 West Fifty-Seventh Street in Manhattan—often referred to as the Triple Nickel—to coordinate their final plans. Then everyone fanned out to prepare for the takedown, which would take place later in the morning in Brooklyn, the Bronx, Manhattan, Queens, and Fort Lee, New Jersey.

The entire Seven-Five squad, twenty-four detectives in all, assembled in the squad room at 4:30 A.M. to get their assignments from Race, Hall, and Mathes. The Seven-Five detectives were split up, joining ranks with federal agents to hit locations all over the city.

Dave was part of a group that included eleven other detectives and federal agents. At 6:00 A.M. they headed out in a caravan of four cars to the nearby Bushwick section of Brooklyn. Their target was Miguel Pons, who handled much of the financial activities of La Compañía, and who was considered highly dangerous. Just the week before, Joe Hall and a DEA agent in an unmarked van had been surveilling Pons and some others when the gang members had realized they were being watched. The drug dealers had shot at the detectives, then taken off after them in a high-speed chase over sidewalks and street islands. The chase ended only when the van drew near the 75th Precinct station house.

The four cars parked near Pons's travel agency at the intersection of Myrtle and Wyckoff, a busy business district, with a train station across the street. The men inside the vehicles waited patiently for their quarry.

At 8:00 A.M., a woman came in and opened the store. Soon after, others arrived, followed a short time later by a well-groomed husky red-haired man, about thirty, wearing a sport jacket and a knit shirt. Eyeing the man, Joe Hall picked up the DEA radio provided for each car and announced, "The subject has arrived."

The dozen detectives and agents swept out of their cars and withdrew their weapons; some were carrying shotguns. Some took positions outside, while the others stormed the agency, yelling for everyone to freeze. The workers inside, terrified and confused, stood motionless. Joe Hall and Dave moved to the rear of the store, where they found Miguel Pons crouched behind a desk. Since Hall had been pursuing the gang for years, he had the honor of slapping the cuffs on

Pons. Searching a nearby back room, Dave and Hank Mathes found a rifle and a shotgun.

In the other locations across the metropolitan area, similar scenes were being enacted. Law enforcement had laid its plans well, and by the end of the morning the takedown of La Compañía was complete. Twelve gang members were arrested and much property seized, bringing the total recovered to thirty automobiles valued at $350,000, one of which was a Rolls-Royce; $450,000 in assets, including houses, cash, and jewelry; an $800,000 yacht; ten guns; and five kilos of cocaine. It was with keen interest that the agents and detectives perused the organization's records, learning that its weekly payroll had been $144,000 and its weekly gross approximately $800,000.

Nineteen murders in New York City were tied to the gang, fourteen in East New York alone. Witnesses came in to identify the suspects rounded up, and as a result the open homicide investigations were officially closed. Some members were, under the federal statute, facing the electric chair, but as it turned out, before trial they pled guilty to the charges and were instead given life prison sentences.

A press conference took place at the U.S. Attorney's Office on the afternoon of March 26, announcing the results of the takedown. Heads of the various agencies involved, including Roger Hayes, the Acting U.S. Attorney; Robert Bryden, chief of the New York office of the DEA; and Joseph Borelli, the NYPD chief of detectives, spoke at the conference, along with Detective Sergeant Mike Race.

Some members of La Compañía had still not been apprehended, the most important of whom was Maximo Reyes. Later the president of the Dominican Republic, Joaquín Balaguer, would appoint Reyes to head the country's equivalent of the U.S. Drug Enforcement Administration. (According to several members of La Compañía, Chelo had contributed $6 million to Balaguer's electoral campaign.) But the takedown effectively brought an end to the violent drug organization known as La Compañía.

With suspects in custody, the Seven-Five detectives began their interrogations. It was the practice of detectives in debriefing prisoners to ask them what they knew about other murders. If the prisoners provided any information that would help the detectives solve any open murders, it might bear favorably on the suspects' prosecutions.

One subject who had been apprehended on March 4, a few weeks before the big takedown, was being grilled by Hall and Mathes when he asked casually, "So what would you like to know about Mikey Corvette?"

The detectives looked at each other in astonishment. Many of the people who worked in the 75th Precinct knew a cop named Mike, who drove a flashy red Corvette. His name was Michael Dowd, and what the informant told the detectives blew them away.

Dowd was a corrupt cop. He had started small, receiving $250 to $300 a week protecting drug dealers in East New York. But he had upped the ante as time passed.

Dowd's services included providing information to the gang about drug busts the precinct squads were planning. He also supplied them with license plate numbers and models of the cars to be used, as well as descriptions of the undercovers. Although it was never proved, a portable radio from the detectives' unit had turned up missing and some of the detectives believed Dowd had given it to the Dominicans so they could monitor police street activities.

As time passed, the informant said, Dowd had demanded more money, eventually getting $3,000 a week from the Dominicans. In turn, he increased his services. Dowd and some of the other cops he banded with went after La Compañía's competition. They went into bodegas, robbed the owners of drugs and money, and sold the drugs to the Dominicans, keeping the money. But Dowd eventually became too expensive, demanding $10,000 for each week's "protection." He grew so greedy the Dominicans eventually put out a contract on him; he was more a liability than an asset.

The prisoners being debriefed by the detectives told stories about how bold the rogue cops were. Police officers in the 73rd Precinct, they said, were dealing drugs right out of their patrol cars.

Seven-Five detectives notified the NYPD's Internal Affairs Division. At the same time, Detective Joe Trimboli of Brooklyn North's Field Internal Affairs Unit had been tracking Dowd and reporting to IAD. The U.S. Attorney's Office was not going to take the word of drug dealers and asked IAD to corroborate the allegations with evidence such as surveillance photos of Dowd consorting with gang members or telephone records from Dowd's home to illicit places of business or vice versa, but IAD seemed to drag its feet.

Dowd was eventually transferred to the NYPD's Whitestone Pound, where recovered stolen cars were stored, and then to the 94th Precinct. He was working that assignment when he was picked up in May 1992 by Suffolk County, Long Island, cops for possessing and selling drugs. Dowd's arrest sparked massive publicity, and soon the so-called Mollen Commission was formed to investigate alleged acts of corruption in the New York City Police Department and to recommend corrective procedures. (Dowd, who was the commission's star witness, was sentenced in 1993 to a prison sentence of fifteen and two-thirds years.) What hurt many of the NYPD cops most was not that Dowd was corrupt; it was that he was locked up not by the NYPD but by another police department.

The whole Dowd corruption scandal was a shock and a great disappointment to the Seven-Five detectives. "I'd take a corrupt cop down in a second," Dave reflected to Smitty. But what really stung Dave was that La Compañía gang members, he had been told by the NYPD's Intelligence Division, had made death threats against him and Joe Hall—the same gang Dowd, a cop from Dave and Joe's own precinct, was getting rich protecting.

For Joe Hall, the takedown was somewhat anticlimactic. For years he had been tracking Chelo, the founder of the notorious La Compañía. Chelo was more than just a bounty for Hall; he was an obsession. What pleasure it would have given Hall to collar the leader of the gang that had littered the streets with drugs and soaked them in blood!

But Chelo was dead. He had been gunned down recently outside the restaurant where he had eaten his final meal, just two days before Joe Hall had planned to arrest him, after a five-year investigation and hunt.

There were other personal emotions tied up in the case for Joe Hall. He had formed somewhat of an attachment—perhaps it was sympathy—for Cabo Lugo, whose two brothers and cousin had been murdered. After the killings, Cabo had fled to the Dominican Republic to avoid being spotted and to convalesce from the hand wound he had received in the poolroom at Norwood and Fulton the day before the triple murder.

During his stay in the Dominican Republic, Cabo communicated frequently with Joe Hall by telephone. Cabo provided information to help Hall track his brothers' killers and to hurt the Maximo Reyes faction of La Compañía.

After two months in the Dominican Republic, Cabo returned to East New York. One day in the Seven-Five squad room Joe Hall told him, "I've been receiving very reliable information, and the word is that you and your buddy Julio are going to be killed. Do me and yourself a favor and stay away from the spots."

"They owe me some money," Cabo objected.

"How much?"

"Fifteen hundred dollars."

Hall stared Cabo straight in the eyes. Cabo was a big fellow, about six feet two, and weighed some three hundred pounds. His arm was still in a sling.

"With all the money you have," Hall said deliberately, "if your life is worth fifteen hundred dollars, then go to the spots. But if you're a smart guy, you'll stay away."

Two days later, Joe Hall received a call at home: Cabo and Julio had been walking on Belmont Avenue to the spot owned by La Compañía at Pitkin and Pine when someone opened fire on them. Julio had escaped injury, but Cabo had been killed.

News of the takedown of La Compañía made the national media. For the people involved, it was also satisfying in that it showed that city police and the feds could work well together in a joint investigation. For Dave and Smitty, the takedown was sweetened by the news that Polova had been picked up in Manhattan. That was the second arrest in the triple—La Ceta had recently been collared by DEA agents in Fort Lee, New Jersey. As it would turn out, Colita would be arrested a few months later.

As they walked out of the squad room late that afternoon at the end of their tour, after a momentous day that had begun in the wee hours of the morning, Dave and Smitty exchanged smiles of quiet satisfaction. The river of blood had been avenged.

18

With the multitude of homicides in the 75th Precinct, squad detectives were always looking to break in new confidential informants. CIs were, after all, an important link to the kind of information that could result in arrests in heavy cases. But breaking in CIs was a delicate process. On one hand, while most CIs had some kind of criminal background— that was why they were in a position to have information on illegal activities, after all—they were putting their lives in jeopardy, and they still had to be protected. On the other hand, detectives could never be quite sure to whom a CI was really loyal, and they always fretted over the possibility that working with a CI put a particular investigation at risk.

But the Seven-Five detectives always seemed to be able to bring in fresh CI blood. Because the assistance of CIs generally resulted in more arrests and consequently higher clearance rates for the detectives, there was even a friendly competition in the squad to develop CIs. Informants were part of the detectives' arsenal of crime-solving tools. Dave himself was becoming pretty good at persuading people to help him, but what he took greatest pride in was his ability to make potential informants believe they had no recourse but to cooperate with him when he really had squat. This was his special talent as a jerkologist.

"I'm here to see Detective Carbone," said the man at the reception desk.

Police Aide Cheryl Pough looked into the squad room and saw that Dave was on the telephone. "Please have a seat," she said to the visitor. "He'll be with you in a moment."

With the telephone pressed to his ear, Dave was watching a murder collar in the holding cell sucking his thumb. Covering the bottom part of the phone with his hand, he hissed to Smitty over his shoulder, "I should have brought in one of my daughter's pacifiers for that nitwit."

Then Pough caught Dave's eye. She gestured to the man sitting in the reception area and pointed at Dave. He nodded and held up a finger, asking the person on the phone if they could continue the conversation later. He hung up and went out to meet his visitor.

"I'm Detective Carbone. What can I do for you?"

"I'm the guy you're looking for."

Ah, yes, he bit, Dave thought, noting the man's thin, muscular body. "Okay. Would you come with me, please?"

Dave led the man to the interview room, where they both sat down. The man was here, Dave knew, in connection with the murder of Rudolf King four days previously. Two gunmen had gone to rip off a stash house and had had a shootout with the enforcer inside. The enforcer had shot and killed one of the robbers, but the other had escaped. Now Dave was looking for the enforcer to charge him with murder. Based on some interviews, he had found out that the stash house where the killing had taken place belonged to the girlfriend of a dealer named Champ. No one could tell him the name of the enforcer, but if Dave could find Champ, he could probably find the enforcer.

Going to another of Champ's drug locations, Dave had put the word out to his friends and associates: Tell Champ to come see me, or I'll come after him and lock him up for murder. It was Champ's stash house, and he, said Dave, would be held responsible.

Dave leaned forward. "Okay, Champ," he said in a friendly tone, "why don't you tell me a little bit about yourself?"

Dave hadn't expected his visitor to be particularly forthcoming, but Champ surprised him. He was a little too forthcoming—so much so, in fact, that Dave realized he had to be wary. Either the guy thought so little of cops that he believed he could get away with anything, or he was just very ballsy and not to be trusted.

But Dave listened with interest as Champ, for the next ten minutes, explained how he had gotten into the drug business. He had been studying engineering in college, he said, and had started selling on the side. The money was irresistible. Realizing he would be able to make more money in drugs than he'd ever be able to earn as a professional, he had decided, much to his hardworking father's dismay, to change careers.

"I'm thirty," he said, "and of the ten years I've been in the drug business, I've spent only four days in jail. It happened after somebody tried to shoot me in the head once and I put up my arm to block it, which is why I've got pieces missing. Look at this."

Champ took off his shirt and showed a thick scar running from his left armpit down to below his elbow, with four bullets lodged in the arm. Then he pointed to his stomach, where two rows of four bullets stuck out under the skin, mementos of other entrepreneurial ventures. "They burn a lot, but I'm proud of them," he said.

Dave looked into Champ's eyes. They were cold and dark and distant.

"I came in because I heard you wouldn't arrest me if I did," said Champ. "They tell me you're a man of your word. Your rep on the street is that you're fair and straight, so let me ask you: Now that I'm here, am I leaving?"

"Yeah, you've got my word, Champ. I said if you came in, you could leave."

Dave gloated. The drug dealer had actually bought into the load of shit Dave had put out. Dave couldn't lock him up for murder—he couldn't prove Champ owned the stash house where Rudolf King had been killed, or that the drugs found there were his. Champ hadn't even been there when the murder had taken place. Champ, in fact, didn't even have to talk to him, and if the dealer had wanted to, he could just have told Dave to go fuck himself. For all the intelligence drug dealers credited themselves with, they weren't all that smart.

"What's your real name?" Dave asked.

"Russell Youmans, but as you already know, on the street it's Champ. Anyway, six months later I shot the guy who shot me. I heard the cops coming and waited for them, told them the guy shot me and I shot him back. I was out of jail in four days."

Champ rambled on, telling Dave more than he had ever expected to hear. Getting what he needed to know from this chump was going to be easy, Dave thought. But could he be trusted?

"I love the feeling of shooting people," Champ observed, and for the first time a light showed deep within his eyes. "My first murder, I went home and felt bad for a few minutes, but then I thought, ah, fuck it, the guy deserved it anyway."

Dave stared at him, trying not to show his disbelief. Nice way to rationalize a murder, he thought.

"I've got twenty to thirty people who work for me now," Champ said proudly. "I don't even know most of their names."

"I want the guy who killed Rudolf King," Dave said.

"Okay, Carbone, I'm going to tell you who it is. It's George Gonzales."

This was too easy. Dave wondered what Champ had up his sleeve.

"Let me talk to him and see if I can get him to surrender," Champ continued. "He's moving around all over the place, but I'll see what I can do."

Champ stood up and looked Dave square in the eyes. "You know, we drug dealers are no different than politicians. It's just that we commit our crimes with guns, they commit theirs with pens."

At the door Champ extended his hand. "Yo, Carbone, you're a pretty cool guy. Where you from?"

Dave was taken aback. Does he really think I'd tell him? he wondered.

"East Bumfuck," Dave replied.

"Where the hell is that?"

"East."

Champ grinned.

The next day Dave received a phone call from Champ.

"You're a straight-up guy," Champ said. "You did let me go. I really can't trust you yet, but I have a good feeling about you."

How nice, Dave thought. "So what do you have for me?"

"Nothing. The guy ran because he didn't want to go to jail for murder."

"No sweat." Dave had already put out a Wanted Card on Gonzales; if he was picked up, the card would pop.

"You want the murder weapon? Some guy in Queens bought it."

"Uh, yeah, that'd be swell," Dave said.

The murder weapon might bolster his case, Dave thought. He already knew the identity of the killer, and he had witnesses, two women who were in the apartment at the time. Having the gun used to kill Rudolf King could nail the case. And possibly, just possibly, if he had the suspect in custody along with the gun, he could use it to persuade the suspect to plead guilty before going to trial. He could use one of his favorite bits of jerkology, the old "I've got your fingerprints on the gun" routine.

"I can take you to the guy who has the gun," said Champ, "but you'll have to dress up as one of the boys."

"No problem. When?"

"Two o'clock tomorrow afternoon."

"Meet me here at one-thirty," said Dave.

It was a brisk, sunny day, the wind blowing heavily. Dave was dressed in jeans, sneakers, and a sport jacket. His hair was slicked back in a ponytail, and he had on two earrings and mirrored sunglasses. At one-thirty, Champ pulled up to the station house in a white Nissan Pathfinder with tinted windows, and Dave hopped in.

Champ looked Dave up and down. "Yeah, you could pass for one of them Mafia dudes," he said, laughing. "Listen, this guy's cool, I know him."

As the Pathfinder pulled out, an unmarked car turned onto Sutter Avenue and followed from a distance.

"The guy's cool," Champ said again. "He owes me a favor. I told him I owe you money, and this would square it. Sort of a favor for a favor."

"Sounds fair to me," Dave said.

"Listen to this," Champ said, turning up the volume of the music on the car stereo to a deafening level. "State of the art, man."

As they cruised into Queens, Dave felt himself growing more tense. He didn't know the owner of the gun, and he couldn't yet trust Champ. He didn't know if he was walking into a setup. He slid his revolver between his legs, praying Smitty and Redmond were on his trail.

Several minutes later, Champ drove down a block of narrow brick homes with small front yards. He pulled up in front of a brown house, and a tall, stocky man standing by the door walked slowly toward the vehicle. He peered in the window on the passenger side at Dave.

Champ turned off the stereo. Dave gripped his revolver.

"You're the guy that wants the gun?" The man had a bold manner.

Dave touched his index finger to the bridge of his sunglasses and pushed them back. "Well, I didn't come here to fucking say hello."

"Yo, man, I told you," Champ interjected. "This is the guy that wants the gun. He has a job to do. You don't want that gun; it's got a body on it. After he gets done with it, he's gonna get rid of it."

"Can you trust him?"

"I brought him here, didn't I? You know me. I ain't gonna bring no cop or nobody here. Give the man the gun."

Dave spoke up loudly, his tone angry. "Yo, motherfucker," he said. "I ain't got no time to play with you. You either give me the fucking gun or I'll go get another gun somewhere else. I trusted my homeboy here. He told me you'd take care of business. I'm a busy man. I don't like to be jerked off, unless it comes in a skirt."

"All right, all right, man, I'll be right back."

A minute later the man reappeared from the house with a paper bag. He set it down on the hood of a car in front of the Pathfinder. He walked away, shouting over his shoulder, "You want it, you come and get it. I ain't handing it to ya."

"Fine, motherfucker," Dave shouted back. "I don't give a fuck."

Dave got out of the car and picked up the bag. He peeked inside.

Sure enough, there was a black 9mm gun, just like the one he had heard was used to kill Rudolf King. He looked up at the man, now standing on his porch. "Yo, man, take it slow," he called out to him jovially. Then he jumped back in the Pathfinder, and Champ drove away.

It was late at night when the overhead bell on the squad-room door jangled. Al Nesbot, a new detective on Team One, walked to the reception area. "Who are you here to see?" he asked the visitor.

The man grinned. "The guinea with the slicked-back hair."

"I guess that's not me," said Nesbot, chuckling. "Carbone!"

In the lounge, Dave told Champ the gun had been tested in the ballistics lab and found to match the bullet in Rudolf King. "It was the gun I was looking for," he said.

Champ smiled. He seemed glad to be of assistance.

Because Champ had proved himself trustworthy, Dave now began to consider cultivating him as a confidential informant. Most drug people hung out not with bank tellers or teachers or insurance salesmen but with other drug dealers, and they went to dance clubs and parties and other places where hit men and sellers and runners talked—or rather bragged—about what they did. Guys like Champ knew who had killed this person or robbed that spot. Having him on the detectives' side would be invaluable. Furthermore, with spots in Brooklyn, Queens, Virginia, North Carolina, and Georgia, Champ had a pipeline to a plethora of information, information that could help Dave—and other detectives—solve a lot of cases.

It was not unusual for ambitious drug dealers like Champ to set up drug spots away from their main base of operations. They ran their drug businesses like corporations, setting up remote spots the same way legitimate companies established branch offices or subsidiaries. In selecting out-of-town spots, they often looked for small or medium-sized towns where local law enforcement lacked the resources to conduct full-scale narcotics investigations. They favored college towns and other places with hip young adult populations; proximity to highways and other major arteries and the overall potential profitability of the area were further considerations.

The dealers would install their most trustworthy colleagues to run and manage the spots. Champ had his brother and closest friends run his remote spots; they in turn hired local people to work them. There was never any fear that the local guys they brought in would get caught up in the entrepreneurial spirit themselves and decide to strike out on their own. There was a penalty for that, and the locals knew it was administered via the barrel of a .357 or 9mm.

Champ still hadn't figured out that Dave had lied about being able to lock him up for Rudolf King's murder. By helping Dave, Champ thought he'd be avoiding a lengthy prison sentence if a judge or jury found him guilty of involvement in the murder. As far as Champ was aware, Dave was protecting Champ's ass. And there was another, perhaps even more valuable, benefit of playing along with the cops. By ratting on the competition, Champ effectively sent rival drug dealers to jail. That was a lot less risky than killing them, and vastly more satisfactory than being killed by them. The cops would do his dirty work for him, and he would become stronger. This is great, he thought. What better way to stay in business?

Although Dave loathed drug dealers, he thought helping them receive reduced sentences or other considerations was an equitable exchange for information if it resulted in solving a murder case. The CI was happy, the police were happy, and the family of the murder victim was happy—and the case was closed. Champ was a piece of dung, but who else was going to give the police information on murders and killings?

"Listen, Russell," Dave said, "you told me you make a quarter of a million dollars a month. You own three buildings, three houses, and six cars. Why don't you get out before you get killed?"

The drug dealer shrugged. "Because then I wouldn't have a rep, man. What good is it all without a rep?"

"You'd be alive."

"You don't dig, man. When you've got a lot of power and money, you want more. You want it all. My business is power and fame, and I live for it." He leaned back in his chair and spread his hands out. "Shit, I really enjoy the prestige of being a drug dealer. You know, I fuck the wives of a lot of famous rappers. It's a power trip for them to sleep with a gangster, and I usually screw at least six different bitches a week. That's why I can't go to jail, man. There's no pussy in jail."

"This is true," said Dave gravely.

"I'll bet you think ghetto people are poor, don't you?"

Dave nodded.

"That's a myth, I'm telling you. We're not poor, we're nigger-rich. We spend all our money while white people save theirs. That's the only difference."

"I see," said Dave. He certainly couldn't say the man wasn't a philosopher.

Champ was feeling expansive. "I've got three rules in my gang," he said. "One, anyone I hire has to be over twenty-one, because kids crumble to the cops. Two, you look your victim in the eye before shooting him. And three, you never kill a priest."

Maybe cops should wear clerical collars rather than bulletproof vests, Dave thought. "Can you help me out?" he asked. "I'm looking to solve unsolved murders."

Champ smiled and looked at Dave's neck. "I like your jewelry, Carbone. You should see me when I go to a rap concert. I'm a fucking golden calf."

Over the next few months, Champ took Team One and their homicide assistants on a number of stakeouts. Riding with Dave and another detective—usually Smitty or Cutrone—in a beat-up old surveillance van, they went looking for murder suspects who Champ had heard would be somewhere at a particular time, and whom he could identify.

The men in the van were backed up by detectives in one or two unmarked cars a block or two away. When Champ spotted a suspect, Dave and whoever he was with leaped out of the van and grabbed him, immediately slipping on handcuffs. They acted so quickly the person was taken by surprise, cuffed before he could reach for a gun, if he had one.

Champ promised to give up several murderers, and within a short time, three homicide cases in Queens and two in Brooklyn were closed out. Champ supplied Dave with details of killings, descriptions of the perps, whatever he could find out about them. For murders out of the Seven-Five, Dave passed on Champ's information to detectives in other squads. Champ also primed Dave with information on other drug dealers—"What a way to eliminate the competition," Smitty observed—and Dave informed Narcotics, which then made several raids, resulting in numerous arrests. "If this keeps up," Dave told Smitty, "I'll be solving half the crimes in this city."

Dave, in turn, helped Champ with some legal problems. Champ had been caught with a gun while out on parole, which was a violation, and he had been charged with urinating in public. His wife had an order of protection against him, and one day he had gone to her house and peed on it. She filed a complaint, and he was arrested.

At the hearing in Queens the judge proclaimed, "I told you if you ever bothered your wife again, I was going to throw the book at you. You're remanded!"

Champ and Dave looked at each other. "This is bad," Dave said, shaking his head. Dave approached the bench and spoke quietly with the judge.

Although Champ had violated his wife's order of protection and had urinated on her house, as far as Dave was concerned the transgression wasn't serious enough to lose a valuable informant over. Dave realized any arrangement to keep Champ out of jail put Champ's wife at risk and wasn't exactly serving her best interests, but then again, catching murderers was important, and he had come to know Champ well enough to believe that if Champ said he would leave his wife alone, he probably would. Still, there was a residue of doubt. How smart could Champ be to risk all his freedom and his wealth—his huge weekly earnings, his real estate holdings, his fancy cars, and much more—by going to his wife's house and pissing on it while he was on probation, just because he was peeved at her?

But any way you looked at it, Dave had decided, someday Champ was going to be caught. Until that time, the detectives might as well use him for what they could get out of him. Dave explained to the judge that Champ wouldn't be worth much to the police in jail, and the judge agreed.

The judge asked Champ and his attorney to stand up. "I was going to throw the book at you because you haven't learned your lesson," she said, addressing Champ sternly, "but I understand you've been helping the police. So I'm giving you another chance. Come back to me in thirty days. In the meantime, don't even think of going near your wife's house. One more violation and you're going to jail, even if the police think you're St. Francis." She shot a hard look at Dave, who nodded acceptance.

A month later, Champ returned to court with his attorney. Dave couldn't come, but the attorney had a letter from him affirming that Champ had continued to help the police solve numerous cases. The judge let Champ stay out on parole.

Soon Champ was calling Dave once or twice a week with tips on murders and drug dealing. He understood that at any point he could be locked up, and he realized Narcotics might already be investigating him, but he trusted Dave and believed Dave would help him if he did take a collar. However, while Dave was soaking up all this valuable information, there was another related development that he found galling. George Gonzales, the enforcer in the Rudolf King killing, had been caught on a routine traffic violation by upstate police, who had run his name with the NYPD Warrant Division. Dave had expected him to do heavy time for murder, but the murder charge was dropped. His attorney argued that although the enforcer hadn't had a license to carry a gun, he had only fired back in self-defense when he himself was shot at. With the murder charge out of the way, King was sentenced to jail for illegal gun possession. Dave was deeply disappointed but not surprised.

It was ten-thirty in the evening, and Team One was in the squad room. It had been a slow night. The detectives were making wisecracks and telling jokes to relieve the tedium of their paperwork.

The phone rang, and Smitty answered it. "Dave, it's for you," he said.

As Dave became immersed in conversation, Smitty glimpsed a type-written manuscript on Dave's desk and idly picked it up. He remembered Dave telling him Champ had brought it in.

Smitty glanced at the first page. "Critical Decision," read the title of the five-page outline treatment for a motion picture. Following the title was a statement of the high concept: "A story of two brothers reaching for their goals. The only thing in their way is each other."

One night when he was home, Champ had told Dave, he had begun to ponder their unlikely relationship. Their bond was one of trust. When Champ had come into the precinct several months ago, he had fully expected to be locked up. He was impressed because Carbone had lived up to his word and let him go, and had helped with some of his legal difficulties, just as he had said he would.

Dave, telling Smitty with some amusement about Champ's screenplay treatment, had commented wryly that trust seemed to be everything to criminals. After Dave had helped Champ out with the peeing incident, he could do no wrong with the drug dealer.

But Dave still couldn't believe Champ hadn't figured out that on that first day in the precinct, Dave couldn't have arrested him. On one level, Dave respected Champ's intelligence—Champ could deliver a dissertation on the economics of setting up dummy corporations or wax philosophical about complex social issues. But on another level, Champ lived a delusion. And that was his downfall. Many drug dealers had plenty of smarts, yet they were ultimately stupid for staying in the business. They got caught up in making a lot of money for easy work. Most of the time, they had managers run their spots, and they only had to make an appearance every now and then to make sure everything was running smoothly. Meanwhile, they were making mucho bucks.

If Champ was shrewd about the law, he might have figured it out.

Certainly, if Dave had been able to arrest Champ the first day they met, that's just what Dave would have done. He would have had to, or risk dereliction of duty. He couldn't let a person wanted for a crime walk out of the precinct without taking any action. What if the next day that person killed somebody, and the investigating detectives found he had just happened to be visiting with Carbone the day before? The city would be open to a major lawsuit, and Dave would probably lose his shield.

But besides leading Champ to believe that cooperating with the police would be a return favor for letting him go, Dave continually impressed the dealer with his knowledge of Champ's activities—another ruse from the detective's bag of tricks. The detective took a little street information and blew it up to make a criminal think the police knew a lot more about him than they really did. Just little bits, such as what kind of car the person drove, or what he liked to drink, could cause the guy to sit on the edge of his seat and worry—"How the fuck does he know that about me?"

Champ knew there were some things he couldn't tell Dave—that he had a gun on him, or that he had just shot somebody—because Dave would have to lock him up. But so strong was his trust in Dave that he fed the detective information that could have gotten him killed. After the Rudolf King killing, Dave had never asked Champ to give up his own people, but only his enemies or acquaintances or others he had heard about, and he knew Dave would never ask him to testify on any information he had passed on to the detective.

In the beginning, Champ had felt at odds with himself for spilling his knowledge to a police detective, but he also realized he didn't have to worry about not going home, nor did he have to look back over his shoulder to see if the detective was going to fuck him somehow. Their understanding was crystal-clear, and Dave had laid out for Champ from the beginning what his job obligated him to do. If anything came up that implicated Champ in a serious crime, their friendly relationship would be at an end; Dave would go after him and arrest him.

So one night at home, Champ, sitting at his computer, reflected on how ironic it was that he was actually able to think of Carbone as a trusted friend, all the while knowing the bond between them was paper-thin and could be severed at any time. Despite himself, he had grown to like Dave, and although he couldn't be sure, he had the sense the feeling was mutual.

Then, suddenly, the creative muse had spoken to Champ. There are two brothers, one a cop, the other a drug dealer. What happens if the cop has to arrest or kill the drug dealer, or the drug dealer has to kill his cop brother? What would each of the brothers do?

This difficult premise was not a far stretch from real life. Champ had many drug spots in East New York. It was not at all unlikely there would be another murder at one of them. Criminals were always looking to rob drug spots, and a drug dealer had to provide armed protection of his spot. Or what if plainclothes cops hit an apartment with a warrant, and one of Champ's men hurt or killed an officer? Under those circumstances, Dave would be under pressure to link the spot's owner to the shooter and get him on conspiracy charges. In either case, Dave would have to bring Champ in and put him in jail. Champ was aware of this, fascinated by it, obsessed by it. He thought it would make a terrific movie.

Dave was also aware of the hazards of working with a confidential informant who was a big-time drug dealer. But it was a necessary risk. Because of the nature of the work, Dave might have to drive to different drug locations where his informants were working to set up a meeting somewhere else, and people might see him and make a complaint or allegation. A drug dealer who was arrested out of state might hand over the detective's card and say he was a CI for the NYPD and had received the promise of immunity in exchange for cooperation. Or he might even try to say he had a corrupt cop in his pocket and would give him up in exchange for having the charges dropped.

That was one of the reasons a detective's job was tough, Dave thought. His job was to make people talk, and in order to do that, he had to "befriend" certain lowlifes, and give a little, but not cross the line—because if he did, he could lose everything he had ever worked for, throw his life away for a piece of shit. Even though Dave solved a lot of murders with Champ's help, if he crossed the line by running a license plate for Champ, for instance, and the department got word of it, the brass would bring the ax down on him. Just one thing wrong, and they wouldn't give a rat's ass that Dave had solved a dozen murders or so with Champ's help. It might have seemed an inconsequential favor at the time, but it would still have been a criminal act. A man's got to know his limitations, Dave reflected.

And so most of the time, Dave lied to Champ and his other informants—Champ was just one of many—if they asked about the cases he was working on, because he knew that they could turn around and use that evidence against him if they got into trouble. Dave usually knew just what to say, when to say it, and how. And he was aware too that at any time these drug dealers could be lying to him. It was a game of wits, in which the winner was whoever lied the most convincingly.

Smitty, bemused, continued reading Champ's screenplay treatment.

```
    It is the order of the NYPD for David to bring in
his brother, dead or alive, or turn in his badge and
gun. It is the order of the mob for Champ to kill his
cop brother. Both of the boys have what is called a
``critical decision.'' When it comes down to it,
they each have to ask themselves: Could I kill my
mother's child?
    Which comes first—blood, money, honor, respect,
or loyalty? How far would either brother go?
    Drug dealers are bad, but not all cops are good.
So think about it.
```

Smitty thought briefly and painfully of Michael Dowd as he turned the page and continued to read.

```
    The movie shows how Champ grew from a little boy
to a man, from poor to rich. He goes through bad
experiences from the time he committed his first
murder to his last. He loses his mother and father
because of his lifestyle, and now all that's left is
his brother, David. David goes through the oppo-
site, although he had support from his wife and the
NYPD. It shows how drug dealers can have a bad impact
on their families. It shows the difference between
a person who wants to be bad and one who can't help
being bad. It tells how just because a person sells
drugs does not mean he or she is all bad. It will
make you laugh and cry and think. It's just about the
truth, which is, sometimes in life we all have a
Critical Decision.
```

Smitty shook his head and threw down the manuscript, then glanced over at Dave. "He's been on the phone a long time," he said to the others.

A minute later, Dave hung up. "Champ just got whacked," he said tonelessly, staring in front of him.

Smitty glanced involuntarily down at the manuscript on Dave's desk. "What happened?" he asked.

"That was a detective from the One-Oh-Three Precinct in Queens, wanting to know if I knew a Russell Youmans. I said, 'Yeah, why?' She said, 'Because he was just killed. And we found your card in his pocket.' " Dave got up and began to pace aimlessly.

"She said he had just come back to New York with two other guys from North Carolina," he continued. "They brought back over sixty thousand bucks and a few kilos of coke. Then his brother and another man barged in, and an argument began because they wanted some of the money and drugs, and Champ wouldn't give it to them. So his brother and his friend just shot all three of them. Killed them in cold blood."

Dave pressed his lips together. Just yesterday Champ had called him from North Carolina to say he was on his way back and wanted to see Dave when he got in because he had information on yet another homicide in Queens. Before Champ left, he had told Dave about a murder in the borough, and Dave had relayed the information to Queens homicide detectives, who had quickly made an arrest on it. He was looking forward to Champ's return; he just hadn't anticipated the dealer would be coming back loaded down with drugs and drug money.

Dave plopped into his chair, leaned back, and looked up at the ceiling, aware of an odd hollow feeling in the pit of his stomach. You have to put things in perspective, he counseled himself. Remember who they are and who you are. Champ was a good informant, but he was nothing more than a drug dealer, and maybe—probably—worse. He had lived in the fast lane and died in the fast lane.

Dave told himself he wasn't going to have any personal feelings about Champ's death. He had cultivated Champ because it was his job, because Champ was a bad buy who was privy to information that could help the police, and their relationship had been purely business.

"Too bad," Smitty observed after a long silence. "He was turning out to be a good informant."

Dave shrugged his shoulders and looked down at the Five in front of him. Then he raised his head. "Ah, fuck it," he said softly, recalling Champ's own rationalization for murder. "The guy deserved it anyway."

19

In a high-crime precinct like the Seven-Five, it wasn't just the residents who were in constant danger, but the police as well. All too often, when an arrest was going down, gang members didn't hesitate to shoot it out with the cops. Other times, when a patrol car was cruising innocently down the block, or an off-duty cop was driving through or shopping or getting a haircut or pursuing some other mundane activity, certain people had the balls to open fire. And the sad part of it, aside from a cop's getting hurt or killed, was that the shooters were often teenagers. The precinct cops couldn't understand it. Why did these youths have such a total lack of respect for authority, and even for human life? There was virtually no chance that anyone who shot at a police officer in the precinct would get away with it, and that was well known. So what drove these kids to shoot a cop and—in one brazen, thoughtless moment—essentially throw their whole lives away?

Dressed in street clothes, Police Officer Eddie Serocki, a friend of Dave's, pushed open the heavy glass front door of the precinct and hung a left, heading home at the end of his four-to-midnight tour this September day of 1991. He wanted to pick up a pack of cigarettes at the bodega down the block before walking to the lot across the street where his car was parked.

Serocki ambled to Linwood, crossed the street, hopped back on the curb, and headed toward Elton. Halfway down the block, a group of a half-dozen teenagers was milling about. Serocki caught the glower of a young man but ignored it and continued on. He reached the bulletproof service window of the bodega and was about to tell the man behind it what he wanted when he felt the presence of several persons behind him. Then an angry voice sounded.

"Fuck you, cop!" Before Serocki could turn around, a hand clutching a semiautomatic pistol rose, and the trigger finger unleashed a shower of bullets.

The detectives in the squad room were busy on the phone or at their typewriters when the series of shots hit the night air. Shots were constantly being heard from the precinct, but these sounded as if they came from right outside the window. The detectives walked briskly to the window and peered out into the dark, but for several seconds they didn't see anything. Then, looking to the right, at the intersection of Linwood and Sutter, they saw a Housing Police car screeching backward down the block.

"Something's up," Dave said.

Immediately after that, they saw a man, doubled over, stumble across Linwood toward the station house.

The detectives ran out of the room, through the north hallway, into a stairwell, down the stairs, and out to the first floor. Just as they emerged from the stairwell, they saw the bloodied man stagger through the door. He cried out, "Sonny, I'm hit!"

Sonny DeSenso, a RIP detective who was standing by the front desk, ran over.

Holy shit! Dave thought, as he ran to help. His buddy Eddie Serocki had been shot. Dave and DeSenso helped the wounded officer over to a chair, his blood dripping on them. A lieutenant behind the desk called a 10-13 over the radio, then announced to those in the room that the midnight tour had just turned out and there were no RMPs left in the precinct parking lot.

"Jack, hold him," Dave barked to Cutrone. "I'm going upstairs to get the keys to one of our cars." There was no time to wait for an ambulance; Serocki looked as if he was going into shock, and Dave knew if he didn't receive medical attention soon, he would die.

Thirty seconds later, Dave returned. Serocki was being half-carried out the back door by two uniformed officers. In the parking lot was a brand-new unmarked Chevy. The two uniforms gently maneuvered Serocki into the backseat, then got in themselves, one on either side. Dave and Cutrone got in the front, with Dave behind the wheel.

Cutrone notified Central over the portable that they were on their way to the hospital, and immediately after, the occupants of the car heard Central putting out the call: "The Seven-Five is presently bringing a police officer shot to Jamaica Hospital."

"Where are you, squad?" the Central operator asked.

Cutrone keyed the radio. "We're taking Atlantic all the way. Block off the streets!"

Although Queens was not on their band, they knew the Queens Central operator was at the same time alerting cops in the adjacent precinct that the unmarked car with the injured cop was heading their way.

Out the lot, left onto Essex Street, five long blocks, and then a right on Atlantic Avenue. The siren blared, the headlights flashed, and Dave's foot inched the accelerator to the floor. Cars pulled over to the side of the road; RMPs with spinning turret lights blocked traffic at intersections from Atlantic Avenue. The precision of coordination was fantastic, Dave thought. Between gasps of pain, Serocki was able to give a description of the person who had shot him: a male black about sixteen years old, about six feet four or five, wearing a blue jacket with white stripes and blue jeans. Cutrone reported the description to Central, which in turn fed it to the cops at the crime scene.

Smitty and Nesbot had cordoned off the area in front of 676 Sutter Avenue, one block from the precinct. The midnight tour had responded to the 10-13 the lieutenant had put over the air, and the area was now swamped with RMPs and uniformed officers. Spectators had also gravitated to the crime scene but were kept at a distance by angry cops.

Well-liked by people in the area, Smitty began soliciting information about who had shot the off-duty police officer. Nesbot had already obtained the direction in which the gunman fled. With much territory to cover in a canvass and search of the area, the night threatened to be long and wearying.

Sharp curves, violent bumps, swerves to avoid hitting other vehicles—the ride was rough and wild, but all through it the cops in the car tried to keep Eddie Serocki talking.

For his part, Serocki recalled the tenets of an advanced survival course he had taken at police headquarters. He was taught that if you're shot and you're aware of it, you must do everything possible to keep your wits about you and not pass out. As long as you can function, you can survive. "I'm alive," Serocki repeated to himself, concentrating hard not to lose consciousness.

The Central operator's voice sounded over the radio. "Five squad, Jamaica Hospital notified and awaiting your arrival."

The pedal was nailed to the floor now, the red needle on the speedometer jumping the one-hundred-mile-per-hour mark. Dave pressed his foot down even harder, practically boring a hole through the floor. As they approached and passed intersections, radio-car sirens Dopplered up and down. Dave negotiated curves and traffic, occasionally letting up a bit on the pedal, then grinding it back down to the floor. Sometimes cars turned onto Atlantic, and Dave realized he was traveling so fast he was beating sector cops to the intersections where they were supposed to halt the traffic.

For a moment Dave's mind flashed back to his days as a volunteer fireman and fire chief. He had qualified to drive pumpers, a ladder truck, and ambulances to fire scenes, and was quite adept at driving at high speeds.

"Oh. Aahh!" The moaning came from the back.

Dave quickly shot a look at Serocki through the rearview mirror. His face was contorted.

"Hold on, Eddie," Dave commanded.

Serocki lay motionless. Seconds later he murmured weakly, "Hey, guys, don't let them put that rubber thing up my dick."

"Yo, Eddie," Dave responded buoyantly. "What are you, embarrassed or something? You're afraid for them to see your wiener, right? Don't worry, if they do have to use anything on you, it'll only be the small hose."

The Emergency Service Unit truck had come and lit up the crime scene like a movie set, its intense halogen beam shining from the giant pole. The area was awash now with precinct, housing, and Emergency Service Unit cops. Smitty continued his canvass and elicited from a young man hanging out on a corner the partial name or nickname of the gunman: Brax.

The street lining the entrance to Jamaica Hospital was paved with cops. As the unmarked car sped into the emergency-room driveway, Dave crunched the brakes. But the car wouldn't quite stop, and it smacked into the loading dock. The engine was smoking so heavily that cops came running over, thinking the vehicle was on fire.

The officers flanking Serocki jumped out of the car, then hospital technicians, waiting outside, extracted the injured cop gently, laid him on a gurney, and wheeled him quickly to the emergency room. Within minutes, police brass started arriving, and the hospital became a sea of uniforms and suits. For an hour, a horde of cops waited in the hospital to hear Serocki's prognosis.

Finally, it came. Serocki had been hit twice. One bullet had entered his left shoulder and broken it into seven pieces. The other had entered and exited his left leg. Serocki was lucky. The bullet that had penetrated his upper chest had missed his aorta by only an eighth of an inch.

Shortly after, a press conference began, attended by Mayor Din-

kins, Commissioner Kelley, Chief of Detectives Borelli, Chief of Patrol
Scott, and other major dignitaries.

"Time to go," Cutrone said, motioning Dave to the door.

Dave's relief that Serocki was going to live was so great that it took
him a minute to get back into gear. It was his habit never to worry
about getting shot or killed or hurt himself; at critical moments like
these, most cops never thought consciously of their own welfare. First
there was fear for the cop who had been felled; then, if he was not
going to die, the adrenaline was converted to anger and an intense
determination to catch the perpetrator. Only later, at home, when the
cops had for the moment shed the physical and psychic armor of the
job, did they get the shakes, seeing terrifying visions of their own bodies torn and bleeding.

Dave, now propelled by a rising rage, charged ahead of Cutrone
through the emergency-room door and threw himself into the car.
There was just one small problem, however, as he found out the next
moment. The transmission of the new squad car they had used was so
damaged it wouldn't shift gears, and he and Smitty had to drive back to
the precinct at a snail's pace.

Thirty minutes later, Dave and Cutrone were at the crime scene,
helping Smitty and Nesbot trace the escape route of the shooter. Housing and city police had grabbed a bunch of people on the street and
held them, but none, apparently, was the shooter. A helicopter was in
the air beaming a light on rooftops. A resident had told the cops while
they were searching that a man who was running down the block had
thrown something onto his roof. Then a patrol cop found a Tec-9
semiautomatic pistol on the roof of a house.

The detectives returned to the squad room, where several teenagers were sitting in the reception area.

"These people are, uh, witnesses," a uniformed officer told them.

Smitty and Dave detected the sarcasm in the officer's voice. They
understood his emphasis on "witnesses" meant they had probably
been with the gunman.

After a few hours of debriefing, three of the so-called witnesses
were willing to cooperate, but all claimed not to know the shooter's
name. They had been placed in separate rooms so they couldn't talk
among themselves, and each one was drilled by detectives, who took
turns going around from one to another of them. Dave sensed one did
know but wouldn't give it up. He nodded to Nesbot and Smitty to bring
him into the interview room.

"The game is over when a cop gets shot," Dave began moments

later. He extended his fingers and slipped off his rings, one at a time, fixing a glare on the young man. He tried to contain his anger. Every police officer identified with a shot cop, because it could easily have been him. The shooting of a cop was a personal attack on all police officers.

Dave unhooked the chain around his neck and placed it on the table next to the rings. He had to remind himself that the person before him was only a witness.

"Yeah, I was there," said the young man glumly. "I saw the guy, but I don't know who he is. I really don't."

"It's time to cut the crap," Dave said. He turned to Smitty and Nesbot. "Let me talk to this person alone. And shut the door on your way out, please."

Dave sat down and wheeled his chair next to the young man's. "You're in my home here, in this precinct, you understand? So don't bullshit me, or you'll insult me. And I don't think you want that to happen." Dave paused a moment to let the meaning sink in. "Now, a cop was shot tonight. Do you know what that means?"

The young man did not respond.

Dave answered his own question. "It means either of two things is going to happen to *you* tonight. One, you're going to be a witness to the shooting. Or two, you're going to jail. And I'll tell you this. We're going to get the guy. There's no doubt about it, I promise you that. And if he says you did it, you'll be behind bars on a long-term basis. A very-long-term basis."

Dave stared at the young man, wondering if he knew he was being handed a bunch of intimidating bullshit. There was no expression on his face. Dave figured he was probably fearing for his life if he gave up the shooter.

"You want to do the right thing, don't you?" Dave said, more softly now. "You don't want to be arrested for having anything to do with a police officer being shot. Because you know what happens when people who shoot cops go to jail, don't you? Wouldn't you rather go home tonight?"

The young man shifted uncomfortably in his chair. "Yeah."

"Well, then, talk to me, because otherwise you're not going home. I'll know you're lying, and when the DA comes here, he'll lock you up."

"Oh, yeah," said the young man, now rather defensively. "Whaddya got on me?"

"For one thing, you'll be charged with acting in concert. Second, by lying or withholding information, you're hindering an investigation and obstructing governmental administration." Dave felt he had enough to charge the young man with these offenses, but the DA would probably drop the charges.

"But I don't know anything," the young man protested earnestly.

"Now, what did I tell you before about insulting me in my home?" Dave's voice rose a notch. "You're really starting to piss me off now." The detective rose from his chair and put his hands on his hips.

"If you want to continue saying you don't know anything, fine. I'll just lock you up, and you can tell your story to a judge. But remember—there's no bail for cop shooters. But we know you were standing next to the shooter, so don't yank my pickle. Now, what's it going to be?"

"Yo, man, that guy's gonna kill me."

"He's not going to kill you, because I'm here. I promise you we'll get him."

"He shot someone before and got off," the youth said plaintively.

"He won't get off this time. Now, one way or another we're going to end this."

"Okay," said the young man, sighing deeply. Then he revealed the shooter's name and gave Dave a description. He added that the guy had shot the cop just to be macho. The kid paused a moment, then spoke again. "By the way, I just thought I'd tell you, they're gunning for cops here in East New York."

There was no limit to the balls these drug dealers have here, Dave thought, recalling that over the past week some of the precinct cops' civilian cars in the parking lot across the street had been set afire.

Smitty was sitting on a desk nearby, in front of the holding cell, when Dave walked out of the interview room. "Did it work?" he asked.

"Does a bear shit in the woods? The guy's name is David Braxton."

Smitty crunched his forehead and then looked at the floor. "Wait a minute," he exclaimed. "I know that guy. Is he tall?"

"The witness said he's over six feet."

"Yeah, that's him. He was involved in a murder last year on one of Jack's cases."

Smitty thought a moment before speaking again. "The DA never authorized his arrest. Braxton and another guy both had guns and shot a fifteen-year-old. But the other guy shot first and killed the kid, so the way the DA looked at it, Braxton only shot a dead kid. You can't go to jail for that, you know."

Just then Cutrone strolled into the squad room.

"Yo, Jack," Dave said. "We need the folder on one of your old cases."

Cutrone combed through the Fives until he came to David Braxton's address. "Here it is," Cutrone said. "455 Barbey Street."

He and a Seven-Three detective in the squad room left to sit on the location in an unmarked van. It was a long shot, but if Braxton was home and tried to flee, they'd take him out.

Then the night duty captain came up with a takedown plan.

At seven o'clock the next morning, Dave and five Emergency Service Unit cops in vests and helmets, carrying M-16s and shotguns, stood before the door of the apartment where Braxton lived. Dave knocked loudly on the door, and seconds later a woman opened it slightly.

"Is your son David home?" Dave asked, wedging his foot deftly between the door and the frame. In Dave's mind, they were going in no matter what.

"Yes," she said in a timid voice. "He's in his room sleeping."

"May I come in and talk to him?"

The woman opened the door, and Dave walked in, followed by the Emergency Service Unit cops.

"What did he do?" the woman asked, her eyes wide, her brow furrowed anxiously.

"He shot a cop. Where's he sleeping?"

The woman gasped, then pointed, her hand shaking, to a back room.

At the foot of the bed was a blue jacket with white stripes, exactly as Serocki had described. The young man had awakened and was staring at the cops. Dave looked at one of the ESU cops, and together they pulled Braxton out of bed. The ESU cops led the prisoner to the hallway, where they cuffed him.

Dave picked the jacket off the bed along with a pair of pants, then turned to Braxton's mother, who stood trembling as she watched the arrest of her son. "You can bring the rest of his clothes to the 75th Precinct if you want," said Dave.

Minutes later, the cops behind the front desk at the Seven-Five looked up when they saw the handcuffed teenager, barefoot and clad in only pants and an undershirt, being escorted through the door.

Dave led Braxton into the interview room. Braxton sat down, still handcuffed. Dave walked behind him and spoke softly into his ear.

"I know what you did. You know what you did. For the next hour, I want you to think about it." Then Dave turned and walked out, closing the door behind him.

An hour later, Dave returned with the Tec-9 recovered at the scene. He laid it on the table and took off Braxton's handcuffs. Then he advised him of his Miranda rights.

"We know this is your gun," Dave said. "Your fingerprints came off it, and it matched the ballistics we covered at the crime scene." Dave paced the floor for several seconds, stepping slowly for effect. Then he sat down next to Braxton.

"Did you know he was a cop?" Dave asked in a confidential tone.

Braxton didn't answer for a moment, then spoke up. "No, man, I didn't."

Braxton admitted to shooting the Tec-9 on the table, but he had shot at somebody else, he insisted, someone who was after him and had pulled a gun out. It was an accident that he had shot the cop.

"We have some of your friends who say that prior to the shooting you said, 'I'm gonna smoke the motherfucker.' And then somebody else said, 'No, man, he's a cop.' And then you said, 'Well, fuck him. I'm gonna shoot him anyhow.' "

Braxton looked scared. "I said, I accidentally shot the cop. I was shooting at somebody else to defend myself. All I can say is I knew I'd missed when I saw the cop at the window go down."

"That's a pretty good story, asshole. But guess what? You're going to jail anyway."

Hours later, after Serocki had picked Braxton's picture out of a photo array that Cutrone brought to the hospital—Serocki saw the shooter because he turned his head when he was shot—and the witness had picked Braxton out of a lineup, an ADA came to videotape Braxton's statement. Braxton didn't deny shooting the cop, but he kept to his story that it had been an accident.

"It's bullshit," Dave told the ADA, explaining how the recovered ballistics matched Serocki's and the witness's story and repudiated Braxton's. The ballistics didn't match where Braxton said he was standing.

Later, he and Smitty drove Braxton to Brooklyn Central Booking. As they lodged him in a holding cell, Dave said, "By the way, we're going to be passing your mom's house on the way back. We'll tell her to put a Room for Rent sign up, because you ain't gonna be using yours for a long, long time."

Thirteen months later, in October 1993, the Serocki shooting case went to trial. First were the Huntley and Wade hearings, or pretrial hearings, in which evidence and statements were ruled admissible or

not for the trial, based on arrest procedures. During such a proceed-
ing, the defense tried to have various elements of the prosecution's
case thrown out. If they could show the arrest had been illegal, the
defendant's rights would be seen as having been violated, and any
statements he had made or evidence collected by the detectives would
be deemed to have been obtained illegally (such as the jacket Dave had
found on Braxton's bed). These statements and evidence would be
barred, weakening the case. So, for example, if the prosecution came
in with two witnesses, a statement, and evidence, and the statement
and evidence were suppressed, the prosecution would be down to two
witnesses. The more the prosecution got in, of course, the better off it
would be.

Dave found that most of his murder cases didn't go to trial, because the defendants pleaded out beforehand. He put together his
cases so well that the suspects usually decided it was better to take eight
or twelve or fifteen years for the murder rather than risk a conviction
and a sentence of twenty-five years to life. But although the case against
Braxton was strong, Officer Serocki had only been shot, not killed, and
Braxton was facing five to fifteen years maximum. A plea bargain
might reduce that to a mere three years, and that was wholly inade-
quate for a cop shooter as far as the DA was concerned.

In the pretrial hearing, Dave took the stand. After three years in
the squad and numerous times testifying, Dave had his own philosophy
about how to handle himself in court.

When he first began having to testify, he was a little intimidated by
the defense attorneys, but his rule was never to show it. After a while,
he realized a cross-examination was just a game of wits. He viewed defense attorneys only as people with a degree who were entitled by law
to cross-examine him in front of a judge and jury. They came into the
courtroom in their silk suits with a pompous attitude, and why? They
were defending some piece of shit who should be locked up for murder. They hadn't investigated the suspect and chased him all over
town. The detectives did the real work. The defense attorneys were
defending someone Dave knew had committed a murder, and they
were going to make Dave look like the bad guy? Hell, no!

Dave understood that defense attorneys were paid to do a job, and
that they did whatever it took to get the job done right. That meant
calling into question the credibility and competence of whoever testi-
fied for the prosecution. In turn it was Dave's aim to do whatever he
could, given the onerous restrictions of cross-examination, to present
himself as sharp and trustworthy and to make the defense attorney,
and his client, look bad.

It all began, of course, with how he had carried out the case. Paperwork occupied a large portion of a detective's work on a case, and the defense attorney was entitled to all that paperwork—everything in the case folder. Through experience and mistakes, Dave had learned what to put down on paper and what to keep in his head. What the defense attorney couldn't see, he couldn't ask about during the trial.

Of course, the detective couldn't break the law, but there were ways to get around it. Consider, for example, the following scenario at a trial.

The defense attorney asks the detective on the stand, "How many times did you go to the house, detective?"

"Four or five times."

"Well, but on this report you wrote that you went four times. Now, which was it, four or five? Did you forget to record the fifth time? What else did you forget to put down?"

Dave learned never to record a precise number when a more general phrase would suffice. Instead of writing "I arrived at the defendant's place of employment at 3:10," he would write "midafternoon" or "around three o'clock." That way he couldn't inadvertently contradict himself on the stand.

Defense attorneys asked prosecution witnesses questions to which they wanted just a yes or no answer. The attorney didn't want the witness to ramble on; he or she wanted to have complete control of what the jury would hear. The detective likewise had a clear agenda of what he wanted to impart to the jury. The conflict often turned into a battle of wits.

"Isn't it a fact, detective," a defense attorney might ask, "that you showed up at the defendant's house?"

And Dave had learned to say, "Showed up? What exactly do you mean by that, counselor?"

"Well, how did you get there?"

"I went in an unmarked auto with eight other detectives."

Dave knew the defense attorney might not want him to say he had gone with eight other detectives; it gave the jury the impression that the defendant was a dangerous criminal. But he figured out a way to get it in. Even if it was stricken from the record, the idea would have been planted in the jury's mind.

"Isn't it true, detective, that my client came to the station house of his own free will?"

Instead of giving a yes or no answer, Dave would say, "What do you mean by that, counselor?"

"How did he happen to come to the precinct?"

Now Dave would be able to give an explanation, rather than a yes or no answer.

"I called his house, and he came to the precinct with his lawyer."

And this would be a strike against the defendant in the jury's mind. If he was innocent, why would he have brought his lawyer?

With experience, Dave learned how to frustrate the defense attorney's intention to elicit yes or no answers. If the defendant had been arrested before—something the detective wasn't allowed to say directly—Dave would try to work into his testimony the fact that he had a picture of the suspect. He hoped it would occur to the jurors that the picture was most likely a mug shot.

Different attorneys had different approaches, but Dave figured out how to apply his basic precepts to any of them and say just what he wanted to say. They had their routines, he had his. Sometimes he was even brazen enough, if he was cut off in answering a question, to finish his answer when asked the next question. The defense attorney would try to get his statement stricken from the record, and the judge might agree, at the same time admonishing Dave, but he had said it, and the jury had heard it—some telling piece of information that could really hurt the defendant.

With a homicide, of course, there was a dead person and one or more perpetrators. Even though each murder was different, the investigations, Dave realized, were basically the same. He remembered Sergeant Race's example of President Kennedy's murder. The investigation for that had been particularly intense, but the steps were no different from those of any other investigation. And there were specialists along the way, like the Crime Scene Unit detectives, to help.

If the defense attorney asked, "How many rounds were recovered, detective?" Dave would say, "I don't know."

"Didn't you see the rounds?"

"Sure, I saw the rounds."

"Well, how many were there?"

"I don't know exactly, counselor. I'm not a ballistics expert, so I didn't collect the evidence. You'd have to ask the crime scene detective, because he knows precisely."

Dave would just have saved himself from potentially contradicting another expert who might be called to testify. If Dave were to say five rounds had been recovered, and the Crime Scene Unit detective said seven, the defense attorney would suggest one of the detectives was lying or had meddled with the evidence.

Dave's rule was, if he wasn't an expert at something, he kept his mouth shut. If he was asked a medical question, he deferred it to the medical examiner. It wasn't his job to answer questions outside his specialty, and it would hurt the case to contradict the specialists. These were points the defense attorney would use in his summation to question the competence and sincerity of the prosecution.

When Dave was a cop and was hanging around in the court building waiting to talk to an ADA, he would go across the hall to a court session and listen to cases being tried. He watched defense attorneys hammer away at cops' testimony, and he tried to learn how to answer questions and handle himself on the stand. He knew the defense attorneys were out to make him look bad, but he hadn't realized how ruthless they could be until he actually went up against them. Dave's pride and ego were too big for him to tolerate being made to appear anything other than competent and polished. He observed to Smitty, "We have to be able to articulate how we investigated the case. Defense attorneys only have to be good storytellers. They're going to try to paint a different picture of what we're describing. But if we've done our job right to start with, the attorney is going to have to tell a false story to get his client off, and to do that, he's going to have to try to make us look like liars and fools. We have to know how to make the truth a more convincing story than his."

During the Serocki pretrial hearing, the defense attorney said to Dave, "Isn't it a fact, detective, that you knocked my client's mother to the ground and then ran into the apartment and arrested him in the back room?"

Dave was thinking ahead.

"No, I didn't," he responded.

The defense attorney looked incredulous. "She's prepared to testify that you knocked her down. Are you calling her a liar?"

Dave pointed behind the attorney to a woman sitting in the courtroom and inquired, "Why don't you ask her yourself, counselor?"

The woman was the defendant's mother. She had been listening to Dave's testimony, which she wasn't allowed to do if she was going to be called to the stand as a witness, which Dave suspected she would be. A witness was not permitted to hear what any other witness had to say, lest it taint his or her testimony. Dave had been waiting for the right moment to drop this bomb on the defense attorney.

The defense attorney turned around and, to his horror, saw the defendant's mother. "Your honor," he said, thoroughly flustered, "my client's mother just walked into the courtroom."

"Counselor, stop right there," said the judge. "I know when anybody comes in or out of my courtroom during a trial. She was sitting here the entire time this detective was on the stand.''

Dave's response had blown away the defense attorney's line of questioning. A year before, he would not have known how to accomplish that, but testifying effectively in court was one more area of detective work in which he had gained expertise by learning how to stay two jumps ahead of the game. It was a deadly serious game, to be sure, but one at which he was becoming a master.

The next day, the trial of David Braxton began. It lasted eight days, and Seven-Five detectives Carbone, Smith, and Cutrone, as well as Officer Serocki, took the stand.

The cops could never quite put their finger on the motivation behind the shooting. Dave attributed it to "bragging rights." It was a big thing for some people to be able to say "I shot a cop" to their peers. But he wondered how great the bragging rights were for shooting a cop in the back.

While Braxton stuck to his story that he hadn't meant to shoot Serocki, that he had been shooting at somebody else, there was no doubt in the cops' minds that this was a total fabrication. Braxton's own friends admitted he had told them he was going to smoke a cop, which, given the group situation, was obviously his way of trying to impress them. Other than that, there was no reason the cops could discern for his despicable act.

Braxton didn't seem the slightest bit remorseful, and Dave even detected a certain insouciance in his attitude—Braxton was a juvenile and knew he wasn't going to go to jail for the rest of his life. All the way through the interrogation, the detectives had had the impression Braxton was a cold kid, unconcerned about what he had done. They were hardly surprised, given the fact that he had previously been identified as a perp in a murder—one whose arrest the ADA wouldn't authorize because he had supposedly shot the victim after he was already dead. In any case, Braxton was not new to violence.

Dave was convinced of Braxton's guilt. Braxton had confessed to owning the gun, to being at the crime scene, and to having fired the shots that wounded Serocki. Whatever reason he gave didn't matter to Dave. Dave was only concerned that Serocki's shooter be put away.

The whole senseless act, in fact, made perfect sense to Dave. People don't need a reason for what they do, he told the others. What galled him was that the shooting had hit so close to home. It was one thing to go on murder cases and see a lot of innocent corpses. It was another to see a fellow officer almost murdered a few doors from the police station. It jolted the cops, made them realize how vulnerable they were, reminded them once again to keep their eyes open at all times. But they also knew it was something they couldn't continually worry about. If they became preoccupied with it, it would interfere with their jobs and their lives. If it was something they couldn't handle, they had no right being cops in the ghetto.

The only thing Dave couldn't figure out was why Braxton would shoot a cop so close to the police station. That was so stupid it was downright perplexing.

The day after the trial ended, the jury returned a guilty verdict. Under New York State law, a juvenile could receive a maximum of eight and a third to fifteen years for attempted murder in the second degree, but the judge gave Braxton only five to fifteen. When Serocki asked the ADA why the judge had knocked it down, he said, "You're lucky he got that much, in Brooklyn."

On February 28, 1993, Police Officer Eddie Serocki retired from the NYPD at the age of thirty-one on a line-of-duty disability pension. Chronic pain from the injury prevented him from taking full-time employment and limited the kinds of jobs he could perform, but he went on to take a position as a part-time plainclothes security guard.

20

The terrain detectives inhabited was littered with hideous corpses and meandering, dangerous pathways to their murderers. It was a dark, somber world that could cast an oppressive shadow on the detectives' private lives if they failed to put up the proper barriers. Most people never got to see this terrain, except for the fictional glimpses provided by novels, movies, and television, but real human beings dwelt in it, feeling its pain and living its horrors.

At first, it had been difficult for Dave not to think about the murder victims he had seen in the Seven-Five. Like a video montage, crime scenes continually played themselves out in his mind. The scenes, the people, the blood—after a while, they had no longer even seemed real. But of course they were, and Dave had realized that he was going to have to keep the carnage from getting to him.

Work at the Seven-Five consisted largely of one macabre crime scene after another, and they no longer bothered Dave very much unless the victim was very young or very old. Dave was able to deal with gruesomely slain bodies because he generally vented in a healthy way—he joked about them.

There was, for instance, the charred remains of a body found in two bags—the limbless torso in one, the legs and handcuffed arms in the other—that had been set on fire. The hands were burned so badly that lifting fingerprints would not have been possible. Dave advised Cutrone, the catching detective, to take a picture of the victim's teeth at the morgue and put it on a poster to send to all the dentists in the area with a caption under the photo reading, "If you recognize these teeth, please contact Detective Cutrone at 1-800-BAG-OF-SHIT."

Then there was the young man who was getting a blow job from a prostitute in a crack den when some kid broke in to pull a stickup and shot the victim. At the crime scene, Dave wondered aloud, "Wonder how it feels to get your head blown off on both ends at once?"

It was better to get his emotions out like that, he figured, than to take them out on his family, regressing into a shell primed by alcohol, or to bottle things up like a Molotov cocktail until some little annoyance set him off. He'd heard about cops screaming to their wives, "A kid died in my arms today, and you're bothering me about taking out the fucking garbage?" He didn't want to become like that, and while he joked a lot, he kept his compassion and knew in his heart when it was appropriate to joke and when it was not.

When a hysterical mother sent her two-year-old son away for the night with friends after her husband had been shot and killed in the apartment lobby, the tot, separated from his mother for the first time, began wailing as he was being carried off into the elevator. In the lobby, amid a sea of cops and detectives, the family friend put the boy down to walk. Careful not to lose his balance, he trod slowly and carefully, still sobbing, through a forest of legs. He came to a wobbly stop in front of the police tape, within arm's length of his father, whose bullet-riddled body rested in a sea of its own blood. The little boy, a pacifier in his mouth, bawled, "Da, Da, Daaaa!"—unaware of the identity of the corpse stretched out behind him. The detectives and cops watched in amazement, and no one, including Dave, uttered a word.

Dave tried not to burden his family with what he saw or how he felt about it, and he was generally successful, remaining mostly silent at home about the grimmer aspects of his job.

But the emotional whiplash manifested itself in other ways, altering Dave's philosophy and comportment, his personality and responses. He became laid back, introspective. If someone cut his car off, shouldered in front of him in a supermarket line, threw a nasty remark his way, he didn't become excited. He just let it pass, dissipate like a noxious odor in the wind.

At times, Dave's impassive attitude drove his wife, Luci, up the wall. Why didn't he honk the horn when another car cut in front of him? Why didn't he give the intruder in the supermarket line a piece of his mind? Why, if they couldn't meet the month's bills, did he shrug and say one of their creditors was just going to have to wait for his money?

"Nothing bothers you," Luci fretted, puzzled at the stories she'd heard about how intimidating Dave could be to perps in the precinct, since he was such a quiet lamb at home. "It's not normal!"

But Dave would be thinking about the four-year-old girl who had been raped and beaten; about the female drug dealer who had come up a little short and got gang-banged, her head crushed with a boulder afterward; about the ten-year-old boy who died after his father shoved a broomstick up his rectum all the way into his stomach.

By comparison, the little annoyances just weren't important enough to worry about anymore. When he was not being a detective, when he was home with his family being a father and a husband, he was too busy being grateful for what he had.

While Dave and his team solved the majority of cases they caught, the unsolved ones bothered them deeply. One murder that festered in Dave's mind was that of an elderly woman named Rebecca Johnson. She had been brutally stabbed, and Dave was having a difficult time proving that Amy Mackson, who lived downstairs from Johnson, had done it. But then another crime took place that enabled him to finally collar his suspect.

Late on the evening of December 19, 1991, violent screams and the sound of furniture being thrown in apartment 6F at 272 Pennsylvania Avenue, the same building Rebecca Johnson had lived in, were heard by neighbors. They called the police, who arrived just minutes later. The cops pounded on the locked door and yelled for someone inside to open it.

Officer John Difillipo gripped the door handle and wrenched it back and forth. Frustrated, he rammed the metal door with his body, then kicked it in the center as hard as he could. People on the floor opened their doors as far as the chains would permit, watching the police stand by helplessly as something horrible was happening to their neighbor. Difillipo stormed the door again, using all his strength to try to break it down.

"Police, open the door!" shouted Officer Florence Gomes.

No response. Gomes raised her portable to her mouth: "Central, have Emergency Service respond to gain entrance to a locked apartment."

Just then the building superintendent came running over, his right hand extended. "I have a key," he said breathlessly. There were two locks on the door. He inserted the key into the top lock. It opened. Then he put it into the bottom lock, but it wouldn't turn.

The screams inside the apartment were agonized. Difillipo continued to give the door mighty kicks, creating booming sounds.

A patrol sergeant and several uniformed officers came running down the hall. They too stood helpless, listening to the blood-curdling screams.

Then out of the sixth-floor elevator emerged the detectives: Dave, Smitty, Cutrone, Nesbot, and Sondra Royal, a recent transfer to the squad, along with Lt. Kevin Perham, the new squad CO. Officer Gomes told the detectives what was going on.

"Sounds like somebody's moving furniture," Smitty said. There were loud thuds from the other side of the door; the officers could see the panel shake as something heavy bumped against it.

A lock snapped open at an adjacent apartment, and an elderly woman emerged and approached the officers. "Somebody jumped out the window. She's lying on the ground," she said urgently. Using his radio, the patrol sergeant notified the police officers on the ground floor to check out the back of the building.

Now the Emergency Service Unit crew emerged from the elevator. Within a minute or two, an officer popped the bottom lock.

Dave turned the handle of the door and pushed in, but it only went an inch and then hit something.

"Fucking door won't move," he grunted.

Smitty joined him in putting his shoulder against the door, but it still wouldn't budge. It took five large cops to inch the door open so the officers could enter. A refrigerator had been wedged up against it.

Inside the apartment, furniture was turned upside down and scattered about. The floor was strewn with clothing. A bathroom wall was smeared with blood, and a steak knife rested in the reddened basin. The door of the medicine chest was ripped off, a heating vent cover sat in the toilet, and on top of the toilet tank was a hammer, its head covered with blood. The shower curtain was torn down and the rod dangled, bent in the middle. In the bedroom, bureau drawers were open, their contents heaped on the bed.

A heavyset black woman was lying facedown on the living-room floor in front of a couch, her face resting on a throw pillow. Her face and chest were covered with blood, there were bruises on her head and face, and her red nightgown and black slip underneath were pulled up above her waist, exposing her panties and legs.

"Hey, Smitty," Dave said in a low voice, "are you having a déjà vu or what?"

"Yeah," grunted Smitty.

The crime scene here was almost identical to that of the Rebecca Johnson murder.

"Creatures of habit, Smitty. They do it the same way every time."

"The only difference here is the victim seemed to put up a fight." Near the victim was a large butcher knife, its seven-inch blade covered with blood.

An EMS technician knelt down and listened for a pulse. Seconds later, he pronounced the woman dead.

Dave turned to all the uniformed cops. "Okay, I want everybody to leave right now," he said. "I don't want this crime scene touched."

As the officers left, a soft cry could be heard from the rear of the apartment. The detectives looked out the window. On the ground, six floors below, lay a woman. A cop was standing by her; two ambulance technicians were preparing to take her away.

To the right of the window was a heap of several white bedsheets tied together, one end attached to the leg of a bed. "Look at this," Dave said to Smitty. "You know, that girl on the ground has something to do with this murder. I think she forgot to grab the sheets on the way down." Dave strained to get a look at the woman on the ground, but it was too dark and she was too far away.

Dave spoke into his portable to Cutrone, who was on the ground floor.

"Jack, go with that girl to the hospital and get a statement from her. I don't think she'll be able to move much, but don't let her out of your sight. We'll catch up with you later."

"If she did it," Smitty said, "she must have been on something to be able haul that refrigerator all by herself to the front door. It took five of us to open it."

"A crackhead, no doubt."

"From the way this apartment looks, whoever did it was probably looking for money or jewelry."

Lieutenant Perham took control of the crime scene. "Dave, you stay here with the body," he said. "Everybody else, see what you can find out."

The woman lay in pain on the bed in the emergency room at Brookdale Hospital. A bone in her right leg was sticking out, and she had cuts on her face, hands, and neck. Doctors and nurses were stabilizing her in preparation for surgery.

The detective walked next to her and bent down slightly. "I'm Detective Cutrone. What's your name?"

The woman's eyes were glazed. "Amy Mackson," she said softly.

"How old are you?"

"Twenty-four."

Cutrone estimated her weight to be two hundred pounds.

"Amy, I need to know how you hurt yourself."

The woman closed her eyes briefly and groaned. Then she spoke, in disjointed phrases. "I . . . went to Mrs. Dortch's apartment. . . . She had some Avon items . . . for me." She squirmed, then went into a brief but violent coughing spasm. "We were talking, and the doorbell rang," she said hoarsely when she had recovered. "Mrs. Dortch . . . she answered the door." Her voice was fading away; Cutrone had to strain to make out the words. "It was a black man. He was . . . about thirty. Light skin, tall and thin. He and Mrs. . . ."

Mackson stopped speaking and, astonishingly, began to snore. Cutrone grasped her shoulder gently, and she immediately opened her eyes again, but they were glazed and unfocused. She nevertheless continued from where she had left off, as if there had been no break. " . . . Dortch were arguing about money. He grabbed . . . a knife, and he stabbed . . . Mrs. Dortch. Oh, oh!" She gave a piercing shriek and began to writhe in pain. Again Cutrone grasped her shoulder, and she went limp. "I . . . tried to stop him," she breathed, "but he attacked me." At this point Mackson, her head rolling aimlessly from side to side, managed to focus her eyes and fix them on Cutrone. "Then he went out the window and up to the roof." She sighed deeply and closed her eyes again.

Cutrone prodded her. "And how did you get hurt?"

Eyes still closed, she murmured, "I jumped out the window . . . to get away."

Cutrone waited out another coughing spasm. "Are you on drugs, Amy? Did you have anything to drink this evening?"

"I do crack. I had some . . . earlier today. I had a quart of beer this evening. Around eight-thirty." She began to moan, her voice rising and falling rhythmically as if she were keening.

The attending doctor caught Cutrone's eye and made a "That's enough" gesture.

Detectives Royal, Nesbot, and Smith were spread out now at 272 Pennsylvania Avenue, talking to people in the hallways and knocking on every door on every floor, to see if anyone had heard or seen anything related to the murder. One man told them he had seen Amy Mackson at the staircase. Others said they had heard loud screams coming from Violet Dortch's apartment not long after; they had recognized the voice as Violet's.

A short while later, the two Crime Scene Unit detectives walked past the uniformed police officers guarding the front door of apartment 6F. As they stood a few feet inside the apartment, Dave watched the look of recognition come over their faces. Detectives Mary Dugan and Mike Sheptuk had also processed the crime scene of the murder of Rebecca Johnson.

"I know what you're thinking," Dave said. "Check everything you can think of, so we can link this bitch to the other murder. She's not going to get away with killing two women."

After Sheptuk photographed the murder victim on the floor,

Dugan placed paper bags over her hands, sealing the openings with masking tape. Violet Dortch might have scratched at her assailant and have skin fiber or hair under her nails or on her fingers, and the bag would protect the evidence for the ME to examine. If necessary, a court order could be obtained to compare epidermis and hair of the suspect with scrapings recovered from the victim.

While the crime scene was being processed, Smitty, Nesbot, and Royal returned from their canvass and shared the statements they had obtained.

Smitty had already spoken with Jack Cutrone, who was at Brookdale and had interviewed the woman who had fallen.

"Are you ready for this, Dave?" Smitty asked. "Guess who's in the ER now?"

"Oh, shit. Amy Mackson?"

"Yep."

"I thought that might've been her. I just couldn't see that far down."

"Jack said she's all cracked out. But apparently after they got her stabilized, they decided to postpone the surgery. We can talk to her now if we want."

A half hour later, Dave, Smitty, and Cutrone were standing before Amy Mackson in the emergency room at Brookdale. The injured woman repeated her story about a strange man coming into Violet Dortch's apartment, demanding money, and climbing out the window and up to the roof, followed by Mackson's leap out the window to escape.

"If the man had already escaped out the window," Dave said, "why would you jump out?"

Mackson stared at the wall and ignored the question.

"Why is there blood on you?" Smitty asked.

Mackson shrugged.

Several minutes later, outside the emergency room, the detectives discussed their suspect. Her story was inconsistent with the crime scene. There was no fire escape in the building, so nobody would have been able to climb up from Violet Dortch's window to the roof, and no man had come out the front door of the apartment. There was no such intruder. Mackson's clothes were covered with blood.

"She did the murder," said Dave. "She went out the window. There was no other way out, so that's the way she went out. She tied the sheets together to climb down, but she was so fucked up she slipped and fell."

"We'll arrest her for the murder of Violet Dortch," Smitty said. "We have enough evidence to show she did the murder, and that there was nobody else. We'll have the ADA ride the case. Since Mackson will probably be in the hospital for another month, we'll post a police officer by her room full-time, then have Corrections take her away when she's ready to be released."

Two ADAs sat in the captain's office filling out court papers charging Amy Mackson with murder in the second degree.

It was just after four o'clock in the morning. Dave and Smitty sat at their desks, taking a break from typing up the Fives.

"Dammit, Smitty," Dave said, "if we'd been able to collar Amy Mackson on Rebecca Johnson, Violet Dortch wouldn't be dead now."

"Our hands were tied."

"I know. But maybe we could still have found a way to get her."

"Don't be so hard on yourself. We couldn't prove it legally, so what are you going to do? There was nothing we could do about it."

"I know, but it still bothers me. Here we targeted a woman, and she killed again."

"Look, we staked out Amy Mackson and her boyfriend. They stayed away from the dealers for those few days. That's just the way it goes."

After the Rebecca Johnson murder, Dave and Smitty had wanted to get Mackson's prints. The easiest way would have been to arrest her on drug charges, which would automatically permit the police to print her. Dave and Smitty put her under surveillance for a few days, but they didn't see her make any purchases. They did the same thing with her boyfriend. If they'd busted him, he might have given her up in exchange for leniency. If you can't arrest the person you want right away, Dave said, you go after the "weak link." But alas, they couldn't catch Mackson's boyfriend either.

"It's unbelievable. Same MO. Same crime scenes. Two single women who lived alone, each knifed and brutally murdered. Mackson got away with it the first time, so she thought she could do it again."

Ah, getting away with murder, Dave thought. So many people did it! Often detectives targeted a suspect but couldn't arrest him or her for murder. They just didn't have enough to charge the person, to prosecute and make it stick.

A killer who murdered somebody when no one else was around, left no fingerprints or evidence behind, destroyed or hid the murder weapon, and never told anyone about it might never even be targeted by the police. If he was targeted but had a good alibi, he might still get away with murder, unless a detective with good skills was able to elicit a confession.

Even when there was a witness, a person could get away with murder if the witness refused to testify. Testifying was a risk; if the jury found the suspect not guilty, when the suspect was released, he would know who the witness was. Was the gamble to put the suspect away worth it?

Joe Howard was right, Dave thought, reflecting on the New Haven detective's philosophy. Being a detective was like wandering in the dark with a little flickering torch, trying to find your way to the truth. But it wasn't enough just to find it. You had to find it in such a way as to be able to preserve it, intact and ironclad, all the way to court and into the skeptical minds of the judge and jury.

As the ADAs finished writing up the charges and Team One finished typing their Fives in the squad room, Police Officer Stacey Riddle stood guard at Brookdale Hospital outside the room in which Amy Mackson was recovering from surgery. Mackson was handcuffed to her bed. "When she's well enough to be released from Brookdale," Dave said in the squad room with some degree of satisfaction, "that bitch will be whisked off in a wheelchair to prison."

In early 1993, Amy Mackson's case went to trial. She was found guilty of murder and, in May 1993, was sentenced to twenty-five years to life in prison.

21

The banquet room of the Eastwood Manor on Eastchester Road in the Bronx was filled with cops dressed casually or in suits. They were seated at tables eating dinner, awaiting the awards ceremony sponsored by the New York Shields, a fraternal organization of local, state, and federal law enforcement officers.

The Seven-Five Precinct Detective Unit was to receive an award for its part in investigating the shooting six months previously of two undercover cops and for arresting the perpetrator.

As Dave sat at the Seven-Five table, filled with Team One and its homicide assistants, he thought back with satisfaction on the arrest.

In January 1993, the undercovers had been shot in their car by a drug dealer who had mistaken them for the guys who had ripped off his spot a short while before. The undercovers had been watching another undercover walk away from the spot after having purchased drugs. The dealer had sprayed the car with bullets; one undercover had been shot in his right hand, the other's eyes had been injured by flying glass from the shattered windshield.

A major break in the case had come from two teenaged girls, who had let it be known to the police that a local resident named Sarge knew who the shooter was. They were supposed to take Dave and a new Team One member, Johnny Mullins, to meet Sarge, but they never showed up at the preset time and place. Dave wasn't surprised, and he was glad they had at least provided a lead. One of the girls had told him they'd set up the guys anytime, especially if there was a reward. They often learned about killings and other crimes because the guys would brag to them in bed. For the girls there was no great emotional attachment. Dave found that under pressure they could be persuaded to give information to the cops, and he told Mullins that girls were often a good source of information on crimes.

Through canvasses and stakeouts, Dave and Mullins managed to find Sarge, who provided the first name of the shooter—he swore he didn't know the last name—and also a drug location where the shooter had once been arrested.

Running the location with the CARS unit, they came up with several names and NYSIIS numbers of people arrested at that location over the past several months. Using the NYSIIS numbers to obtain mug shots of these people, Dave brought Sarge in again to identify the perp, and then he and Detective Al Nesbot staked out various locations where the suspect might be. Soon they found and arrested him.

Leaning back in his chair in the banquet room, Dave recalled his first day on the squad. He had come into the squad room a naive kid, and everybody had busted his chops, trying to unsettle him. Now, four years later, he was an experienced detective who possessed the confidence and skills to handle himself well under pressure.

He had learned a tremendous amount. He could read a crime scene astutely and had a good sense of exactly where to begin an investigation, what direction to take it in, and what turns to make if it wasn't leading anywhere. He was skilled at working around the law when necessary and getting what he needed legally. He could gain the confidence of victims' families and witnesses and inspire them to help as much as they could. And he was also a terrific interrogator, usually successful in obtaining confessions. No matter how rough or intractable the suspects, Dave knew how to play their game until they broke.

This was all based on a foundation of knowledge accumulated from all his experience on the force over the years, and from formal courses he had taken. He was able to assimilate, for example, the Criminal Investigation Course, in which he had attended classes on such subjects as Lust Murder, Estimating Time of Death, Forensic Entomology, Death by Asphyxia and Narcotic Related Deaths, Interview and Interrogation Techniques, Forensic Dentistry, Psychological Profiling, Tracing the Known Fugitive, and Investigating Human Remains. Dave had found that in his current assignment, the ghetto had its own rules and the formal precepts of criminal investigation didn't always apply; but the reservoir of knowledge was there if he needed to draw on it.

Interestingly, by the time of the CIC, after he had been in the Seven-Five squad for a year and had caught forty-three homicides with his team, Dave was already more experienced at murder investigation than most other detectives elsewhere. Indeed, of the approximately one hundred investigators taking the course, including not only detectives from other NYPD precincts but investigators from other police departments and federal agencies, hardly anyone had ever caught so much as a single homicide, although they had vast experience with burglaries, robberies, car thefts, and rapes. Detective Raymond Pierce, the course director and the NYPD's top serial killer profiler, himself a veteran of the Seven-Five squad—or, as he put it, "the Slam-Bam

School of Investigation"—told the class, "If you guys think you have it bad, it's all kindergarten compared to East New York."

And Dave's experience and skills had finally paid off for him. Just a few months earlier, Lieutenant Perham had made Dave a homicide assistant for Team One. No longer did he catch regular cases; it was only homicides now.

Dave was thrilled with his promotion; his goal of becoming a homicide detective had finally become a reality. Thirty-six years old and a homicide detective in the NYPD. Mom would have been proud.

Taking pride in his accomplishment, Dave contemplated himself and his job. To become a detective, a cop had to want to better himself on the job, to embrace new challenges, to enjoy putting together the pieces of a puzzle. But those who wanted to work homicides exclusively were almost a breed apart.

A civilian friend of Dave's had once asked him why he was so dedicated to working homicides, why he spent so much time and effort learning how to be the best at what he did. He had responded, "I love going to murders and finding out how they happened, and figuring out who did it, and then hunting down that person until I finally lock him up. A lot of guys don't like murder. They can't deal with the diet of blood and guts. They can't handle seeing body after body, going to autopsy after autopsy. The smell of death makes them sick. Having to tell people their husband, their father, their brother, their daughter, has been blown away wipes them out emotionally.

"To me, being a detective is very special, but doing homicides is the ultimate. To catch somebody who murdered someone, to be able to put cuffs on that guy and say, 'You're under arrest for the murder of so-and-so'—that's the ultimate satisfaction.

"With murder, you have to do it all yourself from start to finish, because the victim can't tell you what happened. The challenge is putting that whole murder case together. If I want to meet that challenge, if I want to have that satisfaction, I need to be able to do the footwork and the paperwork. I have to know how to fake a suspect out and get him to confess. I have to be able to stick with it when I'm tired and think twenty steps ahead. I have to have my emotions under control so I can be compassionate when it's appropriate and tough when that's what's called for. To be able to put it all together—it takes a whole lot of experience."

The conversations in the room were now interrupted by a speaker at the podium. It was time for the awards to be presented.

Twenty-five minutes into the program, a captain presented plaques to the two undercovers shot in East New York and the Seven-Five PDU. "It's totally out of control in the Seven-Five," he told the audience. "We should have armored cars there on every block."

By now, the whole city was aware of the precinct's reputation. Just recently, a blaring front-page headline in the *New York Post* had called the 75th Precinct "New York's deadliest neighborhood—with a murder every sixty-three hours."

With the frequency of homicides and other cases in the Seven-Five, not every murder case could be solved, and Dave had had his share of disappointments. Chief among them were the Shaun Henry–Robert Dudley murders. His prime suspect, Charlie Brackett, had eluded both him and Joe Howard of the New Haven PD.

Howard had contacted the New Haven field office of the FBI, and agent Ralph DiFonzo, an eighteen-year veteran with the Bureau, was assigned the case. DiFonzo went to federal court and obtained a federal fugitive warrant for a separate charge, Unlawful Flight to Avoid Prosecution. He placed the warrant into NCIC, hoping it would assist the FBI in locating and apprehending Charles Brackett.

DiFonzo then took every name and address Dave and Howard had developed during their investigations and ran computer checks on them. He also ran all Brackett's relatives who were living in the country through the U.S. Immigration and Naturalization Service. All this started a paper trail of Brackett's friends and relatives, and for the next six months FBI agents in Florida, California, Texas, and New York interviewed everyone related to the investigation they could find. Nobody admitted to knowing the whereabouts of Charles Brackett.

Then on January 1, 1993, the national television show *America's Most Wanted* broadcast a reenactment of the abduction and execution of Robert Moody in New Haven, along with an interview with the victim's mother and Detective Howard; Dave's taped interview was canceled after the family of one of his murder victims refused to go on the air.

As a result of the telecast, over one hundred calls were made to the show. DiFonzo followed them all up, but with no results.

Then one day a confidential informant who worked with DiFonzo on cases involving Jamaican gangs called to tell him she had spotted Brackett while on vacation in Belize. The Central American country did not have an extradition treaty with the United States, so plans were made for the CI to return to Belize to try to lure Brackett to the Bahamas, where FBI agents could arrest him so that he could be brought back to the United States to stand trial for murder. The CI, however, had been unable to entice Brackett to leave.

Dave closed out the Henry-Dudley case with an exceptional clearance—the designation for a perp who had been identified but was either in jail in another jurisdiction or in a foreign country that had no extradition agreement with the United States—although he hoped that designation would be only temporary. If it became known that Brackett had returned to this country or had traveled to any country that had extradition with the United States, the case could be reopened.

Dave believed a drug dealer named Tookey was the other gunman in the Henry-Dudley murders, but a relentless hunt had failed to locate him. Later, Dave heard Tookey had been killed in Jamaica.

Dave had many other memories of working in the 75th Precinct. There was Puzzle, the fifteen-year-old who had terrorized the community, killing at least four people and shooting numerous others before he himself was shot down; the murder of two students at Thomas Jefferson High School by a classmate a half hour before the mayor was to speak there on violence in the schools; the cult gang that stole body parts at Cypress Hills Cemetery and engaged in sexual practices late at night on top of the tombstones; the man whose face had been stomped on for an hour by his drunken roommate until his eyes were gone and you could see the coiled gray tissue of his brain through his eye sockets; the "crispy critter" (as the detectives dubbed him) who was beaten up, stabbed, pistol-whipped, chain-whipped, set on fire, pissed on, shot, run over, and scorched again, all on one night, only to be finally done in a few months later by the same perps he would not give up when he was originally hospitalized.

The *New York Post* was right; the Seven-Five was a killing ground. With 105 homicides in 1988, 98 in 1989, 109 in 1990, 115 in 1991, and 92 in 1992, and a record number promised for the current year, it had four to five times more murders than the average New York City police precinct. A war zone, it revolved around its own bloody axis.

After the two undercovers received their award and a standing ovation, the Seven-Five detectives were called to the podium to collect the PDU's plaque. It read: "In recognition of your outstanding contribution to the principles and goals of American law enforcement." Cameras flashed, the detectives returned to their seats, and an hour later they drove back to the Seven-Five to finish out their late tour. Although there was only an hour or two left, that was enough time for a hell of a lot of cases to come in.

Team One's day tour was winding down on a Thursday afternoon late in May. The detectives—Jack Cutrone, Al Nesbot, Johnny Mullins, and Sondra Royal—and their homicide assistants, Dave Carbone, Mike Redmond, and Richie Brew—were engaged in routine tasks when Sergeant George Hohenstein emerged from the bosses' room, a forlorn expression on his face. "We just got a call about a little boy found in a compactor at 185 Wortman Avenue," he said. "Suit up."

Still fresh in Dave's mind were the two baby cases his team had caught—the baby in the gym bag over on Amber Street, and the one he had scooped out of a garbage bag seconds before sanitation men would have thrown it into the truck's rear hopper. He glanced involuntarily at the "Death's Door" sign across the room. It read "53." The baby would be homicide number 54 for the year, after only four months and twenty days. "Fucking unbelievable," he muttered to Nesbot.

When the three unmarked cars pulled up to the Linden Houses project, a large crowd had already formed. Several RMPs were parked on the street, and the crime scene area in the rear of 185 Wortman was taped off.

As the detectives approached the police, patrol officers divided the crowd so they could move through. Everyone stared, shuffling back passively. Dave briefly remembered his early days on the squad, how important the deferential gesture had made him feel—like the Red Sea parting. But it no longer had the same effect.

The compactor room in the basement of the building was a rectangular chamber with dingy cinder-block walls and a web of pipes running along the ceiling. At the far end of the room was the compactor machine, which crushed garbage that slid down the floor chutes and fed it into large green plastic bags. Maintenance personnel periodically checked the bags, and when they were full, tied them up and rolled them on conveyor belts that extended deep into the room.

On the belts now were several swollen bags. One bag had been ripped open in the center, partially exposing the body of a little boy, engulfed in putrid garbage. Only a few years old, he was on his back, his right leg folded and his left leg twisted up unnaturally around its axis at the kneecap, like a corkscrew. Bloodied cuts and scrapes pocked his face and body, and his right ear was lacerated. His eyes were closed and his mouth open. He was dressed in gray "A-Team" pajamas with blue trim over white underwear. The pants legs and his shirt and undershirt were pulled up, and his feet were bare.

The detectives—from Housing Police as well as the Seven-Five squad—and their bosses silently took in the scene, anger and disbelief on their faces. No matter how many atrocities they had witnessed, a young victim always hit a nerve.

Outside, patrol cops kept the ever-growing crowd of curiosity-seekers at bay, fielding their queries. What was going on in the basement? Was the dead child from the project? Someone they knew? Television trucks pulled up, disgorging reporters prepared to deliver the ghastly news live.

The victim had been pronounced dead by EMS, but he wouldn't be removed until the Crime Scene Unit and an ME investigator had arrived and done their work. It was after three o'clock now, and the detectives fanned out for the canvass.

In a little hallway off to the side of the compactor room a man wept, shaking, adamantly refusing to go back into the room. He had gone in to change the sleeve on the compactor. Pulling on the bag to tie it, he had felt something odd, like a hand or leg. He had thought it was a doll until he cut the bag open.

Dave tried to calm him down. "Take it easy," he told the custodian. "We can talk later."

This homicide was already drawing a great deal of attention. Lieutenant Perham and Captain Robert Kinkaid, the new commander of the 13th Division, were there, as well as Lieutenant John Cutter, the CO of the PSA 2 detective squad, and Lieutenant Donald Durando, the Housing Brooklyn Major Case Squad CO. John Harkins, the deputy inspector of Brooklyn North Detective Operations, was on his way over, as well as other brass from the NYPD.

Most of his team spread out now, Dave stood in the compactor room, transfixed by the sight of the little boy in the bag. Involuntarily, he pictured the boy sliding down an upper-floor chute into the compactor and being brutally crushed.

The two crime scene detectives dusted and photographed the area, being extra-meticulous about their work. Now came the difficult part. Dave and one of the crime scene men lifted the child out of the garbage bag and laid him on a blanket on the floor. Hardly any decomposition had set in yet. The corpse was that of an adorable little boy.

The officers took the garbage out of the bag piece by piece and laid it on the floor. There were soda bottles, beer cans, empty containers, chicken carcasses, used sanitary napkins, diapers folded around excrement, decaying meats, cans of food oozing sticky liquids, snot-encrusted tissues, rotting fruit. Dave coughed and flared his nostrils. A crime scene detective tried to lift prints off the cans and glass immediately surrounding the boy. Every piece of garbage would be taken back to the precinct, vouchered, and examined.

A short while later, donning thin rubber gloves, the ME investigator examined the body. It was pin-drop-still in the room. The doctor studied the contusions on the boy's neck, noted blood on the gum below the bottom teeth. He raised the boy's eyelids and observed small, pinpoint-sized bruises called petechiae, which indicated strangulation. Dave stood next to him the whole time, watching and listening carefully to everything he said.

On the sidewalk outside the building, Inspector Harkins stopped Sergeant Hohenstein. "Who's got the case?" he asked.

"I'll check who's up."

"I don't care who's up," Harkins barked. "I want Carbone to catch this one. Let Redmond assist him. I want this solved as quickly as possible."

Technically, Dave was only supposed to assist Team One detectives on homicides. Being put in charge of this already high-profile case was a vote of confidence and a challenge. But because the body had been found in a project, he would share the case with a housing detective out of PSA 2. Frank Ciccone, a savvy twelve-year veteran with a crewcut, was catching, assisted by Peter McMahon from Housing's Major Case Squad.

Back in the squad room, while detectives from the Seven-Five and Housing Police continued to canvass the Linden Houses project, Redmond and McMahon sifted through the vouchered garbage. Dave's cardinal rule floated in his mind: Learn your victim. "No way this little boy's going to be a John Doe for long," he said aloud.

The detectives found papers discarded in the garbage that bore apartment numbers, and they went to the project housing office to check the listings for boys about the victim's age. None of the apartments had a listing for a boy three to five years old, and the canvass yielded no one who had ever seen the boy before.

"If this boy didn't come from the project," mused Redmond, "then where?"

Dave shook his head. "Why did the killer bring him here?"

Child autopsies were always the most difficult to watch. Dave stood next to Redmond, Ciccone, and Eddie Feit in the Kings County Hospital morgue the next day, watching Dr. Arden slice the corpse open. An hour later, Dr. Arden made his preliminary determination: The boy had been beaten and had died of manual strangulation. Some of injuries were postmortem, from the compactor. Dave felt marginally better; at least there was a chance the boy had already been dead when his body had made that hellish journey.

Working from a photograph taken at the morgue, the police artist at One PP in lower Manhattan drew a delicate reproduction of the boy's face to use in seeking an ID. The actual photograph was too horrifying. Taking the sketch back to the Seven-Five, the detectives distributed dozens of photocopies to detectives and cops in the precinct and at Housing, who began to show them around the Linden Houses.

A bus was set up as a command post by the New York City Housing Authority outside 185 Wortman Avenue. Cops who manned the post questioned anybody who walked by and distributed the sketch of the dead boy. The detectives were growing frustrated; the homicide was already a day old, and the little boy was still unidentified.

The media were having a field day. Camera crews milled constantly around the scene and at the Seven-Five, and reporters surreptitiously pestered the detectives for an inside scoop. But the detectives had little to go on until a call came in late in the afternoon. Cutrone answered the phone.

"This is Detective Cauldwell of the Jersey City Police Department," the caller said. "Listen, can you guys help me out?"

Cauldwell was investigating an assault of a Dana Blackledge Poole of Kensington Place in Jersey City by her husband, Stephan Poole, in the early hours of the previous morning. After striking his wife, Stephan Poole had taken her four-year-old son, Kayesean, and driven away. Cauldwell had spoken to Poole by phone twenty minutes ago and had asked him how the boy was. Poole had told Cauldwell to call the Seven-Five Precinct in Brooklyn.

Cauldwell didn't mention the curious fact that Poole had previously called the Jersey City police to tell them Kayesean was in East New York, but the Jersey City police hadn't followed it up. Although the boy's murder had been all over the news the night before, the police there hadn't connected the Jersey City boy's disappearance with the recovered body in East New York.

When Poole found out Detective Cauldwell had the case, he had called the detective directly. With a sinking feeling, Cauldwell had finally put two and two together.

Cutrone immediately picked up the portable and had Central put him through to Dave, who was doing a canvass at the crime scene.

"Hey, Dave, drop what you're doing and get back to the precinct," Cutrone said. "We may know who the baby is."

Ten minutes later, Cutrone filled in Dave, Ciccone, Redmond, and McMahon on his conversation with Detective Cauldwell. Cauldwell, meanwhile, was on his way to the Jersey City Medical Center with a facsimile of the police artist sketch of the boy found in the compactor.

Dana Blackledge Poole, hospitalized with stab wounds, identified the boy in the sketch as Kayesean.

Now things were beginning to move. Mike Redmond ran DMV and BCI checks on Stephan Poole, which yielded an address in Queens and the registration and license plate numbers of a four-door gray 1988 Subaru.

The NYPD's BCI unit reported that Stephan Poole had once been arrested but had little information. Redmond called the FBI. Poole had been arrested in the Army in 1991 for "indecent assault," probably an attempted rape, and had received a dishonorable discharge. Poole was described as a black male with brown eyes, five-ten, 145 pounds. He worked for the New York City Sanitation Department.

Frank Ciccone called New York City Sanitation Operations. Stephan Poole hadn't shown up at work for the past two days; he had called in sick. The staff supplied the Queens addresses of Poole and his parents.

That night the usually bustling Seven-Five squad room was fairly quiet; the detectives were all out. A couple of teams were hitting the Queens homes of Poole's relatives. Another was visiting the place where he worked and talking to supervisors and coworkers. Gradually, a picture of the suspect was emerging.

Stephan David Poole was an enforcement agent for the New York City Department of Sanitation. One of six children born to Gloria and Andrew Poole, he had a twin sister, Stephanie, two older brothers, and two older sisters. His mother seemed protective, while his father was more judgmental, saying his son probably had killed the boy.

That evening, Perham, Cutrone, and Brew interviewed Dana Poole at the Jersey City Medical Center. She told them she was Kayesean's adoptive parent. She had had him since he was four months old, when his mother had given him up.

In Queens, Dave was laying a jerk job on Gloria Poole, who had been receiving phone calls from her son. "Look, Mrs. Poole," he said, "maybe Stephan didn't do it. Maybe he gave the boy to someone else, and that person killed him. We don't know. That's why it's very important for us to talk to your son and find out what happened, why he's running. Next time he calls, tell him to get in touch with us."

On the way back to the Seven-Five, Dave, driving the unmarked Chevy, looked over at Ciccone and Detective Tony DeRita. "Let's dump her phone. If her son calls her again, we'll find where he's hiding out, or at least where the call's coming from."

A half hour later, Dave was seated at his desk, plotting how to find

Stephan Poole. Suddenly his eyebrows went up, an,
Redmond. "You know, Mike, Poole's running aroun,
where," he said. "Now, if I put him into NCIC and th,
and run a check on him, nothing'll pop unless I have an
on him. But I don't want an arrest warrant on him becau,   o
talk to him. There probably aren't any witnesses to the baby   urder,
so I've got to get a confession. With an arrest warrant, he'll have the
right to counsel and I won't be able to talk to him." He pondered the
situation for a few more minutes, then bounced up out of his chair and
grinned. "But there is one way."

Dave sauntered into the bosses' office, where Lieutenant Perham,
Lieutenant Donald Durando, and Lieutenant John Cutter were talking. "Sorry to interrupt," Dave said, "but I was thinking that if Stephan Poole isn't around and hasn't talked to us, he may be dead somewhere."

The three bosses maintained a studied blankness. Carbone was up
to something.

"And if he's dead," Dave continued, "someone may have stolen
his car, right?"

Before anyone could speak, Dave rushed ahead.

"Dana has no idea where their car is, and her husband is missing.
For all we know, he's dead. So if we can't find him and the car is gone
and the wife wants it back . . ." He paused and tried to look innocent.
"I think it's safe to say the car is stolen. Right?"

The men looked at each other and nodded. "We understand,"
Perham said.

"Thank you," said Dave, elated.

Dave immediately returned to his desk and called Dana at the hospital. "We can't find your husband," he said, "and the car is missing.
We think it's stolen. We're going to put a stolen car alarm on it, okay?"

"That's fine," she said.

Just after midnight, Dave called the NYPD's Alarm Board, a unit
hooked up to a national computer system reporting stolen property.
Once a felony alarm was put on the car, if a police officer ran the license plate on Poole's car for any reason, it would come up on the
computer as stolen. There wouldn't be any warrants on Stephan Poole,
just his car. Dave left his phone number for contact information.

Detectives Redmond and Nesbot began their day tour with an interview of one of Stephan Poole's supervisors at the sanitation department. Lieutenant Blanche Riddick said Poole had called in sick on the

20th and 21st and hadn't reported to work. He hadn't yet picked up his paycheck. If he came by the office, she would call the squad. Then the detectives went to the King's County Hospital morgue to meet Kaaron Blackledge, Kayesean's natural mother. She confirmed she had given Dana Blackledge Poole, who was Kayesean's aunt, temporary custody of the boy.

A little after noon, Dave and Ciccone were in the second-floor Brooklyn apartment of Andrew Poole. Stephan's brother reluctantly told them he'd been getting calls from Stephan.

"Do yourself a favor," Dave told him. "Tell him to come in, tell him to talk to us, tell him to say whatever he's gotta say. Right now he's on the run. We don't know what happened. He's got to tell us what he did, what happened to the baby, who he gave the baby to, whatever."

Dave leaned heavily on Andrew Poole. "Listen, I'm gonna be back here every day of the week," he said, emphasizing the words. "I'll be here three times a day banging on your door. I don't want to bother you and the rest of the family, but I have to talk to him. I'll follow you to work, I'll stand outside the stall when you go to the john. I'll sell hot dogs in front of your house if I have to."

"I understand," said Andrew nervously. "If my brother calls or comes over, I'll bring him to you."

The detectives were constantly on the phone with Stephan Poole's mother and wife, trying to pry out any morsel of information that could help them track him down. They reviewed Poole's FBI and Army records to see if they could find any friends or acquaintances from those periods that he might seek refuge with. They thought he might flee to Georgia, Virginia, or Maryland.

"Poole assaulted Dana in Jersey City at around five in the morning," Dave said to his catching partner, Frank Ciccone. "We found the boy the next day in the afternoon. Now why did he come to Brooklyn? We know his beat was East New York, so that could have brought him here, but he's also a weird kind of guy. Maybe he patronized the prostitutes in the building there."

Later they talked to some prostitutes in the project, showing a picture of Stephan Poole that Dana had given them. "He looks familiar," one of the prostitutes said.

The missing Stephan Poole had assumed a kind of looming virtual existence in the detectives' minds, highly charged and sinister but not yet real. So when Ciccone answered the phone in the squad room and a low voice grunted, "This is Stephan Poole," Ciccone nearly dropped the receiver. He recovered quickly.

"Hey, how are you, Stephan?"

"Okay," said Stephan tonelessly.

Ciccone leaned forward, focusing on the tenuous connection, projecting himself over the phone line, intent on making contact. He willed himself to sound cheery and unconcerned. "So, how you feeling?"

"What am I being charged with? What's going on?"

"You're not being charged with anything, Stephan. I just want to talk to you, that's all."

"Okay. So talk to me."

"I'd rather meet you in person so I know it's you. I got all kinds of people calling me and looking for me to tell them things. I can't talk to you unless I'm sure it's you."

"I'd like to know what I'm being charged with before I come in and get arrested."

"You're not getting arrested, Stephan. That's what I'm trying to tell you. We just need to talk to you about it. That's all. What can you tell me about this?"

"Well," said Poole dully, "she tried to stab me, so I got her. And I really feel bad about that poor little kid."

"Do you know what happened?"

"No, I don't. I left him in the apartment when I left that morning."

Ciccone shifted in his chair. He was sweating. "I'd just really like to talk to you about this. I can't say anything more about what I know, because if you're not Stephan, then I could get into a lot of trouble. Can we arrange something?"

"No, we can't. Like *I* said, I'm who I say I am."

And Stephan Poole hung up.

Ciccone slammed the receiver into the cradle.

A few hours later, Poole called back. This time Dave answered.

"I'd like to know what I'm being charged with," Poole began. "What's going on?"

"Did you talk to your brother Andrew yet?"

"Not today."

"Well, we were over there yesterday. We explained everything to him to make it comfortable for you. And like I told him, if you wanted to talk to me, we could do it with him there so you don't feel anxious. All I want to do is talk to you."

Dave consciously filtered the urgency out of his voice.

"We could speak at your brother's house," he continued. "Not at the police station. I'm not looking to do anything to you. Right now we just want to find out what happened."

Poole was quiet. Dave tried again.

"I want to talk to you. I'm kind of like nervous because we're on the phone, and I don't even know if I'm talking to Stephan."

"It's me, all right."

"Yeah, but you don't know if this is Detective Carbone. You know what I'm saying? I don't know who you are. You could be anybody. Now we have to talk. There's no two ways about it."

"I'd like to know what I'm being charged with before I come by."

"I have the case, and I'm not charging you with anything. Okay? Over in Jersey, I don't know if they're going to go through with it. All it is is an assault, a simple assault."

Poole was silent again, and Dave repeated, "I'm not charging you with anything. I just need to find out what happened."

"It's not important, then."

"No. It's very important. You want me to give Andrew a call? You want to give Andrew a call again?"

"You're playing games."

"No, we're not, that's why we're trying to do it with your brother."

There was a click, and the line went dead.

Monday found the Seven-Five and Housing Police detectives continuing to work the case around the clock. They canvassed the Jersey City apartment building where Stephan and Dana Poole lived; brought Gloria Poole to the Brooklyn DA's office to tape her statement; interviewed Poole's twin sister, Stephanie; checked out leads phoned in by anonymous callers; recanvassed the building where the boy's body was found; interviewed other coworkers, relatives, and friends of Stephan Poole; staked out locations where Poole might show up. But there was no sign of Stephan Poole, and there were no more calls from him. Dave decided it was time for him to interview Dana Poole himself.

In the late afternoon, Dave and Ciccone walked into Dana Poole's hospital room. On the bed, wearing a hospital gown, lay a shapely black woman with high cheekbones and big oval eyes. Her face was sad and expressive, and even without makeup, she was curiously attractive. As the detectives drew nearer, they saw with horror that she appeared to be growing a beard.

Dave tried to contain his shock. He hoped his reaction wasn't apparent, because he didn't want to offend her. The other detectives who had interviewed Dana had warned him, but he still felt queasy.

"Dana," he said, pulling himself together, "I know you already went through it with the Jersey City police, but we want to hear it from you firsthand."

Dana Blackledge Poole was composed, anxious to cooperate. When she was given custody of Kayesean four years ago, she began, she had been his granduncle. The child had been born to her fifteen-year-old niece, Kaaron Blackledge, who was too young to care for Kayesean, and Dana had subsequently been appointed the baby's legal guardian. At the time, she was in the middle of a sex-change operation, and was already dressing and acting like a woman. Later, after she had completed the sex change, she adopted Kayesean.

Her doctor had told her she should start dating men. Her friends suggested she meet men through the personal columns, where she could say up front that she was a transsexual. She had placed an ad, and sixty men had responded. But when she spoke to Stephan Poole, she had felt there was something special about him. He understood what a transsexual was, he told her, and they made a date to meet in Manhattan.

"He brought me a rose," Dana said, looking up at Dave, her eyes crinkling a little at the memory.

"That—that was nice," Dave stammered, nonplussed. Despite Dana's discomposing sexual status, Dave found her likable and sincere. She had a very endearing quality, direct and straightforward. "Uh, okay, now can you tell us what happened the day you had a fight with Stephan?"

Dana took a deep breath. "The alarm went off at five o'clock as usual. He said, 'Dana, lay down for a little while. You still got time.' He—he was rubbing up against me. He wanted to make love." Dana glanced at the detectives, then plunged ahead. "But he couldn't get it up, and he started to get rough." Tears were forming in her eyes. "So then Kayesean got out of bed and came over to me. I told him to go back to bed. Stephan was acting so weird. Then he—he pulled a knife from under the pillow and stabbed me in the side.

"I jumped out of bed and ran into the living room, and he followed me and started wrestling me. Then Kayesean came out to the living room, and he looked real scared. I told Stephan to take Kayesean in the other room. I was willing to do whatever he wanted, just not in front of Kayesean. And I didn't have any clothes on, and I'm bleeding." Dana's voice was becoming unsteady.

"So he took Kayesean to the bedroom." She stopped for a moment, deep pain in her eyes, remembering the last time she had seen her beloved child.

She took another deep breath to steady herself. "While he was in the back, I ran out into the hall, but Stephan heard the door open and followed me. He tried to pull me back. He still had the knife, and I think that's when he cut me on my arm. I said, 'I love you, what's going on? What did I do?' But he didn't—he didn't say anything. He never acted like that before." She turned away from the detectives for a moment, head down, shoulders shaking. Then she straightened up and faced them again.

"So then I pulled away from him and ran down the stairs and out the door. There was a man on the street getting into his car, and he saw me, and Stephan coming after me, and he told me to get in, he'd drive me to the police station. Stephan went back in the house, and the man took me to the precinct.

"I got out of the car, and the man just drove off. I went inside the station. And I'm standing there, blood dripping and all naked, and the police thought it was so funny, they stood there looking at me and laughing for about five minutes before they even told me to sit down." Dana's mouth tightened at the remembered humiliation. "And I told them, 'My son is in the house—please someone go there and get him.'

"They took me to the hospital, and I assume they went to my house. They came to the hospital and told me, 'Miss, we knocked on your door and nobody answered.' I said, 'The boy is in the house, he's in there. Why don't you break down the door and try to go in and get him? He's in there!' And then they—they just walked out of the room. And that was it."

Dana's chest began to heave, and her face crumpled. She shook her head from side to side, whimpering. The detectives said what they could to console her. A short while later they left.

Coming in early for a night tour the next day, Dave called Dana with an idea he and Ciccone had discussed the night before. "Can the New York City Police Department monitor your bank accounts?" Dave asked her.

Her voice was strong. "You can do whatever it takes to find my husband."

Working out of the Seven-Five office now, like most of the other housing detectives on the case, Frank Ciccone called the three local airports to run parking-lot checks on Stephan Poole's car. An officer from the Port Authority police at Kennedy Airport reported that a car with Poole's license plate number had entered parking lot number nine on May 21 at 9:25 A.M. and departed two hours later.

In the squad room, Mike Redmond sent a message through Inter-City Correspondence, providing a description of Poole's car and the plate number, noting that Stephan Poole was wanted for questioning in connection with a homicide. He sent the message to a dozen states in the South, Midwest, and West; it would filter down to police at the local level.

Later in the day, Lieutenant Donald Durando was on the phone with a bank supervisor. Five hundred dollars from Stephan and Dana Poole's account had been withdrawn from a bank early that morning in Crestview, Florida.

Durando immediately called Lieutenant Perham in the Seven-Five squad. The detectives would have access to every transaction made with Poole's NYCE, or New York Cash Exchange, card. Five hundred dollars was the maximum amount that could be withdrawn with it from an ATM machine in a twenty-four-hour period. "Let's see if he goes to the same bank again tomorrow," Durando said to Perham.

This was a break, but the case was growing stranger all the time. A phone call came into the squad with another piece of disturbing information about Stephan Poole. In 1989 he had married a woman named Michelle Jenkins, and the couple had settled in Far Rockaway. Three months later, Michelle was dead. The ME had determined the woman died of heart disease related to her obesity, but with the murder of Kayesean Blackledge, some of the detectives were doubtful of that conclusion.

Then the detectives were put in touch with a former girlfriend of Poole's with whom he had had a child. When the baby was born, Poole had seemed jealous of all the attention the baby received. After a petty quarrel, Poole had sent nude photographs of the woman to the supervisor of her job as a school crossing guard, as well as to the local police, telling them she lured young boys from the school into her car. Not long after that he had abused her physically, and she had obtained an order of protection. Poole apparently had a tendency to create chaos wherever he went.

Late Wednesday morning, Lieutenant Durando called the bank and requested a check of Poole's NYCE card again for activity. Another five hundred dollars had been withdrawn at nine o'clock that morning from the same ATM machine in Crestview, Florida.

At noon, Lieutenant Perham summoned Dave into his office. "Go home and pack your bags," he ordered. "You're going to Florida. I just spoke with Chief Borelli, and he wants us to go down there and pick up Poole. You and Joe will be going from the squad."

Lieutenant Durando of the Housing Police was in the room. "Frankie's got the case," he said, "so he'll be going with you, and I'm going to send Tommy with him."

Meanwhile, at the building where Kayesean had been found, Detective Tony DeRita found a young woman who identified the man in the photo he showed her as a man she had seen in the building on the morning of May 20. He had accosted and propositioned her. She had told him no and walked away.

The man, she told the detectives, had been carrying a little boy.

Now the detectives had a witness who put the suspect, Stephan Poole, together with the victim, Kayesean Blackledge, in the building where the boy's body had been found.

By six o'clock that evening, David Carbone, Frank Ciccone, Thomas Harris, and Sergeant Joe Herbert—a veteran who had received nearly a hundred department recognitions and a Medal of Valor—were aboard a plane to Fort Walton, Florida, racing down the runway at La Guardia Airport.

22

At Fort Walton, the detectives picked up the two Ford Tauruses waiting for them at the rental office and drove to Crestview, where they checked in at the local Holiday Inn. Sergeant Herbert called the Crestview PD to announce the four were in town in connection with a homicide and to request a meeting the next morning.

The four New York City officers and the three Crestview, Florida, cops were all dressed in casual civilian clothes when they met for breakfast in the hotel dining room at six-thirty Thursday morning to plan for Poole's arrest if he showed up at the First Bank of Crestview for the third consecutive day to make an ATM withdrawal, as they hoped he would. Sergeant Herbert showed the Florida cops a picture of the suspect.

At seven, an hour and a half before the twenty-four-hour period from the previous ATM withdrawal ran out, the officers distributed themselves around the bank and waited.

At nine-fifteen, Herbert's car phone rang. It was Lieutenant Perham from the Seven-Five. "Poole already hit the bank," said Perham.

"He couldn't have," Herbert protested. "We're right here."

"No, no," said Perham. "Not that bank. The Bank of Mississippi in Biloxi."

Before they left Florida, the detectives obtained a subpoena for the bank's ATM videotape of the previous day, thinking Poole might have altered his appearance somehow. But the quality of the videotape was so poor they could not make out any of the people who used the machine.

They bid farewell to their Florida colleagues and piled into the cars.

Several hours later, the two Ford Tauruses pulled into the parking lot of the Bank of Mississippi in Biloxi. Sergeant Herbert requested the bank's videotape of ATM withdrawals, but the bank wouldn't surrender it without a subpoena.

Dave and Ciccone immediately drove to the local court, pulling the

judge from an ongoing trial. At first annoyed, the judge's face darkened when they told him of the homicide, then hardened when the
detectives told him of the bank's lack of cooperation. The judge arranged for the subpoena immediately. "You all bring this guy back to
me tomorrow, dead or alive," he ordered.

Armed with the subpoena, the two detectives raced back to the
bank to obtain the videotape. Afraid the tape would be of poor quality,
Harris asked where they could go to have it enhanced. A local river-
boat had a casino on board. The casino's equipment enhanced the
tape, but it was still difficult to tell if the man at the ATM machine was
Stephan Poole. If so, he had grown a beard and mustache.

The detectives awoke at five the next morning and met the officers
from the Biloxi PD for breakfast at the hotel an hour later. At eight,
they began their stakeout of the bank Poole had hit the day before.

The sun shone brightly, and there was a breathtaking view of the
Gulf of Mexico from the bank. But they waited in vain. At three o'-
clock, Sergeant Herbert received another phone call from the Seven-
Five. Poole had hit a bank in Conroe, Texas.

"Fuck!" Dave exclaimed. He looked at his fellow detectives, whose
faces mirrored his own frustration.

The initial thrill of the hunt was beginning to wane. How long
would they have to be away from their families? They hadn't planned
on an extended trip, and none of them had packed more than a couple of changes of clothes; they were starting to feel distinctly seedy.

"Yo, Frankie," Dave said. Ciccone was looking particularly discouraged. "Don't look so down. We'll get him."

Ciccone nodded absently.

"Well, at least we're getting to see the country."

Ciccone cleared his throat and spat. "It would feel a lot better if we
were chasing a live baby rather than a baby killer," he said shortly.

Seated in a restaurant, a map spread on the table before them, the
detectives tried to guess where Poole would go next. They had decided
to spend the night in Biloxi and get up early in the morning to hit the
road.

Dave looked up from the map. "I got a feeling," he announced.
"Poole's been going west and south, right? Now, if any of us were on
the run, where would *we* go?" The other detectives, intrigued, stared at
Dave. "I'd go to a highly populated area where I could get lost," he
continued. "There's no place like that for Poole if he continues south,

so I would say—and this is strictly a guess—that he's headed north, for Dallas.''

That was as good a surmise as any. Joe Herbert called the Seven-Five squad room and spoke to Lieutenant Perham.

"We've got a hunch," he said, "and that's all it is, but we'd like to fly ahead and go to Dallas."

Perham told Herbert there was pressure from above to bring everybody in. A chase like this could go on forever and could cost the department big bucks. But the lieutenant said he would see what he could do.

The detectives in the restaurant took the news with great disappointment. Dave and Ciccone decided that if the chase was called off, they would take their vacation time and hunt down Poole on their own.

While they were eating, Sergeant Herbert was called to the phone. A minute later Herbert returned beaming, his thumbs up. Perham had gotten the green light for them.

After dinner, Herbert called the Dallas Police Department and made arrangements to meet the next day to make plans to track down Stephan Poole.

At eleven the next morning, the detectives stood in the Dallas PD detective squad room.

Dave noticed the five detectives in the squad room were all wearing cowboy boots. "This is great!" he exclaimed. "Listen, would you guys do me a favor? Get up and stand over there for a minute."

The Dallas detectives, bewildered, stood across from Dave, Herbert, Ciccone, and Harris. "See all these fine detectives here?" Dave demanded of his fellow officers from New York City. "Now, you all make fun of my fucking cowboy boots."

"No, no, no," Ciccone protested, as Herbert and Harris guffawed. "Dave, we all *like* your cowboy boots."

The Dallas detectives stared at their East Coast colleagues, amused but still perplexed. "I'm probably the only New York City detective who wears cowboy boots every day of his life," Dave explained. "I don't even own regular shoes. But my friends here think that's kind of strange."

Getting down to business, Sergeant Herbert said they had come up with four banks in Dallas where Poole could use his NYCE card to make an ATM withdrawal. He thought they could split up into teams to stake out the locations.

But while the officers were going over the plan, Herbert received a call from the Seven-Five squad. "Stephan Poole was just picked up in Walker County, Texas, by a state trooper," said Lieutenant Perham.

"Well, that saves us a lot of trouble," said Herbert. "How did he get stopped?"

"He was driving his car, and the trooper was doing random license plate checks. Poole's came back stolen, wanted by New York, so he pulled Poole over, took him back to the holding area, and called New York City. And we told them to hold him until you could get down there."

This was precisely what Dave had had in mind when he had put the stolen-car alarm on Poole's car. Dave looked at Ciccone, and the two exchanged a high five. "It worked," said Dave exuberantly. "How about that!"

The four detectives rented two cars for the trip to Walker County. Dave, scenting his prey at last and unreasonably fearful Poole would somehow manage to slip away yet again, had his foot nailed to the accelerator, driving at ninety miles per hour.

"Slow down!" ordered Sergeant Herbert. "Poole's not going anywhere. And I'd like to be around to walk my daughter down the aisle one day."

At 6:00 P.M. in the Walker County jail, Carbone, Ciccone, and Harris sat down with Stephan Poole.

"We've spoken before, Stephan," Dave began. "Do you remember? I'm Detective Carbone, and this is Detective Ciccone. I think you know what we want."

Poole appeared surprised that only a few hours after he had been pulled over on a Texas highway, three New York City detectives were by his side.

"We know you killed the boy," Dave continued. "We know everything. If you're any kind of a man, you'll own up to it."

Poole stared at his feet and remained silent.

Dave stood up suddenly, and Poole shrank back. 'From the moment I caught this case," Dave said, his voice husky with anger and contempt, "I swore I was going to catch the miserable piece of shit who would throw a little boy down a garbage compactor." He walked around Poole's chair and stood behind him, then leaned down and hissed into his ear. "Did you actually think you were going to get away with it?"

Stephan Poole began to confess.

Dave interrupted him. He read Poole his Miranda rights and asked him to sign the card to acknowledge that he had been read the rights, which he did. Then Poole started in again, Dave transcribing his words as he spoke. When he was finished, Dave had him read over the transcript, and both Poole and Dave signed it.

Dave asked Poole to go through his confession once more, this time with a videocamera running. There was no way Dave was going to let Poole beat this rap, and since the Brooklyn DA's office had not been willing to send a DA to Walker County, he had asked a Texas trooper to record Poole's confession on videotape so it would show he hadn't been coerced, threatened, or beaten into telling his story. This tape would become part of the mass of materials to be admitted into evidence in the pretrial hearing, if Poole didn't plead out first. With Dave sitting a few feet away, the Texas trooper focused his videocamera on Poole.

His hair cropped, wearing a white T-shirt incongruously emblazoned with a colorful scene of wild animals, the child murderer sat slightly hunched forward, his hands resting on his legs, his face impassive. Thin and small-framed, he seemed to Dave rather pathetic. There was little emotion in his voice as he recounted his version of the events surrounding the death of Kayesean Blackledge.

"I had a fight with my wife that morning. She said to me, 'I know something that can make you very, very upset.'

"She told me she had been a man before she was a woman. She told me her family and friends and the people she worked with were all laughing at me because I was tricked into believing she was a woman."

This did not sound at all like the Dana Poole Dave had interviewed. She seemed warm, sensitive, and straightforward, and had shown him her personal ad that Poole responded to, which stated she was a transsexual. But even if Stephan could convince a jury it was true, against Dana's own personal testimony, did he really think it constituted justification for murdering a child?

"I told her I was going to take my stuff and leave," Poole continued, staring at his hands. "Then she ran into the kitchen and got a knife, and she tried to stab me. We had a tussle, and I managed to get it away from her. I stabbed her in her right side.

"She ran down the stairs and out of the apartment, and I tried to find her in my car, but she had disappeared." Poole raised his head and looked at the detectives.

"I got Kayesean, and we drove to Brooklyn. I wanted to take Kayesean to one of Dana's relatives there. But I really wasn't too sure what apartment building it was. I was still in shock, thinking what a fool she had made of me.

"Then I drove to my friend Andrew's apartment. A lady coming out let us into the building. I was carrying Kayesean. We took the elevator to the eighth floor, and I walked around trying to find Andrew's name on the door. Kayesean was getting restless, and he was crying. I told him we'd get some breakfast soon, and everything would be okay.' " Poole gazed at Dave, who coldly returned his stare.

Poole looked down at his hands. "But he just cried more and more. So I gave him a slap on the side of his face. He kept crying, so I hit him again, he cried louder and louder. I told him to stop crying, and I—I choked him a little bit." Again Poole looked at Dave. "When I choked Kayesean, he went all limp. He just went totally limp."

Poole paused, shook his head gently, and stared down at the floor. "I was so scared. I didn't want to leave him there." Then he raised his head and met Dave's eyes once more. "So I put him down the garbage chute," he continued, his voice suddenly husky. "I put him down feet first and faceup. I opened the chute halfway, and he fitted in." Poole was still shaking his head, his eyes back on the floor. "I walked from the eighth floor down to the lobby, and then I just drove around for a while."

Poole's chilling testimony sickened Dave. What had bothered him from the beginning was whether Kayesean had been dead when Poole put him in the chute, or rather unconscious and killed by the compactor. Dave decided he didn't really want to know.

Poole finished his confession by telling of his flight from Brooklyn. He had intended to go to Dallas, where he thought he could blend into the large black community and perhaps get a job at Six Flags Great Adventure Park while he decided what he would do next. He had had a feeling the cops were following him, and he had driven all the way down to Conroe, Texas, to throw them off, just in case they were.

The next morning, a judge arrived at the Walker County jail to settle the extradition situation. Poole waived his right to an extradition hearing. He would accompany the detectives back to New York City.

One of the Texas troopers asked the New York detectives if they wanted to go to Willie Nelson's bar later that night. "Hell, yes," Dave said. "We got the piece of shit we wanted. That'll be a cap to a beautiful day."

The detectives went back to their hotel to shower and dress and met the Texas troopers back at the jail. Two of the troopers brought their girlfriends, and a female ADA and her girlfriend came along as well. The detectives were dressed in sport jackets and ties, and Dave wore his cowboy boots.

When the group ambled into the nightclub, the loud music immediately drew their attention to the dance floor. Men and women interlocked at the elbow were circling around, kicking up a storm, and yelling "Yee haw!" and "Yippee-i-o-kiyay!" as strobe lights rained down on them. The place was so crowded that moving around was a challenge to one's agility.

Wood was the predominant architectural feature here, from the wagon wheels to the bar to the sawdust-littered floor. Waitresses zipped around wearing hot pants and tight tops. Over the tops they wore bandoliers with shot glasses inserted in the bullet slots, and holsters at their hips presented bottles of Tequila. Holders on their belts contained small salt shakers.

The strangeness of it all made Dave think he was in a time warp, carried back to the Old West. Then he was reminded of a country-and-western music show on TNN. Whatever it was, it was delightful, and he was drawn into the excitement and frenzy.

At the bar, a young woman in a cowboy outfit with a bright smile and buck teeth started up a conversation with Dave.

"Y'all aren't from Texas, are ya?"

Dave grinned. 'Is it that obvious?"

"Well, you're cute as a button, but you gotta lose that tie."

Dave cleared his throat and looked around, realizing how out of place he must look in his silk suit, despite his cowboy boots. "You know, you're right," Dave said to the girl, taking off his tie.

Feeling a bit looser, Dave tapped the shoulder of the ADA who had come along with them and motioned to the dance floor, and the two boogied out and joined the gyrating dancers.

Later, the DJ, tipped off by one of the Texas troopers, picked up his microphone and made a dedication. "For those four guys from New York who chased that scoundrel through the states and got him in Texas," he said, "this song's for you. Take him back to New York where he belongs."

As the DJ finished speaking, the thumping opening of Hammer's "Too Legit to Quit" blared over the loudspeakers.

The next morning, the four New York City police officers drove with their prisoner to the Dallas–Fort Worth airport for the return flight home. Poole's capture in Texas was all over the local media. People in the airport stared as Poole was escorted through. His limbs were confined by leg irons and handcuffs that were chained to a locked belt, and he had to shuffle as he was being led.

"What do you think is going to happen to me?" Poole asked after takeoff.

Dave leered at him. "You were a corrections officer once. You know what happens to people who kill children. It's not going to be a party in jail. I think you're gonna have to hit the weights, because you're not that big. If I remember what some of the prisoners do down there, you might get a taste of your own medicine."

Five minutes later, Poole fell asleep. He slept through the rest of the trip. Dave couldn't believe it.

Waiting at La Guardia Airport was a throng of media people and television cameras. The detectives escorted Poole out the rear of the plane. A minute later, several police cars drove out to the runway, and Poole was put in an unmarked vehicle.

Within an hour, the cars pulled onto Sutter Avenue in East New York. Television news trucks were parked all around the precinct, and the police had closed down the street to traffic. Dozens of reporters and news cameras waited at the front door to record the successful conclusion of the interstate manhunt.

The unmarked cars pulled up to the front. Poole didn't want to leave the car and had to be dragged out. Dave wouldn't let him cover his head with his jacket. "You had balls enough to kill a little boy," Dave said with disdain, "you got balls enough to show your face on national TV."

Dave and Ciccone flanked Poole. Grabbing him by the elbows, they led him inside the precinct. A woman screamed, "Baby killer! Why did you kill the baby?"

As the press conference was getting underway on the first floor of the precinct, the detectives led Poole into the squad room on the second floor. When the squad-room door opened, the overhead bell jangled. All eyes in the room looked up. The detectives gave a standing ovation to Dave, Ciccone, Herbert, and Harris as they walked in. Poole was put into the holding cell.

A couple of hours later, Lieutenant Perham ordered pizza for the squad. The lounge was mobbed as several boxes of pizza were brought in and stacked on the table. The Seven-Five squad detectives sat or stood, watching the evening news lead off with the story of Poole's capture. In the room were Dave, Mike Redmond, Al Nesbot, Jack Cutrone, Sondra Royal, Johnny Mullins, Richie Brew, Jerry Rupprecht, Dave Coleman, Jessy Gonzalez, Neil Tasso, Charlie Zammet, Phil Saurman,

Tommy O'Donnell, Joe Falcone, and Steven Amalfitano, as well as Captain Kinkaid and Police Aide Cheryl Pough. Lieutenant Perham told Dave and Sergeant Herbert, exhausted from their six-day pursuit, to go home and rest up. A couple of hours later, Mike Redmond, Peter McMahon, and Jerry Rupprecht took Stephan Poole in to Brooklyn Central Booking to be lodged for arraignment the next day.

Resting in her Jersey City home, Dana Poole watched the evening news with intense interest. Her wounds were still painful, but at least she had the satisfaction of knowing her husband had been found and arrested. She would never get over the loss of the little boy she had come to love so dearly. She wondered how he would have developed, what his interests would have been. She remembered his voice, his smile, his laugh, his gentleness, his innocence. And she had to work hard to block from her psyche the harrowing pictures her imagination kept forming of his horrible end. She stared at the television set, her heart leaden with despair.

On the south shore of Long Island, it was dark in the little girl's bedroom. Dave knelt beside her bed. A faint lunar light penetrated the curtains, so he could make out her still form. He watched her lie there for a few minutes, feeling the emptiness of the night as her body breathed quietly, calmly.

He pondered for a moment how death was a natural part of his life now, an occurrence assimilated into his routine, like eating. After what he'd seen, he realized, nothing bothered him anymore. Nothing shook him up, nothing surprised him, nothing depressed him for very long. He was as stolid as a piece of rock, impervious to abrasion no matter how severe the forces that acted upon it.

He thought of his mother and wished achingly that she could be with him, but he took solace in the fact that for the first time in several years, there were signs the rest of his family was healing, coming back together. He hoped in time his brothers and sisters and father would forge a closeness such as they had enjoyed so long ago. For when the job is all over, if you don't have family and love to return to, what's left?

He stood up and leaned over. Placing his fingers on the sleeping girl's face, he stroked it gently, then kissed her cheek. Then he stood straight and turned. At the door, a woman's body was silhouetted by the moonlight, on her face a faint, wistful smile. Walking over to her, he gripped her hand in his and led her out, quietly closing the door of the little girl's bedroom, savoring the moment, not thinking about tomorrow.

EPILOGUE

The child homicide case never went to trial, because the suspect, Stephan Poole, pled guilty in January 1994, just as pretrial suppression hearings were about to get underway; Poole subsequently received a sentence of twenty-five years to life. During the months after Poole's arrest, David Carbone gave a lot of thought to his future in the NYPD. With the successful clearance and high media profile of the Poole case, he was becoming better known both in and out of the department. Not only had the case been featured in all the print and television media of New York City, but Carbone was even reaping national publicity. His name was mentioned in large-circulation consumer and professional magazines, and he was invited back onto the nationally televised *Sally Jessy Raphael Show* for his third appearance within a few months.

The publicity was fine—as ''stars'' in their own right, detectives as a breed rarely eschewed it—but foremost in Carbone's mind was how to further hone his skills and instincts to become the best detective he could. That meant continuing to work homicides—as many as possible—and receiving a promotion in grade. He wanted to remain a detective, and he wanted to work no other cases than murder.

For several months, Detective Mike Redmond, the Seven-Five squad's veteran sage, had been urging Dave to transfer to the Brooklyn North Homicide Task Force. Although the Seven-Five Precinct Detective Unit was one of the busiest squads in the city, and one of the few to catch its own homicides, a homicide task force was the most prestigious assignment in the department. Its members were known strictly as homicide detectives, and they used their expertise to help other detectives in the borough. As detective reputations went, a detective on a homicide task force was considered the elite of the elite.

''It's time for you to make a career move, Dave,'' Redmond counseled him. ''The task force will be a better place for you to advance.''

Dave knew Redmond had his best interests at heart. Dave had only the highest respect for Redmond, who was practically a father figure to him, and the older man's advice was essentially a sanction.

Dave had no doubt he was ready. He had investigated hundreds of murders since he had come into the squad four years earlier, as well as 716 nonhomicide cases in the three years before he was assigned to investigate homicides exclusively. These latter cases included assaults, burglaries, missing persons, kidnappings, car thefts, child abuse, forgeries, and violations of orders of protection. Of this enormous volume of cases, Dave had cleared almost 92 percent, and he had solved virtually the same percentage of his homicides. Given the immense workload in the squad and the fact that numerous cases were worked simultaneously, Dave was well satisfied with his stats. The cases he hadn't been able to clear remained a source of frustration, but no detective could possibly solve every one of his cases.

To some, like Detective Joe Howard of the New Haven PD, with whom Dave had worked tracking multiple murderer Charles Brackett, David Carbone was the personification of the young hotshot New York City detective. Dave's positive attitude and apparently boundless energy, his relentless gallows humor, his ability to remain upbeat even in the goriest and most morbid crime scenes, and his droll New York accent had led Howard to peg him as a "hot shit." Even when Howard was doing exaggerated impressions of Dave to detectives in his squad after getting off the phone with him, Howard's respect for the New York City detective was intense. "In his investigations he has a pretty set idea of what he's going to do fifteen, twenty steps down the road," Howard told his men. "He figures things out way ahead of time. Hanging with him is like hopping on and off a moving freight train."

Still, there were others who didn't cotton to a detective's cutting a larger-than-life image. To these detectives—including some in his own squad—David Carbone appeared to be trying to draw attention to himself. But that was just Dave's style, and to all who knew him, there was no denying that Carbone was an aggressive, hardworking, and perspicacious detective.

In early December 1993, after having discussed his intentions with Seven-Five squad CO Lieutenant Kevin Perham and 13th Division CO Captain Robert Kinkaid, and receiving their approval, Dave paid a call on Inspector John Harkins, the commanding officer of Brooklyn North Detective Operations. Harkins knew Dave fairly well; he had assigned Dave a number of cases, including the compactor homicide, because he knew Dave got the job done.

"Inspector," Dave began, "I'd like to move on in this job, to move up in grade. You've known me for a while, and I think you know what kind of work I do. I've had—"

Harkins interrupted. There was no need for any explanation, he said. He knew Dave's track record, what kind of detective Dave was. Everything he'd ever asked of Dave, Dave had accomplished. It was clear Dave was looking for a transfer, and Harkins was amenable. "Would you like to go to the homicide task force?"

"Yes," said Dave, nodding vigorously.

"It's a good place to be. I'll make a few phone calls and get back to you."

Although Dave's good work and high case clearance rate were undeniable, he was still rather young to be in a homicide task force. Most of the detectives in these units were older men, with twenty or more years on the job. Dave had only half that time, and only five years of that as a detective catching homicides.

So when three days later, back in the Seven-Five, Captain Kinkaid called Dave into his office, his news was a welcome surprise. "Your transfer letter is on my desk," he said. "Just so you know, I'm signing the letter with regret, because I'm losing a great detective. I'm sorry to see you go, but you deserve it, and it's a great advancement."

Although excited about his new move, Dave was also sorry, in a way, to be leaving the Seven-Five squad, which had been his second home for the last four years. He had worked closely with these people and had built an attachment to them. But in a big police department like the NYPD, with its sundry units and precincts, positions and assignments frequently changed, and cops knew that moving up on the job required them to be on the move laterally as well. Indeed, the squad itself had changed significantly over the years. Smitty was gone, now a sergeant in the Bronx, and Dave's team now consisted of Jack Cutrone, Al Nesbot, Johnny Mullins, Jessy Gonzalez, Richie Barrios, Dave Coleman, Mike Redmond, and Richie Brew. Mike Race and Jimmy Owens had retired, and Redmond would be retiring in a year.

There was no doubt that Dave's chances for improving his grade would be better in a homicide task force than in the Seven-Five squad. Despite the squad's having some excellent detectives—Mike Redmond and Jerry Rupprecht had almost thirty years on the job now—it had not one first-grade detective. Grade promotions were hard to come by, and the Seven-Five traditionally had not received the respect it merited. Of the entire NYPD Detective Bureau of approximately 4,000 detectives, only 125 had the designation of first grade, and 400 of second grade. All the others were third-grade detectives like Dave. So, as sad as he was to leave, he knew that advancement meant being on the go.

And as friendly as he was with his colleagues on the squad—and with other cops in the department, for that matter—the socializing and banter was mostly on the job. At work or at police meetings or retirement, promotion, or holiday parties, Dave was as gregarious as they come. But these days he rarely socialized with cops when off duty. Most of his free time was spent with his family or working on his house.

On January 2, 1994, Dave reported for his first tour of duty with the Brooklyn North Homicide Task Force, based out of the 90th Precinct in Williamsburg, Brooklyn. He had already met the unit's commanding officer, Lieutenant Ronald Peragine, when he went to introduce himself after being notified of his transfer by Captain Kinkaid. Peragine had explained to him that as a member of the task force, Dave would be assisting detectives in eight precincts in Brooklyn North (all but the 73rd and 75th precincts now) who caught homicides. He would be responding to crime scenes and using his expertise to help them solve the case, then moving on to the next. With the number of murders in Brooklyn North, that promised to be a great deal of work. In the previous year alone, there had been 488 homicides in Brooklyn North, the most of any borough task force in New York City.

Dave had been assigned by Peragine to a team in the unit, and there was an unexpected surprise. In his team was José Torres, his old RIP partner and mentor. Now they would be reunited as homicide partners.

In his second day in the task force, Dave caught a baby murder, and then another baby murder shortly after that. But then Lieutenant Peragine assigned him to continue work that he had begun shortly before leaving the Seven-Five squad—investigating murders by violent Brooklyn-based drug gangs.

In the Seven-Five squad room one day, Dave had received a telephone call from his old partner, Joe Hall, who was now an investigator for the Office of Special Narcotics. Hall told him of a new concept developed by Attorney General Janet Reno, the Violent Drug Task Force. A local task force composed of FBI agents, Office of Special Narcotics investigators, and NYPD detectives was forming to investigate violent New York City drug gangs, and since Dave knew a lot about East New York drug gangs, he could be a big help to the group. Would he join?

Lieutenant Perham and Captain Kinkaid had both given approval to Dave for this assignment, and it had occupied the bulk of Dave's time before he left the squad.

Now, Lieutenant Peragine gave permission to continue with the drug task force not only to Dave but to Joe Torres as well. Together, they would assist the group in targeting violent Brooklyn-based drug gangs and trying to solve any murders related to the gangs. Several months later, in October 1994, the U.S. Attorney's Office for the Eastern District of New York held a press conference to announce that the Violent Drug Task Force had arrested nineteen Brooklyn drug gang members for murder, and that numerous other arrests were impending.

Dave's promotion to the Brooklyn North Homicide Task Force was complemented by an event that occurred in his personal life, enriching the one area where it was empty. One day, Dave called his father, from whom he had been estranged ever since their falling-out following his candidacy for fire department chief seven years earlier. They met, went for a long walk, and decided to arrange a family meeting. One week later, the immediate family gathered at Dave's father's house to talk about the discord in the family, and why Dave had gone his own way. It was a difficult discussion, but the family ties were strong, and Dave was able to reconcile with his father and most of his brothers and sisters. The balance in his personal and professional life, the first he had achieved since becoming a detective, brought Dave immeasurable satisfaction.

Dave is happy to be working in Brooklyn. There are many fine and beautiful sections in the borough, to be sure, but gangs and murder are rampant and may continue to be so for the indefinite future, offering many opportunities for the determined crime fighter. Whatever the future may bring, no one can foretell, but Dave relishes as a personal mission the chance to hunt down killers. As a cog in the great crime-fighting machine that is the NYPD, he has resolved to devote his career to controlling the carnage. He has faith that no matter how ferocious, malign, and tough the killers are, he will bring them to justice.

ACKNOWLEDGMENTS

Rarely does a book have an editor whose interest in its subject goes profoundly beyond the professional. Gerald Howard, the editor of *The Making of a Detective,* is the son of a New York City police detective, the late Harry Howard. I was fortunate to have an editor who not only was intimately associated with the world of detectives, but also deftly guided my unfolding and shaping of the story presented herein.

I feel fortunate also to have agents who genuinely care about their authors and stint no effort when it comes to furthering their authors' careers. My agents, Lynn Chu and Glen Hartley, were enthusiastic about this project from the beginning, and they fed me doses of inspiration through the occasional lulls in the taxing and draining writing process. I shall always be grateful to Lynn and Glen, who ably and diligently guided me and who are also my trusted and dear friends.

It is rare for a civilian to be granted access to the inner sanctums of the police world, and the New York City Police Department is an especially close-knit organization. I knew from the start that my access was an extraordinary and unprecedented privilege, not to mention a dream come true for me. To all the people who made it possible, I am very grateful.

Permission to conduct my study was granted by the New York City Police Department. Lieutenant Raymond O'Donnell got the ball rolling, and the final consent came from Suzanne Trazoff, who at the time was the Deputy Commissioner of Public Information. Once the green light was given, Thomas J. Scotto, president of the Detectives' Endowment Association, set the wheels in motion.

The next protagonist in this bureaucratic drama was Lieutenant Kevin Perham, the commanding officer of the 75th Precinct Detective Unit. It was the "lieu's" squad and squad room, and he did not have to let me in, allow me to talk to his detectives, or permit me to come and go freely. But he couldn't possibly have been more amiable and accommodating. Kevin Perham is a consummate professional in every aspect of his life, and I am lucky to have had the opportunity to work with him.

I would also like to thank everyone in the Seven-Five squad who was present during my research, many of whom went out of their way to help me feel at home there. Many are still in the squad, some have transferred, and others have retired, but they are, altogether, the following: Captain John J. Finn and Captain Robert Kinkaid; Detective Sergeant Michael S. Race (who provided much extra assistance in his off-duty hours); Sergeants George Hohenstein, Joe Herbert, Tommy Morris, and Robert McDonald; Detectives Richie Brew, Michael Redmond, Alexander Smith, Al Nesbot, Jack Cutrone, Joe Hall, Sondra Royal, Jerry Rupprecht, Al Kennedy, Butch Neacy, Tom Buda, James Curran, James Owens, Tom Maher, Jeff Wright, Thomas O'Donnell, Phil Saurman, Steve Amalfitano, Neil Tasso, Mike Oliver, Dave Coleman, Johnny Mullins, Jessy Gonzalez, and Richie Barrios; and Police Aide Cheryl Pough. Others I'd like to thank at the precinct are RIP detective Joseph Vigiano, officers Janet Barry and Eddie Serocki, and Police Aide Yanira Oquendo.

Of course, tremendous gratitude is due the main subject of this book, David Carbone, who gave unstintingly and unremittingly of himself for over two years. At first somewhat skeptical of my intentions, Dave eventually opened up his professional and personal life to me completely. I not only stood in his shadow at work, but called or beeped him at all hours of the day when I wasn't with him, and he always willingly and gracefully answered my requests for information, no matter how elementary or complex. Dave's wife, Luciann, and daughter, Danielle, not only endured my taking Dave away from them during the precious few hours he had free, but welcomed me into their home and patiently submitted to probing interviews themselves, graciously enduring my incessant intrusions into *their* personal lives.

Other Carbone family members and relatives who shared insights with me are Joseph Edward Carbone, Lillian McMurray, Rose Murer, and Phyllis Carbone. I'd like to thank them and all the other members of the Carbone family.

Several members of the NYPD, many still active and some subsequently retired, shared technical information with me or told me stories from field work or patrol. I am indebted to all of them. At the risk of omitting some names, I will venture to list them: Bill Brino, Tony Tota, Jerry Donohue, Henry Fieldsa, Ray Pierce, José Torres, Joseph Heffernan, Herbie Holman, Steven Fiorica, Luis Bruno, Jim Martin, Lawrence Ursitti, and Tom Barbagallo. I would also like to thank detectives Eddie Feit, Tony DeRita, Thomas Deutsch, Vaughn Munro, Pete McMahon, and Frank Ciccone who worked out of the New York City Housing Police Department's Police Service Area 2 in East New York before housing, city, and transit police merged into one force. The assistance of Detective Joe Howard of the New Haven Police Department and Special Supervisory Agent Ralph DiFonza of the Federal Bureau of Investigation is also much appreciated.

I am very grateful to City Medical Examiner Dr. Thomas A. Andrew of the New York City Office of the Chief Medical Examiner, who spent several hours explaining autopsies and pathology to me.

Others along the way who helped, outside the department, were Theresa Denson, a former NYPD Central operator, Gaetano Pernice, and Carmine and Rose Babino. Sadly, Carmine, who enthusiastically told me about his experiences with Detective Carbone when Dave was a patrol officer, passed away before the manuscript was completed, but he was delighted that a book was being written about Dave, whom he regarded as a hero.

Bruce Cameron of *Law and Order* magazine gave me many opportunities to increase my knowledge of police management and other aspects of law enforcement through article assignments. I will always be grateful to him, as well as publisher H. Scott Kingwill, and the rest of the courteous and professional staff of *L & O*.

My close and respected friend Judith Stein once again lent me her considerable talents by reading the manuscript and offering many valuable suggestions. Her honest and sharp insights strengthened the book and are much appreciated.

My skillful and conscientious typist, Nancy Constantine, patiently deciphered the chicken scratches of this antiquated writer who still likes to churn out a first draft on a legal pad. A fervent police buff who learned the lingo as she went along and followed the detective's metamorphosis portrayed in these pages, she's now ready, I think, to go out and process her own crime scenes.

My parents, Philip and Mazie, provided regular moral support over the phone. My son, Glenn, provided a rapt audience for the tales of heroic detective exploits. Stepdaughters Elyssa and Lauren were also swept up in the excitement of the project.

And finally, it is with my full love and gratitude that I thank my wife, Marla, who endured my seemingly interminable absences while observing at the precinct or holed up in my office at home writing. She knows the scoop only too well by now, but still, it is never easy.